REGULATING VICE

Regulating Vice provides a new, interdisciplinary lens for examining vice policy and focuses that lens on traditional vices such as alcohol, nicotine, drugs, gambling, and commercial sex. *Regulating Vice* argues that public policies toward addictive activities should work well across a broad array of circumstances, including situations in which all participants are fully informed and completely rational and other situations in which vice-related choices are marked by self-control lapses or irrationality. This precept rules out prohibitions of most private adult vice and also rules out unfettered access to substances such as alcohol, tobacco, and cocaine. Sin taxes, advertising restrictions, buyer and seller licensing, and treatment subsidies are all potentially legitimate components of balanced vice policies. *Regulating Vice* brings a sophisticated and rigorous analysis to vice-control issues, an analysis that applies to prostitution as well as drugs, to tobacco as well as gambling, while remaining accessible to a broad social science audience.

Jim Leitzel teaches public policy and economics at the University of Chicago. He received his PhD in economics from Duke University; he has taught at Vanderbilt University and Duke University and served as the Academic Coordinator at the New Economic School in Moscow. Jim has been a National Fellow at the Hoover Institution at Stanford University and an Atlantic Fellow in Public Policy based at the Department of Economics of the University of Essex. His previous books include *Russian Economic Reform* and *The Political Economy of Rule Evasion and Policy Reform*. Jim is the founder of Vice Squad (vicesquad.blogspot.com), a blog devoted to vice policy.

D1086914

Regulating Vice

MISGUIDED PROHIBITIONS AND
REALISTIC CONTROLS

JIM LEITZEL

University of Chicago

CAMBRIDGE
UNIVERSITY PRESS

CAMBRIDGE
UNIVERSITY PRESS

32 Avenue of the Americas, New York NY 10013-2473, USA

Cambridge University Press is part of the University of Cambridge.

It furthers the University's mission by disseminating knowledge in the pursuit of
education, learning and research at the highest international levels of excellence.

www.cambridge.org
Information on this title: www.cambridge.org/9780521706605

© Cambridge University Press 2008

First published 2008

A catalogue record for this publication is available from the British Library

Library of Congress Cataloguing in Publication data
Leitzel, Jim.
Regulating vice : misguided prohibitions and realistic controls / Jim Leitzel.
p. cm.
Includes bibliographical references and index.
ISBN- 978-0-521-88046-6 (hardcover) – ISBN- 978-0-521-70660-5 (pbk.)
1. Crimes without victims – United States. 2. Crimes without victims – Europe. I. Title.
KF9434.L45 2008
345.73027–dc22 2007034889

ISBN 978-0-521-88046-6 Hardback
ISBN 978-0-521-70660-5 Paperback

To Jed, Mike, Julius, and other friends of long standing

Contents

Tables and Boxes

Preface

Craft against vice I must apply.
                        – Shakespeare, *Measure For Measure*

When I arrived at the University of Chicago in the fall of 1998, I was asked what courses I might like to teach. I suggested Regulation of Vice, and it is to the credit of the university that, without further ado, and without any questioning of my motives, the course duly appeared on the spring schedule. *Regulating Vice* has grown out of that course.

Each spring, during the first class meeting of Regulation of Vice, I provide a few disclaimers, which are appropriate here as well. I am not a lawyer, nor am I a physician, and I often am wrong. (I am not wrong about not being a lawyer or physician, however.) Please do not mistake anything that appears in *Regulating Vice* as legal or medical counsel; it is not. This book is about public policy toward vice, not private policy, and you should beware of basing your personal vice-related choices on anything in these pages. If what you really need is treatment for a vice problem, then please seek help right away. *Regulating Vice*, alas, will not be of assistance.

Calling an activity a vice is not considered to be a form of praise; nor is referring to a person as vicious regarded as a compliment. In this book, however, vice and vicious are used as neutral terms, intended neither to denigrate nor commend. "Vicious" is employed in a manner quite at variance with everyday language, standing in as an unassuming synonym for "vice related." Vice issues often are highly charged, and hence the choice of terminology can be fraught with implicit associations. An example is "sex worker," the use of which is sometimes seen to signal an attempt to normalize prostitution as just another profession. These sorts of signals are unintended in my selection of terminology – though I do believe that some forms of adult prostitution should be legal and regulated.

Regulating Vice discusses directly a variety of vicious behaviors, and I like to believe that the ideas pertain to essentially all vices. I also like to believe that my approach to vice applies globally. (Indeed, there seems to be no end to the things I like to believe.) Nevertheless, most of the specific applications and examples are drawn from the United States. My decision to make United States policy the focus of *Regulating Vice* mainly follows from constraints of time, space, and familiarity. The relative neglect of other countries is most pronounced with respect to the "Vice Verdicts," summaries of court cases derived almost exclusively from U.S. Supreme Court decisions. These summaries are provided in recognition of the important role that the judiciary plays in developing vice laws. "Vice Verdicts" also illustrate the influence of vice regulation upon public policy more generally, through the determination of the limits of constitutional rights to free speech and freedom from unreasonable search and seizure, for instance.

I am a blogger; surely this is one of the more dispiriting phrases in the language. But it isn't as bad as it sounds: I am part of a group blog, Vice Squad (vicesquad.blogspot.com), devoted to explorations of vice policy. Many of the topics that are touched upon in *Regulating Vice* have graced the webpages of Vice Squad. Citations to Vice Squad in the footnotes are given with the date on which the relevant posts appeared, but for ease of exposition, the lengthy URLs are not provided. All of these posts can be found by going to vicesquad. blogspot.com and clicking on the appropriate month in the archive listing. Citations to other webpages generally include complete URLs.

My debts are many, and I fear that most of them will go unacknowledged here. But a start can be made by reference to the course from which this book developed. Regulation of Vice initially was modeled after a class that I knew about at Duke University, taught by my friend Phil Cook. Thanks to Phil for the inspiration, as well as for many helpful insights over the years. My teaching assistants for Regulation of Vice – Sheldon Lyke, Nicole Eitmann, Paul Goyette, Petr Barton, and Martina Smith – have been stellar. Chapter 7, on the Internet, grew out of a short handout for class that Sheldon and I jointly prepared years ago. Hundreds of University of Chicago students have improved this book over the years; five who merit special mention are Will Baude, Evan Haglund, Dmitriy Masterov, Jessica Ianotti, and Kathleen Rubenstein.

Comments from Mark Kleiman and Rob MacCoun have refined my thinking. Others who have lent their assistance at various stages include Nicole Eitmann, Michael Alexeev, Mary Ann Case, Phil Cook, and Peter Reuter. John Berger at Cambridge University Press has been supportive and pleasant throughout. I have been blessed with two first-rate research assistants, Ryan Monarch and Alexandra (Ali) Cirone. Ryan delved into many vice topics for me over the years and eventually even joined the Vice Squad team. Ryan also collected the data that, in updated and expanded form, became the statistical appendix. Ali was the first person besides me who read a complete draft, and she regularly provided wise counsel. My Vice Squad partners have been a constant encouragement. Thanks to everyone who helped.

Much of the progress on the manuscript was made during a six-month secondment at the University of Chicago Paris Center. Many thanks to College Dean John Boyer and College Masters John Kelly and Constantin Fasolt, along with the Center Director Robert Morrissey and the outstanding Center staff, for their assistance in making my Paris stay possible. Richard Taub kindly stepped in to more than fill my shoes back at the Hyde Park campus, with aid from Lee Price. My Paris friends were more helpful than they can know in sustaining the development of *Regulating Vice*.

My family and friends have been supportive beyond measure. It is to old and dear friends whom I dedicate this book, including many who will go unnamed here. Among the named old friends are Jed, Mike, Julius, Janice, Joselyn, Jim, Fallaw, Chris, Shlomo, Geoff, Cliff, Barry, Will, Bob, and Nikkie.

Introduction

THE VICE CONTRARIAN

Imagine a vice policy contrarian, someone who rather recklessly advocates the wholesale overturning of our current vice regulations. What would such an outspoken contrarian have to say? Perhaps she would start with something along these lines:

> Tobacco kills more than 400,000 Americans each year, while we temporize with smoking areas and excise taxes and Surgeon General warnings: ban the sale of cigarettes. Alcohol is responsible for some 75,000 deaths annually in the U.S., and yet we tolerate alcohol, even actively promote it. The manufacture of alcoholic beverages should be immediately banned. Pornography assaults us from every billboard, television, movie screen, Internet connection, and magazine rack. Even supposed "literature," like D. H. Lawrence's *Lady Chatterley's Lover*, is sufficiently sullied with smut to make it unfit for human consumption: we can happily throw such soft-core babies out with the bath water of hard-core porn, by making it illegal to peddle filth. Adultery, premarital sex, sodomy, all sorts of sexual perversions, are not only common, they are celebrated – to the threat of our civilization. Signaling our disapproval through the criminal law would be a better policy than the current anything goes, "if it feels good (or even if it feels bad), do it" approach. Swearing has somehow managed to become *de rigueur* on the street, on the airwaves, and in the theater, immeasurably coarsening our social life. Public profanity could safely be countered with modest fines to encourage civility. Gambling is another vile yet pervasive presence, with state lotteries, Native American casinos, and Internet bookies at every turn, ruining countless lives, and for what gain? To enrich the hucksters who proffer such money-for-nothing schemes? We must take away the legal and societal imprimatur from wagering.

But our imagined policy reformer is a contrarian, not a Puritan. She doesn't want to prohibit any and all vice: she only wants to ban those vices that are currently legal or tolerated. For forms of vice that are now illegal, she recommends the lifting of controls:

> To start with the seemingly most difficult case, heroin should be legal. Heroin is a useful medicine, both as a cough suppressant and pain killer, and when available in known dosages and without adulterants, not much of a threat to health. Yes,

some people might abuse heroin were it legal, but many more people will use heroin responsibly and benefit from it. For similar reasons, cocaine should be legal, too. (The case of marijuana is so obvious that it barely merits mentioning – of course pot should be legal, the threat to health being so small.) In fact, the whole notion that certain drugs should be available only with a prescription is itself wrongheaded. If you are an adult and are facing a severe illness and think you can find some solace in a drug, why do you first have to convince a doctor that your desire for the drug is legitimate? We can keep intact most of the prescription system, but eventually there must be some escape clause, so that a sufficiently motivated adult is able to procure a drug legally without the approval of the officially sanctioned health overlords. Finally, adult heterosexual prostitution should be legal, offering as it does both lucrative employment opportunities and some comfort to the lonely or undesirable.

Our vice policy contrarian certainly is peculiar. But while we are discussing imaginary characters, please meet my friend Mr. Twentieth Century, born on January 1, 1901, and hobbling now a few years past his due date into the twenty-first century. Mr. Twentieth Century has lived all of his life in Chicago. And Mr. Twentieth Century has endured through times when every one of the contrarian's suggested reforms has been the duly constituted Law Of The Land. Tobacco: cigarette sales banned in fifteen states (including, briefly, Illinois) during the early years of the twentieth century, with Kansas being the last state to end the prohibition in 1927. Alcohol: manufacture and sale banned nationally, 1920–1933, some municipal and county-level prohibitions still in force. Distribution of hard-core pornography: vigorously suppressed until the 1960s and not entirely free from control by the criminal law to this day. *Lady Chatterley's Lover* (which contains frank sexual language): completed in 1928 but legally circulated in the United States only after 1959. "Deviant" sex: continues to be illegal in many states, though a 2003 Supreme Court decision effectively legalized adult, consensual, private sodomy, either heterosexual or homosexual, throughout the United States. Cursing: state and municipal laws outlawing cursing and blasphemy remain on the books, though blasphemy prosecutions are probably precluded by a 1952 U.S. Supreme Court decision. Gambling: no state lotteries in the twentieth century until 1964, and casinos legal only in Nevada until 1978; sports betting still illegal in almost all states. Heroin and cocaine: legal until 1914. Marijuana: legal as a matter of federal law until 1937. Prescription drug system: monopoly provision of drugs through "prescription only" established after 1938 for non-narcotics. Prostitution: legal in much of the United States in the first two decades of the century, with brothel prostitution currently legal in some counties in Nevada.

So, on average, centenarians have been vice contrarians: all of the contrarian's proposed reforms have held sway during the previous hundred years in our democracy. The point of this exercise in imaginary characters is to convince you that our current vice policies aren't eternal, fixed in stone. Vice policies have undergone a revolution in the lifetime of Mr. Twentieth Century, and there is no reason to suspect that they won't do the same thing during the reign of Ms. Twenty-first Century. Future centenarians are likely to be vice contrarians, too.

Why am I trying to so hard to convince you of this? Why risk your wrath by inventing mythical beings simply to indicate the obvious, that vice policies change over time? Because somehow we have a tendency to view our current vice laws perhaps not as immutable, but as more-or-less correct, and no longer susceptible to radical revision. Of course alcohol is legal. Of course heroin is illegal. Of course states conduct lotteries. Of course potent medicines are available only by prescription. We somehow think of our current approaches to vice as natural, not seriously open to question, even though these approaches are relatively recent phenomena. Within twenty or fifty or one hundred years, our vice policies once again could undergo massive upheaval.

Not only could our vice policies in fifty years look much different than they do today, I think that there are good grounds to think that they will indeed be substantially revised. This conclusion can be reached irrespective of the merits of today's policies, for two related reasons. First, the oscillations that centenarians have seen in vice policy are a recurrent and widespread occurrence, long pre-dating the twentieth century. Second, much of the impetus for the historical variation in regulations is that vice itself "implies moral ambivalence, that is conduct that a person may enjoy and deplore at the same time. As a corollary, moral ambivalence generates controversy over public policy concerning certain activities."[1] Unlike attitudes toward consistently reviled crimes such as robbery and murder, then, the stance toward vice is marked by vacillations that induce significant swings in regulations. Of course, bad laws in any policy field will generate incentives to reform, and there is reason to believe that some of our current vice policies are far from optimal. But the properties of vice, as explored next, engender rule changes even when current policies are tolerably designed.

VICE – IT EVEN SOUNDS COOL[2]

Despite longstanding, widespread, and often deserved condemnation, vice has retained its popularity. A catalogue of today's prevalent vices would include the excessive consumption of alcohol, tobacco, and illicit drugs. Activities such as gambling, prostitution, and viewing pornography would also make the list. Most of these activities were considered to be vicious centuries ago, members of the venerable vice categories of substance abuse, illegitimate sexual

---

[1] Skolnick (1988, p. 10).

[2] I borrowed the locution from a t-shirt popular at Duke University circa 1990 that read "Duke – It Even Sounds Cool."

relations, and wagering. Other behaviors that sometimes seek to be designated as vices do not have the same illustrious heritage: shopaholics and chocoholics are recent arrivals to the vice bestiary.

What qualifies as a vice? Certainly perceptions of both pleasure and wickedness are part of the equation.[3] But beyond fun and iniquity, vices typically exhibit three characteristics. First, they suggest excess. The consumption of alcohol is not a vice – rather, the excessive or abusive consumption of alcohol constitutes a vice.

The term "vice" as traditionally applied to substance abuse, illegitimate sex, and gambling is not as broad as the classical conception. For Aristotle, vices helped to locate virtue, which "is a mean between two vices, that which depends on excess and that which depends on defect; and again it is a mean because the vices respectively fall short of or exceed what is right in both passions and actions, while virtue both finds and chooses that which is intermediate."[4] As Aristotle recognized, for pleasurable activities, where temperate behavior is virtuous, one is more likely to find excessive indulgence rather than deficiency.[5] So the vice of intemperance implies a surplus, not a shortage, of pleasure seeking. But for Aristotle, too little pleasure seeking, too little hedonism, is just as vicious as too much. For our purposes, however, we look only at the excess, not the deficit side, of the Aristotelean vice ledger.

A second characteristic of a vice, indeed, one that often features in dictionary definitions, is that vice is not a one-time or infrequent indulgence but, rather, represents a pattern of behavior. Vice, according to *The Oxford Universal Dictionary*, is "1. Depravity or corruption of morals; evil, immoral, or wicked habits or conduct; indulgence in degrading pleasures or practices. 2. A habit or practice of an immoral, degrading, or wicked nature." So someone who every now and then has a bit too much to drink cannot be said to be a creature of vice, by this reckoning, if the indulgence is sufficiently irregular.[6] Vice is associated with habits, and bad (though pleasurable) habits at that.

A third feature of vice, and one that holds important implications for appropriate regulations, is that the direct ill effects of vice generally are borne by the person who engages in the vice. A person who drinks too much suffers the hangover herself. A person who gambles too much loses money that is his or, at least at the time of the loss, is under his control. This is not to say that the indirect

---

[3] Vice "implies pleasure and popularity, as well as wickedness." Skolnick (1988, p. 10).

[4] Aristotle, in *Nicomachean Ethics*, Book II, Chapter VI.

[5] Aristotle, *Nicomachean Ethics*, Book II, Chapter VII, 1107b. In general, temperance does not mean abstinence, though temperance societies in the United States in the nineteenth century eventually promoted abstinence from alcohol, not temperate consumption, as a goal.

[6] An alternative approach, suggested by Socrates, is that vice doesn't imply a bad habit so much as habits themselves generate the conditions of virtue or viciousness: "Then virtue is the health and beauty and well-being of the soul, and vice the disease and weakness and deformity of the same? . . . And do not good practices lead to virtue, and evil practices to vice?" Socrates, as recorded by Plato, in *The Republic*, Book IV.

effects of vice do not exact an enormous price from intimates of alcoholics and pathological gamblers or victims of drunk drivers – clearly their suffering is immense. But the direct effects of using alcohol, like those of using ketchup, are primarily sustained by the consumer him or herself. Further, except for the pleasure of indulging, those direct consequences of vice tend to be negative – an excessive devotion to exercise or Shakespeare generally is not viewed as vicious.

There are common situations in which significant, direct repercussions from vice fall upon someone other than the vice consumer. "Secondhand" smoke from cigarettes might damage the health of proximate nonsmokers, and drug use by pregnant women can harm their fetuses. Nevertheless, for the most part, vice conducted in private is "self-regarding" behavior, to employ the terminology of John Stuart Mill.

An objection might surface at this point: surely alcohol and ketchup differ in ways that carry grave consequences. People are much more likely to become a nuisance, or worse, to others through alcohol abuse than they are through excessive consumption of ketchup. (Has anyone ever ruined his life, and the lives of those around him, from too much ketchup?) But most people who consume alcohol do not ruin their lives with it – that trait it shares with ketchup. And even if all users of alcohol and ketchup did ruin their lives, alcohol and ketchup consumption would still qualify as self-regarding activities, while robbery, for instance, would not. Most of the direct negative effects of robbery are sustained not by the robber but by his victim. So every country outlaws robbery, whereas the regulatory approach taken to alcohol varies considerably across time and place. A vice need not be, and often is not, a crime, though some vice, like heroin addiction in a society where heroin is prohibited and hence expensive, promotes criminal behavior as a secondary effect. When vice is criminalized, it is, to use a once-common phrase that has fallen out of favor, a victimless crime.

The excess, habit, and self-regarding features are not sufficient to distinguish vice from other activities, such as exercise, that usually are not considered to be vicious: vice also suggests that wickedness is mixed with the pleasure. That is, for many people, vice implicates morality, or rather, immorality. Risky, habit-forming, self-regarding recreational activities, such as skiing or scuba diving, are not vicious, because no one views these recreational pursuits as immoral. Drinking, drug-taking, and nonmarital sex often are considered to be immoral, and this consideration has played a central role in the regulation of vice over the years. As with vice policy, however, perceptions of immorality are neither universal nor immutable.

But taking perceptions of immorality as given, a traditional vice exhibits excess, is habitual, and produces direct consequences that fall nearly in their entirety on the person engaging in it. These common traits imply that approaches to regulating vices as disparate as gambling and injecting heroin involve a shared set of principles. Within the class of illicit drugs alone there are vast and important variations that influence the appropriateness of alternative regulatory structures; nevertheless, it makes sense to discuss public policy toward alcohol, gambling, prostitution, and so on, within a common framework.

The "habit" and "excess" characteristics of vice might not apply to occasional indulgers such as social drinkers, small-time lottery players, or weekend marijuana smokers. Nonetheless, we will consider the full range of users, light as well as heavy drinkers (and gamblers, and tokers, and so on), when we examine regulations, even though only for the habitual or heavy drinkers does alcohol consumption meet all of the standard markers of vice. The bulk of the ill effects associated with vicious activity tend to derive from a relatively small number of excessive users or addicts. But "the bulk" is not the whole: many of the costs of alcohol use are attributable to those who are occasional drinkers – and similarly with respect to other vices.

Why devote much time or attention to studying vice? First, as its long-term popularity suggests, vice is inherently interesting, it continues to amuse. But concern with vice is stoked by factors beyond curiosity or prurience. Public policy relating to vice is of prime, personal relevance for almost everyone, in ways that housing policy or even national defense policy are not. For many Americans, vice will serve as their unintended introduction to the criminal justice system: drunk driving and possession of illegal drugs are the two most common reasons for arrest.[7] Few families have been untouched by tragedies associated with drug, alcohol, or gambling abuse. Even for those in households not directly connected to vice, if we could find such people, vice nevertheless plays a major role in shaping their constitutional rights. In the United States, the extent to which speech is protected against government control is set, in large measure, by Supreme Court decisions concerning attempts to regulate pornography and erotic dancing. Much of the government's scope for conducting searches has been mapped out by judicial rulings pertaining to investigations aimed at illegal drugs. Wiretaps were countenanced by the Supreme Court in an alcohol bootlegging case, and later a warrant requirement for electronic bugs was instituted via a Supreme Court decision involving an interstate gambling operation.[8] There is no avoiding it: the policy issues surrounding vice are immense and continual and have implications well beyond vice's own significant ambit. If that isn't enough of a reason to concern yourself with the regulation of vice, perhaps you can be persuaded by Milton, poet of paradise, who argued that familiarizing yourself with vice can help you to understand its opposite:

> Since therefore the knowledge and survey of vice is in this world so necessary to
> the constituting of human virtue, and the scanning of error to the confirmation

[7] See the Appendix.
[8] *Olmstead v. United States*, 277 U.S. 438 (1927), and *Katz v. United States*, 389 U.S. 347 (1967).

of truth, how can we more safely, and with less danger, scout into the regions of sin and falsity than by reading all manner of tractates and hearing all manner of reason? And this is the benefit which may be had of books promiscuously read.[9]

Onward then, promiscuously, for what I hope constitutes "knowledge and survey of vice."

ECONOMICS AND VICE, AND MORE ON KETCHUP

Trying to understand vice and its regulation is a hopelessly interdisciplinary undertaking. Medicine, law, psychology, sociology, history, economics, and many other fields of knowledge are implicated in providing insight into vice. Vice isn't brain surgery – rather, it concerns brain surgery and lots of other specialties, too. (Rocket science, by and large, is not one of them.) I am an economist, however, and though I try to do all that becomes an author, I privilege the economics approach.

What advantages, or perhaps I should say features, are offered by an economic approach to vice? Economics is the science of choice and in theory, at least, should be as applicable to choices to grow opium poppies or inject heroin as it is to choices to grow tomatoes or eat ketchup. Indeed, the rational choice framework of economics has proved its worth in a range of applications, including such nontraditional settings as decisions to get married, to have children, or to commit crimes. Nevertheless, it is hard to look at the choices of a homeless heroin addict and to view these choices as being the result of some rational decision calculus – hard, but not impossible, given years of economics training. Even homeless heroin addicts at least seem to conform to the "law of demand," the notion that if the price exacted to engage in an activity is raised, people will lessen their involvement in the activity. The extent to which an addict can be said to make rational choices, and what difference it makes for policy, will be examined in some detail in Chapter 2.

If addicts are incapable of making decisions that contribute to their well-being, then there is little reason for society to respect those choices, just as society does not respect the choices of those who are adjudged to be insane. Children represent another subset of humanity whose choices are not given full societal warrant.

Most people who choose to engage in vice are neither addicts, insane, nor children, however; hence, the rationality of their choices is generally not suspect. A choice taken rationally has the feature that it provides the decision

[9] Milton, *Areopagitica*. But why turn to Milton when the voice of Fanny Hill, heroine of John Cleland's (1985 [1748/9], pp. 187–8) famous eighteenth-century pornographic novel, *Memoirs of a Woman of Pleasure*, can serve the purpose?: "if I have painted vice all in its gayest colours, if I have deck'd it with flowers, it has been solely in order to make the worthier, the solemner sacrifice of it, to virtue."

maker with the highest possible "net benefits," relative to all of the other options available at the time of the choice – where the net benefits are judged from the point of view of the decision maker. Many people consider themselves to be better off by drinking alcohol, or by smoking marijuana, or by going to a casino, or by having sex with a prostitute – just as they view themselves as being better off when they have ketchup on their burger. So a second feature of the economics approach to vice is that vicious activity is viewed as having benefits. The existence of benefits might be obvious, but public debate regarding vice policy is typically conducted as if vices were some sort of mysterious activities that involve only costs. Even supporters of liberalized vice regulations are unlikely to point to the good features of the activities: when is the last time you heard someone argue that there really isn't enough pornography available or that it would be a welcome change if the extent of prostitution would grow? The policy discussion, rather, is almost always conducted in terms of the lessening of evils, ways to minimize the extent or the harms of vices, as opposed to maximizing their net benefits. Those who take a public health approach to vice, or view addiction as a disease, for instance, frequently ignore potential benefits as they look to ameliorate the medical hardships associated with drinking or drugs.[10] The economics approach employed here instead tries to keep the benefits of vice in mind, too, even when the explicit discussion involves minimizing harms.

If choices are viewed as rational, then to some extent, society can leave adults alone in their vice-related choices, just as society has little interest in my ketchup-related choices. But only to some extent: if the decision maker does not face the full panoply of costs and benefits, then his or her choices, though rational, will be skewed. A burglar might be rational, but in making decisions, he (rationally) ignores the losses his choices directly impose on his victims. If he considered these costs, he probably would not burgle, though he might offer to buy those items he particularly covets. Is a drug user more like a burglar or a ketchup eater?

The point is, for now, that the economics approach views this as a meaningful question. In economics terminology, the issue concerns the extent to which the costs and benefits of a decision are "internal" or "external." Sometimes economics is viewed as being exclusively about money, but this is far from the case. An economic approach to regulation considers the full range of costs and benefits, those that can be quantified and those that can't be quantified. If you are unhappy because someone a thousand miles away is smoking a marijuana cigarette in a safe manner without directly or even indirectly harming anyone else (except for your unhappiness), in theory, an economic approach would

---

[10] Public health researchers tend to use population-level analysis, whereas economists focus on individual choice. Cook and Leitzel (1996) talk about the public health versus economics approach to gun regulations.

take your distress into account in evaluating alternative policy regimes toward cannabis.[11] Economics looks to include all costs and benefits, monetary or not. The key distinction, again, is between those costs and benefits that the decision maker bears and those that are imposed on others. A rational decision maker who takes all costs and benefits into account can safely be left alone – his choices, aimed at his own self-interest, will have the Adam Smith property of simultaneously promoting the welfare of society.[12] But if the decision maker does not face the full range of consequences from his choices, that is, if there are spillovers or "externalities," then intervention might be required to ensure that social welfare is not sacrificed to the private interests of the decision maker. And so we have laws condemning burglary, but leave adults free to make their own ketchup-related decisions. My earlier contention that engaging in most forms of vice is primarily a "self-regarding" activity implies that, with respect to externalities, a typical drug user is more like a ketchup consumer than a burglar. Indeed, it is the self-regarding nature of vice that generates moral ambiguity. Burglary and murder are not similarly self-regarding, and there is little ambivalence underlying their condemnation and criminalization.

The coincidence between private choices and the public good, however, depends not just on the absence of externalities but also on the rationality of the decision maker. We have already noted that addicts and rationality do not appear to be all that closely paired. But drug use and the consumption of other vices present rationality concerns not just for addicts but also for occasional users. (That is, I am now suspicious of what I claimed, a few paragraphs ago, was not generally suspect: the rationality of vice choices by nonaddicted adults.) Alcohol, drugs, tobacco, and gambling are like ketchup in that they involve primarily self-regarding decisions. But they still differ from ketchup in that people (nonaddicted people) are more likely to regret their drug-related decisions than they are their ketchup-related decisions. This is not true of everyone – some people who use illicit drugs, for instance, no doubt are every bit as reasoned in their drug use as in their ketchup consumption, and maybe some otherwise deliberate folks go wacky with the ketchup in ways they later rue. But all in all, vices are particularly susceptible to lead to regrettable individual decision making, even in isolated, acute instances among nonaddicts. (The regret might manifest itself on the "supply" as well as the "demand" side, from part-time strippers and drug

---

[11] In practice, your unease would get little or no attention, because it is hard to quantify and, more importantly, it is too easy to fake – even people who barely care might claim that they care quite a bit, if by such dissembling they could influence policy outcomes. Choices that are made when your own resources are on the line – as opposed to answers to survey questions about how much you care – are typically given more weight.

[12] To avoid libeling Adam Smith, let me note that (1) there were many areas where he favored some government influence over decisions, and (2) his reference to the invisible hand in *The Wealth of Nations* was specific to a very circumscribed setting; see Grampp (2000). Further, the precise coincidence of individual choices with the social good generally requires such unrealistic conditions as undistorted, competitive market prices.

sellers along with occasional cyberporn consumers or drug users.) We have legitimate reason to worry about whether typical choices with respect to vices serve the interests of the decision maker as well as the interests of the rest of us.

Beyond overarching issues of costs and benefits, externalities, and rationality, economics brings some specific competencies to the study of vice. The basic supply and demand framework applies to vice markets as to other markets, and regulatory policies can usefully be delineated into demand-side (targeting users) or supply-side (targeting producers, traffickers, and sellers) approaches. Economists have learned a good deal about regulation of industries, such as public utilities and airlines, and some of those regulatory lessons apply in vice settings, too. Public finance specialists study taxes, tax evasion, and black markets, and their insights also have relevance for vice. Finally, economists have conducted many quantitative studies that help to answer such questions as how the consumption of cigarettes responds to a higher tax, a ban on advertising, or the provision of antismoking ads.

So economics offers an approach, and it offers some tools to generate information. Nevertheless, an early lesson for anyone who undertakes the "knowledge and survey of vice" is humility, the recognition of how little we know. What is addiction? Are chemical addictions (drugs) like behavioral addictions (viewing Internet pornography, gambling)? How do people substitute among drugs? Will a crackdown on marijuana or Ecstasy lead to more use of alcohol and perhaps more drunk-driving deaths? How will the long-run effects of a drug- control policy differ from the short-run effects? Are regulatory walls stable? For instance, is it possible to shield teens effectively from substances that are legally available to adults? Does tolerance of cannabis make it more problematic to limit the consumption of "hard" drugs like heroin? Do state-operated lotteries generate forces that lead to legalization and commercial promotion of other forms of gambling? Although we are not completely at sea with respect to answers to these questions, we are pretty far from shore. Other questions are perhaps more fundamental and maybe harder still to answer. Should pornography be freely available, and even difficult to avoid? Do we want to respect personal freedom to use drugs, perhaps encouraging habits that will ruin many lives, or do we want to put folks in jail for carrying around a substance that they occasionally like to consume? These broader questions come close to asking, what kind of society do we want to live in? Neither economics nor rocket science is of much help in providing answers to questions like these. But economics can help us to understand, to some extent, the kinds of worlds that will be generated by alternative policies regulating vice.

THE $3\frac{1}{3}$ STANDARD VICE CONCERNS

(1) Kids; (2) addicts; (3) external harms; ($3\frac{1}{3}$) endangered health and other negative impacts on nonaddicted adult consumers – already mentioned in the

previous discussion, these constitute the standard $3\frac{1}{3}$ vice concerns. At first glance, perhaps they look like four concerns. They only sum to $3\frac{1}{3}$, I maintain, because harms suffered by nonaddicted consumers (or producers) don't quite rate as a full unit, equivalent to each of the first three concerns. The rationality of decisions made by kids and addicts is questionable. Choices made when some of the costs of those choices are borne by others carry no presumption of equivalence between private and public benefit. But if you are a normal adult, why should there be public concern, even only $\frac{1}{3}$ of a concern, over those aspects of your decisions that do not harm others?

In self-regarding areas other than vice, we generally don't question adult consumption of goods or activities, even if some risk is involved. If people want to scuba dive, ski, or mountain climb, then they jolly well can, even though these are quite risky activities. Although we might want to find ways to make such activities safer, we don't look on their practitioners as hopelessly misguided souls, and we certainly don't put them in jail for indulging their curious recreational preferences. We respect skiers' abilities to judge the risks and benefits for themselves and to make their own skiing-related decisions. But for the traditional vices, as noted, we might have some concern about the rationality of decisions even by nonaddicted adults: more concern than we have with their ketchup or skiing decisions (approximately zero) but less concern than we have for the vice choices of kids and addicts. Approximately $\frac{1}{3}$ the concern, I will arbitrarily maintain. Whether the vice is gambling or pornography, smoking or heroin use, the standard $3\frac{1}{3}$ concerns dominate the effort to construct a desirable regulatory environment.

One "cost" of vice that I have not explicitly included among the standard concerns is productivity losses. Sometimes these are prominently featured when the costs of vice are being tallied: "alcohol abuse costs so many billion dollars in reduced productivity" is not an uncommon trope.[13] But laziness, video games, skiing, lunch, or almost any use of time not directly tied to production are also sources of productivity losses. (Every minute you other folks are not working is lowering my standard of living. Now get back to work!) As we don't know how much productivity from others we have the right to expect or demand, any calculation of productivity losses is bound to be arbitrary. Of course, part of the reason that we don't see calculations of the productivity cost of lunch is we trust adults to make rational decisions about their lunch habits. We are less sure of vice-related decisions (and the recent rise of obesity makes us less trusting of those lunch decisions, too). But to some extent, that uncertainty is implicitly taken into account as a component of the $\frac{1}{3}$ concern

---

[13] See, for instance, National Institute of Alcohol Abuse and Alcoholism (2001) and the general discussion of cost estimates in Single (n.d.). Somewhat inconsistently, those who highlight productivity losses associated with vices rarely include the incomes of drug sellers, say, as one of the benefits of vice.

identified previously, the negative impacts of vice upon nonaddicted adult indulgers. Vice consumers will tend to have lower earnings if their vice habits reduce their productivity. Beyond this implicit accounting, however, we should be wary of counting "productivity loss" as part of the social cost of engaging in vice, skiing, or anything else.

It is not only on the cost side that analyses of vice policy frequently include some questionable elements. Proponents of legalization of a currently prohibited vice often point to the tax revenue that might be raised following legalization. Indeed, significant tax revenue can be collected from sales of a legal vice – current sin taxes on alcohol, tobacco, and gambling are cases in point – but that revenue does not represent a net social benefit from legalization; rather, tax revenue is a transfer, a cost borne by those who pay the tax and a gain to those who are beneficiaries of the subsequent government spending. The distributional consequences of the tax might be a relevant policy consideration, but unless the tax is correcting for some other distortion – and we will later see that vices frequently are associated with significant distortions – tax revenues are not a social gain, handy though they might be for the stereotypical cash-strapped government, and despite the prominent role that the prospect of increased tax revenues plays in the politics of vice policy.[14]

A related element of vice regulation that rightly receives attention in policy debates is the extent of resources devoted to the regulatory regime. For outlawed drugs, these include the costs of police officers, courts, and prisons, and the diminished enjoyment of life by those imprisoned for drug-law violations. For legal vices like alcohol, these resources include myriad licensing boards, inspectors, and enforcers, as well as courts and prisons for those who run afoul of the system. All else equal, of course, it is best to minimize the amount of resources that have to be devoted to regulating vice or virtue.

Productivity and budgetary effects pertain to a whole range of public policy issues. What separates vice from other policy areas is the centrality of the $3\frac{1}{3}$ concerns, those dealing with kids, addicts, externalities, and the costs borne by nonaddicted vice participants.

HARM REDUCTION VERSUS ZERO TOLERANCE

Having recently extolled the benefits of vice, let me now ignore them. Consider the costs of vicious activity, both the harms suffered by vice participants and the external damage imposed upon people other than the relevant decision maker – that is, other than either the producer or the consumer of vice. Drinking involves

---

[14] If the tax corrects for underpricing of a vice (perhaps because of otherwise neglected externalities or "internalities"), then the revenue might involve a net social gain. Further, a second-order benefit might be available from vice tax revenue if the revenue is raised with less distortion via a vice tax than by some alternative means (an income tax, say). Chapter 5 elucidates some of these points.

increased violence, for instance, and more car wrecks. In both cases, it is not the drinking per se but, rather, subsequent behaviors, fighting or driving recklessly while impaired, that are directly responsible for many of the costs that drinkers impose on others and themselves. Nevertheless, these costs are tied sufficiently closely to drinking that we can account them to be overall costs of alcohol consumption. Policy can change the relationship, however; it might be possible to alter the regulatory regime in ways that will lead to more drinking but fewer auto accidents.

It turns out that this is where much of the debate about vice policy centers: reducing social harms from a vice as opposed to reducing the prevalence of the vice itself.[15] Alcohol Prohibition in the United States led to a fall in alcohol consumption; eventually, however, a consensus emerged that the social costs associated with drinking and the enforcement of Prohibition, including violence, corruption, and the poisoning of consumers through adulterated beverages, were higher than they would be under an alternative regulatory regime where alcohol was legal – even if legal alcohol meant more drinking would take place. The experience of Prohibition was sufficiently searing that the consensus remains, more than seventy years later: there is essentially no support for a return to national-level alcohol prohibition in the United States, even though such a policy could reduce the consumption of alcohol. (Another reason why repeal of Prohibition is itself not ripe for repeal is that many people recognize the benefits of alcohol consumption – they enjoy wine with dinner or a beer at the game. Research suggests some additional benefit from moderate alcohol consumption for the middle-aged in the form of improved cardiovascular health. Alternatively, the existence of benefits from drug use or prostitution is rarely conceded publicly, even by those who find private pleasure in these activities.)

The trade-off between prevalence and harm exists because stricter control of a vice typically has two effects: it reduces the amount of the vice produced and consumed and, simultaneously, raises the average social cost of that vicious activity that manages to take place anyway, despite the stricter regime. Whether total social costs rise or fall depends on which of the effects dominates, the lower level of activity or the higher cost per vicious incident.[16]

As the current policy toward illicit drugs in the United States is quite punitive, the issue of reducing harm versus reducing consumption generally presents itself with respect to potential liberalization or medicalization of drug policy. Free needle exchanges, for instance, make it easier for addicts to use heroin or other injectable drugs. In a sense, such programs subsidize the use of

---

[15] Here I have used the term "prevalence" to refer to total consumption. For some purposes, it makes sense to follow MacCoun and Reuter (2001, p. 10) and to define prevalence as the number of users. Then total consumption equals "intensity," the number of doses per user, multiplied by prevalence.

[16] MacCoun and Reuter (2001, pp. 10ff.) were the first to stress the centrality for vice policy of the trade-off between the number of vice incidents and the average harm per incident.

heroin, and in themselves, may well lead to more heroin use.[17] Nevertheless, the point of such exchanges is to lower the costs of heroin use, by reducing needle sharing and thereby limiting the transmission of HIV and hepatitis. Other "harm reduction" measures that might, as an unintended but perhaps unavoidable side effect, also increase the prevalence of illicit drug use include subsidized methadone maintenance for heroin addicts and the provision of devices to test the purity of drugs like Ecstasy.[18] (Methadone maintenance might reduce external costs by making junkies less likely to steal, to become infected with HIV, or to lose their jobs, whereas drug purity testing primarily protects the users, that is, reduces internal costs.) Stricter enforcement, alternatively, tends to raise the levels of violence in the distribution network and the costs of the administration of justice, while potentially lowering the amount of the drug distributed and consumed.

"Extreme" policies starkly illustrate the trade-off. Legalization of drugs under a regulatory regime similar to that for alcohol (taxed and regulated but wide availability for adults, a loosely enforced prohibition against older teenagers) would end the violence that is associated with current drug markets, diminish the adulteration of drugs while standardizing purity (thus helping to prevent unintentional overdoses), and reduce police and judicial costs and corruption; simultaneously, an increase in use of the formerly illicit drugs would be likely. Alternatively, a strict zero tolerance campaign would have essentially the opposite effects, curtailed use but greater harm per use.[19] That such a trade-off often exists means that the relative desirability of various policies will, unavoidably, depend on values – in general, one vice-control policy cannot be said to be clearly better than another. Consider the provision of heroin at low cost in a safe environment to those adjudged to be addicts. (This policy, called "heroin maintenance," has been undertaken in Canada and some European countries, with many beneficial consequences.[20]) Suppose that we know that this policy will have a net monetary cost of zero, but that it will lead to two additional people becoming heroin addicts annually as well as one fewer death per year from heroin overdose. Should this policy be adopted? If you think that it should be adopted, what if the number of new addicts per overdose life saved is not two, but two thousand annually? Two hundred thousand? How

[17] In practice, needle exchange programs do not seem to promote heroin use, and by putting addicts in touch with treatment alternatives, they can combat such use. The Centers for Disease Control and Prevention, in their December 2005 report on Syringe Exchange Programs [SEPs], note: "Studies also show that SEPs do not encourage drug use among SEP participants or the recruitment of first-time drug users." The report is available at www.cdc.gov/idu/facts/AED_IDU_SYR.pdf (accessed March 4, 2007).

[18] As with needle exchange, methadone maintenance in practice does not seem to promote drug use – rather the opposite, actually. See www.drugpolicy.org/library/research/methadone.cfm (accessed March 4, 2007).

[19] A zero tolerance policy might not actually cause use to decrease; see Caulkins (1993).

[20] Small, Drucker, and Editorial for *Harm Reduction Journal* (2006).

many new addicts would it take before you would prefer a policy that avoids those new addictions, even though it would mean sanctioning an additional overdose death each year? Does the extent to which heroin addiction imposes external as opposed to internal costs factor into the decision? Whatever your answers to these queries, it is clear that intelligent people of goodwill could disagree over whether heroin maintenance is a desirable policy.

Not all vice-control policies are beset by the prevalence versus cost trade-off. Prevention programs, such as the provision of accurate information concerning the dangers of drugs, can lead to lower prevalence without any concomitant effect on the social costs per use. Indeed, by reducing demand, a prevention program might decrease the price of illicit drugs and in turn decrease the violence associated with dealing in the less lucrative black market. In practice, needle exchange and methadone maintenance also seem to reduce costs without increasing prevalence.[21]

The harm reduction dilemma presents itself in many areas of social policy other than vice. Those who extol zero tolerance in some vice arenas might, somewhat inconsistently, find themselves on the side of harm reduction in another context. Should it be legal to abandon a newborn infant? Won't legalizing baby abandonment lead to more abandonments? Perhaps – but those abandonments that do take place can be made safer for the infants; that is, the right type of legalization might reduce harm, even if more babies are deserted. Or at least that is what the state of Texas thought in the late 1990s (under then-Governor George W. Bush) when it adopted a law shielding parents from prosecution if they abandoned their infant by bringing the baby to an emergency medical technician.[22]

FUTILITY?[23]

While there aren't many voices publicly extolling the virtues of vice, eloquent explication of the perils of prohibition is not uncommon, especially for relatively safe illegal drugs like marijuana. Sometimes an explicit analogy is made to the experience of alcohol Prohibition. The costs of a drug prohibition, by such reckonings, are simply not worth the gains in the form of reduced consumption. But sometimes the argument goes further and becomes the assertion "prohibition doesn't work" or, perhaps, in the face of significant demand for a drug, "prohibition can't work." Why? And "doesn't work" relative to what? The standard reasoning here is that motivated users and profit-seeking sellers

[21] See notes 17 and 18.

[22] See Dara Akiko Williams, "California Debates Measure to Set Rules for Abandoning Babies," *Chicago Tribune*, February 2, 2000, p. 9. For other zero tolerance versus harm reduction policy instances, see MacCoun and Reuter (2001, p. 389).

[23] The rhetoric of futility and perversity claims was explicated in Hirschman (1991); see my discussion of Hirschman's approach in Leitzel (2003).

will always be able to evade government controls and find each other. Prohibition, by this reckoning, is futile, a small and leaky dam that is unable to cope with the floodwaters of market forces, so that the prevalence of drug use under a prohibition is similar to what would occur in some legal regulated market, like that for cigarettes in the United States.

The problem with this argument – which, again, is surprisingly common – is that it is wrong. Prohibition can "work," especially if working is taken to mean reducing consumption relative to the levels that would prevail in an unfettered or lightly regulated marketplace. There might be high costs, and they might be sufficiently high as to render prohibition foolhardy, but a policy of prohibition is not doomed to futility.[24] Of course, there might be alternative regulatory schemes that also lower consumption, and with fewer associated harms: such policies would then dominate prohibition. But in some dimensions, prohibitions can work. If not, then perhaps we should eliminate drug prohibitions not just for adults but also for children.

Sometimes critics of prohibitions go beyond the futility argument, by arguing that consumption of a drug actually increases under a prohibitory regime. (Social scientist Albert O. Hirschman refers to such reasoning as the "perversity argument."[25]) The usual idea underlying the perversity argument applied to vice prohibitions is that there is an allure to contraband, a forbidden fruit effect. That some such appeal for outlawed goods (and even outlawed people) exists is undoubtedly the case, if introspection can serve as a reliable guide. But the claim that such an effect dominates, that consumption increases in the face of an enforced prohibition, is highly suspect. There is no reason to think that vice is an exception to the usual law of demand; therefore, a prohibition that raises the effective price of consuming a drug should lead to diminished drug consumption. Although intuition tells us that there is something to this forbidden fruit argument, it also tells us that if the prohibition on drugs and prostitution were lifted, we would immediately see more drug use and more acts of prostitution. My intuition suggests that for many who currently abstain, the only issue would be which vice to try first. (Nevertheless, to speculate even more recklessly, I imagine most supporters of these prohibitions do not see themselves as being directly and personally helped by the bans – i.e., they probably do not think that if it weren't for the illegality, they would become involved in drugs or prostitution.)

The point is, the easy resort to futility or perversity claims generally doesn't stand up to scrutiny. If it did, those arguments would carry the day: who would support a costly and violence-inducing prohibition if it were sure to

---

[24] Indeed, one might suspect – if one were sufficiently intemperate to question motives – that many of those who argue against drug prohibition on the grounds of futility actually oppose prohibition precisely because it is not futile.

[25] Hirschman (1991).

either heighten or to have no effect on consumption of a dangerous product?[26] Rather, trying to determine desirable vice policies requires a serious inquiry into the full array of consequences arising from alternative regulatory regimes: arguments against prohibition must be made of sterner stuff than confident assertions of futility or perversity. A prohibition generally doesn't make "the problem" worse; rather, a ban exacerbates some problems, creates some others, and alleviates some others. Judgment is required in ranking alternative vice-control policies, and reasonable people needn't all reach the same conclusions.

TOWARD A THESIS

It is not just conclusions that may differ. I have suggested that policy surrounding a variety of vices, from alcohol to heroin to prostitution, can be approached through a shared set of principles. But what principles are appropriate? This is the issue to which the next three chapters are devoted. First, I examine John Stuart Mill's attempt to develop a principle to govern social intervention in individual decision making, one he applied both to vice regulation and to policy more generally. Mill's "harm principle" argues that adult self-regarding activity should be free of societal constraint. I then augment the harm principle analysis with a look at our understanding of the nature of addiction.

These preliminaries lead me to suggest that a type of "robustness principle" should govern the regulation of vice: public policy toward addictive or vicious activities engaged in by adults should be robust with respect to departures from full rationality. That is, policies should work pretty well if everyone is fully informed and completely rational, and policies should work pretty well even if a substantial number of folks are occasionally (or frequently) irrational in their vice-related choices. "Working well" entails coming to grips with the $3\frac{1}{3}$ standard vice concerns of kids, addicts, externalities, and harms to nonaddicted adult users.

Working well when everyone is rational – the first part of the "robustness principle"– rules out prohibitions of most private adult vice. Working well when many folks are poorly informed or irrational – the second requirement of robustness – rules out unfettered access to traditional vicious goods such as alcohol, tobacco, or cocaine. Mandated information provision can go a long way toward overcoming problems with a lack of knowledge, but even

---

[26] Someone who understood that drug consumption, for instance, would increase under a ban might still support the prohibition if he or she believed that the law should nevertheless signal social disapproval of drugs. The "sending the wrong message" argument is curiously asymmetric: it rarely is used to argue for the criminalization of currently legal but morally questionable acts such as extreme rudeness or sexual promiscuity. Further, the actual message sent by drug laws might be much different than that of social disapproval of drugs. On the "sending the wrong message" argument, see MacCoun and Reuter (2001, pp. 389ff.), Husak (2002, pp. 56–7), and Kaplan (1998 [1988], p. 96).

well-informed people are susceptible to rationality shortfalls in the vice world. By this reckoning, high taxes, advertising restrictions, and subsidies focused on prevention and treatment are all potentially legitimate vice policies. Our current drug prohibition, of course, does not meet these guidelines, and I argue that the empirical record of U.S. alcohol and drug prohibition lends more credibility to the pertinence of the robustness precept.

The robustness principle shares with John Stuart Mill's harm principle an important consequence that already has been identified but is worth highlighting: adults should not be put in prison simply for engaging in vice, at least when their vicious behavior is carried out in private. Public manifestations can rightly be controlled, and forms of vice consumption or associated activities that directly threaten others (such as drunk driving) can be prohibited. As markets are generally public, buying and selling fall within the ambit of vice manifestations that legitimately can be regulated. But a drug user, found in possession of a small amount of a drug intended for his future personal consumption, should not be punished. Adults engaged in voluntary sexual behavior in private should not have to fear the criminal law, though possibly certain steps could be required to ensure the informed and voluntary nature of the activity. Friday night low-stakes poker games at Lou's house should not be a matter of concern to the local magistrate. I should be able to sip a glass of wine or eat some fatty foods, in the privacy of my own home, without worrying that a neighbor will notice and bring down upon me the forces of law and order. Come to think of it, a cookie sounds pretty good right about now.

I

The Harm Principle

When and how should the government (or society, more generally) intervene in the activities of individuals, and when should individuals go about their business free of government constraint?

The pioneering text addressing this issue is *On Liberty*, written by John Stuart Mill and published in 1859. Mill gave a simple answer to the question of the propriety of social compulsion, one that has become known as the "harm principle":

> ... the only purpose for which power can be rightfully exercised over any member of a civilised community, against his will, is to prevent harm to others. His own good, either physical or moral, is not a sufficient warrant.

Social coercion exercised over you for your own well-being, in the absence of "harm to others," is a violation of your individual liberty. Of course, Mill quickly offers the necessary child-excluding qualification, "that this doctrine is meant to apply only to human beings in the maturity of their faculties."[1]

Mill noted that, in the absence of a general principle, society was apt to intervene in individual decision making in circumstances where the intervention would likely be unhelpful and to fail to intervene when intervention was merited. The harm principle is useful in part because its application in most cases accords well with the intuitions developed in liberal democracies.[2] For instance, under the harm principle, the government has no business regulating what color I paint my living room, but society does have an interest in ensuring that my children are protected against abuse and have access to education. The principle also accords well with the standard economics approach to regulation (which is unsurprising as Mill authored the text that dominated economics instruction during the latter half of the nineteenth century). Government, according to this view, should intervene in activities among adults only in the presence of externalities.[3] The costs and benefits of various actions that

---

[1] Mill (1978, p. 9) is the source for the two initial quotes from *On Liberty*.

[2] The word "liberal" here is employed in the nineteenth-century (Millian) sense of being focused on individual liberties.

[3] Monopoly power might present another rationale for government intervention. Indeed, any departure from first-best competitive conditions, in theory, could generate an efficiency rationale for

accrue directly to the decision makers can best be weighed by the individuals in question. Only external effects, those that are imposed on nonconsenting others, provide a potential rationale for social intrusion into individual choice.

Most vice is what Mill referred to as "self-regarding" conduct, which does not directly harm other people, though it may harm the person engaging in it. Therefore, the harm principle presents a barrier, though not necessarily an insuperable one, to the societal regulation of vice. Victimless crimes would disappear in a Millian world – consensual adult behavior that does not involve a (nonconsenting) victim would not be criminalized.[4]

Simple to state, the harm principle has proven to be complex in application, an art as much as a science. Mill's concepts of self-regarding and other-regarding activities do not draw clear, unambiguous lines between different behaviors: "To make a satisfactory distinction between these two sorts of conduct requires the kind of practical, historically informed, and commonsensical, although unrigorous, analysis that Mill undertook in chapter 4 ["Of the Limits to the Authority of Society Over the Individual"] of *On Liberty*."[5] Nevertheless, the harm principle certainly seems to rule out general prohibitions against adult indulgence in most vices: there would be no such thing as an illegal drug, for instance, were a straightforward interpretation of the harm principle the guiding force underlying our vice laws. Likewise, prostitution and all other forms of consensual sex involving adults typically would not be criminal matters. Drugs and sex could still be regulated and, perhaps, even regulated quite strictly, under the standard established by the harm principle, but the private use of drugs and private exchanges for sex could not be forbidden to adults. Those strict regulations themselves would run up against the harm principle, once they became so stringent that they approximated a total ban.

Despite the general accord of the harm principle with the tenets of liberal democracies, Mill's rule has never attracted anything like unanimous consent. So one way to justify prohibition of some vice is simply to reject the harm principle, an approach that I will pursue in Chapter 3. A second possibility is to accept the harm principle but to argue that prohibition is not inconsistent with Mill's criterion. Here I will examine this second challenge to the harm principle in the case of drug prohibition.

How can drug use be criminalized without rejecting Mill's thesis? Prohibitionists reconcile their preferred policy with the harm principle via a number of

---

government intervention, and the government might also adopt regulations for distributional, as opposed to efficiency, concerns.

[4] There might be "crimeless victims," however. Mill's principle provides a necessary condition that must be met before societal intervention into adult decision making can be countenanced. Once this condition is met, once it is clear that an activity involves "harm to others," it still does not mean that any policy restricting the activity is justified. Although harm to others provides a necessary condition, it is not a sufficient condition vindicating any and all coercive policies.

[5] Posner (1992b, p. 438).

arguments, which correspond to the $3\frac{1}{3}$ standard vice concerns. One approach invokes the permissible exceptions to Mill's general rule: decisions made by children or those adult decisions that are made by individuals who are not "in the maturity of their faculties." Two and one-third of the $3\frac{1}{3}$ standard vice concerns enter here: kids, addicts, and harms imposed on nonaddicted adults from the questionable rationality of their vice choices. A second approach to harmonize Mill's principle with drug prohibition adopts an expansive notion of what constitutes "harm to others." This approach corresponds to the remaining standard vice concern: externalities. Mill's own interpretation of his harm principle, however, appears to rule out drug prohibition, despite the standard $3\frac{1}{3}$ vice concerns.

KIDS

Children are widely regarded as being fit subjects for prohibitions against consuming or producing vice, at least in the absence of parental supervision. There are many tricky issues, such as identifying an appropriate minimum drinking age or age of consent for sexual activities, but the conviction that the law can and should attempt to shield children from unbridled vice is all but universally accepted. The difficulty for the harm principle comes when regulations undertaken to further the interest of protecting children from vice involve collateral restrictions on adults.

For a moment, consider an imaginary world where both children and drugs have different properties than they have in our real world. Our imaginary children make the switch from childhood to adulthood instantaneously upon reaching their eighteenth birthday. Our imaginary drugs have the property that, while they are very enjoyable but completely harmless for adults, children who use the drug immediately perish. The imaginary children share one property with real ones, however – even though they know that drug use will result in terrible consequences for them, many kids might use drugs anyway, if they get the opportunity. How should adult drug use be controlled in such an imaginary world?

Essentially, every effort would have to be made to prevent youth contact with the fatal substances. One possibility would be that the adult market would be unrestricted, but that if any adult were found to be responsible for "leakage" of the drug to a child, the adult would face huge, possibly capital punishment. But I doubt that this regime would work, at least if adults found the drug so alluring (despite the potential legal penalties for misappropriation to children) that use remained popular. Drugs would leak to children, and those unlucky or careless adults who had a hand in the seepage would be severely punished. Only those who are caught and convicted would receive the punishment, however, and it might turn out, in practice, quite difficult to identify the adults involved in any specific case of drug use by a child. I suspect that the drug control regime that would be adopted in our imaginary world would involve extremely tight controls on adult drug use and possibly even prohibition (including prohibition of manufacture, sale, distribution, and so on), as an all-but-necessary means to protect against childhood drug use.[6] If there were no children, adult use would be unregulated. But the interest of protecting children, in our imaginary world, requires such vigilance that the liberty of adults to use the drug might be completely overridden. It would be a case of what some drug policy experts have termed "reluctant denial": the drug is denied to adults only because the diversion of the drug to rightly proscribed users, children, cannot easily be controlled in the absence of the adult prohibition, and the harms attendant upon that diversion are immense.[7]

The imaginary world parable points to one justification for a drug prohibition that is potentially consistent with the harm principle – even for a drug that involves no direct harm to those who do not use it (nor, in this fanciful example, does the drug harm those adults who actually do use it). Though there is no immediate, direct "harm to others" from adult use of the drug, the indirect harms are sufficiently closely associated with adult use and are so significant, that adult use really does constitute harm to kids. But even such harm only indicates that a prohibition is not perforce a violation of the liberty of adults to use this dangerous drug. If there are regulations short of prohibition that can effectively and cost-efficiently control the harm to children, then these regulations would be preferable to a ban.[8] Even if such efficacious controls are not available, a prohibition might be unwise, if the ban does a poor job at reducing the use by children or reduces that use while imposing other, possibly more significant, harms, such as widespread killings that take place in attempting to evade or enforce the ban.

Fortunately, in the actual world, kids are not as fragile as they are in our imaginary world. Further, prohibitions are not necessarily effective, nor are regulatory regimes short of prohibition completely ineffective. These considerations combine to make "reluctant denial-style" prohibitions relatively uncommon. Lots of substances that could be harmful to children are legal and, in some cases, like household cleaning products, essentially unregulated. (Alternatively, it is far from clear that heroin and cocaine, for instance, would be legal for adults even if these drugs posed no danger to children.) In general, society is

---

[6] Even more substantial changes in the organization of society would probably result from such a fatal combination of children and drugs; specifically, children might be segregated from adults, to the extent possible, until the children turn 18.

[7] "Reluctant denial" is discussed in MacCoun, Reuter, and Schelling (1996, p. 336).

[8] Here I am invoking what Pope (2000, p. 431), quoting Dworkin (1988, p. 126), terms "the principle of the least restrictive alternative." Mill (1978, p. 94) subscribes to this principle, too: "... leaving people to themselves is always better, *caeteris paribus*, than controlling them. ..." A similar principle is employed in First Amendment jurisprudence in the United States, which (in some domains) requires regulations that serve some compelling interest to be designed in such a way as to minimize collateral constraints upon speech.

unwilling to deny adults all access to materials or substances simply because their use by children would be injurious. Potential harm to children serves as a compelling reason for regulations concerning availability and consumption of some materials, including regulations holding adults responsible if kids are damaged by access resulting from adult negligence, but rarely is such potential harm sufficient to justify a complete, across-the-board prohibition, on adult possession or use as well as sale and manufacture.

Sexually explicit literature provides one instance where potential harm to children at one time did lead to reluctant denial for adults. The longtime standard, both in the United States and the United Kingdom, for whether a book could be suppressed as obscene was whether the book tended to "deprave and corrupt" minds vulnerable to such influences.[9] One problem with this standard is that it makes the most vulnerable mind the arbiter of the availability of literature to all potential readers, vulnerable or not. As the renowned American judge Learned Hand put it in a 1913 obscenity case, the "deprave and corrupt" test would "reduce our treatment of sex to the standard of a child's library. . . ."[10] This reduction or bowdlerization might be appropriate (àla reluctant denial) if the harm from failing to so censor were immense; but as there are alternatives to suppression that also can reduce the availability of obscene material to children, and as the harms attendant upon a child falling upon a copy of *The Decameron* or *Ulysses* or even material more salacious do not seem to be all that significant, complete prohibition of literature on the basis of supposed harms to children is inappropriate.[11]

Maybe drugs are different, more like the drug in our imaginary world than sexually explicit material in the real world. Maybe adult access to recreational drugs, even if regulated, opens channels that would not otherwise exist for making the drugs available to kids, and with this availability comes significant harm. Drug policy expert John Kaplan thought so, based in part on the experience with alcohol and tobacco, as he indicated in his influential 1988 article that argued against the legalization of hard drugs: ". . . legal access for adults makes a drug de facto available to the young."[12] But there are different degrees of availability. It is one thing for a drug to be available to those kids who invest enormous resources in tracking it down. It is something else entirely if every high school cafeteria table has its own supplier.

---

[9] The "deprave and corrupt" standard comes from the 1868 British case *Regina v. Hicklin*; see the discussion in Heins (2001, pp. 28ff.).

[10] The excerpt from Judge Hand's opinion is quoted in Heins (2001, p. 36).

[11] Of course, much of the censorship of works such as *Ulysses* or *Tropic of Cancer* actually may have been motivated by moral disapproval and not by perceived harms to children with precocious literary tastes.

[12] Kaplan (1998 [1988], p. 98). Hawkins and Zimring (1988, p. 201) make a similar point with respect to pornography: "[P]ornography cannot be made freely available in mainstream retail channels for adults and be made scarce for children."

Even if the legal availability of a drug to adults implies some availability to youths, the force of that implication in recommending a prohibition for adults depends on the relative availability of the drug to the young under a regime of prohibition. It cannot be taken for granted that drugs that are legal but regulated for adults will be more available to kids than drugs that are prohibited. Teen access to a prohibited drug depends upon many factors, including the extent of enforcement of the prohibition and the fashionableness of the drug. Certainly various illicit drugs are readily available to inner-city youths; indeed, employment opportunities in the distribution chain of such drugs also appear to be widely available to kids in the inner city. Many American teenagers find it easier to acquire marijuana, a prohibited drug, than alcohol or cigarettes, substances widely and legally available to adults, though prohibited for kids.[13] (Nor do kids appear to be commonly employed in the chain of distribution for alcohol.) Many American high school seniors, inner-city or not, can expeditiously procure pot. For each year since 1975, between 82 and 91 percent of twelfth-graders surveyed as part of the Monitoring the Future project have indicated that marijuana is either fairly easy or very easy to obtain.[14] Further, the harmfulness of drug use by children is not simply a function of the prevalence of that use. Prohibition might, for instance, lead to less drug use (by both adults and kids) than in a legal, regulated market, but the potential to overdose might be higher under prohibition because the strength of a dose would not be standardized.

Nevertheless, significant leakage of a drug to children from a legal adult market combined with substantial harm from that leakage provides one rationale for a drug prohibition, even for committed Millians. Note the use of the qualifier "significant," which indicates the extent to which application of the harm principle is a matter of judgment. Given the evidence concerning marijuana availability and the employment of young children in some sectors of the illicit drug trade, I generally do not think that any marginal increase in availability to kids through leakage from a legal adult market would be significant enough to justify, in itself, an adult prohibition of a recreational drug – but others might legitimately disagree. (Leakage is particularly unimpressive, I would maintain, in establishing the desirability of a ban on adult possession, as opposed to sales or manufacture.[15]) One difficulty of making categorical pronouncements here is that drug legalization would undoubtedly have different consequences for

---

[13] Results of a survey of 1,000 teens (12 to 17 year olds) published in 2002 indicated that 34 percent found marijuana easier to purchase than either cigarettes or beer, with smaller percentages choosing the legal goods as the easiest to buy; see CASA (2002). The 2004 edition of the yearly survey found that cigarettes were easier to buy than marijuana, which was easier to buy than beer; CASA (2004). The annual Monitoring the Future surveys consistently show that marijuana is less readily available to teens than alcohol or cigarettes, however.

[14] See Table 13, "Trends in Availability of Drugs as Perceived by Twelfth Graders," in Monitoring the Future (2004).

[15] Husak (2002, pp. 71–2) provides a more extensive argument against the justification of a prohibition of adult drug possession by way of concerns with leakage to adolescents.

different kids. Those youths who live in neighborhoods where drugs are already rife would probably see a decrease in drug availability through legalization and regulation – for these kids, drugs are essentially unregulated under the prohibition regime. But for kids who live in neighborhoods without widespread drug markets, it is possible, even likely, that some forms of legalization would lead to increased availability.[16]

For a variety of crimes, adolescents are typically not punished as severely as are adult offenders. Not being in "the maturity of their faculties," kids are not treated as harshly as adults when they violate laws. This observation applies as well as to violations of laws concerning drug prohibition as to breach of other rules. As a result, kids possess a comparative advantage (relative to adults) in working in the supply side of prohibited drugs – an advantage that is reinforced by restrictions on youth labor in legal enterprises and structural impediments (such as poor schooling) to legal market success. Adult sellers of illicit drugs seem to have few compunctions about employing kids to help distribute their product and even fewer scruples over vending to the underage.

Another kid-related issue that holds implications for the regulation of drugs is that adults who are addicted to hard drugs by and large do not make good parents. That is, perhaps a legal adult market for a drug does not increase the use of the drug by kids or does increase use but with a lower level of overall harm to kids. Nevertheless, if such availability leads to child neglect on the part of parents, then adult drug use still involves "harm to others" that might provide a second kid-based rationale for a prohibition.

In *On Liberty*, Mill addressed this type of harm to others – the neglect of duties, including parental duties, stemming from indulgence in a drug or another vice. If vice indulgence would necessarily or with a very significant probability lead to such neglect, then a prohibition might be in order:

> ... when a person disables himself, by conduct purely self-regarding, from the performance of some definite duty incumbent on him to the public, he is guilty of a social offence. No person ought to be punished simply for being drunk; but a soldier or policeman should be punished for being drunk on duty. Whenever, in short, there is a definite damage, or a definite risk of damage, either to an individual or to the public, the case is taken out of the province of liberty, and placed in that of morality or law.[17]

But if the risk of damage to others is not so immediate, then punishment should be targeted at the infliction of damage and not at the behavior that "caused" the imposition of harm:

> If, for example, a man, through intemperance or extravagance, becomes unable to pay his debts, or, having undertaken the moral responsibility of a family,

---

[16] Boyum (1998) argues that this is one of the factors underlying the seeming political unpopularity of the legalization of currently illicit drugs. See also Becker, Grossman, and Murphy (2004).

[17] Mill (1978, pp. 79–80).

becomes from the same cause incapable of supporting or educating them, he is deservedly reprobrated, and might be justly punished; but it is for the breach of duty to his family or creditors, not for the extravagance. If the resources which ought have been devoted to them, had been diverted from them for the most prudent investment, the moral culpability would have been the same.[18]

Although child neglect is a bad thing, therefore, it does not serve as a Millian rationale for a drug prohibition, unless any consumption of the drug as assuredly leads to child neglect as drunkenness on duty leads to severely diminished performance by a police officer. Someone who had once neglected a duty through his indulgence in a vice, however, could be prohibited from future indulgence, as Mill noted, without the prohibition constituting an unacceptable limitation on individual liberty.[19] A parent who became neglectful or abusive under the influence of drugs or by a fixation on finding and using drugs could face a drug prohibition targeted personally at him or her – a policy still consistent with the harm principle.[20]

VICE LUNACY

A second approach to justifying a drug prohibition without abandoning the harm principle is to note that when it comes to making choices about drugs, and particularly those choices that are made while under the influence of drugs, adults share with children the feature of not being "in the maturity of their faculties." When a heroin addict wakes up in the morning, is his decision to go out in search of a fix the decision of a fully reflective agent? Perhaps not. We will look more fully into the rationality of vice-related choices in the next chapter. But the easier case is that in which the person is already intoxicated. Mill makes it clear that coercion is permissible in this situation: restraining someone who is already drunk from having another round or from driving home is not a prima facie violation of the individual's liberty, as the person is "in some state of excitement or absorption incompatible with the full use of the reflecting faculty. . . ."[21]

Those who appeal to the irrationality of vicious choices by nonintoxicated adults need not invoke harm to others as a rationale for intervention. Harm to the decision maker is sufficient rationale for regulation, if no deference is given to the rationality of those decisions – just as if the decision maker were a child. But for Mill, informed decisions to use a drug or to take a drink or to gamble or to engage in other risky behaviors (by the nonintoxicated) are not

---

[18] Mill (1978, p. 79).   [19] Mill (1978, pp. 96–7).

[20] Prohibitions specific to an individual are already employed to some extent, in the case of both illegal drugs and alcohol. In the United States, for instance, many individuals on probation or on pretrial release have their freedom conditioned on remaining drug or alcohol free.

[21] Mill (1978, p. 95).

themselves evidence that a person is irrational. Potentially dangerous behavior ought to be warned against, not prohibited. The person deciding to engage in risky behavior may well be making an ill-advised choice. But "[a]ll errors that he is likely to commit against advice and warning are far outweighed by the evil of allowing others to constrain him to what they deem his good."[22]

What if Mill's approach were rejected, in the sense that it were generally agreed upon that choices in the vice arena tend to be marked by irrationality and, hence, could be very strictly controlled, perhaps up to the point of legal prohibitions? First, such a blanket provision for government coercion would be dangerous because then any activity that the government or a majority of the electorate did not care for might be defined as a vice and prohibited.[23] (Of course, this danger has been realized in many ways in many nations over the course of history, leading to such regulations as bans on theaters or dancing or opium or rock and roll.) Second, once decision makers are regarded as irrational, a whole host of problems arises. If people are irrational, what makes us think that they will respond as expected to the incentives created by regulations or by a prohibition? Why will the threat of jail deter such capricious beings? In other words, the basis for judging a vice amenable to prohibition – the irrationality of decisions – in part would also serve to undermine the rationale for any attempt to regulate consumption of the vice via the criminal law because the efficacy of regulations themselves is based on the ability of people by and large to respond appropriately to incentives.[24] Lunatics are not held criminally responsible for actions that they cannot control. Nevertheless, a version of the irrationality argument will be pursued further in Chapter 3.

THE UBIQUITY OF HARM

The notion that drug taking or some other vice might justly be prohibited if the activity involves "definite damage, or a definite risk of damage, either to an individual or to the public" is the source of another argument that attempts to reconcile the harm principle with drug prohibition. The idea is to point to serious harm to others from drug use, harm that is sufficiently likely to occur that an individual's drug taking could not be characterized as self-regarding activity. For such an approach to succeed in justifying prohibition under Mill's standards, the external harms from drug use would have to approximate those brought about by a drunken police officer – the potential (though quite uncertain) harms of drug-induced neglect of familial duties would not be sufficient.

[22] Mill (1978, p. 75).
[23] The U.S. Supreme Court noted the undesirable prospect of a "vice exception" to the First Amendment, which might lead to the possibility of censoring speech surrounding any activity that the government labeled a vice; see *44 Liquormart, Inc., v. Rhode Island*, 517 U.S. 484 (1996).
[24] The irrationality of vice consumers, however, would not be a reason to forgo regulations on manufacture or sale, as opposed to possession and use.

Social scientist James Q. Wilson adopts a version of the "significant harms-to-others" approach:

> John Stuart Mill, the father of modern libertarians, argued that people can only restrict the freedom of another for their self-protection, and society can exert power over its members against their will in order to prevent harm to others. I think that the harm to others from drug legalization will be greater than the harm – and it is a great harm – that now exists from keeping these drugs illegal.[25]

For Wilson, an individual's drug use apparently involves "definite damage, or a definite risk of damage," to the public, like that of a drunken cop. Wilson is not alone: "Today, the harm principle is being used increasingly by conservatives who justify laws against prostitution, pornography, public drinking, drugs, and loitering, as well as regulation of homosexual and heterosexual conduct, on the basis of harm to others."[26]

Just about any activity that harms the person engaging in it also harms those who are attached to that person, as Mill recognizes: "I fully admit that the mischief which a person does to himself may seriously affect, both through their sympathies and their interests, those nearly connected with him and, in a minor degree, society at large."[27] One family member's addiction to alcohol, drugs, or gambling frequently throws a household into misery. At the societal level, insurance involves the pooling of risks, so a person who takes actions that make it more likely he or she will collect insurance payments harms the other members of the risk pool.[28] Some health care costs are publicly subsidized, so the ill health of many drug addicts harms the rest of society. Pathological gambling can increase the rate of bankruptcy and drive up borrowing costs for everyone. Of course, as noted, Mill would permit the punishment of those who violate family and societal duties through their vicious activity, or through any other cause. But the harm principle would not countenance prohibiting an activity simply because a small percentage of those who engage in it will subsequently violate such duties. (As with the harm principle generally, the determination of a threshold for when probable harm is large enough to justify societal coercion is more of an art than a science, though Mill provides some contours.) Further, minimizing the potential to require publicly subsidized health care is not an obligation that society can legitimately impose upon individuals, without opening the way to regulation of the minutest aspects of our activity, from what we eat to how much we exercise to what time we go to bed to how we spend our leisure hours.[29] Nevertheless, it would probably not be

---

[25] Wilson (2000).
[26] Harcourt (1999, p. 139).
[27] Mill (1978, p. 79).
[28] This claim assumes that the risk has not been appropriately priced in the insurance premium.
[29] As Mill (1978, p. 80) writes, "If grown persons are to be punished for not taking proper care of themselves, I would rather it were for their own sake than under pretense of preventing them from impairing their capacity of rendering to society benefits which society does not pretend it has the right to exact."

an invasion of individual liberty to require private insurance for individuals who choose to engage in exceptionally risky ventures, those activities that involve a very significant risk of claiming societal resources. Mountain climbers, intent upon scaling a peak that frequently has required expensive rescues of previous would-be climbers, might have to post a bond in advance to pay for the rescue services that they, too, might require.

When the risk of damage to the interests of others is sufficiently large, as in the case of the drunken police officer, society can try to use the law to prevent harm. Without an ample risk of harm to others, however, the criminal law is an inappropriate tool for regulating vice. How certain is "harm to others" from occasional indulgence in a vice? Typically, drug users and gamblers indulge in ways that are not particularly problematic for their close friends and relations. Even for cocaine and crack cocaine, drugs whose consumption can be strongly reinforcing, only a small percentage of people – less than 10 percent, and perhaps as little as 1 percent – who use these substances develop into habitual consumers.[30] In the United States, where most adults have gambled, about 1.2 percent can be classified as pathological gamblers.[31] Although external costs from addiction are high, these costs are insufficiently certain to arise from experimental or occasional indulgence to justify criminalization of drugs or gambling.

> But with regard to the merely contingent or, as it may be called, constructive injury which a person causes to society by conduct which neither violates any specific duty to the public, nor occasions perceptible hurt to any assignable individual except himself, the inconvenience is one which society can afford to bear, for the sake of the greater good of human freedom.[32]

Again, to justify the use of coercion, Mill's explication of the harm principle requires that conduct directly and perceptibly harm some "assignable" individual. Nor can would-be prohibitionists simply assert that they are harmed by the conduct of others: there must be some perceptible harm:

> There are many who consider as an injury to themselves any conduct which they have a distaste for, and resent it as an outrage to their feelings; as a religious bigot, when charged with disregarding the religious feelings of others, has been known to retort that they disregard his feelings by persisting in their abominable

---

[30] According to the National Survey on Drug Use and Health, in 2003, more than 34 million Americans (12 and older) had used cocaine at least once in their lives. Cocaine treatment admissions in 2003 came to nearly a quarter million people, about 0.72 percent of the lifetime users. See Haasen and Krausz (2001, p. 160) for the contention that cocaine addiction affects a subset of less than 5 or 10 percent of cocaine users. Eldredge (1998, p. 11), states that "Fewer than 1 percent of those who try cocaine become daily users," a contention based on data he discusses on page 2.

[31] *Gambling Impact and Behavior Study* (1999).

[32] Mill (1978, p. 80). But also see the discussion of "garrison thresholds" in Feinberg (1986, pp. 21–3). Feinberg's four-volume *The Moral Limits of the Criminal Law* provides a painstaking analysis of the harm principle and related concepts. Other important modern examinations of the Millian harm concept include Hart (1963) and Packer (1968).

worship or creed. But there is no parity between the feeling of a person for his own opinion and the feeling of another who is offended at his holding it, no more than between the desire of a thief to take a purse and the desire of the right owner to keep it.[33]

The tenor of *On Liberty* makes it clear that Mill views the harm principle as generally forbidding legal prohibitions on vice, in contrast to the reasoning of James Q. Wilson. Occasionally, Mill is even more explicit on this issue. In particular, he attacks the "Maine Laws," state-level prohibitions on alcohol that were then current in the United States and were in some danger of being exported to England.[34]

Generally, therefore, the exceptions to the harm principle for children and lunatics are insufficient, by Mill's reckoning, to justify all-encompassing prohibitions. Further, the fact that harm to yourself generally involves, as a consequence, some harm to your close connections and society also fails to render vice prohibitions acceptable.

ON LIBERTY ON DRUGS

A more systematic survey of the implications that the harm principle holds for vice regulation provides a sounder basis for deciding whether to accept or reject Mill's approach. With our discussion of *On Liberty* behind us, let's try to engage in "the kind of practical, historically informed, and commonsensical, although unrigorous, analysis that Mill undertook. . . ."[35] We can venture to be more specific about the types of policies toward alcohol and other psychoactive drugs that are consistent with the harm principle. In some cases, Mill speaks definitively: for instance, he says explicitly that drunkenness alone should not be illegal, but for many issues, there is room for considerably divergent interpretations of how to apply the harm principle. I'll suggest one plausible application of Mill's approach to drug policies in this section; what is perhaps most surprising is that many extremely restrictive policies do not conflict with the harm principle.

Recall first that harm to drug users themselves is not a sufficient warrant to coerce sane, adult individuals into abstaining from drugs. The $3\frac{1}{3}$ part of the standard $3\frac{1}{3}$ vice concerns, harm to the vice consumer herself, carries essentially zero weight in a Millian universe. Mill would not object to strict controls on principle if the drug use would, with a high probability, directly cause harm to others. ("Whenever, in short, there is a definite damage, or a definite risk of damage, either to a individual or to the public, the case is taken out of the province of liberty and placed in that of morality or law."[36])

---

[33] Mill (1978, pp. 81–2).
[35] Posner (1992b, p. 438).
[34] Mill (1978, pp. 86, 94–5, 99).
[36] Mill (1978, p. 80).

In what ways do drugs cause harm to others? Equivalently, what are the external costs of drug use? Drug policy expert Mark Kleiman offers one potential accounting of "harms to others" associated with drug use: dereliction of duty; crime; nuisance; health damage; drain on common resources; risk-spreading and cross-subsidy effects; leading others to use drugs (in epidemiological fashion); and "notional" damage.[37] (Notional damage is the possibility that some people are made unhappy or disgusted simply by knowledge of others' drug use.)

Kleiman's list of potential external effects of drug use consists of those effects associated with drug use per se, independent of the regulatory regime. Many of the costs commonly associated with drugs, including the drive-by shootings and the bulk of the fatal overdoses are primarily artifacts of the existing regulatory structure, however. Under the influence of some drugs – alcohol is the preeminent example, but cocaine and PCP would also qualify – people might be more likely to commit violent crimes, though even this tendency involves the social setting and many factors beyond the drug's chemical properties.[38] (Those under the influence of nicotine, opiates, or marijuana do not appear to be increasingly predisposed toward violence, although in the past, these drugs, too, have been thought to be violence inducing.) With the particularly notable exception of alcohol, the perceived relationship between drug use and crime is primarily a side effect of prohibition.

Briefly, then, consider Kleiman's first three external costs, dereliction of duty, crime, and public nuisance. We have already seen that the harm principle does not prevent police officers and soldiers from being punished for being drunk on duty because their inebriation presents a definite risk of damage to the public. More generally, dereliction of duty (such as failure to provide for children) could be punished, whatever the cause. But the potential for drug taking to lead to this outcome is not sufficiently direct and certain to justify making drugs illegal. Likewise, the crime engendered by some types of drug consumption – violence by drunks, for instance – is not sufficiently direct and certain to stand as a basis for outlawing drugs. The external harm that arises from creating a public nuisance, like the harms from dereliction of duty or drug-induced crime, could provide a reason to punish those who create public nuisances. Again, however, the public nuisance associated with some drug use is insufficiently direct and certain to justify drug prohibitions (though some less-stringent regulations aimed at minimizing nuisance would not unduly restrain the liberty of drug consumers). If a person had once been violent under the influence of alcohol or drugs, then a prohibition specific to that person would be appropriate.

---

[37] Kleiman (1992, chapter 3).

[38] Sullum (2003, pp. 205–8) indicates that there is scant evidence for a link between PCP and violent behavior.

Table 1.1: *John Stuart Mill as drug czar: a capsule summary of drug policy screened through the harm principle[a]*

Prohibitions of manufacture or possession: These would not be allowed for any drug that offered even the remotest hope of benefiting (or failing to damage) someone.[b] Individuals who had previously harmed others while intoxicated, however, could be subject to a specific prohibition. Kids could be prohibited from using drugs. Further, those "doped up" at the time of attempted purchase could justly be refused service, just as bartenders can refuse to serve intoxicated customers, on the grounds that such patrons are "in some state of excitement or absorption incompatible with the full use of the reflecting faculty...."[c]

Prohibitions on sales: Some drugs, such as marijuana, can rather readily be produced at home. In such cases, legal markets for the drug are not required, as the ease of home preparation protects the liberty of adults to consume the drug. If sellers are "indispensably required" for procuring the drug, however, then prohibitions upon sales are unallowable infringements on liberty.[d] The Maine laws or national alcohol Prohibition in the United States, which outlawed sales but not purchases or consumption of alcohol, were inconsistent with individual liberty. Mill believed that in the case of alcohol legal sales were a near necessity for consumption. But in general, prohibitions on sales are a close call. Buying and selling is a public act and hence not a species of self-regarding conduct. Trade can be prohibited without violating individual liberty, as long as there exist accessible alternative channels through which consumers can acquire drugs.

Regulations (short of prohibition) on sale: Many controls are allowable and potentially desirable, including registration of sales for the purpose of crime control, sanitary or worker-safety regulations, licensing of sellers, and opening hours restrictions. Limiting the number of sellers simply as a means to discourage consumption (as opposed to being an aid in enforcing other regulations) is an infringement on the liberty of potential purchasers, however.[e]

Prohibitions or regulation of advertising: Such restrictions on sellers, who have a pecuniary interest in intemperance, may be justified. But private individuals can freely advise or induce other adults to use drugs.[f]

Mandated provision of health and safety information: Warning labels and other information concerning risks can be required. As Mill notes with respect to an obligation to label poisons, "the buyer cannot wish not to know that the thing that he possesses has poisonous qualities," and "liberty consists in doing what one desires."[g]

Special taxation: This is not justified if the goal of the taxation is to reduce consumption.[h] If the goal is the collection of necessary government revenue, however, then drugs could and should be taxed, up to the point of maximum revenue collection.[i]

Prescription-only regimes: To make drugs available only by prescription generally cannot be countenanced, as a prescription regime places too great a burden upon those who have legitimate, including recreational, uses for the drugs.[j] Some "nonrecreational" drugs involve externalities that might justify a prescription regime, however. In particular, antibiotic use harms others by contributing to the buildup of resistant strains of pathogens; so, antibiotics could be subject to a prescription regime as a means of countering socially excessive use.

License requirements for legal purchase or use: If the conditions for qualifying for a license are that the buyer or user indicate he or she understands the risks involved in consumption, or the conditions might aid in the enforcement of other legitimate regulations, then such a licensing system would not fall afoul of the harm principle. But a licensing system for adult buyers could not be adopted simply as a means of reducing consumption.

Regulating intoxicated behavior: Prohibiting an intoxicated person from engaging in certain types of activity (such as driving under the influence) is not a violation of individual liberty, if the behavior presents a definite risk of harm to others. Public intoxication might justifiably be regulated – Mill notes that many acts that are not harmful in themselves can nevertheless be restricted in public manifestations.[k] Private intoxication, however, cannot be prohibited, at least for those adults with no prior record of harming others while intoxicated.

---

[a] In the United States, "drug czar" is the informal sobriquet for the person who heads the Office of National Drug Control Policy.

[b] See Mill (1978, p. 95).   [c] Mill (1978, p. 95).
[d] Mill (1978, p. 99).   [e] Mill (1978, pp. 96, 100).
[f] Mill (1978, pp. 97–8). In the United States, a broad advertising ban for a legal product might be construed as being inconsistent with First Amendment protection of the freedom of speech.
[g] Mill (1978, pp. 95 and 96).   [h] Mill (1978, p. 95).
[i] Mill (1978, p. 100). Strictly speaking, Mill's injunction that goods like alcohol should be highly taxed is consistent with but not a consequence of his harm principle – it stems from other considerations of desirable public policy. Mill's general support for free trade, too, is not a consequence of harm principle reasoning.
[j] Mill (1978, p. 96) is explicit on this point.   [k] Mill (1978, p. 97).

When the health of nonconsenting others is damaged by an individual's drug taking, as by secondhand smoke, then legal controls are justified. Whether the actual damage to health caused by secondhand smoke (or similar remote health effects from other drug use) is sufficiently direct or certain, given current evidence, is less clear; certainly, the extent of exposure matters, and would make intervention more justified in those places where nonsmokers are involuntarily subjected to frequent exposure of relatively high concentrations.[39] Where such effects exist, regulations are not inconsistent with the harm principle – though the regulations should not be more restrictive of individual choice to use drugs than is necessary to prevent the negative external health consequences.[40] Cigarette purchase and consumption must be allowed, while smoking legitimately can be banned in some public areas.

Kleiman's remaining types of external costs (drains on common resources, risk-spreading and cross-subsidy effects, leading others to use drugs, or

---

[39] Controversy over the dangers of secondhand smoke was reignited with the 2003 publication of a study in the *British Medical Journal* that indicated no link between lung cancer or heart disease and exposure to secondhand smoke. See "Claim That Passive Smoking Does No Harm Lights Up Tobacco Row," by Sarah Boseley, *The Guardian*, May 16, 2003, p. 1 (international edition).

[40] Again, I am invoking "the principle of the least restrictive alternative"; see Pope (2000, p. 431) quoting Dworkin (1988, p. 126).

"notional" damage) do not appear to me to rise to the Millian level to justify prohibition. Such costs generally do not constitute "perceptible hurt to any
assignable individual. . . . "[41]

So, the interpretation offered here of Mill's approach does not provide all
that much scope for legislation overriding the personal liberty of adults to
engage in vice, even when accounting for the kids and externality exceptions.
Although some strict controls are consistent with the harm principle, channels
for legal adult consumption of recreational drugs must remain open, from
Mill's point of view. Table 1.1 offers a summary of the implications of Mill's
harm principle for drug policy.

The next chapter will look at addiction, and Chapter 3 will then revisit the
applicability of the harm principle to vice policy.

[41] Mill (1978, p. 80).

2

Addiction: Rational and Otherwise

Addiction is a slippery, hard-to-define concept. The one element of addiction that is commonly agreed upon is that addiction involves "reinforcement": consumption of the addictive good or activity today increases the desire to consume the good in the future. By this reckoning alone, caffeine, cocaine, alcohol, nicotine, opiates, gambling, sex, exercise, chess, listening to music, watching television, playing video games, eBay, eating Chinese food, reading, and religious observance are addictive for many people. Public policy responds mainly to those potentially addictive substances or behaviors that tend to bring on severe adverse effects: whereas some people read too much, the negative consequences of "readaholism" are insufficiently widespread or dangerous to make book addiction a pressing social concern. But the detrimental effects arising from excessive indulgence in alcohol, nicotine, cocaine, and gambling, among other vices, foster efforts at social (and sometimes governmental) influence or control.

Beyond reinforcement, other markers of addiction include tolerance, withdrawal, and craving. Tolerance is present if a given level of enjoyment of the good or activity requires higher and higher doses over time. Withdrawal implies that a failure to consume the good leads to adverse psychological or physical symptoms. Craving exists if an individual is beset with an almost overwhelming desire for the addictive good or activity; addicts who relapse following a period of abstinence often attribute their backsliding to intense craving. Not all addictions seem to involve tolerance, withdrawal, or craving, however.

Partly as a result of discomfort over the slippery notion of addiction, some people prefer to speak of physical and psychological dependency.[1] Physical dependence on a drug, like physical withdrawal, involves a consistent pattern of bodily symptoms when the drug is withheld; the use of alcohol, tranquilizers, caffeine, or opioids can be accompanied by physical dependence.[2]

---

[1] See Bakalar and Grinspoon (1984, p. 38).

[2] Not all cases of physical dependence involve addiction, however. Some patients given opiates for pain relief suffer withdrawal symptoms when their drug use is curtailed, though such patients have none of the other characteristics of addiction. Carnwath and Smith (2002, p. 160).

Psychological dependence involves craving; cravings themselves can be influenced by cues, as when desire for a drug is stoked by reentering an environment in which the drug was used in the past. Cocaine and amphetamines are drugs not closely associated with overt physical dependency, but they are associated with psychological dependency, probably related to chemical changes in the brain induced by previous drug use.

In general, both physical dependency and craving are consequences, not causes, of addiction; that is, heavy usage leads to physical dependency and craving, though these factors can then reinforce heavy usage.[3]

Relative to "addiction," the notion of dependency does not significantly reduce the ambiguity surrounding patterns of compulsive consumption because it is hard to know when someone's bad habit becomes a dependency.[4] Nevertheless, empirical definitions of dependencies on various substances or activities have been adopted by psychiatrists, providing a measure of objectivity. Dependence is said to be present if a patient exhibits more than a certain number of compulsive-type behaviors. Gambling is said to be pathological, for instance, if the gambler manifests any five from a list of ten characteristics, including lying about gambling, betting with higher stakes to maintain the thrill, becoming irritable when not gambling, engaging in illegal activity to feed a gambling habit, and "chasing losses," that is, continuing to gamble after dropping significant sums (out of desperation to make good previous losses). Substance dependence is diagnosed if at least three of seven drug-related conditions are present simultaneously over the course of a year; the conditions include tolerance, withdrawal, and a persistent though ineffective desire to quit or cut back.

Addiction frequently is depicted as a type of enslavement, where the addict is not so much choosing to consume the good or activity as the good or activity is undermining the basis of rational choice for the addict. A related approach, and one that is popular with many treatment programs, is to view addiction as a disease. The "enslavement" and "disease" viewpoints render suspect the application of economic theory to addictive behavior, as economic analysis is generally based on notions of "utility maximization" by rational individuals. Government intervention into the market for addictive substances might be warranted, even in the absence of externalities, if individual choices in this arena are irrational: the standard liberal (Millian) notion of respecting the freedom of adults to make decisions concerning self-regarding activities is undermined if those free choices demonstrably and systematically do not serve the best interests of the decision makers. Nor can the choices be viewed as all that free, if they are the product of diseased or enslaved minds.

---

[3] Caffeine consumption equivalent to less than one cup of coffee per day can lead to some physical withdrawal symptoms. Goldstein (2001, p. 215).

[4] See, e.g., Bakalar and Grinspoon (1984, pp. 38–46).

Box 2.1: *Definitions and descriptions of addiction*

A medical definition of addiction: "a condition induced in certain higher mammals by chronic administration of central nervous system depressants like alcohol, barbiturates, and opiates, in which a gradual adaptation of the nervous system to the drug causes a latent hyperexcitability that becomes manifest when the drug is withdrawn and produces physiological symptoms that are interpreted as a physical need for the drug."

– James B. Bakalar and Lester Grinspoon, in *Drug Control in a Free Society*[a]

A psychiatric description of Substance Dependence (the American Psychiatric Association does not employ the term "addiction."): "The essential feature of Substance Dependence is a cluster of cognitive, behavioral, and physiological symptoms indicating that the individual continues use of the substance despite significant substance-related problems. There is a pattern of repeated self-administration that usually results in tolerance, withdrawal, and compulsive drug-taking behavior."

– *Diagnostic and Statistical Manual of Mental Disorders*[b]

"[A]ddiction results when the reward system of the brain is hijacked by chemical substances that played no role in its evolution."   – Jon Elster, in *Strong Feelings*[c]

"By addiction we mean a specific psychological state in which the drug takes up an overriding importance in the person's life."

– Tom Carnwath and Ian Smith in *Heroin Century*[d]

"The basic definition of addiction at the foundation of our analysis is that a person is potentially addicted to c if an increase in his current consumption of c increases his future consumption of c."

– Gary Becker and Kevin Murphy, in "A Theory of Rational Addiction"[e]

"Addiction is a chronic, relapsing disease, characterized by compulsive drug seeking and use, and by neurochemical and molecular changes in the brain."

– National Institute on Drug Abuse, *Heroin Abuse and Addiction*

"After reviewing the addiction literature, one might be inclined to conclude that there are as many definitions of addiction as there are investigators conducting research in the area."   – Glenn D. Walters, in *The Addiction Concept*[f]

"...the phenomenon of addiction is mysterious to the point of being sphinx-like."

– Rachel Green Baldino, in *Welcome to Methadonia: A Social Worker's Candid Account of Life in a Methadone Clinic*[g]

---

[a] Bakalar and Grinspoon (1984, pp. 36–7).
[b] *Diagnostic and Statistical Manual of Mental Disorders* (1994, p. 176).
[c] Elster (1999c, p. 53).   [d] Carnwath and Smith (2002, p. 160).
[e] Becker and Murphy (1988, p. 681).
[f] Walters (1999, p. 5); to be fair, Walters notes that the quoted sentence is "somewhat of an exaggeration."
[g] Baldino (2000, p. 153).

RATIONAL ADDICTION

Does addiction actually imply irrationality? Two economists at the University of Chicago, Gary Becker and Kevin Murphy, launched the theory of rational addiction in 1988. Becker and Murphy maintain that "addictions, even strong ones, are usually rational in the sense of involving forward-looking maximization with stable preferences."[5] As odd as it might seem at first, Becker and Murphy argue that people choose to become drug addicts in much the same way they choose to consume ketchup or to buy shoes.

The rational addiction approach allows the standard tools of economics to be applied to the large variety of choices that involve potentially addictive substances and activities, just as economics applies to ketchup consumption. The application of economic reasoning might not be a notable advantage if rational addiction's implications were widely at variance with the actual conduct of addicts. But it turns out that much compulsive behavior is consistent with the rational addiction approach. Furthermore, rational addiction generates plausible explanations for common but somewhat peculiar drug-related phenomena, such as cold-turkey withdrawals and cyclical binge/purge behavior. The theory of rational addiction also suggests how the pain of divorce, illness, or other temporary events can lead to long-term changes in the use of addictive goods.

A capsule summary of rational addiction theory begins with the description of a potentially addictive good (a drug, say) as having the quality that the consumer's current satisfaction from the drug depends on the extent of previous drug consumption. Other factors such as price will also influence current drug use, but the amount of past consumption plays a key role in generating today's demand for the drug. In keeping with the notion that addiction involves reinforcement, the more you have consumed in the past, the more that you will choose to consume now, holding all other factors constant.

What separates rational addiction theory from most other approaches is that the basic description just provided is understood by the consumer as well as by the armchair addiction theorist. So when you make a choice to consume an addictive drug today, you recognize that today's consumption will increase your desire for the drug tomorrow. Indeed, if you knew that tomorrow you could not possibly acquire any of the drug, you would be less likely to consume it today. Alternatively, if you knew that availability of the drug would increase tomorrow, you would consume more today. (Essentially, there will be a "sale" of the drug tomorrow, so you know that you will consume more tomorrow; but you can take additional advantage of the sale by stoking tomorrow's demand for the drug via higher consumption today.) In the terminology of economics, yesterday's, today's, and tomorrow's consumption of the drug

---

[5] Becker and Murphy (1988, p. 675). An important precursor to the rational addiction literature is Stigler and Becker (1977).

are "complements," like bread, peanut butter, and jelly, or hooks, lines, and sinkers: the more you have of one component of these related goods, the more you want of the other components.

Rational addiction theory, therefore, incorporates the notion that a decision to consume an addictive good today holds implications for tomorrow – implications that are understood by the drug user. You might say that the full "price" of consumption of the drug today to you isn't just the current market price, but also includes the cost to you of the future consumption that will be induced, via reinforcement, by today's drug use.[6] But why should your future consumption represent a net "cost?" Isn't it a benefit? Won't you decide to take the drug in the future only if by doing so you are better off than you would be by abstaining from drug use? Well, yes and no. Yes, relative to not consuming the drug tomorrow, you may well be better off by consuming it – that is, the augmentation to tomorrow's satisfaction from tomorrow's drug use can be positive, in comparison with no drug taking tomorrow. (And this gain in satisfaction from taking the drug tomorrow is more pronounced the larger your drug consumption is today.) But today's drug use can lower the *level* of overall satisfaction tomorrow, even as it preserves *gains* to satisfaction from future drug use. Current drug taking induces more drug taking tomorrow, while simultaneously hindering tomorrow's overall happiness. If you enjoy today's drug use sufficiently, then, or don't care all that much about tomorrow, you might choose to consume the drug today. When you make such a decision, you are fully aware that by taking the drug today you will continue to take the drug tomorrow, and that today's drug use will have a negative effect on tomorrow's aggregate satisfaction.[7]

The complementarity among past, current, and future consumption of an addictive good suggests that some individuals – addicts – will consume very large amounts of the drug over time, whereas many other people will consume little or none of the good. The more highly reinforcing a drug, that is, the more addictive the drug, the smaller the number of individuals who will be moderate consumers: the consumption patterns of highly addictive goods tend to take on an all-or-nothing character. Nevertheless, if an addict can somehow desist from using the drug for a little while, the effects of his past consumption on his current and future desires begin to dissipate. He may then be able to make a transition to near-complete abstinence from the drug. Treatment programs aim to facilitate this transition by rendering the drug unavailable for

---

[6] The "full price" of drug consumption today is explored more rigorously in Becker and Murphy (1988, pp. 678ff.).

[7] Incidentally, the formal model of addiction developed by Becker and Murphy has been appropriated by others who do not fully subscribe to the notion that addiction represents rational behavior. The popularity of the model stems, in part, from its success in characterizing today's drug use as lowering tomorrow's satisfaction, while simultaneously raising the value of more drug use tomorrow. See, e.g., Elster (1999b, p. xi) and O'Donoghue and Rabin (1999).

a time, by speeding up the depreciation of the drug-desire-promoting effects of prior consumption, and by raising the perceived value of abstinence or moderate consumption. New information about the negative consequences of consumption can also cause rational addicts to desist: the large decline in the prevalence of smoking following the 1964 U.S. Surgeon General's report on the health risks of cigarettes is consistent with the rational addiction approach.

From the point of view of rational addiction, the seemingly compulsive consumption associated with addiction is not solely a property of the physical or chemical characteristics of a good; rather, addiction involves an interaction between a person's preferences and his or her opportunities, which include the possibility of consuming a good that can spur habitual use. Given that goods or activities that are addictive for some people are not addictive for others, this aspect of rational addiction theory has much to recommend it. Rational addiction theory is similarly congruent with the fact that even a given individual might be addicted to a good at one point in his or her life but abstain from or be a moderate consumer of the same good at other times.

The future effects of current consumption of an addictive good are completely foreseeable in the basic rational addiction model. No one becomes an addict by mistake. Why would anyone rationally choose to become an addict? One possibility, already suggested, is a short-term perspective, a lack of interest in the future. As addictive drugs tend to be pleasurable at first, bringing their pain in the long run, someone who doesn't value the future will be more likely to choose to become addicted. (Kids might be particularly likely to make decisions that suggest a perspective overly skewed toward immediate gratification.[8]) Even people with a longer time horizon might "choose" to become addicts, however, if their other prospects are not very attractive. For Becker and Murphy, those who are addicted to harmful substances are probably not happy people – the reason they have chosen to become addicted is because life circumstances have offered them some unpalatable alternatives – but they would be even less satisfied if government policy took away from them the possibility of indulging their addiction.[9] Temporary conditions, such as the pain of a divorce, could render someone's other alternatives so unappetizing that addiction has appeal, relatively speaking, despite its negative long-term consequences. Further, while compulsive drug users might wish to be able to avoid the costs of their addiction, they don't really regret their decision to become addicted, as they realize that it was the best among their limited alternatives. So government can't make people better off (at least directly) by making drugs artificially scarce, even if such policies would reduce or eliminate addiction. Rational addiction theory implicitly incorporates the Millian view toward drugs

[8] See the discussion of this issue in O'Donoghue and Rabin (2001, pp. 33–6).
[9] Becker and Murphy (1988, p. 691). The unenviable life circumstances, of course, may themselves be partly due to less-than-sterling previous decisions by the addicts.

as self-regarding behavior: if the only harmful effects of drug use fall upon the (rational adult) drug users themselves, the government should not interfere in drug-taking decisions, as any coercion in such realms will tend to do more harm than good.[10]

The lack of regret over drug-related choices that is a marker of the rational addiction approach is not inconsistent with repeated, failed attempts by addicts to stop consuming the addictive good or behavior.[11] People who have chosen addiction might still be better off if they could find some method, some treatment, that would reduce the deleterious effect that their past drug use has on their current happiness, that is, if they could stop being addicted without the process of stopping itself causing great misery. Nor does the fact that addicts express dissatisfaction with their predicament imply that irrationality is at work:

> The claims of some heavy drinkers and smokers that they want to but cannot end their addictions seem to us no different from the claims of single persons that they want to but are unable to marry or from the claims of disorganized persons that they want to become better organized. What these claims mean is that a person will make certain changes – for example, marry or stop smoking – when he finds a way to raise long-term benefits sufficiently above the short-term costs of adjustment.[12]

In casual conversation, it often is claimed that addicts are unresponsive to increases in the price of the drug they consume: heroin addicts need their daily fix, and they will raise whatever funds are necessary, by means fair or foul, to get it. Surprisingly, rational addiction theory suggests that price increases that are permanent, not temporary, can have a substantial impact on the demand for an addictive good. If you know that a drug is expensive, and that it will continue to be expensive for years, you recognize that the high price will to some extent discourage you from consuming the drug in the future. But as current consumption and future consumption are complementary, knowledge of higher future prices would actually cause you to reduce current consumption – even if today's price is low! Again, rational addiction theory runs counter to approaches to drug dependence that equate addiction with some sort of disease or enslavement, in which addicts are completely undeterred by a high price for their drug.

Alternatively, temporary increases in drug prices, such as might be brought about by a police crackdown on illegal drug markets, will not have much of an

---

[10] Starting from a situation of prohibition, however, the theory of rational addiction suggests that a legalization that would greatly decrease effective prices for drugs would lead to significant increases in consumption and addiction. See Becker, Grossman, and Murphy (1991, pp. 240–1).

[11] "Indeed, rationality implies that failures will be common with uncertainty about the method best suited to each person and with a substantial short-run loss in utility from stopping." Becker and Murphy (1988, p. 693).

[12] Becker and Murphy (1988, p. 693).

effect on consumption, according to the rational addiction approach. Current consumption, recall, is influenced by both past and future consumption. The temporary crackdown, because it is temporary, holds little sway over future prices. Past consumption is a bygone; it has already been determined. A short-lived policy will not significantly alter the effect of either past or future consumption on drug utilization today. As a result, current drug use will not be expected to fall very much in the face of a fleeting price increase induced by a crackdown known to be temporary.

That current demand for a drug will depend on what people expect their future consumption of the drug to be provides the key prediction through which rational addiction theory can be tested. The forward-looking behavior characteristic of rational addicts can be contrasted with myopic behavior, whereby past drug consumption might stimulate current consumption (i.e., the drug displays reinforcement; it is habit forming), but the addict does not take into account the interaction between current and future choices. Myopic individuals don't see the link between today and tomorrow, so tomorrow will play no role in today's choices. For a completely myopic person, tomorrow is always infinitely far away.

This difference between myopic and rational addiction can be put into the service of an empirical test of the rational addiction model by looking at whether expected future consumption and, by extension, expected future prices for the addictive good help to determine current consumption. A rational addict who correctly anticipates lower prices for her drug in the future will expect to consume more of the drug in the future; by complementarity, this will cause her to increase her consumption today. A non-forward-looking, myopic addict's current consumption of the drug will not be similarly influenced by expectations of future consumption. Empirical analyses based on this divergence between rational and myopic behavior have generally been favorable to the rational addiction approach.[13] (Such investigations usually involve cigarette consumption or some other legal addictive behavior, as the data are considerably better for legal activities than they are for illegal ones.) The central tenet of economics, that higher prices reduce the quantity demanded for almost any good, is supported by empirical evidence concerning addictive substances.[14] Also consistent with rational addiction is the common finding that those higher prices lead to larger declines in drug use in the long run than they do in the short run.

Perhaps the main stumbling block for the theory of rational addiction is that addiction is so personally costly that it is hard to imagine anyone, even someone

[13] See, e.g., Becker, Grossman, and Murphy (1991); Grossman (1995); and Gruber and Köszegi (2000).

[14] Strictly speaking, economic theory predicts a negative relationship between price and quantity demanded only for price changes that do not involve "income effects." In practice, higher prices, even without compensation for income effects, lead to lowered demand.

with poor alternatives, choosing to become an addict. When high-performing, seemingly content people ruin their lives because of alcohol, cocaine, or heroin addiction, it looks even less like a rational choice. With full knowledge of future consequences, choosing to become an addict would seem to be analogous to someone with a severe peanut allergy nevertheless choosing to consume peanuts. For the most part, it isn't done: people with allergies to peanuts not only choose not to consume peanuts, they also take elaborate measures to avoid accidental peanut exposure or consumption. In the Becker and Murphy world where people understand the future consequences of their current drug use, it seems that essentially all potential drug addicts should treat drugs the way that people who are allergic to peanuts treat peanuts; yet, potential drug addicts do not behave this way in the real world: many "choose" addiction.

This particular chasm between real-life addiction and rational addiction theory is easily bridged. The basic Becker-Murphy model, in which people perfectly foresee future developments, can be modified to include uncertainty about the future.[15] In the modified model, people are aware that by consuming cocaine today, say, there is some possibility that they will develop an addiction. But a possibility is not a certainty; most cocaine users do not become addicts and perhaps most sporadic users view the potential benefits of occasional cocaine consumption to be worth the risk that they could develop a serious addiction. Those who become addicts, then, do not regret the gamble they took, though they do regret the outcome. Just like a person crossing a street knows that he might get hit by a car, but chooses to cross anyway because it is better on average than staying in bed all day, potential addicts choose a generally desirable, but risky, path. Most make it across, but some get hit hard by the bus of addiction – an addiction, in this view, that is voluntary but not intended.[16] In either the original or extended version of the rational addiction model, if an addict had to do it all over again, given the same preferences and information as he or she had the first time, the addict would make the same choices.

Rational addiction theory strikes many people as so implausible that it is often dismissed out-of-hand. Addiction treatment programs typically do not invoke a rationality perspective, though they do try to alter the perceived costs and benefits of decisions to use drugs. Twelve-step style, Alcoholics Anonymous–type recovery programs center upon a disease model of addiction that is almost completely at odds with rational addiction theory. Nor do most addicts describe their experience as one of rational choice. Part of the gulf between rational addiction and other views of compulsive behavior is tied to the nature of rationality in dynamic contexts.

---

[15] This extension of rational addiction theory appears in Orphanides and Zervos (1995). It is critiqued in Elster (1999c, pp. 183–6).

[16] "Addiction is voluntary, yet it is not intentional." Orphanides and Zervos (1995, p. 741).

TIME INCONSISTENCY

Current pleasure but future pain: this standard dynamic profile of a drug's effects presents a second challenge to the theory of rational addiction, whether in its original or modified garb. An initial issue in this intertemporal context concerns a person's preferences. The economics discipline typically takes preferences as given, thereby excluding value judgments about individuals' inclinations. Rationality involves making choices that are consistent with one's preferences, but the content of those preferences is not restricted within the standard economic approach. The decision of a depressed person to commit suicide, then, might be viewed as a rational act by some economic theorists. In a Latin phrase popular among economists, "de gustibus non est disputandum," you can't argue about tastes.[17]

But would it really be rational to inject some drug, if by doing so, you would gain an hour's worth of pleasure, followed by a lifetime of misery? Are all trade-offs that people make between current pleasure and future pain worthy of respect as being rational decisions, given the person's preferences? What if a 15-year-old truly had no interest in her future self? She would undertake any activity that promised current pleasure, irrespective of the extent of future pain; she might drive recklessly, take drugs, engage in unprotected sex, perhaps rob banks. Can her extreme discounting of the future be regarded as rational, and hence, her decisions, to the extent they are "self-regarding," be accorded the standard Millian deference? Certainly a case can be made for social control of such wildly short-sighted behavior: "Just as we must at times make reasoned judgments about whether a particular thirty-five-year-old is a fit guardian for a particular fifteen-year-old, so, too, we must at times make reasoned judgments about whether the fifteen-year-old is a fit guardian for her thirty-five-year-old self."[18]

Even accepting that a person's preferences are rational, irrespective of the person's willingness to trade future pain for current pleasure, there is still a problem with how this voluntary trade-off might change over time. Rational addiction theory invokes the assumption that consumers are not only forward-looking but also that their intertemporal preferences possess a certain coherence.[19] "Time consistency" (or dynamic consistency) is the term that is given

---

[17] This Latin phrase also serves as the title of the influential article by Stigler and Becker (1977).

[18] O'Donoghue and Rabin (2001, p. 38). For Mill, of course, there is no deference to self-regarding actions unless they are taken by people who are "in the maturity of their faculties," and perhaps 15-year-olds do not qualify on this score. But the point applies just as well to 18-year-olds or 21-year-olds. Becker and Mulligan (1997) examine the possibility that people can choose their rate of time preference through "investments" in patience; their model suggests that addicts will not invest heavily in patience. The resulting impatience then helps to magnify the addiction still further.

[19] This critique of rational addiction is drawn from Gruber and Köszegi (2000), though the basic notion that time inconsistency could present a challenge to a rational model of addiction was noted by Stigler and Becker (1977, p. 89). A seminal article on dynamic inconsistency is Strotz (1955).

to the requisite coherence. Someone whose preferences display time consistency would be able to plan future behavior today (contingent, perhaps, on such things as future prices) and would stick by that plan in the future. Someone with time-inconsistent preferences, alternatively, might develop an optimal plan today but decide not to follow the plan tomorrow. What the person now thinks will be his best choice one year from now, will, when the year has passed, no longer appear to be his best choice – even if no new information or options become available.

There is substantial evidence that individual choices are not time consistent.[20] Further, departures from dynamic consistency are rather systematic, not random, and apply widely. People tend to be more impatient when making decisions concerning the present and near future than when they make decisions concerning the more distant future. Would you rather have $1,000 today or $1,075 in one week? Many people would prefer the immediate $1,000. What if, instead, the choice were between $1,000 to be received precisely 227 days from today, or $1,075 to be received precisely 234 days from today? In this case, many people would choose (today) to wait the extra week (in 227 day's time) for the additional $75. People are typically less willing to postpone gains in the present than they are when making decisions about the future. When 227 days go by, and people are then asked to choose between an immediate $1,000 or $1,075 in one week, these same people will presumably revert to preferring the immediate $1,000 – they would not want to follow the plan they viewed as optimal 227 days earlier. This is the sense in which their choices do not display time consistency.

Regret is one of the markers of dynamic inconsistency, and one that appears to be particularly connected with decisions that involve current pleasures paired with future costs. Many people regret overspending or saving too little money, for instance. (The source of the word "addict" is the Latin word "addictus," which in Ancient Rome referred to those imprudent or unfortunate souls whose excessive debts led to their being enslaved to their creditors under judicial order.) Such people tend to view their previous decisions as shortsighted, which is not to say that these people will become more forward-looking in the future. It is as if we are two people, a prudent Dr. Jekyll and an intemperate Mr. Hyde, but it is our capricious, imprudent self who is making our current decisions about whether to have a beer, play a video game, or pick up smoking. Looking back as Dr. Jekyll, we regret Mr. Hyde's previous choices.

That dynamic inconsistency is at least part of the issue with addiction is lent credence by the fact that many addicts seem to engage in a struggle for

One additional concern with the rational addiction approach is that, for most substances (excluding cigarettes), the probability that a casual user will transform into an addict is fairly low, and there is abundant evidence that people have trouble appropriately weighing risks involving low-probability events.

[20] See, e.g., Loewenstein and Thaler (1989) and O'Donoghue and Rabin (2001).

self-control, a struggle between the desire for the drug and the desire to quit.[21] Addicts frequently describe their predicament in precisely these terms, as if they were two separate people battling for dominance of the decision-making power.

From this vantage point, managing a potential addiction amounts to asking how Jekyll can control Hyde. If Mr. Hyde were truly a different physical person whose conduct Dr. Jekyll wanted to regulate, presumably Jekyll would try to impose rules to govern Hyde's behavior, or even take preemptive actions that would force Hyde to behave in a manner acceptable to Jekyll. The same sort of approach is used by many individuals in dealing with their internal control issues: people adopt private rules or other strategies for pre-commitment.[22] Sometimes people invest in self-control devices designed to lower the payoff from future indulgence – investments that are hard to square with the notion that vicious choices are fully rational and time consistent.[23] Personal rules along the lines of "no dessert," "exercise every morning," "only two beers," and "keep no alcohol at home" seem to be among the best ways to bolster self-control.

The adoption of personal rules goes along with a common mental bookkeeping change, in which a single decision is not viewed in isolation but, rather, as part of a connected series of decisions.[24] What if experience has taught someone that eating one potato chip will almost inevitably lead to eating half a bag, and regret? He is currently faced with the possibility of eating one chip. He would prefer one chip to none, but he prefers no chips to having eaten half a bag. If the current "chip or no chip" decision is viewed in isolation, he will choose to eat that chip – and then the reinforcing qualities of potato chips will cause him to eat more and more until he has consumed half a bag, and regret has consumed him. So he might view the initial situation not as a choice between no chips and one but between no chips and half a bag, and this view of the choice problem might provide or augment the willpower that allows him to forgo the first chip.

Rules that help to promote self-control are used by nonaddicts all the time and in part might explain why they remain nonaddicts. Once addicted, the situation is less amenable to the adoption of and adherence to simple rules.

---

[21] Bakalar and Grinspoon (1984, p. 46) refer to the "paradox of habit," where a person views her actions, simultaneously, as being her own and not her own.

[22] See Elster (1999c, p. 74) and Schelling (1984, 1996).

[23] Though the discussion here has focused on time inconsistency, there are alternative approaches within the field of behavioral economics that involve different types of departures from full rationality. For instance, people might be subject to "projection bias," where they overestimate how similar their future preferences will be to their current preferences; see Loewenstein, O'Donoghue, and Rabin (2003). Or, their decisions might be excessively controlled by "visceral factors," in a manner that they neither fully anticipate nor appreciate in hindsight; see below, and Loewenstein (1996).

[24] See Ainslie (1992, pp. 142–62).

The rules might still be adopted, but they are not adhered to, as Dr. Jekyll noted:

> Strange as my circumstances were, the terms of this debate are as old and commonplace as man; much the same inducements and alarms cast the die for any tempted and trembling sinner; and it fell out with me, as it falls with so vast a majority of my fellows, that I chose the better part and was found wanting in the strength to keep to it.[25]

There is no simple solution to the perils of addiction, indeed, just the opposite it is a fiendishly perplexing status from which to escape. For many addicts, however, the road to recuperation seems to involve the complete overhaul, rather than the control, of Mr. Hyde. Addicts who recover do not simply give up a bad habit or adopt and follow one or two rules; rather, they often undergo a more general self-transformation.[26]

DYNAMIC INCONSISTENCY AND RATIONALITY

So, time inconsistency creates a sort of Jekyll-Hyde internal combat, the control of which frequently proves confounding.[27] But are dynamically inconsistent Jekyll-Hydes irrational? In other words, what happens if people are forward-looking and rational but not time consistent?[28] For one thing, their current consumption decisions will continue to depend on expected future consumption, as in the standard rational addiction approach.

Recall that the usual empirical tests of the rational addiction model allow us to compare rational addiction with myopic behavior; however, such tests do not permit us to determine whether rational individuals are time consistent or not, as both time-consistent and time-inconsistent rational people are forward-looking. The difference between rational/time consistent and rational/time inconsistent is evident, though, with respect to regret. With dynamic inconsistency, rational people (or at least their Dr. Jekyll incarnations) will tend to regret their past consumption of drugs, which they now view as excessive. As we have already seen, rational, time-consistent addicts would have no such regrets.

---

[25] Stevenson (1981 [1886], p. 91).

[26] Bakalar and Grinspoon (1984, p. 46) make this point with respect to reforming alcoholics. See also, e.g., the chapter entitled "Epiphany" in Baldino (2000, pp. 123–7).

[27] An important issue is the extent to which people recognize that their choices are subject to dynamic inconsistency, the extent to which they are "sophisticated" or "naive"; see O'Donoghue and Rabin (1999).

[28] This is the subject of Skog (1999) and O'Donoghue and Rabin (1999). Another possibility, examined by Braun and Vanini (2003), is that consumption of a habit-forming good might alter time preferences in a present-oriented direction. From such a standpoint, addicts tend to discount the future heavily, not because of an innate impatience but, rather, because their past drug consumption has rendered them impatient.

Box 2.2: *Thomas De Quincey, rational addict?*

Varieties of addictive experience are as numerous as addicts, so it is reckless to draw any generalizations from a single case. Nevertheless, one account of addiction, Thomas De Quincey's *Confessions of an English Opium Eater*, is fully deserving of its status as a classic, not just of addiction literature but of English literature more broadly. The *Confessions* combines penetrating insight with impressive style, in a work whose initial 1821 publication also can stake a claim to temporal priority among most addiction reminiscences.

An "opium eater" is someone who takes opium by drinking it in an alcoholic tincture called laudanum. In De Quincey's time in Britain, opium was legally available without a prescription; its pain-alleviating qualities led to its use as medicine for a variety of ailments, even for children, and, in some cases, to abuse. De Quincey's chapter on "The Pleasures of Opium" is quite laudatory – the name "laudanum" was given to the opium tincture by the famed sixteenth-century physician, Paracelsus, from a Latin word meaning "worthy of praise."[a] So impressive is De Quincey's descriptions of the joys of opium that the passages might provoke a rational individual to initiate opium eating – were this paean not succeeded by "The Pains of Opium," prefaced by De Quincey's "long farewell to happiness . . . farewell to smiles and laughter."[b]

According to the *Confessions*, De Quincey first took opium for relief from a toothache. The toothache eventually subsided, but De Quincey's regular opium eating did not. He continued to use opium for pleasure, perhaps once every three weeks or so but without addiction. After being a satisfied opium user for nearly ten years, though, under an acute case of emotional and physical distress, De Quincey increased both the frequency and the dosage of his opium consumption until he became a habitual, addicted user. (De Quincey's experience in this regard is more general: many addicts use their drug of choice in a controlled manner for a long time before succumbing to addiction.)

De Quincey traces the origins of his emotional distress to some wrenching events that occurred when he was 17 and living on his own in penurious conditions in London. In making this connection between his youthful distress and his later opium eating, he does not absolve himself of blame for his addiction: the London sufferings themselves, De Quincey writes, "grew out of my own folly." Indeed, De Quincey depicts his subsequent use of opium in terms that cohere well with the theory of rational addiction:

> I, for my part, after I had become a regular opium-eater, and from mismanagement had fallen into miserable excesses in the use of opium, did nevertheless, four several times, contend successfully against the dominion of this drug; did four several years renounce it; renounced it for long intervals; and finally resumed it upon the warrant of my enlightened and deliberate judgment, as being of two evils by very much the least. In this I acknowledge nothing that calls for excuse. I repeat again and again, that not the application of opium, with its deep tranquilising powers to the mitigation of evils, bequeathed by my London hardships, is what reasonably calls for sorrow, but that extravagance of childish folly which precipitated me into scenes naturally producing such hardships.[c]

An "enlightened and deliberate judgment" to remain a regular opium eater is perhaps one type of addiction. De Quincey, however, also provides a brief account of the opium-related behavior of his acquaintance, the celebrated writer and philosopher Samuel Taylor Coleridge. De Quincey tells us that Coleridge, in his effort to control his opium craving,

> went so far as to hire men – porters, hackney-coachmen, and others – to oppose by force his entrance into any druggist's shop. But, as the authority for stopping him was derived simply from himself, naturally these poor men found themselves in a metaphysical fix, not provided for even by Thomas Aquinas or by the prince of Jesuitical casuists.[d]

De Quincey then reports a typical conversation between Coleridge and one of his hirelings, culminating in this flourish from "the Transcendental Philosopher":

> An emergency, a shocking emergency, has arisen – quite unlooked for. No matter what I told you in times long past. That which I *now* tell you, is – that, if you don't remove that arm of yours from the doorway of this most respectable druggist, I shall have a good ground of action against you for assault and battery.[e]

De Quincey's own use of opium, then, may have been governed by his "enlightened and deliberate judgment," but Coleridge's behavior, at least as depicted by De Quincey, can scarcely be characterized in those terms.

---

[a] Carnwath and Smith (2002, p. 5).   [b] De Quincey (1986, p. 96).

[c] De Quincey (1986, p. 147); this passage is from De Quincey's 1856 revision of his original 1821 *Confessions*.

[d] De Quincey (1986, pp. 144–5); this passage, like the preceding and subsequent ones, is from De Quincey's 1856 revision.

[e] De Quincey (1986, pp. 145). The italics in the quote are De Quincey's.

Perhaps more importantly, time inconsistency could greatly alter the appropriate policy toward drugs or other potentially addictive goods, even if it is accepted that users are rational.[29] If individuals themselves are composed of time-specific entities who have different preferences, then John Stuart Mill's notion of "harm to others" could be construed to include "harm to your future self" – harm that you will not fully take into account, as your future self will have different preferences than your current view of that person's preferences. "Internalities" is the term applied to these "internal externalities."[30] Personal rules that help us to precommit to low consumption of a potentially addictive good or otherwise fortify our self-control are one method to give our future selves their due.

Public policies, like personal policies, might want to respond to the internalities that arise when a person's "current" self imposes costs on his or her

---

[29] This is the argument of Gruber and Köszegi (2000).

[30] The term "internalities" derives from Herrnstein et al. (1993).

"future"self; that is, the government might be in a position to help Dr. Jekyll control Mr. Hyde.[31] (Further, such interventions do not violate Mill's harm principle, once internalities are accepted as an instance of external harms.) Taxes are a convenient lever by which government can reduce consumption of targeted, potentially addictive goods. In the case of cigarettes, to induce current consumers to take into account the full costs they impose on their otherwise underrepresented future selves, it has been estimated that an additional tax of $1 per pack of cigarettes might be justified.[32] If the measure of happiness is a person's long-run preferences (i.e., Dr. Jekyll's preferences), such a tax can contribute to a smoker's happiness – a startling revision of the standard economics notion that a consumer cannot be made better off when the price rises for a good she already purchases.[33]

VISCERAL FACTORS[34]

Although time inconsistency can generate regret over decisions to use drugs, by itself, it does not imply that drug-related decisions are irrational – though whether it is Jekyll or Hyde who is the rational one does become somewhat muddied.[35] Even accepting that rational people can be dynamically inconsistent, there remains unease with viewing addiction as a rational choice. Time inconsistency alone doesn't seem sufficient to explain addictive behavior, for various reasons. First, as noted, the disregard for the future displayed by some choices seems well beyond the range of rationality.[36] Second, not all of a person's choices seem to suffer from time inconsistency. Rather, there is an identifiable subset of decisions that appears susceptible to the excessive influence of short-term considerations. Sometimes the mere appearance of a cue can cause craving and drug use, even though there is no reason to think that the cue itself alters the rate at which an individual values present versus future costs and rewards.[37] Someone who in the past habitually drank red wine with

---

[31] On internalities, see, e.g., O'Donoghue and Rabin (1999).

[32] Gruber and Köszegi (2000). The additional tax is relative to the amounts commonly prevailing in the United States at the end of the 1990s.

[33] Gruber and Mullainathan (2002).

[34] This section draws heavily upon Loewenstein (1996). Ainslie (1999) provides a critique of the visceral factors approach to addiction.

[35] Jekyll himself felt the ambiguity: "Though so profound a double-dealer, I was in no sense a hypocrite; both sides of me were in dead earnest; I was no more myself when I laid aside restraint and plunged in shame, than when I laboured, in the eye of day, at the furtherance of knowledge or the relief of sorrow and suffering [Stevenson (1981 [1886], p. 79)]."

[36] One incident that suggests excessive interest in present satisfaction occurred when a man, finding himself in the driver's seat of his car as it was sinking in a pond, chose to smoke some crack before exiting the vehicle. See the post on Vice Squad, August 16, 2004.

[37] Loewenstein (1996, pp. 277–8) also notes that the "preference reversals" induced as time passes in the face of dynamic inconsistency should not all take place at the last possible moment, but they often do: pregnant women often override their earlier decisions not to take painkillers during childbirth, but they rarely change their minds until labor commences.

pasta meals can, even years later, yearn for wine when presented with a plate of spaghetti.

For those types of decisions that tend to be overly influenced by short-term considerations, people might select alternatives while being fully aware that their choices do not serve their long-term best interests. Economist and addiction researcher George Loewenstein "attributes this phenomenon to the operation of 'visceral factors,' which include drive states such as hunger, thirst, and sexual desire, mood and emotions, physical pain, and craving for a drug one is addicted to."[38] A significant visceral factor, like pain, can produce the sort of present-oriented choices that might be suggestive of dynamic inconsistency, but only with respect to choices connected with the relevant visceral factor. "Further, at even greater levels of intensity, visceral factors can be so powerful as to virtually preclude decision making. No one *decides* to fall asleep at the wheel, but many people do."[39]

That choices respond to visceral influences is not evidence of irrationality. Visceral factors influence preferences, and rationality consists of choosing the best means to satisfy one's preferences. Loewenstein argues, however, that people consistently underestimate the strength of the compulsion that visceral factors will exert on their future choices. Unlike rational addicts, then, who perfectly foresee and indeed can consistently plan their future choices today, those who will respond to visceral factors tomorrow cannot fully perceive, today, the sway of visceral effects on future decisions. (If their foresight were perfect, they might engage in the sort of precommitment strategies that are employed by time-inconsistent decision makers.) Further, the underestimating of visceral factors holds when people look back at their previous choices, too: people forget the extent to which their earlier decisions were driven by their then-current visceral concerns. (People also underestimate the extent to which the choices of others are motivated by visceral considerations.) This systematic misunderstanding of choices is not consistent with fully rational behavior.

Loewenstein offers many fascinating illustrations of choices influenced by visceral factors, and many others can be imagined.[40] People will be more likely to buy cookies if they are hungry, of course, but whatever their level of hunger, they are more likely to buy cookies if they can smell the cookies. A rational addict might purchase large quantities of his drug at one time, and store them for future use; actual addicts, though, have a hard time storing drugs for later consumption – the immediate availability of the drug will induce a craving in them for immediate use. Drug addicts who succumb to a craving, when they look back upon it later, cannot understand why they lapsed – they do not fully appreciate, after the fact, the strength of their previous hunger for the drug.

---

[38] Loewenstein (1996, p. 272).   [39] Loewenstein (1996, p. 273).

[40] The "cookies" example is from page 279; the underestimation of craving in hindsight, from page 278; and the "informing" example, from page 283, of Loewenstein (1996).

Box 2.3: *Akrasia: weakness of will*[a]

acrasia – The state of mind in which one acts against one's better judgement;
weakness of will, 'incontinence' . . .
Oxford English Dictionary

The struggle between visceral influences and rationality in decision making is an
old one, and the debate was joined by Socrates and Aristotle. Can it be that a
person understands the best course of action, but nevertheless chooses a different
path? To employ the Greek terminology, can a person be subject to *acrasia* (or
akrasia), knowing the better but choosing the worse? Surely cravings can get the
better of us, our reason can be overcome by passion. Socrates asked: "When men
are overcome by eating and drinking and other sensual desires which are pleasant,
and they, knowing them to be evil, nevertheless indulge in them, would you not say
that they were overcome by pleasure?"[b]

Socrates employed the question, er, Socratically. He argued that someone who
knew the action that best served his interests would take that action. Failure to take
the preferred action was not evidence of acrasia, but rather of a lack of knowledge of
what choice is best. A man who seemingly knows the better but chooses the worse
actually mismeasures the various beneficial and costly consequences arising from
an action. For Socrates, choices that appear to be the result of the decision maker
being "overcome by pleasure" are, in reality, the result of ignorance. In a sense,
given his incorrect information, an overindulgent man is making rational choices.

Aristotle noted that this contention by Socrates "plainly contradicts the observed facts . . . "[c] After carefully parsing various meanings of "knowledge," however, Aristotle ends up in substantial agreement with Socrates. For Aristotle, someone who lets passion overrule his reason concerning what action to choose is in a
sort of temporary state of ignorance. While such a person may appear to be lucid
and to possess knowledge, that appearance is deceptive. "It is plain, then, that incontinent people must be said to be in a similar condition to men asleep, mad, or drunk.
The fact that men use the language that flows from knowledge proves nothing . . . "[d]
Those who "know" the better while choosing the worse, at the time of the choice,
do not really "know." But they recover knowledge, and, presumably, regret their
choice: "The explanation of how the ignorance is dissolved and the incontinent man
regains his knowledge, is the same as in the case of the man drunk or asleep . . . "[e]

---

[a] Mary Anne Case brought the classical debate about akrasia to my attention.
[b] *Protagoras*, 353; Plato (1952, p. 60). See also *The Republic*, pp. 439–43.
[c] *Nicomachean Ethics*, Book VII, 1145b; Aristotle (1952, Vol. II, p. 395).
[d] *Nicomachean Ethics*, Book VII, 1145b; Aristotle (1952, Vol. II, p. 397).
[e] *Nicomachean Ethics*, Book VII, 1147b; Aristotle (1952, Vol. II, p. 397).

Similarly, those detainees who inform on friends when goaded by interrogators using sleep deprivation, cold, or hunger, have a hard time forgiving themselves later because, in retrospect, they cannot appreciate the potency of the visceral factors that pressured their revelations or fabrications.

Adding credence to the theory of the influence of visceral factors on decision making is the fact that brain chemistry is altered by visceral factors, or rather, we experience visceral conditions such as sleepiness through changes in our brain chemistry. Drugs likewise alter brain chemistry, and as with decisions made under the influence of other visceral factors, the drug decisions of addicts are apt to appear to be irrational, or as not being the result of a deliberate choice at all.[41]

ADDICTION AS A DISEASE

Neurobiological factors play a key role in much drug use. The reward structure of our brains (and of animal brains) provides a motive toward behavior that is generally beneficial for the individual (or his or her genes), activities such as eating, drinking, and sex. One main channel for reward in humans is dopamine neurotransmission within a part of the brain known as the medial forebrain bundle.[42] Addictive drugs, including alcohol and nicotine, have differing and complex effects on brain chemistry, but they all stimulate the dopamine reward mechanisms, despite being unconnected to the beneficial behavior that the reward system developed to motivate. In all likelihood, it is this stimulation that makes drug use so reinforcing. "[A]ddiction results when the reward system of the brain is hijacked by chemical substances that played no role in its evolution."[43] In other words, drug addiction can be viewed as a disease, an unhealthy physical condition.

Much of the evidence concerning the effect of drugs on the brain, and thereby on behavior, is drawn from studies on animals. Addiction does not seem to occur to nonhuman animals in the wild.[44] In experimental settings, however, animals can be induced to press a bar repeatedly for a reward of a drug like cocaine, to the exclusion of all else. (They can be induced similarly to push a bar when pushing results in a direct electronic stimulus to the reward area of their brain.) "[A] monkey will self-administer [cocaine] to exhaustion – not eating, not drinking, and ignoring opportunities for sexual activity. Eventually,

---

[41] Bernheim and Rangel (2004) provide a model of addictive behavior that shares many features of Lowenstein's visceral factors approach. Bernheim and Rangel, however, posit a specific mechanism through which visceral factors affect choice. Under the influence of visceral factors or cues, people employ cognitive shortcuts; as a result, decisions do not involve the full reflective faculties. In other words, people's judgment is impaired in identifiable circumstances, including situations generally associated with addiction. Recognizing their susceptibility, people attempt to manage their exposure to cues.

[42] In this section, I rely primarily on Gardner (1999) and Goldstein (2001).

[43] Elster (1999c, p. 53).   [44] Bakalar and Grinspoon (1984, p. 41).

such a monkey will die taking cocaine – of starvation or dehydration or sudden heart stoppage caused by the drug excess in the body."[45]

The "short-term benefit, long-term cost" nature of drug use also is reflected in brain chemistry. Acute administration of a drug produces the brain reward. Long-term drug use, however, tends to cause "homeostatic" adjustments in the brain. The excessive dopamine presence created by the drug use leads the brain's own reward circuitry to become degraded in various ways. One result, apparently, is tolerance and withdrawal symptoms. More of the drug is needed to achieve the same hedonic effect, and the absence of the drug leads to unpleasant feelings, anhedonia. These longer-term effects on brain chemistry from drug use, of course, can themselves reinforce the desire to use the drug.

This brief description of the neurobiology of drug use is hopelessly over-simplified. The precise mechanisms through which drugs affect the brain are multifarious and to some extent remain unknown. For example, the central role played in addiction and relapse behavior by cravings induced by environmental cues suggests that drugs influence the part of our brain that forecasts how much we will enjoy some activity and not just the part that provides the reward during consumption.[46] (The hypothesis that addictive drugs play primarily upon drug "wanting," as opposed to drug "liking," their hedonic effect, has been put forth and developed by Terry Robinson and Kent Berridge.[47]) Within-session effects can be different from both acute and chronic impacts: an initial dose of cocaine might lead to sensitization, where the closely following dose has a larger, not a smaller impact, than the first dose.[48] Nevertheless, that the general brain reward mechanism is at play with most addictive drugs is suggested by the phenomenon known as "cross-priming" – a small dose of one drug tends to produce a craving in an addict for another substance, his usual drug of choice.[49] Despite cross-priming, however, drugs are not perfect substitutes for one another. A heroin addict or an alcoholic will not fully be satisfied by the nicotine in a cigarette, even though all three drugs tend to enhance dopamine neurotransmission. Amazingly, behavioral addictions such as pathological gambling seem to involve brain chemistry in ways that are not dissimilar from those of drug addiction.[50]

---

[45] Goldstein (2001, p. 59).

[46] See the discussion in Bernheim and Rangel (2004).

[47] See, e.g., Robinson and Berridge (1993, 2001).

[48] See, for instance, Goldstein (2001, p. 183).

[49] Gardner (1999, p. 74) and Elster (1999c, p. 83).

[50] See, e.g., Gardner (1999, pp. 78ff.), and Waal and Mørland (1999, p. 132). Recently it has been reported that some patients taking dopamine agonists to treat Parkinson's disease develop an unexpected side effect: a newfound compulsion to gamble. See "Parkinson's Treatment Linked to Compulsive Gambling," Scientific American.com, July 12, 2005, available at http://www.sciam.com/article.cfm?chanID=sa003&articleID=0008C23C-CEE1-12D2-8EE183414B7F0000 (accessed on July 18, 2005).

The disease view of addiction lends itself to understanding drug use as an act initiated by a patient, a victim of disease, to medicate his affliction. Some people have a brain reward system that is relatively underdeveloped, so the "artificial" stimulation of drugs or gambling might be needed for their brains to function "normally." This view is particularly compelling in the case of opiate addiction because there are some naturally produced opiate-like substances, endorphins (from "endogenous morphines"), in the brain. (Cannabinoids – psychoactive compounds found in marijuana – also occur naturally in the brain.) Someone with "too few" endorphins might rationally treat his condition by ingesting morphine, heroin, or some other opioid. For such a person, narcotics use could compensate for his inborn deficiency, just as diabetics rely on insulin injections to make up for their own natural shortcoming. In a sense, both junkies and diabetics use drugs to become "normal."[51] Users of nonopiate drugs likewise might be compensating for a neurobiological condition, a substandard dopamine neurotransmission system. This condition has been termed "reward deficiency syndrome."[52] For those individuals with reward deficiency syndrome, drug use might not be a free choice, much less a rational choice.

The degradation of the brain's own reward circuitry that follows heavy drug use implies that even people who cannot initially be characterized as suffering from reward deficiency syndrome end up suffering from a form of that condition. They start out as "normal," but they experiment with a drug, and they really enjoy it. They naturally seek to repeat that pleasurable experience by taking the drug again, and again, and again. Homeostatic adjustments within their brain then begin to kick in, so that their "baseline" level of pleasure is degraded. Eventually, taking the drug still provides a pleasure boost, but because their baseline has shifted, the drug only makes them feel normal, the way they felt without any stimulus before their addiction. Potentially addictive drugs or activities are a trap: a known trap but nonetheless a subtle one.

If addiction is primarily or exclusively a biological phenomenon, perhaps we can identify addicts in advance, just as we can identify infants with diseases before they are symptomatic. Science has uncovered genetic markers for increased susceptibility to a variety of addictions. The identical twin of an alcoholic has something like a 6-to-8 times greater chance of being an alcoholic than does a nonrelative.[53] Further, the biological basis for addiction suggests that pharmacological treatments might be available to "cure" addiction, and indeed, pharmacological agents are used in addiction therapy. (Such agents currently fall well short of a cure, however.) Nicotine patches or gum, which provide nicotine to the brain while bypassing the lungs, can help wean smokers

[51] Robson (1999, p. 200). Also, see the discussion in Goldstein (2001, p. 101) and Baldino (2000, p. 154).
[52] See Blum et al. (1996).   [53] Schuckit (1999).

from cigarettes. Methadone or other opiate agonists are used in the treatment of heroin addiction. Daily administration of methadone can dampen the euphoric effects of heroin and prevent opiate withdrawal symptoms, without inducing the sharp high and "nodding off" that are common responses to heroin injection. Pharmacological agents that would provide the rough equivalent of the methadone/heroin relationship are actively being sought for cocaine and other addictions. It is even possible to imagine the development of a "vaccine," which, once taken, might offer long-term protection against the reinforcing, hedonic effects of some addictive drugs or activities. Imagination isn't even required: in the case of cocaine, an experimental vaccine already exists.[54]

THE ANTI-DISEASE VIEW

Neurobiological correlates and effects of drug use do not, in themselves, imply that drug use is involuntary. Nor are addictions genetically predetermined, despite genetic influences on drug-using behavior. Most children of an alcoholic will not become alcoholics, while most alcoholics have nonalcoholic parents.[55] Many people appear to be addicted to some substance or activity at one point in their life, but not at other points.[56] The overwhelming majority of U.S. soldiers addicted to heroin when stationed in Vietnam did not continue as heroin addicts after they returned to the United States.[57] Even animals given regular (though not continuous and intravenous) access to cocaine regulate their intake, and those in less isolated, more social environments, take fewer drugs.[58]

Psychological mechanisms play a role in what seem to be predominantly biological drug-related processes, like tolerance. A large dose of a drug administered to an addicted animal in a familiar environment will not cause the animal any major health problems, while in a new environment, the same dose might kill the animal.[59] A formerly addicted animal will revert to addiction quickly if returned to the same environment in which it consumed drugs in the past. Nicotine gum is more effective than nicotine patches in helping some people give up cigarettes, presumably because gum allows people to deliver nicotine on demand.[60] This, too, suggests a psychological component to addiction.

---

[54] See, e.g., the Yale University news release, dated March 10, 2000, entitled "Anti-Cocaine Vaccine Produces Antibodies, Shown To Be Safe In Yale Researcher's Phase 1 Study," available at www.biopsychiatry.com/cocaine/vaccine.htm. There is some evidence that a monthly injection of the opioid antagonist naltrexone helps alcoholics control their drinking; see the Vice Squad post from April 7, 2005.

[55] See Schuckit (1999).

[56] This point has been emphasized by addiction researcher Stanton Peele; see, e.g., Peele (2001).

[57] See, e.g., Carnwath and Smith (2002, p. 87).

[58] Peele and DeGrandpre (1998).   [59] Elster (1999c, p. 67).

[60] Elster (1999c, p. 54). But as Goldstein (2001, p. 60) notes, humans also enjoy spikes in the concentration of a drug, and it may be that nicotine gum provides spikes as opposed to the near constant nicotine concentration offered by a patch. Goldstein (2001, p. 131) also reports, contrary to Elster,

Drugs affect our brains, but our responses to our altered neurochemistry vary with our attitudes and our environment.[61] Drug use is not a purely biological phenomenon.

Just as a person's genes do not dictate his or her drug use, neither do psychological factors. The idea of an "addictive personality" is largely discredited, in part because it is hard to predict who will become an addict on the basis of personality traits.[62] "In fact, alcoholics appear to have nothing in common which differentiates them from the rest of us, except that at some time in their lives they are regarded by others or regard themselves as persistent users of alcohol in a way that is harmful to themselves, their families, or society."[63] Nevertheless, in studies of normally functioning adolescents, an increased likelihood of experimenting with drugs is associated with general sensation or novelty-seeking behavior.[64] Children who are deviant in other ways also have a much higher incidence of drug use. (Of course, illegal drug use itself can magnify existing shortcomings: it is difficult for a heroin addict to lead an otherwise normal life, not so much because of the drug itself, but because of the burdens that illegality places on the user.[65]) Like genes, psychological factors influence addiction, but again like genes, psychology does not completely predetermine drug-related behavior.

Even so-called psychological factors have some biophysical substrate. Consider the following situation.[66] Pain is induced in an individual, who then receives an injection of an opiate such as morphine, causing the pain to disappear. This procedure is repeated a few times daily, for some time. Then one day, after the pain is induced, the injection that is given contains no morphine nor any other active ingredient; it is a placebo, and the subject is unaware that the injection does not contain morphine. Nevertheless, the pain will be relieved by the placebo, once the shot has come to be associated with the removal of pain. The twist occurs if the same experiment is run, but the placebo shot includes some of the opioid antagonist naloxone. In this case, the placebo will no longer relieve the pain. In other words, it appears as if the placebo effect induces the emission of the brain's natural opioids, and hence the effect can be overcome if an opioid antagonist is administered. The "psychological" placebo effect seems to have a physical underpinning.

The notion that alcoholics have little in common beyond unhealthy heavy drinking takes on even more force when all addictions, chemical as well as

---

that nicotine patches work better than gum, in part because the absorption of nicotine through the mucous membranes of the mouth is too variable.

[61] See Zinberg (1984); Bakalar and Grinspoon (1984, p. 42).

[62] Bakalar and Grinspoon (1984, pp. 42–3).   [63] Bakalar and Grinspoon (1984, p. 53).

[64] See, e.g., Gardner (1999, pp. 80ff.).

[65] Bakalar and Grinspoon (1984, p. 43) and Goldstein (2001, p. 89).

[66] This paragraph is based on "13 Things That Do Not Make Sense," by Michael Brooks, NewScientist.com news service, 13 March 2005.

Some researchers have developed approaches to addiction that are profoundly at odds with the disease view. Herbert Fingarette offers one notable alternative in his book *Heavy Drinking*, which is subtitled *The Myth of Alcoholism as a Disease*. Though Fingarette's book concerns drinking alcoholic beverages, the general tenor of his argument can be applied to other drug addictions as well.[a]

Fingarette characterizes what he terms the "Classic Disease Concept of Alcoholism." This concept maintains that, first, "[a]lcoholism is a specific disease to which some people are vulnerable."[b] Second, individuals who are vulnerable to alcoholism will contract the disease if they begin to drink. Third, the disease has an inevitable, standard progression, in which the alcoholic moves from social drinking to loss of control, then to heavy drinking with blackouts and withdrawal. Fourth, the disease is incurable, so abstention is the best hope. Though few people are steadfast proponents of all four components of the Classic Disease Concept of Alcoholism, it is very influential; for instance, it is essentially the view adopted by the well-known recovery program Alcoholics Anonymous.

Loss of control constitutes the central premise of the disease concept. There is some confusion over whether the loss of control applies to the decision to take the first drink – apparently not, since abstinence is presumably the way out – or only after the first drink. But if control over the first drink remains, how can alcoholism be associated with a loss of control? Experiments show that perceived costs and benefits matter to the drinking decisions of alcoholics; that is, these decisions are not consistent with the loss of control model. Further, many alcoholics at times choose to drink moderately or to abstain. The notion that heavy drinkers have an uncontrollable urge or craving (perhaps after the first drink) is not supported by the evidence, either; the social setting matters, for instance.

Loss of control is not the only aspect of the disease view that is inconsistent with the evidence. According to Fingarette, none of the tenets of the Classic Disease Concept of Alcoholism are scientifically valid. Neither the ineluctable progression of the "disease," nor the necessity of abstinence for a cure, are borne out by the experiences of many heavy drinkers.

Physical withdrawal symptoms are commonly pointed to as biological causes for alcoholism. A vicious circle is sometimes suggested, in which drinking increases tolerance, and higher tolerance therefore means that more alcohol is needed to avoid withdrawal. But more than one-third of alcoholics have no withdrawal and tolerance symptoms. Nor do those who suffer from withdrawal have an insatiable need for alcohol. Physical symptoms are more consequence than cause of heavy drinking.

Neither withdrawal nor any other single factor dictates heavy drinking. As there is no single cause of "alcoholism," so there is no single cure. About one-third of heavy drinkers improve over time without any treatment. Disease-oriented treatment programs do not seem to be better at reducing alcohol intake than does the "natural" course of alcoholism: the "very label *treatment* thus seems a deceptive misnomer."[c] Although they frequently are based on the notion that alcoholism is a disease, most recovery programs, including Alcoholics Anonymous, offer little in the way of medical interventions.

Fingarette presents an alternative to the disease view. Heavy drinkers are those for whom drinking has become a central activity in their way of life.[d] In this sense, drinking for alcoholics is like religion, food, reading, or a vocation might be for other people. The drinking behavior of alcoholics is a result of a long series of choices that coalesce into making heavy drinking a central life activity.

Why would anyone make such destructive choices? Fingarette suggests that we are all myopic – his is neither a disease nor a rational addiction approach. We respond to current problems, drifting into habits, without necessarily seeing the long-run consequences. "For the person challenged by personal problems, heavy drinking is one of the culturally available responses, however imprudent and self-destructive."[e]

To outsiders, the failure of an alcoholic to reform in a beneficial way seems surprising. But altering something that has become central to one's life is no simple matter, whether that "thing" is patterns of reading or eating or drinking. "Internal and external factors – bodily constitution and age, intellect and education, cultural and ethnic norms, economic and domestic circumstances – limit one's potential for change and one's alternatives."[f] For a heavy drinker to revert to moderate drinking or abstention requires a major change in lifestyle, and such a change does not come easily.

---

[a] Fingarette (1988, p. 7). Another prominent opponent of the disease view of addiction is Stanton Peele; see. e.g., Peele (1989), and his website at www.peele.net/index.html (accessed January 1, 2007).

[b] Fingarette (1988, p. 2).   [c] Fingarette (1988, p. 73).

[d] Fingarette (1988, pp. 99ff.). The "lifestyle model" of Walters (1999) is highly congruent with Fingarette's approach to addiction.

[e] Fingarette (1988, p. 103).   [f] Fingarette (1988, p. 105).

---

behavioral, are considered. There are important similarities among those who smoke a lot of cannabis and those who snort a lot of cocaine, among those who are addicted to heroin and those who are addicted to shopping. Some alterations in brain chemistry appear to be among those similarities, but that does not mean that these behaviors are of a kind, as alike as pennies. Bats fly and birds fly, but bat wings and bird wings are the result of two separate developmental processes.[67] In the terminology of evolutionary biology, bat wings and bird wings are analogous (similar in function), but not homologous (similar in origin). So it may well be with the addictions – they have some close behavioral and even physiological analogies, but they are not, at root, the same phenomenon:

> ... since a unified theory of addiction presupposes that the central addictive phenomena are homologous rather than analogous, and since many causally important features of addiction do in fact exhibit analogy rather than homology,

[67] See the discussion of homology and analogy in Waal and Mørland (1999, pp. 141–4).

the prospects for a unified theory are somewhat dim. It is not a question of a causal theory of the development of wings but different factors that influence the ability to fly in itself.[68]

Even different individuals suffering from the "same" addiction might be analogues, not homologues. Perhaps some forms of alcoholism, including the most severe cases, are "caused" by genetic factors, while other forms of alcoholism lack a congenital basis.[69] In any case, "[w]e are far from a situation in which neurobiological research explains addiction. What is explained is aspects of behavior and neurobiological changes that would understandably influence choice processes."[70]

COMPARATIVE ADDICTIVENESS

"CIGARETTES ARE HIGHLY ADDICTIVE
Studies have shown that tobacco can be harder to quit than heroin or cocaine."
– From a set of more than a dozen health warnings, one of which must
appear prominently on every cigarette pack sold in Canada.[71]

The politics of U.S. domestic tobacco regulation changed in April 1994 when, in sworn testimony before a congressional subcommittee, the chief executives of the seven leading tobacco companies all testified that they did not believe that nicotine was addictive. The difficulty of defining "addiction" implies that these statements were not entirely without justification. Nevertheless, they contradicted the commonsense, shared understanding of the term addiction (as well as contradicting some of the companies' own internal documents) and helped to nurture the belief that the companies were willing to mislead for profit.[72]

Granting that nicotine is addictive, an obvious undertaking is to compare nicotine's addictive potential with that of other drugs, such as alcohol and cannabis, or even of other vices, such as playing slot machines. Obvious, but somewhat misguided: under any definition, the addictiveness of a vice depends on the precise format of its consumption, along with personal characteristics and expectations of the consumer and the environment in which consumption occurs.[73] Even the regulatory climate can alter the reinforcing qualities of a vice. For instance, a prohibition that renders drug access and quality to be

---

[68] Waal and Mørland (1999, p. 142).   [69] See the discussion in Blum et al. (1996).

[70] Waal and Mørland (1999, p. 143).

[71] The warnings and their accompanying pictures, which must make up 50 percent of the packaging, can be seen at www.hc-sc.gc.ca/hl-vs/tobac-tabac/legislation/label-etiquette/graph/index_e.html, visited June 29, 2006.

[72] On the alteration in attitudes toward tobacco companies dating from 1994, see Bogus (2000, pp. 1361–72).

[73] That is, addictive potential depends on drug, set, and setting, to employ the well-known triad of Zinberg (1984).

unpredictable imparts an intermittent reward structure to the search for the drug, a sort of gambling dimension that could add to the addictiveness of drug taking.[74] By these lights, a categorical statement that nicotine is more addictive than heroin (or vice versa) is inappropriate or virtually devoid of meaning. The Canadian smoking warning above is somewhat better, as it only implicates a subset of users in suggesting that tobacco "can" be harder to give up than heroin or cocaine.

Nevertheless, addictive potential is perhaps the main determinant of what separates vice from other elements of self-regarding behavior, at least if the addiction is viewed as carrying highly negative consequences. Some substances and activities, in general, seem to be more habit forming than others. But formalizing this impression is not easy. One approach in the case of substance consumption has been to examine the likelihood that an occasional user of a drug becomes a habitual user.[75] Another approach is to try to gauge the difficulty in quitting a habit once acquired. Under both methods, nicotine in the form of cigarettes seems to be the most addictive among the common drugs, whereas marijuana tends to be much less habit forming; alcohol, heroin, and cocaine fall somewhere in between. Alternatively, rankings of drugs can be developed by experts among a variety of (somewhat overlapping) addictive dimensions, such as the build-up of tolerance, the extent of withdrawal symptoms, and the reinforcing nature of consumption.[76] Substances vary significantly among the criteria. For instance, alcohol withdrawal is very serious and potentially fatal; cocaine use typically presents milder withdrawal symptoms but tends to be more reinforcing than alcohol consumption. In terms of public attitudes and public policy, general perceptions of dangerousness are probably more important than addictiveness per se: caffeine use is fairly addictive but is not viewed as particularly dangerous – and substances containing caffeine are openly sold to children. Perceptions of dangerousness, however, are themselves dependent upon the existing policy environment. Criminalized drugs become disproportionally favored by, well, a criminal population, and then the characteristics of these users reinforce the perception that the drugs themselves are inherently dangerous. Public and private marketing campaigns can downplay or exaggerate the hazards of drug use.

One attempt to isolate the "inherent" dangerousness of a drug compared

... the severity of health effects for heavy users of different substances in their most harmful common form. By the rough rankings in this comparison alcohol

---

[74] Carnwath and Smith (2002, p. 108).

[75] See Table 3.4 in Institute of Medicine (1999).

[76] See "Is Nicotine Addictive? It Depends on Whose Criteria You Use," by Philip J. Hilts, *New York Times*, August 2, 1994. Also see *Prime Minister's Strategy Unit Drug Report* (2003), where an assessment of potential addictiveness (page 11) lists heroin and crack at the top, LSD, cannabis, and ecstasy at the bottom, and alcohol and tobacco in between. For an update, see the Vice Squad post from March 25, 2007.

ranked highest, with tobacco and heroin in the middle and marijuana at a lower level, in terms of number and seriousness of particular health harms.[77]

The multitudinous ways in which drugs can be compared with respect to addictiveness or dangerousness lead to different rankings, of course. But one typical outcome is that marijuana is found to be less addictive or dangerous than alcohol or nicotine. (This result is not universal: on a scale of intoxication potential, marijuana ranks ahead of nicotine.) Nevertheless, marijuana is much more strictly controlled in the United States than either alcohol or nicotine. It is a "Schedule 1" drug, one that cannot be prescribed by doctors. Schedule 1 drugs are supposed to present a high potential for abuse, while lacking an accepted medical use; heroin is a Schedule 1 drug, as are hallucinogens such as LSD, mescaline, and psilocybin (found in "magic mushrooms").

The relatively strict policy regime that has been established in the United States with respect to marijuana and for hallucinogens such as LSD and psilocybin mushrooms seems anomalous from the viewpoint of comparative danger.[78] These drugs are almost surely less addictive and less harmful than either alcohol or nicotine. Marijuana and the hallucinogens also hold promise for medical and psychological uses;[79] marijuana already is part of the legal pharmacopeia in some countries. Nevertheless, more than 700,000 arrests are made in the United States annually for marijuana or hallucinogen possession.

RESPONSIBILITY

Should drug users be held responsible for their decisions to use drugs? Should addicts be held accountable for other criminal acts that are undertaken either under the influence of drugs or to serve the needs of drug acquisition? If addiction is a disease, shouldn't addicts be excused for their habits or for their actions, even otherwise criminal actions, that flow from their addictions? Could a heroin addict who is charged with theft (a theft motivated by the desire to pay for heroin) use her addiction as a defense? The legal system is continually faced with such questions, and some of the current answers are discussed a bit later. Our own, personal response to addicts and their behavior is also colored by how we think about these questions. Are addicts who commit crimes sick, or are they weak, or are they bad – or all three?[80]

---

[77] Room (2006, p. 166).

[78] See, for instance, Courtwright (2001, p. 189).

[79] On recent medical and psychological uses for psilocybin, see Griffiths et al. (2006) and "Study: Psilocybin Relieves OCD Symptoms," December 20, 2006, at www.dailyadvance.com/health/content/shared-gen/ap/Health_Medical/Psilocybin_Study.html, visited January 1, 2007. The Drug Policy Alliance maintains a helpful webpage on Medical Marijuana at www.drugpolicy.org/marijuana/medical/ (accessed January 1, 2007).

[80] Bakalar and Grinspoon (1984, pp. 55ff.).

Many addiction recovery programs, including Alcoholics Anonymous, Narcotics Anonymous, and Gamblers Anonymous, explicitly adopt a disease perspective toward their respective addictions. Nevertheless, these programs do not absolve the addict of responsibility for his or her behavior – quite the contrary, they emphasize personal accountability. Further, though they maintain that addicts have a disease, their recovery programs center on nonmedical techniques aimed at building the resources for improved self-control. The inconsistency is manageable. For some treatment purposes, it appears, addiction can profitably be viewed as a disease and possibly even an infectious disease.[81] Simultaneously, for other aspects of treatment (bolstering self-control) and for the purposes of the criminal law, the personal responsibility of the (diseased) addict can still be maintained. A similar approach applies to other diseases that can alter behavior: people who suffer from bipolar disease or diabetes, for instance, are held responsible for managing their condition.[82]

For serious crimes, "a pattern of addiction or alcoholism has never been an excuse for denying responsibility."[83] Nevertheless, many people are willing to be indulgent of less serious social indiscretions if the perpetrator "had a bit too much to drink." Chronic addicts, however, often become unsympathetic characters – compassionate social workers find themselves "blaming the victim" (the client or patient) when they deal extensively with junkies.[84]

With the current state of scientific knowledge, we have essentially no alternative but to hold addicts responsible for their criminal acts, even if the crimes were motivated to feed a habit. We simply cannot tell which drug users are truly unable to control their behavior and which are not. (Further, we have good reason to suspect that almost every addict has some level of self-control. Addicts are not in the habit of shooting up directly in front of police officers.) Alternatively, if drug addicts were not judged to be responsible for their criminal acts, then all drug-using criminals could claim to be addicts or under the influence of overwhelming visceral factors, and again, we simply wouldn't know if this claim were valid. Some people, intending a criminal act, would first become a drug user, to purchase immunity from responsibility, just as some people purposely drink to increase sociability or engender courage. And even if biological considerations make drug use an overwhelming necessity for addicts, it is the drug use that is the necessity, not bank robbery, car theft, or other crimes.[85]

At first glance, it might seem as if holding addicts fully responsible for their crimes is excessively harsh. But the alternative of not holding addicts responsible for criminal activity would, in practice, likely be even harsher.

---

[81] See, e.g., Goldstein (2001, pp. 12–3, 308), and Carnwath and Smith (2002, p. 79).

[82] See the discussion in Bonnie (2001). [83] Bakalar and Grinspoon (1984, pp. 48–9).

[84] See, for instance, Baldino (2000, pp. 79ff., 103ff.).

[85] This notion is a theme of the Federal Appeals Court opinion in *United States v. Roach* (2002), 296 F. 3d 565, the shopaholic case discussed below.

Policy toward those who are not regarded as responsible, such as children and the mentally ill, tends to be very coercive. Civil commitments already take place with respect to mental patients and sexual offenders deemed to be dangerous to themselves or others. If the actions of addicts are beyond their control, could Millian self-regarding addicts, those who commit no crimes (other than purchasing or possessing their illegal drug, perhaps), be forced into treatment or institutionalized?[86]

In other words, the disease view of addiction potentially provides a considerable justification for strict drug regulations. If we go further and view addicts not just as diseased in themselves but as carriers of a latent epidemic, then there is an even greater rationale for coercive measures based on public health considerations. Forced institutionalization of addicts could be undertaken in the name of quarantine. The "civil" alternative to control by the criminal law need not be more humane. Civil commitment proceedings lack the full evidentiary and procedural safeguards of criminal trials – and increase the possibility of injustice and abuse:[87]

> The most important restraint on our treatment of sick people is the requirement that the patient feel ill and want to be cured; the most important restraint on our treatment of criminals is the requirement that they have committed some harmful act. If the condition of addiction to certain drugs or the habit of using them is an illness and a crime, both restraints may come to seem unnecessary.[88]

ADDICTION SUMMARY

This chapter started with a claim that the concept of addiction is slippery, and perhaps, the remainder of the chapter has largely served, unintentionally, as a warrant for that claim.

One possibility is that addiction is not all that special, that it represents a rational choice, just like any other. Drug policy experts frequently dismiss rational addiction theory out of hand or mention it only in passing.[89] Nevertheless, as noted earlier, rational addiction theory has some attractive properties, and even imperfect theories can provide useful lenses for viewing the world. One of the attractive features of rational addiction theory is that it affords good reason for rejecting some common but unconsidered statements, such as that heroin addicts will do whatever it takes for their daily fix. In general, the law of

---

[86] Krongard (2002) argues that a 1997 Supreme Court case, *Kansas v. Hendricks*, 521 U.S. 346, could open the way for civil commitment of substance abusers, in part because one of the qualifying conditions has been weakened from possession of a "mental illness" to possession of a "mental abnormality."

[87] Bakalar and Grinspoon (1984, p. 49).   [88] Bakalar and Grinspoon (1984, p. 59).

[89] See, e.g., Kleiman (1992, p. 116) and MacCoun and Reuter (2001, p. 64n).

demand holds with respect to addictive as well as nonaddictive goods: higher prices reduce consumption.[90]

Rational addiction theory, in its expanded version that incorporates uncertainty about the future, views addiction as a gamble gone bad, and maybe not a ridiculous gamble for a user to take. This, too, seems consistent with much evidence and at least suggests that many choices concerning drugs are not made haphazardly. Rational addiction theory also points the way to how the effects of temporary policy changes are likely to differ from those of permanent policy changes.

But there's more: the part of compulsive behavior that rational addiction theory doesn't capture. First, there is the Jekyll-Hyde internal control problem. That people are dynamically inconsistent in their choice behavior seems likely, so in this respect, at least, individuals indeed contain multitudes – alas, multitudes of contradictions, different selves with different preferences. In some settings, visceral factors or environmental cues play a large role in decision making, sometimes to the point of exercising dictatorial control. And the neurobiology of addiction suggests strong physical motivations for some compulsive behavior. Both "reward deficiency syndrome" and the influence of visceral factors and cues imply that decisions are not fully volitional.[91]

Whether addiction should be considered a disease may be largely a matter of the definition of disease. Addiction is surely not a disease with a single cause or a single cure. It does resemble certain diseases in being a chronic, recurring condition and one that can be ameliorated but not necessarily cured. In these respects, addiction is similar to rheumatoid arthritis.[92] There is a volitional element in addiction, but this is true of many diseases, too, even infectious diseases – people make choices which put them at a greater or lesser risk of contracting the disease. For some addicts, viewing their predicament as a disease might be helpful, even if it is not descriptively accurate.[93] Addicts themselves struggle with gauging the extent to which their condition is physiological, a disease, as opposed to a moral failing, a weakness of will.[94]

The incoherence of views toward addiction is a long-term phenomenon. Addiction traditionally has been perceived as some (possibly incompatible) combination of moral failure (poor or weak, but rational choices) and disease. The relative strength of these dual approaches changes over time, though not primarily as a result of improved scientific information. The "disease" portion

---

[90] Of course, a negative relationship between price and usage would be consistent with a wide variety of addiction theories, not just rational addiction. Elster (1999a, p. 259) distinguishes "choice-oriented behavior," which is "sensitive to rewards and punishments," from fully rational behavior.

[91] Loewenstein (1996, p. 289) and Bernheim and Rangel (2004).

[92] Goldstein (2001, p. 309).

[93] Though it could also be otherwise, as Fingarette notes – for instance, adopting a disease view might convince those who have problems with a drug, though not all of the "symptoms," that they are not addicted nor in need of treatment.

[94] See, e.g., the insightful passage in Knapp (1996, pp. 269–70).

of this ambivalent view toward addiction has garnered strength in the past two centuries, and now serves as perhaps the most important justification for strict controls on drugs.[95]

Attitudes toward addiction are incoherent for a reason. Costs and benefits affect the decisions of the least rational among us. In general, addicts and other consumers are forward-looking and possess preferences that do not change capriciously: in this sense, most people make "rational" choices most of the time, and some people are rational almost all the time. Nevertheless, even the minimally "akrasiatic" individual is not fully rational; all of us have self-control problems, which can and do vary with time, place, and circumstances. Excessive myopia and problems with self-control appear to explain many of the common departures from stark textbook versions of rational choice. Addicts are particularly likely to have self-control problems on matters that connect with their addiction, and further, for an addict, almost all relevant decisions connect with their addiction. So, addicts have less effective foresight than nonaddicts, lessening the value of the rational addiction theory in terms of how to help addicts, even though that theory is successful at offering explanations for why addictions affect some people and not others, and why even addicts sometimes consume their drug compulsively and sometimes do not.

ADDICTION, SELF-CONTROL, AND VICE POLICY

Addictive potential provides a rationale for strict control over a vicious good or activity, but addiction alone is neither a necessary nor a sufficient condition for rigorous vice laws. Prostitution frequently is criminalized, though few people are considered to be addicts to prostitution, either as customers or as prostitutes.[96] Coffee addiction is a widely (though not universally) recognized condition, but coffee consumption is legal and unconstrained even for children.[97] Pursuits such as stamp collecting appear to be addictive for some people, though as the "sufferers" of numismatic addiction do not seem to be greatly harmed by their habit, and as the external costs of their curious habit also appear to be minimal, the law leaves them at peace.

There is no clear demarcation between addiction and more widely shared self-control deficiencies. Addiction and harms to nonaddicted adult vice participants form $1\frac{1}{3}$ of the standard vice concerns, but in practice, they meld into a single issue. If there were no addicts – perhaps a pharmacological cure for addiction becomes available – self-management shortcomings by nonaddicts

---

[95] Bakalar and Grinspoon (1984, p. 35).

[96] On addiction to sex, as opposed to prostitution, see Chapter 6, however.

[97] Satel (2006, p. 494) questions the addictiveness of coffee and caffeine more generally: "In short, coffee drinking resembles more a dedicated habit than a compulsive addiction [reference omitted]."

would still provide a good reason to regulate vice.[98] The elimination of the possibility of addiction might even inspire more people into vice involvement, giving increased scope to the "typical" self-control problems and for "treatment" of nonaddicted but heavy vice consumers. Of course, one of the significant costs of self-control shortcomings in the vice domain is that a user might develop an addiction. Nevertheless, vice policy, both in theory and in practice, need not be highly contingent upon the current extent or understanding of addiction.

Recent history suggests a very limited connection between the scientific understanding of addiction and regulatory activities: it is hard to trace changes in vice policy to advances in thinking about addiction that have come about in the past few decades.[99] Addiction is given prominence in adopting or defending vice policies, but the substance of the policies themselves seems largely immune to alterations in the prevalence or understanding of addiction.[100]

VICE VERDICTS (I): ADDICTION AND INTOXICATION

Addiction and intoxication present persistent challenges to the legal system. If addiction is a disease as opposed to a choice, can it be made illegal? Can a person be held responsible for actions, such as stealing to raise money for heroin, that are taken as a consequence of addiction? If addicts are assumed to be legally responsible for their actions, should they nevertheless be treated more leniently than nonaddicted people who engage in similar behavior? Can a person who is intoxicated while committing a crime really be said to possess the *mens rea*, the "guilty mind" that is often a necessary component of a finding of criminal responsibility? All of these tricky issues have been the subject of litigation in the United States.

Robinson v. California (1962): Addiction as a Crime

Lawrence Robinson was arrested when a Los Angeles police officer noticed needle marks and other signs of narcotics use on Mr. Robinson's arms. Mr. Robinson did not appear to then be under the influence of narcotics nor to be suffering withdrawal symptoms. A police officer testified that the marks were several days old. Nevertheless, a California law made it a misdemeanor to be "addicted to the use of narcotics." At his trial, Mr. Robinson denied that

---

[98] MacCoun (2003) looks at a hypothetical elimination of drug addiction and its effects on the overall drug problem.

[99] This conclusion echoes MacCoun (2003), which suggests that the recent behavioral economics theories of addiction have held little import for drug policy.

[100] See Room (2006a) for a similar point about the international control of drugs.

he was addicted to narcotics; indeed, he claimed never to have injected drugs and that the marks on his arms were due to an allergic condition. The trial judge instructed the jury that Mr. Robinson could be found guilty if he had the "status" of being an addict – a status that subjected him to arrest at any time before reformation. The jury returned a verdict of "guilty." Robinson lost again on appeal, and then his case was taken up by the U.S. Supreme Court.

Robinson won at the Supreme Court.[101] Justice Potter Stewart authored the opinion of the Court: "We hold that a state law which imprisons a person thus afflicted [with the perhaps voluntarily contracted 'disease' of addiction] as a criminal, even though he has never touched any narcotic drug within the State or been guilty of any irregular behavior there, inflicts a cruel and unusual punishment in violation of the Fourteenth Amendment.... Even one day in prison would be a cruel and unusual punishment for the 'crime' of having a common cold."[102] The Robinson case made it conceivable that the Supreme Court would go further and eventually find that drug addicts or alcoholics were not responsible even for criminal acts that they committed while intoxicated or desirous of buying drugs because their "disease" rendered them unable to choose to obey the law.

Powell v. Texas (1968): Public Drunkenness

A test case came six years later, in *Powell v. Texas*.[103] According to the arresting officer, Leroy Powell was walking down a public street in Austin, Texas, staggering as he walked and smelling of alcohol. Powell was convicted of being "found in a state of intoxication," and the conviction was upheld (and the fine doubled to $40) upon appeal to the Travis County Court. This 1966 arrest itself was far from an isolated incident for Mr. Powell, who estimated that he had been arrested about one hundred times in similar circumstances in the past. Later, he was to be arrested at least twenty more times for public intoxication. The Travis County Court issued findings of fact submitted by Powell's defense team. These included the claims that Powell suffered from the disease of chronic alcoholism, which undermined his ability to resist drinking, and made his choice to appear in public in an intoxicated state one taken under

---

[101] *Robinson v. California*, 370 U.S. 660 (1962).

[102] One important aspect of this case is that it applied the Eighth Amendment's ban on "cruel and unusual punishments" to the states via the Fourteenth Amendment. The first ten amendments to the Constitution directly bind only the federal government. Most of these protections have been extended to the states, however, through their judicial "incorporation" into the Fourteenth Amendment, which in part says "nor shall any State deprive any person of life, liberty, or property, without due process of law; nor deny to any person within its jurisdiction the equal protection of the laws."

[103] 392 U.S. 514 (1968). Most of the details concerning the *Powell* case are drawn from Robinson (1999).

the compulsion of the disease. The Travis County Court did not find that these "facts" constituted a defense to the charge of public intoxication.

The Supreme Court upheld Mr. Powell's conviction on a 5-4 vote, though in their preliminary deliberations the justices apparently split 5-4 in favor of overturning the conviction.[104] Four separate opinions were filed, with no opinion for the Court. Justice Thurgood Marshall wrote an opinion for himself and three other justices who voted with the majority. Marshall noted that Mr. Powell was not convicted because he was an alcoholic but because of his public behavior, which both created hazards and offended sensibilities. Thus, Mr. Powell's conviction was not a "cruel and unusual" punishment, which would be precluded by the Eighth Amendment. Further, Marshall averred that "we are unable to assert that the use of the criminal process as a means of dealing with the public aspects of problem drinking can never be defended as rational." (The item in Justice Marshall's plurality opinion claiming that Mr. Powell was not punished for having the "status" of an alcoholic was necessary to make the argument consistent with *Robinson v. California*.) Justice Byron White also voted to uphold the conviction but added a separate opinion, in which he noted that there was no evidence that Mr. Powell was unable, because of his condition of alcoholism, to remain off of the streets. In other words, Powell's condition had not put his actions beyond his control.

In the aftermath of the *Powell* case, public intoxication was decriminalized in many states, with a new emphasis on encouraging treatment for alcoholism.[105] This change was stimulated, in part, by a Presidential Crime Commission that, in 1967, endorsed a noncriminal approach to public drunkenness. Arrests for public intoxication have fallen markedly since *Powell* – for many cities, drunkenness previously had been the most common basis for arrest – though troublesome drunk individuals are often detained under other charges. Recall that John Stuart Mill, while believing that intoxication should be legal, nevertheless would not have found criminal controls on public intoxication to be an infringement on liberty: many acts that are not harmful in themselves can justifiably be restricted in public manifestations.

Montana v. Egelhoff (1996): Too Drunk to Deliberate?

The traditional common-law rule held that voluntary intoxication not only did not constitute a valid excuse for criminal acts committed while intoxicated but, rather, that such intoxication actually exacerbated the degree of guilt.[106] There has been some refinement in that position; for instance, in some U.S. states, it might be difficult to gain a conviction on a charge of premeditated murder,

[104] Robinson (1999, p. 427).

[105] See the discussion in Kelling and Coles (1996, pp. 43–49) and in Bakalar and Grinspoon (1984, p. 48).

[106] Much of the discussion of *Montana v. Egelhoff* is based on Carter (1999).

if the killer was extremely intoxicated at the time of the killing. Nevertheless, such an offender could be found guilty of second-degree murder. Despite these refinements, the general refusal to recognize intoxication as a mitigating factor in crime still has substantial backing. The Supreme Court helped to firm up this position with its ruling in *Montana v. Egelhoff* (1996).

The state of Montana passed a law that said that a defendant's intoxicated condition could not be used to help determine the existence of a mental state that is an element of an offense. Mr. Egelhoff was being tried for two counts of "deliberate homicide," which means that he was charged with purposely or knowingly causing two deaths. An hour after Mr. Egelhoff was arrested (next to two bodies with gunshot wounds in their heads), his blood-alcohol content was measured at .36, four-and-a-half times the standard in the United States for drunk-driving arrests. Mr. Egelhoff argued that the Montana law did not provide him with the "due process" guaranteed by the Fourteenth Amendment; he contended that he could not confront the state's claim that he acted deliberately with evidence of his intoxicated condition at the time of the crime. The Supreme Court did not accept this argument and upheld the Montana statute: "The people of Montana have decided to resurrect the rule of an earlier era, disallowing consideration of voluntary intoxication when a defendant's state of mind is at issue. Nothing in the Due Process Clause prevents them from doing so. . . . "[107]

United States v. Roach (2002): Shopaholism

Elizabeth Roach pleaded guilty to a charge stemming from her embezzling more than $240,000 from her employer. The embezzled money fueled shopping trips, the extent of which Ms. Roach wanted to keep from her husband. The trips themselves may have been Ms. Roach's way of dealing with her depression, just as many drug addicts are said to indulge in drugs to self-medicate mental illnesses. The trial judge was more lenient to Ms. Roach than the twelve to eighteen months in prison (among other punishments) called for by federal sentencing guidelines: along with a fine and restitution, he imposed six months of home confinement and six weeks of work release rather than a prison term. The judge found that "her offense was motivated and caused by her compulsive shopping and depression and that she had a significantly impaired ability to control her behavior."[108]

The government appealed the downward departure from the sentencing guidelines, and a three-judge federal appeals panel found the trial judge's

---

[107] *Montana v. Egelhoff*, 518 U.S. 37 (1996), at 19.

[108] This is the language used by the appeals court in summarizing the trial judge's finding; *United States v. Roach* (2002), 296 F. 3d 565, at 6.

leniency misplaced.[109] They remanded the case back to the original judge for resentencing; he reluctantly complied, ordering Ms. Roach to spend twelve months in prison.[110] Neither depression nor shopping addiction – technically known as "oniomania" – was accepted by the appeals panel as a valid reason for reducing penalties for embezzlement. What if the embezzlement was motivated by the need for money to feed a heroin or cocaine addiction, as opposed to oniomania? Once again, the chances for leniency would be slim: the federal sentencing guidelines explicitly note that, while significantly reduced mental capacity could justify a "downward departure" from the prescribed punishment, this is not the case if "the impairment was caused by the defendant's voluntary use of drugs or other intoxicants."[111]

In the end, a joined pair of Supreme Court cases concerning drug sentences spared Ms. Roach from a full year in jail.[112] In these cases, the sentencing guidelines themselves were found to be advisory, not mandatory. Ms. Roach subsequently was resentenced; in addition to the already rendered fines and restitution, this time she was ordered to undergo three months of work release, nine months of home confinement, and five years of probation to help her continue with her psychotherapy.[113]

---

[109] *United States v. Roach* (2002), 296 F.3d 565. See also "Oniomaniacs Come out of the Closet," by Jeff Stryker, *New York Times*, July 21, 2002, Week in Review, p. 2.

[110] The prison term has been stayed pending an appeal; see "1 Year in Prison for Shopaholic Embezzler," by Kate N. Grossman, *Chicago Sun-Times*, June 7, 2003, p. 5.

[111] U.S.S.G. § 5K2.13.

[112] *United States v. Freddie J. Booker* and *United States v. Ducan Fanfan* 543 U.S. 220 (2005).

[113] See the Vice Squad post from August 23, 2005.

3

The Robustness Principle

John Stuart Mill's harm principle, as interpreted in Chapter 1, is consistent with extensive regulation of addictive substances and activities. Nevertheless, the harm principle rules out prohibition (backed by criminal penalties) of adult participation in vice, as well as prescription-only regimes for drugs. Regulations that are directly motivated at reducing adult engagement in vice also do not satisfy Mill's criterion.

Addiction and self-control shortcomings call into question the relevance or the appropriateness of the harm principle's application to vice. The harm principle will not apply, under Mill's own conception, if vice participants are not "in the maturity of their faculties," or are "in some state of excitement or absorption incompatible with the full use of the reflecting faculty." The harm principle perhaps should not be applied, even when Mill's preconditions are met, if "harms to self" inflicted upon vice participants are quite likely and significant. John Kaplan suggests that the harm principle is both inapplicable and unfitting in the case of drugs:

> No nation in the world follows [Mill's] rule regarding self-harming conduct, and the rule is probably unworkable in a complex, industrial society – particularly one that is a welfare state. Mill's principle, moreover, seems singularly inappropriate when it is applied to a habit-forming, psychoactive drug that alters the user's perspective as to postponement of gratification and his desire for the drug itself.[1]

At the same time, a refusal to accept the harm principle sets one up to endorse some highly unpalatable policies. Islamic countries legitimately might forbid the eating of pork. (Such a prohibition, Mill wrote, could not even be "censured as religious persecution" because "nobody's religion makes it a duty to eat pork."[2]) Or it might be made a criminal offense to fail to accept the Roman Catholic religion or for a priest (even a non-Catholic priest) to marry. Puritanical rules against both public and private amusements, including painting your living room yellow, are another possibility. Mill asks, "... if

---

[1] Kaplan (1998 [1988], p. 95).   [2] Mill (1978, p. 83).

mankind are justified in interfering with each others' liberty in things which do not concern the interests of others, on what principle is it possible consistently to exclude these cases?"[3]

To reject the harm principle, then, is to accept that sometimes we can interfere with the self-regarding behavior of other adults. And this is not a principle that people are willing to see consistently applied; so,

> ... unless we are willing to adopt the logic of persecutors, and to say that we may persecute others because we are right, and that they must not persecute us because they are wrong, we must beware of admitting a principle of which we should resent as a gross injustice the application to ourselves.[4]

Is the harm principle inapplicable or inappropriate when applied to vice policy? The likelihood of severe "harms to self" from engaging in the traditional vices is rather low: the vast majority of participants suffer no serious ill effects from vice-related activities.[5] Nor do self-control lapses and the nature of addiction altogether negate the force of the harm principle: decisions concerning potentially addictive substances and activities generally cannot be said to be insane or irrational. Indeed, most vice-related decisions appear to be both rational and self-regarding. Many others suggest irrationality or implicate dynamic inconsistency. Mill's harm principle would allow social intervention with respect to the irrational decisions, but generally it is not possible to know which choices are rational and which are irrational. It simply isn't clear when someone's consumption of a drug or an activity crosses the line from acceptably safe to overly risky or when their indulgence crosses the threshold from "regular" to "compulsive."

The dilemma is as follows: if we reject the harm principle, we establish a precedent to repress all sorts of self-regarding behavior, which is not a practice that anyone supports when it is their own behavior that is being repressed. If we accept the harm principle, then Mill's reasoning suggests that we cannot adopt policies with the primary aim of reducing adult vice – even though many adult vice decisions may well be less than rational and involve serious negative consequences. In the case of drugs, resistance to the generally appealing harm principle tends to come in the form of Mill's near dismissal (in terms of public policy) of the problem of dangerous drugs and the harms that such drugs inflict upon some of their adult users.[6] We seem to have available only two disagreeable alternatives: (1) accept the harm principle and give up on trying to use public policy to protect adults against dangerous drugs or (2) reject the

---

[3] Mill (1978, p. 84). [4] Mill (1978, p. 84).

[5] This observation appears to be accurate even though prohibition can push vice participation in a more extreme direction: the use of heroin instead of opium or morphine, for instance. See Chapter 4.

[6] John Kaplan (1998 [1988], p. 93) poses the issue this way: "Probably the central problem with the solution [to our drug predicament] of legalization is that it ignores basic pharmacology. There is such a thing as a dangerous drug...."

harm principle and open the way to treating the self-regarding choices of adults to whatever manner of control garners political popularity.

THE ROBUSTNESS PRINCIPLE

A less disagreeable compromise is available, one that is crafted by Mill himself in his discussion of commodities that can be used both for beneficial purposes and for the purpose of committing crimes. With respect to poisonous chemicals or similar dual-use articles, Mill endorses regulations that aid in deterring the nefarious use, while not being too burdensome upon those consumers with innocent intent. "Such regulations would in general be no material impediment to obtaining the article, but a very considerable one to making an improper use of it without detection."[7] We saw a similar balancing act applied to Mill's condemnation of prescription-only systems: the requirement of having to first obtain permission from a licensed physician is too onerous a burden to impose upon drug consumers, even though such a requirement would help insulate problematic users from drug misuse.

We should forge a similar compromise when constructing vice policy. Some adult vice-related consumption is harmful and (arguably) less than rational; further, we cannot easily distinguish rational from irrational choice with respect to vice. This leads us to the robustness principle, as described in the introduction. Public policy toward potentially addictive activities should be robust with respect to departures from full rationality. Vice policy for adults should hold up pretty well if everyone is always well-informed and fully rational, and it should work well, too, even if some or many vice-related choices are irrational. We require this robustness precisely because we cannot ascertain how much vice is rational, nor distinguish the rational component from that which flows from a degradation of the reflecting faculties.

A robust vice policy will provide some support for those who are uninformed or struggling with self-control in their decision making. The provision of such support should not impose substantial costs upon those whose vice-related decisions are marked by rationality. One example of a policy that satisfies the robustness principle is a requirement for purchases of heroin, say, to be made with at least three days' notice – where the notice would be revocable by the adult would-be purchaser at any time during the ensuing waiting period. Rational heroin consumers, and even rational addicts, can then assure themselves of a steady supply, but those struggling with self-control issues will not be able to immediately satisfy an unforeseen craving and can cancel an impulsive order when their decision-making faculties are controlled by their more considered selves.

[7] Mill (1978, p. 96).

The robustness principle has been fashioned by combining the harm principle with (1) the notion that vice-related choices are particularly likely to fall short of full rationality and (2) the Millian idea that regulations aimed at harmful activities should not impose large costs upon their non-harmful counterparts. Robustness accepts that some drugs (and other vices) are dangerous, and that public policy should aim, in part, to reduce the damage that drugs wreak upon their users. But it does so while also recognizing limits to the harm that the policies themselves can impose on rational drug consumers. Prohibition of drug possession (in personal use amounts) is not compatible with the robustness principle, though many strict controls are acceptable. What the robustness principle demonstrates is that acceptance of those strict controls does not imply that the only governing principle is the logic of persecutors; drugs can be highly regulated without opening the door to legal prohibitions upon pork, or priestly marriages – or drugs.

The robustness principle parallels more general regulatory approaches that have been developed in recent contributions to behavioral law and economics.[8] The "asymmetric paternalism" of Camerer et al. (2003), for instance, is a precursor to advocating policies that offer aid to less-than-rational people, while imposing at most small costs upon rational individuals. The advance purchase requirement for heroin is asymmetrically paternalistic; mandatory disclosure of the risks of heroin use by sellers is another policy that meets the robustness principle and is asymmetrically paternalistic. Moderate sin taxes (see O'Donoghue and Rabin, 2003) likewise can satisfy robustness while being asymmetrically paternalistic. Robustness also coheres with the "libertarian paternalism" of Sunstein and Thaler (2003).[9] Libertarian paternalism accepts that any policy regime will influence individual decisions and suggests that policies be designed in such a way as to push those decisions in the presumably desirable direction – while making it easy for those who desire to head elsewhere to choose otherwise.

The main rationale for the robustness principle lies in ignorance. We can't easily judge when a habit becomes an addiction or when rational consumption involves dynamic inconsistency or shades into compulsion. Therefore we want to avoid a regulatory regime that only makes sense if there is no such thing as vice rationality, or an alternative regime that only works well if everyone makes considered, sober judgments about his or her vice participation. What we tend to end up with when we avoid these extremes is vice controls that offer some assistance to those who are misinformed or struggling with self-control issues, as long as those controls do not impinge significantly upon those who

---

[8] See, e.g., O'Donoghue and Rabin (2003), Thaler and Sunstein (2003), Sunstein and Thaler (2003), Camerer et al. (2003), and Loewenstein, O'Donoghue, and Rabin (2003).

[9] See Vice Squad posts of February 9, 2004, and January 23, 2007.

are rationally vicious. In the realm of adult self-regarding vice, robust public policies can inform, entreat, and induce – but not compel.[10]

A robust vice policy regime will stand up pretty well if our knowledge or situation changes, and our knowledge and our situation are constantly changing. Tomorrow we might learn that moderate alcohol consumption has more severe negative health effects than our current understanding indicates. The next day evidence might arise that moderate Ecstasy consumption promotes mental health with little risk of addiction. A robust regime has already taken these possibilities – and their opposites, that alcohol has more benefits and Ecstasy more costs than previously believed – implicitly into account. We are quite unsure about the extent of rationality governing the use of these substances, so robustness instructs us to choose policies that operate effectively whether the case for rational use improves or deteriorates. (This property of hardiness in the face of altered circumstances is not exhibited by either broad vice prohibitions or laissez-faire.) There might be good reason to adjust even a robust regime at the margins if our understanding of costs and benefits changes, but not to radically revise that regime. Robust rules build-in substantial tolerances for errors in our understanding.

The robustness principle in itself does not characterize "best practice" among drug policies; like Mill's harm principle, it proposes a necessary condition that a legitimate vice-control regime must meet, but it says little about the overall desirability of a regime that satisfies the robustness condition. Rarely can an individual policy measure be said to be robust or not robust in isolation: robustness is a feature of policy regimes as a whole, not specific rules. Nevertheless, adherence to the robustness principle eliminates those forms of control, such as broad criminalization, that are not respectful of adult informed, rational decision making within the vice arena.

Imposing a robustness standard does not eliminate the need for judgment. When do the regulatory costs imposed upon rational participants become unacceptably high? Advance purchase requirements and moderate sin taxes have already been highlighted as potential components of a robust vice-control policy. But as the restrictions steadily become more stringent – the required lead time lengthens, or the tax rises – eventually these measures will no longer comply with the robustness principle. Identifying a suitable threshold requires analysis and discernment, and the threshold can change as experience accumulates.

Robustness is a useful precept beyond vice policy, particularly where there exist significant departures from perfect information. A major virtue of democracy as a form of government, for instance, is that it is robust with respect to the personal qualities of politicians: democracy operates well when enlightened leaders are at hand, and it also works tolerably (though less well) when

---

[10] Compare with Sunstein and Thaler (2003).

leaders are shortsighted, cruel, or venal. Democracy represents a compromise. Democratic institutions purposely make it harder for exceptional leaders to guide a country in desirable directions, to ensure that a bad person temporarily in charge will not be in a position to inflict enormous damage. A theoretically better system would be one with expansive executive powers when an enlightened leader is in charge but much more limited powers when a mediocre or diabolical person holds the reins. But we cannot easily judge (or agree upon) who is enlightened and who is diabolical, so democracies institute a system of checks and balances that constrain leaders of any stamp. The theoretical benefits of basing the extent of power granted upon the character of the current executive are not available in practice. Similarly, the optimal vice controls that would not interfere with rational adult choices while guiding the decisions emanating from diseased or irrational minds are not viable in practice.

HARM VERSUS ROBUSTNESS: THE CASE OF DRUGS

The main difference between the robustness principle and the harm principle with respect to their ramifications for vice policy is that the robustness principle allows for regulations to be aimed directly at reducing harms suffered by adult vice consumers themselves. Indeed, the robustness principle might require such regulations, on the grounds that their absence could result in a regulatory regime that is woefully ineffective in the face of widespread vice-related ignorance or self-control problems. To aid the comparison between the harm and robustness principles, the discussion here will be restricted to drug policy.

Consider again Table 1.1 from Chapter 1. The strictest controls – most particularly, prohibition of drug possession – are as incompatible with the robustness principle as they are with the harm principle because such strict controls fare poorly when imposed upon rational drug consumers. The differences between the principles are revealed in those settings where Mill specifically rules out policies that are intended, first and foremost, to restrict adult drug consumption. With respect to (1) regulations on sellers; (2) taxation; and (3) licensing requirements for legal purchases, Mill would permit controls that serve other legitimate ends, even if those controls have the collateral effect of making it harder for people to consume drugs. He would not accept these measures, however, if they were aimed directly at reducing drug use.

The robustness principle, alternatively, would permit the adoption of some controls designed solely to reduce adult drug use. Limiting the number of sellers (or their hours of operation) to render it somewhat inconvenient to procure drugs impulsively, therefore, is permissible under the robustness principle – as long as the restrictions do not become significantly burdensome for those whose drug consumption choices are fully considered. Similarly, buyer licensing (or some other hurdle to drug availability) would not run afoul of the robustness principle, even if the licensing had no other purpose than to reduce damage inflicted upon drug users by rendering procurement more arduous. Sin taxes, for Mill, are constrained to be no higher than the revenue-maximizing level. For robustness purposes, such taxes are limited by the burden that they place upon rational consumers. This limit could exceed or fall short of the revenue-maximizing amount.

For further illustration, let's look at the possibilities for regulating heroin under the robustness principle. Heroin use can be immensely dangerous; nevertheless, the use of heroin involves little direct harm to others. (That is, doped-up heroin fiends do not typically go on crime sprees induced by heroin's pharmacological properties. Heroin is a narcotic, a drug that tends to induce listlessness, not violence, though individual responses to heroin vary widely.[11]) How strict can the heroin regulatory regime be made without violating the robustness principle?

First, kids could be prohibited from purchasing or possessing heroin, and anyone could be prohibited from selling or otherwise transferring heroin to underage consumers. But if this prohibition is no more effective than current prohibitions on kid purchases of alcohol and cigarettes, then too many kids will be using heroin.[12] So, we must invoke collateral regulations on adults to reduce the porousness of the ban on youth access to heroin. (Such child-protecting measures are consistent with both the harm and the robustness principles.) In particular, adults could face a quantity restriction on how much heroin they can purchase (each month, say). The purpose of this quantity restriction is not to reduce adult consumption but, rather, to prevent a lone rogue adult from supplying heroin to an entire high school. That is, quantity restrictions for adults can be adopted with the intention of helping to police the black market against youth (or ineligible adult) access, under either the harm or robustness principles. Similarly, purchases could be required to be arranged in advance or sales could be made only through mail order with verified delivery to adults so that the heroin equivalent of teenagers waiting outside the convenience store to pay an adult to buy them a six-pack of beer would be foreclosed.

The robustness principle (unlike the harm principle) allows us to go beyond those quantity limits and advance-purchase requirements that help to shield teens from adult drug access. Further quantity limitations – that is, quotas more restrictive than those that would "optimally" preclude youth access – could be adopted as a way of restricting adult usage. These quotas could not be so tight,

---

[11] When heroin is illegal, however, the expense of a heroin habit (combined with the difficulties addicts have in holding regular employment) leads many addicts to engage in crime to raise money for the drug. On the heterogeneity of responses to heroin and other opiates, see Chapter 5 in Carnwath and Smith (2002).

[12] It might reasonably be argued that "even one kid using heroin is too many"; however, a regime of prohibition (for both children and adults) results in a good deal of teen use of heroin, as is evident in both Europe and the United States. So the fact that the child prohibition would be imperfect under a legal regime for adult heroin use is insufficient in itself to deny heroin to adults.

however, as to render it difficult for a rational adult addict to maintain himself in his heroin habit. Quotas that significantly restrict adult addicts would run afoul of the robustness principle, for being too costly upon (potentially) rational consumers. Similarly, using the robustness standard, there is further scope for advance purchase requirements – that is, requirements that go beyond what is needed to police the black market. Even prolonged advance purchase mandates do not impose significant burdens upon considered use. A month-in-advance purchase regulation could be part of a robust heroin policy regime, even if such a rule offered no more of a barrier to black-market acquisition than a twenty-four-hour advance notice requirement.

To implement the quantity restrictions, there must be a method to identify consumers and to keep track of their purchases. Adults would need some sort of credit card–like identification to record their purchases and check the totals against a database. Do all adults automatically qualify for such a card, which is essentially a license to purchase limited amounts of heroin, or are there special conditions that must be met before someone is deemed eligible for a drug license?

In the terminology of Mark Kleiman, the issue is whether the authorization to purchase comes in the form of a "negative license" or a "positive license."[13] A negative license is one that is automatically available to all adults; however, someone who creates a public nuisance, drives a car recklessly, or commits another crime under the influence of heroin, or who diverts the heroin to youths, or in any way imposes harms on others through heroin use or distribution, could then have his or her heroin license revoked. In other words, with negative licensing, socially destructive behavior connected with heroin use would result in a prohibition specific to the wrongdoer – a policy that, as we have seen, also is consistent with Mill's application of his harm principle.

A positive licensing scheme is one where adults must meet other qualifications before they can acquire the credentials to purchase heroin. (Drivers' licenses include a positive element, in that applicants for such licenses generally must pass road tests, written tests on the traffic law, and vision tests.) In the case of heroin, adults might have to provide evidence that they understand the dangers of its use. As with negative licenses, positive licenses could be revoked for misbehavior, in the same manner in which drivers' licenses are revoked. A positive licensing scheme involving a test of knowledge of the dangers of drugs is, I believe, consistent with the robustness and harm principles. But a sane adult who understands the risk of heroin cannot be prevented from using it, as "liberty consists in doing what one desires," and " . . . no one but the person himself can judge of the sufficiency of the motive which may prompt him to incur the risk. . . ."[14] Under the robustness principle, adults could face a positive licensing scheme, wherein to receive the right to purchase limited

---

[13] Kleiman (1992, pp. 98–101). [14] Mill (1978, p. 95).

quantities of heroin, they would have to pass a test concerning the risks of use and perhaps the laws surrounding heroin and their license would be subject to revocation if they harmed others through their heroin-related activity.[15]

One advantage of a licensing scheme for heroin is that private responses could help keep the costs of heroin misuse low.[16] Employees in sensitive positions might face the absence of a heroin license as a job requirement. Insurance companies might offer lower rates to policy holders who opt to forgo a heroin license.

Abiding by the robustness principle does not imply that private sellers need be countenanced. Heroin could be distributed only through state stores, for instance, and as noted, an advance purchase requirement could be imposed. Advertising could be banned, and the heroin could be subject to a substantial (though not prohibitive) tax.[17] It is requisite to avoid taxes that are so high that incentives to evade the taxes spawn a flourishing black market. Presumably, the advantages of receiving heroin of a known purity would make black-market heroin a very imperfect substitute for the legal supply. As a result, heroin taxes could probably be quite significant, as excise taxes often are for alcohol or tobacco, without generating massive underground sales and without imposing too heavily upon rational consumers.[18]

License holders could be given the option to precommit not to purchase any heroin for a period of time, say, one week or even one day, in a binding way. That is, the government could provide a mechanism to help people voluntarily manage the self-control problem that is an obstacle for many drug users, drinkers, or smokers. In moments when their cravings are not intense, individuals might choose to limit their possibilities for future (legal) consumption for a few days, even if they are unwilling to forestall those possibilities indefinitely by relinquishing their license. (Such opt-outs are not uncommon

---

[15] Incidentally, heroin maintenance programs, in which existing addicts qualify to receive supplies legally, are a type of positive licensing scheme. Maintenance is a quite strict licensing regime, as the "test" for receiving a license requires, not knowledge of the risks of heroin but establishing a verifiable addiction.

[16] Kleiman (1991, pp. 99–100). The extent to which private employers can discriminate in hiring, firing, and promotion decisions on the basis of off-the-job, legal behavior, currently varies by state in the United States. Some states do not allow, for instance, employers to discriminate on the basis of off-the-job smoking or drinking. In the case of the currently illegal drugs, I think that there is much to be said for not extending such a nondiscrimination clause when these drugs first become legally available. In the long run, however, it is possible that the absence of nondiscrimination laws might render rational drug use too onerous to satisfy robustness.

[17] A ban on advertising of a legal good might not satisfy the demands of the First Amendment in the United States, of course, but the point here is to indicate the contours of a drug policy consistent with the robustness principle alone.

[18] Legal access to opioids would likely induce a shift away from heroin use toward less potent drugs such as opium; the introduction of opioid bans frequently has instigated a shift in the other direction, toward heroin use, just as alcohol prohibition in the United States instigated a shift from beer to more potent spirits.

in the regulation of gambling.) Or, users could choose a license that permits them some heroin but an amount less than the legal quantity limit.[19]

With the robustness principle as the basis of drug policy, therefore, a very restrictive regime over heroin could be implemented. Children could be forbidden from acquiring drugs, and adults could be required to be licensed before purchasing limited amounts of heroin. Commercial sales and advertising could be prohibited, and significant sin taxes could be imposed. Adults who wanted to acquire heroin, and whose past use had not resulted in any wrongful conduct, would have a safe and legal means to do so.

Alternatively, an extremely liberal policy toward addictive goods such as heroin would not be countenanced under the robustness principle. (This is opposed to the situation with the harm principle, under which laissez-faire would be a consistent policy.) The requirement that public policy lead to tolerable results in the face of significant departures from rationality suggests the necessity of aiding actual and potential addicts with their self-control. Licensing, taxation, and advance-purchase requirements for some addictive goods, then, might be near requirements imposed by the robustness principle and not just consistent with it. Information provision about addiction treatment options (such as now occurs in the form of phone numbers for help with problem gambling printed on lottery tickets) and even publicly subsidized access to treatment are other policies that might be necessary to reduce the harms suffered by less-than-rational users.

Any or all of the specific policies toward heroin, including buyer and seller licensing, mandatory waiting periods, and tests indicating the understanding of dangers, might prove to be a bad idea. The simultaneous adoption of a whole array of such policies, before any small-scale testing, is almost surely a bad idea, with undertones of intricate, utopian-style reforms that smack of the worst sorts of social engineering. In presenting elements of potentially robust policy regimes, I have been offering illustrations, not suggestions. My suggestion is that we adopt the robustness principle as a guide to our vice policies. With that guide in place, experimentation across communities and nations will reveal the specifics of workable (and robust) regulatory mechanisms.

COMPARING ROBUSTNESS TO OTHER VICE POLICY REGIMES

The robustness principle states that a vice regulatory regime should work well irrespective of the precise extent of rationality or addiction associated with vice. Such an approach could be mistaken, in at least two directions. It could be that we should adopt whatever policies are needed (potentially including

---

[19] Further, taxes could be repositioned from being ad valorem or specific to consisting of a single, annual license fee. See O'Donoghue and Rabin (2003).

prohibition) to combat compulsive vice consumption, independently of how those policies affect the rational users (who may not even exist). Or it could be that we should let adults fend for themselves, that we shouldn't be willing to impose upon rational vice consumers just because others are weak.

(1) Ignoring the interests of rational vice participants

To think more about the possibility of a vice-control regime that ignores the interests of putatively rational consumers while discouraging irrational vice, consider an "ideal" ban. This vice ban works cheaply and efficaciously and is fully complied with. Such a ban eliminates all of the $3\frac{1}{3}$ standard vice concerns, addiction and internal harms as well as the problems posed by kids and externalities. The question of the desirability of such a ban amounts to asking whether we would be better off if alcohol (or heroin, gambling, or prostitution) never had been discovered or invented. I find it hard to answer "yes" to any such question. All of these vices have their passionate defenders. All of these vices have their opponents, too, some of whom would be quite happy to conclude that the world would be a better place with one fewer vice. John Kaplan opens his fine 1983 book, *The Hardest Drug: Heroin and Public Policy*, with a paragraph outlining the massive ills attributable to heroin; he concludes the paragraph with the summary sentence, "Heroin never should have been invented."[20]

One complication, however, is that we can't be sure about what activity people would substitute toward in the face of such an efficacious ban. Would the elimination of heroin cause more people to abuse prescription drugs, to sniff glue, or to smoke crack? In the case of prostitution, theologians such as Augustine and Thomas Aquinas reluctantly supported the practice as a "lesser evil": they thought that rape, divorce, and the keeping of mistresses would be spurred by the unavailability of prostitution.[21] So even for an ideal ban, vice prohibitions may be unwise, or at least I am much less willing than John Kaplan to state unequivocally that the world would be a better place in the complete absence of a specific vice. Once we add in all the ways in which a real-world prohibition differs from our idealized version (see Chapter 4), including violent black markets, police corruption, and the discouragement of research into beneficial vice impacts, then I become even less confident that we can identify a vice ban that actually makes the world better off relative to a legal, controlled (robust) alternative. The best case for a prohibition, I think, can be made for a vice with a very small and not very committed following, so that a ban on legal production might be enough essentially to eliminate the

---

[20] Kaplan (1983, p. ix).

[21] See, for example, "Prostitution in the Middle Ages: Prostitution and the Canon Law," on Deca-meron Web, at http://www.brown.edu/Departments/Italian_Studies/dweb/society/sex/prostitution.shtml; and for Aquinas in particular, see Dever (1996).

market, without the need for overt enforcement. (As fashions change, though, today's unpopular vice might become tomorrow's fad.) For any vice with a sizable constituency, a ban in practice will not eliminate the market, and then the legal, taxed, and regulated alternative begins to look better. And the regulatory regime option does not require arresting individuals whose only real crime, it seems, is to have different tastes than the majority. Nor does the robust alternative open the door to all manner of repression of unpopular pursuits.

The currently legal vices illustrate that prohibition is not required to adequately address the $3\frac{1}{3}$ standard vice concerns of kids, externalities, addiction, and harms to nonaddicted adult participants. (This observation is not meant to suggest that all is optimal with respect to the regulation of legal vices, or that the current regulatory regimes are consistent with the robustness principle.) Consider tobacco and alcohol. Amazingly complex regulations governing the production, distribution, and use of these substances have evolved. By and large, such regulations are obeyed (at least when some enforcement is applied), with significant taxes collected. When it is clear that a vice-related problem is being underaddressed, as was true in the past of drunk driving (and I believe to some extent remains so), the political process adjusts. Alcohol and tobacco policies in the United States are not even particularly contentious, relative to the universe of governmental affairs, from public education to national security. A legal, regulated regime for prostitution and drugs could yield similar outcomes. Problems with these vices will not be eliminated through movement to legal policy regimes, but the overall consequences will be tolerable (and desirable relative to the prohibition alternative), while their regulation will become nothing extraordinary, just prosaic planks in the deck of public policy.

Or perhaps the currently illicit vices (including, in the United States, some drugs, prostitution, and Internet gambling) are so different from today's legal vices that attempts to regulate them outside of a prohibitory regime will prove disastrous. It even could be the case that a robust regime requires prohibition in the case of heroin and cocaine, in that any legal availability for recreational use would impose tremendous costs upon multitudes of kids and irrational adult consumers. Likewise, prostitution providers and their customers might be put in extreme peril via a policy of legal regulation. That is, while robustness specifies that a policy regime work well regardless of the extent of rational vice participation, working well must be judged relative to the policy alternatives. Perhaps any legal, regulated regime works so poorly in comparison with even an ineffective and costly prohibition that the ban is required by the robustness criterion.

Why do I think that legal, regulated regimes will work for the currently illegal vices? First, there is nothing inherently special about the addictive properties of illegal drugs relative to the legal alternatives. For many (perhaps most) individuals in various settings, no doubt some forms of consumption of opioids, methamphetamine, or cocaine are more addictive than alcohol or nicotine. For other people, the addictive calculus runs in the opposite direction, while the personal and social costs of addiction tend to be lower under a legal regime. Second, when cocaine and heroin were legal, they caused problems, of course, but problems that appear smaller to similar problems today under prohibition. Habitual cocaine use in the United States is more common today, in both absolute and per capita terms, than in the peak pre-prohibition years.[22] For opiates, the per capita extent of addiction may have been similar or even greater circa 1900 than now, but the shift to heroin and injection, along with the marginalization that comes with illegality, have raised the costs of today's opiate addiction.[23] "It is hard to deny that opiates have become a far greater social problem since the passage of the Harrison Act."[24] Third, the pre-prohibition era for narcotics before 1914 in the United States was one of near free availability, not a system with significant taxes or controls. Information disclosure about the ingredients in patent medicines was not required until the Pure Food and Drug Act of 1906, and hence many people habitually consumed substances that they did not know contained cocaine or opiates. The 1906 act led to greatly diminished use of opiates, as informed consumers found such drugs less attractive than did those who didn't know what they were imbibing. (This response to new information was later paralleled by the remarkable 50 percent decline in smoking prevalence in the United States in the generation following the Surgeon General's Report of 1964.) Drugs such as heroin, methamphetamine, and cocaine can be amazingly reinforcing, such that occasional use converts to habitual use. That very property makes these drugs quite unpopular in overall terms: most people quite rightly want nothing to do with recreational use of these dangerous substances. The chaotic, unhealthy, and unrewarding lives of drug addicts are a persuasive form of counteradvertising, and when legalization takes the trade out of the black market and ensures information provision about the hazards, there is little reason to think that large increases in abusive drug consumption will increase. Finally, the illegal drugs generally have close analogues (such as some antidepressants) rather easily available legally with a prescription, so already a type of regulated supply is in place, lowering

---

[22] See MacCoun and Reuter (2001, pp. 183–204).

[23] Addiction is hard to define, so it should not be surprising that statistics on the number of addicts are full of uncertainty. Nevertheless, one estimate is that at the pre-prohibition opiate use peak around 1900, there were some 250,000 opiate addicts in the United States; today's estimates for U.S. heroin addicts are on the order of 900,000. (The number of heroin addicts pre-prohibition was very small.) By this reckoning, the number of opiate addicts has increased by a factor of 3.6 between 1900 and 2000, which matches the extent of U.S. population growth: from 76 million in 1900 to 273 million in 2000. Persons addicted to diverted pharmaceutical opioids would make the comparison of today to 1900 even less favorable. For the 250,000 opiate addicts figure in 1900, see Musto (1999, p. 5). Courtwright (1982, p. 9) suggests that "there were never more than 313,000 opiate addicts in America prior to 1914."

[24] Kaplan (1983, p. 65).

the additional risks of across-the-board liberalization.[25] That prostitution can be made available legally without irreparable tears in the social fabric is currently being demonstrated in many places, from Australia and New Zealand to Switzerland, Germany, and rural Nevada. A similar point applies to Internet gambling, many forms of which are at least quasi-illegal in the United States, but legal in much of the rest of the world.

(2) Near laissez-faire

In contrast to prohibition, the opposed alternative of letting adults look after themselves is pretty close to John Stuart Mill's harm principle position. Potential vice participants should be well-informed about the likely consequences and dangers from indulgence, and issues concerning kids and externalities must be addressed. Once these preconditions are met, laissez-faire advocates would suggest that the public response to any residual self-regarding vice activity is essentially exhausted. (As we have seen, a Millian vice regime nevertheless can be quite strict, through policies that reduce externalities or that serve other legitimate goals while secondarily inhibiting vice.) The difficulty with this argument, I have maintained, is the affinity of addiction to disease and the problem with vice self-control even among nonaddicts; in Mill's terms, vice consumers might often be in some state "incompatible with the full use of the reflecting faculty" – and hence at least partially exempt from the deference that generally should be paid to adult self-regarding decisions. In an unregulated market, vice producers will have strong incentives to try to target the self-control shortcomings of their potential consumers; sellers will have a pecuniary interest in encouraging addiction.

Robustness's main advantage over laissez-faire is that it is, well, robust. If it turns out that rationality always and everywhere prevails, then laissez-faire is presumably superior to robustness. But importantly, not by much. Robustness limits the costs that can be imposed on all of those rational vice participants. Further, if laissez-faire really is a first-best strategy, competing jurisdictions that impose differing robust regimes will eventually reveal that fact – while in the meantime the departures from those first-best free-market policies will not be very costly, given the criterion of robustness.

If some adults are not rational in their vice-related choices, then robustness begins to look better than laissez-faire. Even in this case, however, it might be argued that we should deal with the problematic folks after they reveal themselves, rather than treating everyone like a child or an addict just because some people eventually will prove to be childish or addicted. Frequently, sole

[25] Judge Richard Posner notes the current availability of legal close substitutes to illegal drugs in his blog post of March 20, 2005, available at www.becker-posner-blog.com/archives/2005/03/, accessed March 5, 2007.

reliance upon after-the-fact, ex post measures is not the best way to conduct public policy.[26] Punishments are costly to carry out; if an ounce of prevention can be purchased cheaply, it often is a wise buy. Licenses, car registration, and insurance are required of would-be drivers in advance, even though we could simply wait and fine or otherwise punish dangerous drivers after their identities are divulged through their accidents. Drunk driving is illegal, despite there being no direct public interest in a driver's blood alcohol content: the social concern is with safe driving, not with whether the motorist is sober. Thomas Hobbes noted that individuals typically and uncontroversially apply the same preventive approach to their private affairs, despite opportunities for the application of after-the-fact measures: ". . . when taking a journey, he armes himselfe, and seeks to go well accompanied; when going to sleep, he locks his dores; when even in his house he locks his chests; and this when he knowes there bee Lawes, and publike Officers, armed, to revenge all injuries shall bee done him . . ."[27] After-the-fact punishments are frequently unavailable, and even when they are available, complementing them with some before-the-fact controls is often sensible.

Again, the robustness-based vice exemption from our usual deference to adult self-regarding behavior is only a partial exemption. Preemptive controls hold the potential to be extremely oppressive, as Mill noted: "The preventive function of government . . . is far more liable to be abused, to the prejudice of liberty, than the punitory function; for there is hardly any part of the legitimate freedom of action of a human being which would not admit of being represented, and fairly too, as increasing the facilities for some form or other of delinquency."[28] Those policies that help guide vice decision making in the direction of rationality will become very expensive (in terms of the welfare of rational vice producers and consumers) if they establish substantial barriers to informed use. Unless we are absolutely certain that there is no such thing as rational, informed vice consumption, significant impediments are unwise. That is not to say that an unfettered vice marketplace is a good idea.

(3) Harm minimization

Alongside prohibition and laissez-faire, harm reduction or harm minimization presents another alternative to robustness in governing vice. In the cases of illicit drugs and commercial sex (see Chapters 4 and 6), policy reforms that reduce harms often simultaneously comport well with robustness; however, in a rigorous accounting, robustness and harm reduction must eventually diverge. A harm reduction approach ignores the conceivable benefits of vice, while

---

[26] See Chapter 5 in Leitzel (2003).   [27] Hobbes (1970 [1651], p. 85).
[28] From *On Liberty*; Ryan (1997, p. 116). I employed both this quote and the previous passage from Hobbes in a similar discussion in Chapter 5 of Leitzel (2003).

robustness allows for the possibility that such benefits might be substantial and hence aims to make those benefits available. Millions of seemingly normal American adults currently risk arrest by buying and consuming marijuana. They apparently believe that their personal gains from marijuana use are sufficiently great to justify that risk, and robustness accepts that they might well be right. Harm reduction ignores user views about the benefits of pot, though it might counsel decriminalization or legalization to reduce the overall harms tied to marijuana and its regulation.

A strict harm reduction policy does not make sense if there are any potential benefits to be had. To illustrate this claim, imagine once again a world in which all people are perfectly law abiding. Consider the regulatory approach to ketchup, under the notion that one in one thousand ketchup consumers will spill his ketchup and badly stain his new trousers. Prohibition of ketchup would be a harm-minimizing strategy, by eliminating the nasty stains. Prohibition would also require essentially no resources to implement and enforce, given our assumption of lawful behavior. But it would be an extremely costly policy in terms of the benefits of ketchup that must then be forgone by 999 of every 1,000 would-be customers.

The reason that harm reduction and robustness tend to go together in the cases of illicit drugs and prostitution is that the current prohibitions are themselves the primary sources of most dimensions of harm associated with these vices. Robustness does not countenance adult vice prohibition, and harm reduction around drugs and prostitution likewise requires less punitive policy regimes than those that currently hold sway in the United States. With reasonable (robust) policies in place, however, further harm reduction may well not point in a desirable direction – just as reducing highway speed limits to thirty miles per hour is not necessarily a good idea, despite the possibility such a reform offers of reduced rates of fatal automotive accidents. Further, once a robust regime is implemented, it becomes harder to know what additional measures would promote harm reduction: the elimination of the vice ban also eliminates the main catalyst of harm. All of the remaining policy alternatives harbor risks, and the accounting of relative risks is uncertain; some risks are more obvious or direct than others. A currently legal vice – smoking – provides an example. An increased tax on cigarettes might induce more consumers to purchase loose tobacco and roll-their-own cigarettes, while the resulting increase in unfiltered smoking could raise health costs.

(4) Medicalization

One further challenger to robustness, also associated (like harm reduction) with a sort of public health approach to vice policies, consists of prescription-only regimes for drugs. If a prescription is easy to obtain, and acquisition requires only knowledge of the risks of drug consumption, then a prescription system is a form of buyer licensing consistent with robustness. If such a licensing scheme is desired, there is no need to involve physicians, as nonmedical professionals can be trained to provide the requisite information and ensure that it is understood. In general, a prescription regime, though, is intended to imply that recreational use of drugs will not be countenanced: the prescriptions are reserved not for all informed adult would-be consumers, but only for those already suffering from addiction. These types of prescription systems are neither robust, nor, in the case of drugs for which significant demand for recreational use exists, harm minimizing. And as with harm reduction, prescription-only legal availability of drugs performs poorly relative to robust regimes if there is the possibility of beneficial recreational use.[29]

Another medical approach to vice control, one that can be combined with prescription-only drug access, is the provision of treatment "on demand" to drug and alcohol abusers.[30] Easy availability of treatment might be a requirement of a robust regime toward heroin or alcohol, for instance. This is true even though the success rate of most treatments tends not to be all that impressive, at least if success is measured by putting an end to an individual's problematic drug or alcohol use. Nevertheless, treatment can greatly reduce the social costs of drug and alcohol abuse, even as it falls short of bringing about a significant fall in the number of drug or alcohol abusers.[31] And in comparison with treatments for other ongoing medical conditions, drug and alcohol treatment meets the typical standards. A 1997 U.S. National Academy of Sciences report noted that "Extensive research has shown that treatment for addiction is as effective as treatments for other chronic, relapsing medical conditions."[32]

Within a regime of drug prohibition, the ready availability of treatment cannot in itself satisfy robustness. Most drug and alcohol users – with the exception of heavy smokers – are satisfied consumers in no need of treatment. Robustness requires legal access to drugs for adults, though it may also require information provision of treatment options, and easy access to those treatments that are available.

(5) Expedience or caprice

Actual vice policy in general does not reflect any of the approaches compared previously. Vice policy making in practice might even be characterized as

---

[29] Prescription-only regimes are not necessarily a good idea for "nonvicious" drugs, either; indeed, a case can be made for rolling back the prescription-only approach to many drugs in the United States. Like the interpretation of the Mann Act that ended up prohibiting noncommercial, consensual interstate travel by lovers (see Chapter 4), the invention of "prescription-only" nonnarcotic drugs appears to have been unintended by those who wrote and passed the relevant 1938 legislation; see Temin (1979).

[30] Massing (1998) makes a strong case for a large increase in the availability of drug and alcohol treatment in the United States.

[31] See, e.g., Reuter and Pollack (2006).

[32] *Dispelling the Myths about Addiction: Strategies to Increase Understanding and Strengthen Research* (1997, p. 87).

irrational, in that the array of benefits and costs of a vice, and how these differ among control regimes, do not seem to be given much notice. Rather, features that seem to be of minor import for the theoretical comparison of the desirability of various controls exert enormous influence over vice policy.

Overall popularity is of foremost importance. All else equal, more popular drugs, for instance, will have an easier time avoiding punitive controls – a result that is at least consistent with a recognition that the costs associated with prohibition tend to be higher for more popular substances. Legions of drinkers protect alcohol from prohibitionist pressure, while the declining number of smokers in the United States contributes to the adoption of stricter controls on smoking.

Moneyed interests, of course, also are politically influential. A drug produced by a major pharmaceutical firm seems to stand a better chance of legality, at least via prescription, then unpatentable drugs that can be produced in your basement. Pills based on the main active ingredient in cannabis are patented by pharmaceutical companies and legal in the United States, while (unpatentable) marijuana is not eligible for legal acquisition at the federal level for medical uses, even by prescription. The connection of a vice with a respected institution – church, police, industry – will add to the vice's own respectability. In many places with otherwise strict gambling controls, church-sponsored gambling (including bingo) is legal and accepted. One the other hand, existing state revenues or private profits that might be threatened by a new drug or vice are a source of tougher legislative scrutiny.

The personal characteristics of those who are perceived as typical drug users traditionally have been instrumental in shaping policy. The introduction of gin to England was not controversial until price declines in the early eighteenth century made the distilled spirit available to poorer people; likewise, the temperance movement in the United States was spurred by the availability of cheap whiskey to the masses in the early part of the nineteenth century. The first U.S. federal vice prohibition applied to smoking opium, which was largely the province of Chinese immigrants working in the west. (The opium that formed the essential ingredient in the elixirs taken by the middle class went untouched at the time.) The prohibitions on marijuana and cocaine gained political currency in part through perceived associations with Mexicans (in the case of pot) and African Americans (in the case of coke).[33] The decline in smoking prevalence during the past fifty years has rendered cigarette consumption in the United States to be a lower-class vice, helping to stoke the calls for stricter controls.

Horrific crimes and high-profile deaths also have been common drivers of drug policy. Astounding claims for crimes committed under the influence of marijuana or cocaine preceded those bans in the United States, and the 1986 death of renowned college basketball player Len Bias precipitated a

---

[33] Musto (1999, pp. 5–8, 219–20).

further crackdown on coke. The Swiss absinthe ban (later adopted by other nations) was motivated by the 1905 murders of a pregnant woman and her two young daughters by her husband. The murderer was a very heavy drinker who consumed an extraordinary amount of alcohol both the day before and day of the murders. His two glasses of absinthe were literally a drop in the bucket of his imbibing, but a petition to ban absinthe was drawn up in the wake of the murders, and eventually succeeded; the Swiss ban lasted almost a century.[34]

In short, the predominant approach to vice control is neither robustness nor some other principled guide such as harm minimization or medicalization; rather, political expedience seems to rule the roost, the lone survivor once principles are eschewed. In the United States in recent decades, expedience has generally meant that perceived new drug threats are met by an enhanced version of the current prohibition: more severe penalties, a widening of the prohibition to encompass precursors, paraphernalia, or devices to confound drug tests, and additions to the list of controlled substances.

New modes of consumption of old drugs can attract the same prohibitory impulse. In the mid-2000s some bars around the world began to offer "alcohol inhalers," in which about half a shot of alcohol is vaporized and mixed with oxygen. It takes about twenty minutes to consume this half-a-shot via inhalation, and that is also about how long it took for alcohol inhalers to be banned, from New South Wales, Australia, to Suffolk County, New York, and various U.S. states. These bans were adopted in the absence of any evidence of increased harm from alcohol inhalation relative to alcohol drinking. The almost reflexive prohibitory response to a new vice isn't entirely devoid of reason, of course, given the large social costs that new vices often have entailed. But strict, nonprohibitory regulatory regimes can control these social costs, without bringing on the many downsides of prohibition, including overriding the liberty of individual adults to make their own decisions in self-regarding matters without fear of arrest.

The reflex toward prohibition is far from universal, however. If the previously mentioned factors line up favorably – if the middle-aged upper middle class is the major consumer of the vice and if respected institutions are prominently involved – then the control regime can be excessively indulgent. Some prescription drugs popular with relatively wealthy individuals have become common and frequently abused without attracting prohibitory interest.

The general absence of a principled approach to vice regulation means that vices tempt us into unthinking controls, which can lead to the extremes of being overly harsh or overly obliging. The large swings in vice policy noted in the introduction also result from the lack of a principled approach to vice

---

[34] See the Vice Squad posts of July 30, 2004, and August 23, 2005. The U.S. ban on sales of absinthe only applies to those varieties with detectable amounts of the compound thujone; see the Vice Squad post of May 11, 2007.

control. Without some mooring, vice control is led by fears and prejudice, and it always seems to be your vice, not mine, that requires restraint.

ROBUSTNESS AND THE PUBLIC SPHERE

Robustness aims to be protective of kids and addicts, while simultaneously protecting rational adult vice participation. But the adult vice participation that it protects is vice conducted in private. A robust regime does not require that injecting heroin in public be tolerated; nor does it necessitate legal public drinking, pot smoking, or, for that matter, cigarette smoking. Publicness serves as a transmitter of external costs. If legal public vice activities are too hard on children, addicts, or anyone else, then these behaviors can rightly be controlled.

Robustness thus permits (and perhaps, in some instances, requires) suppression of vice in the "public square." Gambling must be allowed under a robust regime, but slot machines and lottery ticket sales can be restricted to out-of-the-way, though not terribly inaccessible, venues.[35]

In the case of pornographic images or obscene utterances, public display and public consumption are almost the same thing. By the time you recognize an image or epithet as obscene, you have already "consumed" it. So social control over pornography or verbal obscenities in the public sphere does not violate the robustness principle (though in the United States some controls would run counter to the First Amendment). Again, this does not make any claim for the overall soundness of any given control: robustness is a necessary feature of desirable vice policies but not a sufficient condition. Whether the harms from any involuntary exposure to public porn or expletives are significant enough to require prohibition under a robustness regime is debatable.

In some locales in the United States, it is difficult to lead a sort of "average," everyday existence without significant exposure to alcohol or gambling – in the form both of advertisements and of commercial sales. This constant exposure, or constant deliberation to avoid exposure, can be particularly trying for alcoholics or pathological gamblers in recovery or those battling self-control problems (while also being distasteful to those with moral objections to alcohol or gambling). A robust regime can restrict this exposure, as long as it does not impose too heavily upon rational vice consumers. And again, it is even possible that restricted exposure is required by robustness, if the additional harms inflicted through uncontrolled exposure are significant.

Public manifestations of vice legitimately can be controlled under the robustness standard. Many nations, states, and localities have adopted so-called public smoking bans that apply to indoor smoking in restaurants and other private workplaces. But restaurants are not fully in the public sphere: in market

---

[35] Compare this with the "sumptuary" regime toward the lottery described by Clotfelter and Cook (1989, pp. 241–49).

economies, restaurants are privately owned and operated. Restaurant customers and workers are volunteers. (This is much different than the situation facing some visitors to public buildings such as courthouses or motor-vehicle offices.) Vice controls imposed upon restaurants cannot easily be justified based upon the "publicness" of these spaces.

Robustness applies to overall vice policy regimes, however, including controls over privately conducted vice. If people are addicted or routinely "undercount" their future health in their current decisions, then regulations that increase the representation of future selves in private decisions or counter addictive tendencies might make sense. In my estimation, broad public smoking bans that apply to private bars and restaurants do not satisfy robustness, by being too constraining upon those whose decisions to eat or work in smoky environments are fully rational. Nevertheless, many other smoking-related regulations for restaurants would not be so imposing, while potentially being beneficial to those who undervalue (from their own long-term point of view) their future health. Mandated nonsmoking areas within private bars or restaurants, for instance, do not seem to violate the robustness principle.[36]

---

[36] There is a brief return to smoking regulation in restaurants in Chapter 5. See also the Vice Squad post from October 23, 2003.

4

Prohibition

Prohibition is one social response to vice. Prohibition, however, doesn't go far in characterizing a policy regime. Precisely what is prohibited? In the case of drugs, is possession prohibited? Sale? Manufacture? Purchase? Marketing of related paraphernalia? In the case of prostitution, is all prostitution prohibited, or just streetwalking? Is soliciting illegal? Are clients (buyers, johns) engaging in a criminal act? Is it illegal for someone to "live off of the proceeds" of prostitution? Once it is clear precisely what behavior is prohibited – and it might not be all that clear – there is still the issue of how intensely the prohibition is policed, and what sanctions are imposed on those who are found to be in violation. Swimming is prohibited in Lake Michigan off the promontory near where I live, but lots of swimming takes place there during the summertime despite the ban, and sometimes publicly paid lifeguards are on duty in areas where, officially, swimming is banned. In the Netherlands, possession and sale of cannabis is officially illegal, but government licensed "coffee shops" openly sell marijuana and hashish. The term "prohibition" connotes uncompromising rigor, but prohibitions themselves range over the full spectrum from very lax to very strict controls.

Attempts to gauge the effects of a vice prohibition require not only specifying the precise nature of the prohibition and its enforcement but also the relevant alternative policy regime. Furthermore, the impact of a ban in one locale depends on the policies pursued in other jurisdictions. The relatively liberal regulatory regime on cannabis and prostitution in the Netherlands, for instance, generates a good deal of vice tourism, and Las Vegas was put on the map thanks to its comparative tolerance of vice.

To be concrete, consider a drug prohibition where manufacture, trafficking, and sale are all illegal, and where all these activities have appreciable enforcement efforts arrayed against them with significant penalties applied to violators. Assume that drug purchase and possession, too, are illegal, though the penalty for these offenses may or may not be severe. Essentially, the typical regime currently applied to marijuana in most U.S. states is the style of prohibition that I have in mind; this regime violates the robustness standard, of course, by being much too punitive toward potentially rational adult marijuana consumers.

As an alternative, take the standard U.S. regulatory approach toward alcohol and tobacco. Considerable taxes are applied to these items, substantially raising their prices over what they would be in an uncontrolled marketplace. Sales to and purchases by kids are prohibited – in the United States, a "child" is someone under age 21 in the case of alcohol and under the age 18 in the case of tobacco. Alcohol and tobacco are widely available to adults in most parts of the United States, though there remain many dry counties and municipalities that prohibit alcohol sales. Further, the legal provision of alcohol must conform with a host of regulations, especially for locations licensed for on-site consumption. Opening hours, the length of the bar, the number of tables, whether the words "saloon" or "bar" can appear in the name of the business, promotional activities, and many other features of such establishments are frequent objects of state and local controls.

What would happen if we were to replace the current cigarette or alcohol regulatory framework with a marijuana-style prohibition? It goes without saying that the prohibition of alcohol or cigarettes would not end the sale or consumption of these items. A black market would develop. The size and character of that market would depend on the details of the prohibition and the nature of enforcement. In general better organized black markets are less violent than those that are disorganized – witness the mayhem in U.S. cities when the recognized turf distribution among drug-selling gangs becomes unsettled. Prohibitions tend to decentralize production, too; instead of a few large beer or liquor manufacturers, thousands, maybe millions of individuals would become bathtub gin producers, just as marijuana is now cultivated by many people who otherwise have little interest in horticultural pursuits. (Tobacco growing for personal consumption is not a similarly popular past time.)

Although a prohibition will not eliminate sales, it will tend to raise the price of the prohibited substance. "Price" is meant in a rather encompassing fashion here, where the inconvenience, risk of arrest, and danger of acquiring the banned substance are all elements of a higher price, beyond the actual monetary cost of the prohibited drug. The higher price leads to a lower quantity demanded. This reduced consumption is the obvious impact of prohibition and just about the lone impact that can be said to hold any social advantages – though some people might argue that a second advantage of prohibition is that it signals social disapproval of the banned activity. Those who adhere to the theory of rational addiction would not find any societal advantage from reduced adult consumption, unless the high price compensates for otherwise disregarded externalities associated with the use of the banned substance.

Although a higher "full" price is a likely outcome of prohibition, it is not a logical necessity. The taxes and other mandates that apply to legal but regulated vices are not relevant for black-market sales. Some types of business costs, such as advertising, might also be greatly reduced for black-market suppliers. It is possible, then, for retail prices to be higher under regulation than prohibition, especially if the nonmonetary costs associated with the risk of violence or arrest are not taken into account. Prices for marijuana in the Netherlands, where small sales in licensed cafes are de facto legal, do not seem to be appreciably lower than in the United States, where marijuana remains criminalized in most states.[1] Boston University economist Jeffrey Miron has argued that alcohol prices in the United States during Prohibition may actually have fallen relative to their level in the previous legal market, though this is not the conclusion of most observers.[2] Surely the typical effect of an enforced prohibition is to raise the full retail price relative to that which prevails under a standard legalized regime. If the prohibition price were not higher, presumably there would be a substantial black market even under legalization, motivated not by a (nonexistent) ban but for purposes of tax evasion.[3] Perhaps in recognition of this problem, however, taxes on alcohol and tobacco in the United States are generally calibrated so as not to induce widespread evasion. Indeed, a sufficiently high tax would replicate most of the outcomes of a ban, that is, a "prohibitory" tax generates a rough equivalent of a prohibition.

Beyond a higher price, what are the effects of a policed vice prohibition? The production and distribution of the prohibited substance (or activity, like gambling) become criminal activities. Those who work in this industry are unable to turn to the police for protection against thieves or violent competitors, nor can they turn to the courts to enforce their contracts. They must either self-protect or buy their protection from the local underground supplier. The inability to use formal enforcement methods has been the major reason organized crime has long been associated with vice provision, though sometimes the protection is provided by the official police, in exchange for a cut of the proceeds.[4] In any event, the production and distribution of an illicit good tends to be marked by much higher levels of violence than occur in the dissemination of legal goods.[5] Consumers (and uninvolved bystanders) are often exposed to this violence when they patronize the illegal sellers. Those sellers themselves are more likely to be youths: severe sentences for adults convicted of drug selling provide a comparative advantage for the underaged. The recruitment

---

[1] MacCoun and Reuter (2001, p. 241).

[2] Miron (1999b). Warburton (1932, pp. 112–3, 164, 240) indicates that the alcohol prices facing those who did not consume home-produced alcohol were some three or four times higher under Prohibition than they were before World War I.

[3] In a legalized regime, furthermore, the same level of enforcement resources that was applied under a prohibition presumably could be targeted directly at any residual black market; these resources, aimed at a smaller illicit market, should be sufficient to raise the black-market price above the price that was established when all transactions were illegal and policed.

[4] "The" underground supplier because the provision of protection tends to be monopolized within an illicit industry or a neighborhood. If you are protected by the second-most-powerful provider, you are not protected. See Gambetta (1994).

[5] Miron (1999a) provides empirical evidence that stricter enforcement of alcohol and drug prohibitions in the United States has led to higher overall levels of violence.

of kids into selling helps to fuel the violence because kids typically are unable to defend themselves against adult predators without being armed.[6]

A given drug can be packaged and ingested in many ways. With a ban, the necessity to minimize exposure to law enforcement, as well as the higher price per dose, become key determinants of the popularity of drug variants. The general rule is that prohibition promotes more concentrated forms of the drug and methods of delivery that produce more hedonic impact per dose.[7] During alcohol Prohibition in the United States, there was a significant substitution away from beer toward higher-proof spirits; the end of Prohibition saw a reversal of this phenomenon. Beer is bulky and hard to store, whereas distilled liquors are much more compact – holding total alcohol content constant – and needn't suffer from unrefrigerated storage and transport. As a result, spirits are easier to distribute in an undetectable manner. Similarly, the banning of opiates made injection more attractive than smoking as a mode of ingestion, and heroin more popular than the less-potent morphine.[8] Some commentators attribute the invention and spread of crack, a smokeable form of cocaine, to enforcement of the prohibition on cocaine.[9]

The incentive to switch from opium or morphine to heroin use in the face of a prohibition is one version of a more general phenomenon, regulation-induced substitutions among drugs. Marijuana use is easier to detect via drug tests than is LSD use, and marijuana is bulkier and harder to conceal, so a drug prohibition backed by testing might encourage movement away from marijuana toward LSD, as well as increased alcohol consumption.[10] Correspondingly, a loosening of the teenage alcohol ban in the United States might lead to reduced marijuana use.[11] High effective prices for cocaine indirectly promote the production and consumption of methamphetamine. As noted in the Introduction, these types of substitutions are important determinants of the overall effects of vice regulations, but they are hard to predict, potentially unstable, and may not even be amenable to identification after the fact.

The illicit nature of trade in a banned commodity implies that buyers have little or no recourse against manufacturers or sellers who produce a fraudulently inferior or adulterated product. Quality control suffers. In the case of

---

[6] Polsby (2000, p. 176).

[7] The notion that tighter controls increase the potency of a drug has been encapsulated as the "Iron Law of Prohibition" by Cowan (1986). Sometimes the higher concentration and the method of delivery can work in "opposite" directions. Increases in the purity of street heroin in the past twenty years or so have led to an increase in smoking heroin relative to injecting.

[8] Kaplan (1983, pp. 7, 64–5).

[9] See, e.g., Cowan (1986); however, others evidently disagree: "The war on drugs cannot plausibly be blamed for the development of the crack cocaine trade...." Polsby (2000, p. 175).

[10] See, e.g., Sullum (2003, pp. 116–7).

[11] There is conflicting evidence over whether alcohol and marijuana are complements or substitutes, and there is no reason to expect that the answer has to be the same at all times and places and for all subsets of consumers; see the discussion and references in Conlin, Dickert-Conlin, and Pepper (2001).

illicit drugs, uncertainty over contents and potency leads to unintentional over-doses, sometimes with fatal consequences. Drug sellers do try to "brand" their product, or provide free samples, but all in all, drug composition and quality are much less assured in an illicit market than in a legal one.

Finally, drug use can be beneficial, even if personal pleasure is not considered to be a benefit. Most drugs used recreationally, including tobacco, distilled alcohol, cocaine, and heroin, first became significant elements of commerce through their perceived medicinal properties.[12] One result of a prohibition is a slowing down or cessation of research to discover and develop beneficial uses of banned drugs. Like an enhanced price, this outcome is not a logical necessity of prohibition. With an appropriate regulatory regime, a drug can be banned from recreational use while medical research involving the drug is legal or even encouraged. Nevertheless, it seems to be the case that in practice, making a drug illegal dampens research into its medicinal uses, and reduces the frequency of its therapeutic use. (Further, users of the banned drug are more likely to withhold the fact of their use from medical authorities, potentially compromising their care.) In the United States, the prohibition on opiates discourages physicians from treating pain aggressively, especially given legal actions that have been taken against some doctors whose use of opiates does not conform to standards satisfactory to the police. Marijuana continues to face a federal ban even for medicinal use in the United States, though many states have sanctioned medical marijuana, and informal prescription of marijuana by oncologists is common.[13]

BENEFITS OF DRUG PROHIBITION

The chief potential advantage, or perceived advantage, of a vice prohibition is reduced prevalence. But there is more to the story, or at least, the benefits of reduced prevalence can be fleshed out somewhat.

The relative advantages of drug prohibition depend on the precise alternative under consideration. One option would be to maintain the ban on drug manufacture and sale (the supply side), while decriminalizing possession and use of personal-use quantities (the demand side). (Criminalized supply but legal demand would essentially re-create, for the case of drugs, the policy environment facing alcohol during national Prohibition in the United States.) In general, drug prohibitionists aim their arguments against much more liberal regimes, either a prescription system or something akin to current day alcohol regulation.

Perhaps surprisingly, careful defenses of drug prohibition relative to a legal but regulated regime are not exactly thick on the ground. There have been some influential prohibitionist voices, however, including those of UCLA social

---

[12] See, e.g., Courtwright (2001).   [13] Doblin and Kleiman (1991).

scientist James Q. Wilson, the late law professor John Kaplan of Stanford University, and former U.S. "drug czar" William J. Bennett.[14] Many prohibitionists – though not Bennett – exclude marijuana from their case against legalization or decriminalization. Drawing on these contributions and others, I will try to offer below a sort of advocate's brief, a composite version of the arguments for the prohibition of cocaine and heroin, relative to substantially more liberal policy regimes.

A POLEMICAL CASE FOR DRUG PROHIBITION (OR AGAINST THE LEGALIZATION OF COCAINE AND HEROIN)

It is not a close call: prohibition dominates legalization on each of the $3\frac{1}{3}$ standard vice concerns of kids, addicts, externalities, and negative impacts upon nonaddicted adult users. Let's examine them in turn.

Legal availability of cocaine and heroin for adults will make these drugs widely available to kids, too. Certainly the experience of alcohol and tobacco cannot give any comfort to would-be legalizers on this score. The increased prevalence of heroin and cocaine under legalization also means more irresponsible parenting, more child abuse and neglect, more crack babies and newborns addicted to opiates.

Legalization will bring more addiction and probably a lot more addiction. Drug prohibition, despite its problems, has actually put most Americans out of harm's way with respect to heroin or cocaine. "Even though large amounts of heroin can be produced outside the United States, and it is almost impossible to interfere with drug smuggling across our borders, heroin has long been practically unavailable to most people in most of the nation."[15] If you would rather have heroin be as available as alcohol, go ahead, legalize. And you shouldn't put faith in the idea that we can increase availability without increasing addiction. History has shown again and again that heightened availability to habit-forming substances means heightened addiction. Physicians offer a current example: easier access to drugs has long made for extremely high rates of drug abuse among doctors, despite their enormous educational and social advantages.[16] Imagine what even easier access will do to those who have fewer resources with which to combat addiction.

So legalization means substantial increases in the number of children using hard drugs and in the number of addicts. Not surprisingly, then, we can look forward to large increases in social costs, beyond the crack babies and child neglect already mentioned. Nodding off heroin addicts will send their cars

[14] Schaler (1998) provides an excellent compendium of both pro- and antiprohibitionist views. Of special note among the prohibitionists, beyond Wilson and Bennet, are the articles by John Kaplan and David Courtwright reprinted in the Schaler volume. Husak (2002) also examines the arguments for drug prohibition, though his book provides a strong case for the decriminalization of drug users.
[15] Kaplan (1983, p. 88).   [16] Courtwright (1998 [1993], p. 85).

careening over roads and sidewalks. Unemployment rolls will swell. Although some of the crime inherent in black-market sales will be ended, swarms of addicts will still be breaking car windows for CD players and burglarizing homes for the money for their next fix. Coked-up addicts will unleash sprees of Burgessian ultraviolence. Under a legal regime, you might claim, we would tax drugs to raise their price and thereby reduce consumption and addiction. But the high taxes, in combination with the residual prohibitions against teenagers and others, will continue to spur a crime-ridden black market, while simultaneously increasing incentives for addicts to steal to support their habits.[17] "Legalization will give us the worst of both worlds: millions of *new* drug users *and* a thriving criminal black market."[18] And yet legalizers would have us believe that one of the chief advantages of their policy regime would be a decrease in crime!

Addicts and kids aside, what about all of those new, casual drug users who would spring up under legalization? They would have the usual run of acute problems, the emergency room visits, the occasional deaths from heroin overdose or from cocaine-induced heart failures. Of course, there may be some substitution toward less harmful methods of consuming these drugs – but don't bet on it. With millions of new users, the social costs of drug use will rise in any case, whatever the ingestion mechanism. The avant garde would set the trend: what party would be complete without some opium or maybe speedballs, heroin/cocaine combinations? Give Madison Avenue its due, too. The packaging and marketing of drugs would be vastly improved – Easy Injecto, for those who won't settle for snorting!

Oh no, the legalizers say, it won't be like alcohol, marketing of drugs will be controlled, perhaps prohibited. There won't be an opium café on every corner, not every 7–Eleven will sell crack. But look at what their alternative suggests: the state will be taxing drugs heavily but will not allow advertising or easy availability to stoke demand. Right. Gambling has become legalized in the past thirty years or so, and state governments take in huge revenues from lotteries and casinos – have you noticed how well marketing has been controlled in the case of gambling? I can't even send an e-mail without the state of Illinois reminding me that I could become a millionaire if I only played the lottery. "Tax revenues, like drugs themselves, can be addictive."[19] So we can expect addict-like behavior from those reaping the revenues.

Legalizers love to point to the Prohibition era in the United States as an argument for legalizing drugs.[20] We eventually recognized the folly of alcohol prohibition, goes the argument, and likewise we will one day shake our heads that not all that long ago, Americans thought it made sense to make heroin illegal. But the alcohol Prohibition analogy is so imperfect as to be useless or

---

[17] See Wilson (1998 [1990], p. 57) and Courtwright (1998 [1993]).
[18] Bennett (1998 [1990], p. 65).   [19] Courtwright (1998 [1993], p. 89).
[20] Kondracke (1998 [1988], p. 109).

worse. Most Americans never really supported a nationwide alcohol prohibition to begin with, and pre-Prohibition drinking was extremely commonplace –
even most cops drank – not akin to the few million heroin or cocaine users
today, who make up just a small percentage of the population.[21] As a result,
alcohol prohibition was an attempt to use the threat of prison to eliminate a
behavior that was accepted and deeply embedded in the culture of many or most
Americans. (And even in the case of alcohol, the "socialization" of this drug
doesn't prevent untold harm associated with its consumption.) Drug prohibition is no such beast. It is an attempt to stop the spread of insidious products –
products like refined cocaine and heroin that didn't even exist 150 years ago,
and by no means have been socialized by centuries of use. It is doubtful that they
could be socialized, their isolated forms being so much more potent than the
leaf chewing or opium smoking of some cultures in the past. Even individuals
in today's coca leaf–chewing cultures succumb to addiction when transplanted
to cities where crack is smoked.[22]

Education and treatment are two policies that tend to be revered by drug
legalizers. But it is the current criminalization of heroin and cocaine that renders
these strategies efficacious.[23] Imagine the message sent to children in trying
to prevent them from turning down the path to addiction if drugs were legal.
How will they respond to information about the dangers of heroin when they
see that, at age 18 or 21, they can buy and consume it at will? Some say that
under drug prohibition, forbidden fruit is tempting. You want temptation? Try
telling kids that the fruit is only forbidden until they are 18! And fear of legal
penalties is one of the main spurs for current users to seek treatment to help
them over their addiction. Take that spur away, and you sentence hundreds
of thousands, perhaps millions of current users to more years of destructive
living, and the rest of us to mandatory sentences of picking up the pieces.

Some legalizers are more modest, opting for prescription mechanisms
instead of more general access to drugs. Under such a regime, physicians
would be allowed to prescribe heroin or cocaine, presumably only to certified
addicts. The idea is that, by taking addicts out of the black market, we make
their lives easier and more productive, while simultaneously greatly shrink-
ing the demand for illegal drug sources. In theory, prescription regimes sound
wonderful – if only existing addicts get the drugs, we could have lower social
costs with no increase in addiction. In practice, alas, prescription regimes have
been and will be anything but wonderful. As Britain found out with its heroin
prescription system in the 1960s, prescription systems leak.[24] The legal drug

---

[21] The point that current illicit drug use involves a much smaller portion of the population than did
    alcohol use during Prohibition is made by Levine and Reinarman (1993).

[22] I came across this claim once but cannot recall the source; nevertheless, the general notion that
    addiction rates vary with the form, dosage, and delivery system of a drug is not controversial.

[23] Wilson (1998 [1990], pp. 58–9).

[24] Both Wilson (1998 [1990], pp. 52–3) and Kaplan (1998 [1988], pp. 94–5) view prescription systems
    as being too leaky to be viable.

Box 4.1: *A Pro-prohibition sampler*

"Probably the central problem with the solution [to our drug predicament] of legalization is that it ignores basic pharmacology. There is such a thing as a dangerous drug...." – John Kaplan[a]

"Tobacco shortens one's life, cocaine debases it. Nicotine alters one's habits, cocaine alters one's soul." – James Q. Wilson[b]

"I find no merit in the legalizers' case. The simple fact is that drug use is wrong. And the moral argument, in the end, is the most compelling argument."
– William J. Bennett[c]

"I don't think that you can argue against the fact that the costs in homelessness, unemployment, welfare, lost productivity, disability payments, school dropouts, lawsuits, medical care costs, chronic mental illness, accidents, crime, child abuse, and child neglect would all increase if we in fact legalized drugs."
– former attorney general of California Daniel Lungren[d]

---

[a] Kaplan (1998 [1988], p. 93).   [b] Wilson (1998 [1990], p. 59).
[c] Bennett (1998 [1990], p. 67).   [d] Lungren (2000, pp. 180–1).

---

access for addicts that is designed to kill off the black market has just the opposite effect, it stokes the black market. Even treating heroin addicts with legal methadone fuels demand and raises social costs. Already in Denmark, the "liberal dispensation of methadone has made that drug the principal cause of drug overdose deaths...."[25]

No one can fully be comfortable with the current war on drugs.[26] But any policy regime arrayed against these dangerous substances is sure to be beset with difficulties. You shouldn't let the problems of prohibition lead you to look for a magic bullet, an easy alternative that will set things right. If such a panacea existed, some country would have stumbled upon it long ago, and we would all have adopted it by now. The siren song of legalization is a particularly dangerous folly. It is simply too risky – not only because it will lead to huge increases in problems associated with the standard $3\frac{1}{3}$ vice dimensions but also because once it has had this effect, what then? Can we reinstate prohibition after a failed legalization? Yes, but with three or four or ten times the number of addicts fueling the black market. If you don't like the black market now, wait until you see what you get after a failed liberalization! The current regime, from that perspective, will look like a golden age of drug regulation. So even if the analysis above is likely to be wrong, even if there is only, say, a one-in-five chance that significant increases in drug-related costs would occur

---

[25] MacCoun and Reuter (2001, p. 270).   [26] Kaplan (1998 [1988], pp. 92–3).

with legalization, it is a policy gamble not worth taking.[27] Following a failed legalization, "there is no way to put the genie back in the bottle, and it is not a kindly genie."[28]

In a way, though, the sort of weighing of costs and benefits and $3\frac{1}{3}$ dimensions and the rhetoric of policy science is secondary to what is most at stake. "The simple fact is that drug use is wrong."[29] It is the moral dimension that separates our treatment of another very dangerous psychoactive drug, nicotine, from that of cocaine or heroin.[30] Unlike nicotine, these drugs alter personalities in ways that destroy human character. Legalizing heroin and cocaine is to give social imprimatur to this destruction of character. The destruction of society itself will follow, as the night the day. And then there will be no one left to pick up the pieces.

<h2 style="text-align:center">A TEMPERATE REJOINDER TO SOME OF THE ARGUMENTS
OF THE PROHIBITIONISTS</h2>

OK, convinced? Are the prohibitionists right?

With respect to many of their specific claims, alas, it is hard to say. The effect of a prohibition depends on details of the nature of the ban and its enforcement, and the outcomes under legalization depend on nuances of the regulatory regime. The balance might tilt in different directions with different drugs. It certainly cannot be taken for granted that increased prevalence implies increased costs along the standard $3\frac{1}{3}$ dimensions. As seems currently to be the case with marijuana, some young poeple might find it easier to get the prohibited goods than their legal counterparts, or kids might be employed in distributing the contraband. One of the more emotionally compelling arrows in the prohibitionists' quiver, the epidemic of crack babies in the 1980s, was hyped well beyond what the actual evidence indicated.[31] Controlled but legal availability of cocaine need not lead to worse parenting – after all, the "crack baby epidemic" took place under a regime of strict prohibition, and drug legalization will mean that fewer parents are in jail. Increased addiction might be fostered under a prohibition, as mainstream social controls erode and people avoid treatment for fear of publicizing their illegal activity. The reduced use that is the main rationale for a prohibition is not equivalent to reduced abuse.[32]

---

[27] The irreversibility of legalization argument features prominently in both Wilson (1998 [1990], p. 62) and Kaplan (1998 [1988], pp. 100–101).

[28] Wilson (1998 [1990], p. 55). The quote is taken a bit out of context. The more complete version is, "But that social experiment is so risky as to be no experiment at all, for if cocaine is legalized and if the rate of its abusive use increases dramatically, there is no way to put the genie back in the bottle, and it is not a kindly genie."

[29] Bennett (1998 [1990], p. 67).   [30] Wilson (1998 [1990, p. 59]).

[31] See, e.g., Goldstein (2001, pp. 190ff.) and Emmett (1998). See also "Crack Babies Do Not Have Lower IQ: Study," by Charnicia E. Huggins, Reuters, May 25, 2004.

[32] See, e.g., Johnson (2000, p. 15).

This is the point of harm reduction strategies that might increase prevalence while combatting the costs of addiction. Externalities might rise under a ban, as black markets spawn violence and high prices motivate addicts to steal. (Most of the violence that is associated with illegal substances is not due to the pharmacological properties of the drugs; rather, the crimes are motivated by standard black-market conditions and the desire to raise enough money to pay the high drug prices that prevail under prohibition. Violent crime in the United States during the twentieth century is positively correlated with the enforcement of drug and alcohol prohibition: more stringent prohibition, more crime.[33]) Casual, nonproblematic users will face the prospect of jail under prohibition, itself a significant social cost. In none of the $3\frac{1}{3}$ dimensions can we be confident that a ban will make matters better, even for a prohibition that "works" in terms of reducing prevalence. Further, drug prohibition imposes significant external costs through its influence on policing and civil liberties, as is detailed later in this chapter.

Regulations typically can be more finely tailored than criminal prohibitions to try to limit the most harmful aspects of vice indulgence. Part of the tailoring would involve some targeted bans. These can include residual prohibitions on sales to youths, as well as bans on public uses or sales during legally mandated closing hours, and so on. Penalties for drug transfers to kids could be increased under legalization, and the enforcement resources now aimed broadly can be, in part, focused on the youth market. Taxes, information campaigns, and other controls can try to push consumers toward safer drug formulations and ingestion methods. The prevalence of cigarette smoking in the United States has been nearly halved during the past fifty years, without introducing a ban, and most kids do not smoke, despite the legality of cigarette sales to adults.[34]

Treatment and education do not require the threat of imprisonment to make them effective, even if it is true that some people in need of treatment only seek it out when legal difficulties arise. Alcohol treatment does not appear to be inferior to treatments for illegal substances. The fact that a drug is illegal generally will make a user who has avoided arrest even less willing to seek help and less likely to confide in others who might be able to offer guidance. Pairing illegality with treatment also means that scarce treatment slots will be taken up not by those most in need of help with their addiction but, rather, by those whose legal situation is most likely to be improved by attending a treatment program.

Drug use (and vice more generally) is governed not just by public regulations but by private, social controls. Following a legalization, some employers still will choose to test employees for the use of certain drugs; insurance companies, too, might discriminate against (legal) drug users. Social norms doubtlessly change along with drug laws and perhaps can foster more responsible drug

[33] Miron (1999a).   [34] See, e.g., Gruber (2001).

use once the elimination of prohibition severs the chief connection between drugs and criminality. But because drug control depends on much more than the legal regime, we are on very shaky ground whenever we try to forecast what the world will look like if drugs were legal.[35]

This uncertainty about the future under legalization has become a plank in the prohibitionists' platform, often through their irreversibility contention: if we try legalization and it fails, the legalization will be very hard to undo. Once we legalize and see burgeoning prevalence and addiction, the argument goes, any reversal of the policy would be met by an even more formidable black market than currently exists. Ironically, the argument that legalization is hard to reverse renders prohibition hard to reverse.

Accepting the irreversibility argument, however, does not rule out legalization. Rather, it suggests that we look at gradual approaches to legalization that clearly would be possible to reverse if social costs mount. The obvious reform along these lines is to reduce the enforcement of drug prohibition in a targeted way.[36] The Dutch approach to cannabis is a case in point. Although cannabis is not legal in the Netherlands, enforcement policies have rendered private use essentially legal. If problems arise, enforcement can be altered; such an adjustment occurred in 1995, when the Dutch significantly lowered the amount of cannabis that a licensed coffee shop could sell to an individual without fear of legal consequence.[37] If reduced (and perhaps better targeted) enforcement provides tolerable outcomes, full legal licensing of limited sales could be tried, too, perhaps to a very restricted subset of people – and if that trial works, the licensing system could slowly be expanded. If it doesn't work, the licensing could be eliminated. Admittedly, such gradual approaches will not provide irrefutable evidence concerning the full panoply of effects that would accompany a broader, official legalization, but they can be very suggestive, and reversible, experiments.

Imagine the situation in the United States in 1913, when heroin and cocaine were available without a prescription. A prohibition has been proposed. Consider the following argument against adopting the prohibition: maybe after prohibition the use of these dangerous drugs will fall to negligible levels. But can we count on that? What if, over time, use rises? Then we will be jailing thousands of people, perhaps (it sounds crazy, but it is conceivable) hundreds of thousands, simply because they want to consume one of these drugs. The judicial costs, the violence spawned by the huge black markets, the accidental overdoses brought about by uncertain quality will all be enormous. Children might even be recruited to work in the black market to avoid the criminal penalties imposed upon adults. Perhaps you say, OK, if the outcome is as frightening as that, we can simply get rid of the prohibition, we can return to

---

[35] Husak (2002, pp. 154ff.).

[36] Leitzel and Weisman (1999).

[37] MacCoun and Reuter (2001, p. 249).

Box 4.2: *Some typical effects of a policed drug prohibition, relative to a market regulated like tobacco and alcohol*

1. Development of a black market
2. Higher effective price for the drug
3. Decreased consumption of the drug
4. Dispute settlement by violence
5. Recruitment of the underaged into drug sales and purchases
6. High incomes and status for successful drug sellers
7. Sales of more concentrated forms of the drug
8. Concentration levels and other dimensions of quality unverifiable, variable
9. Unintentional overdoses rise
10. Increased reluctance to summon medical help in the event of an overdose
11. Slowdown of research into beneficial aspects of the drug
12. Increased arrests
13. Police at increased risk of violence, corruption
14. Constitutional rights decay in face of imperatives of black-market policing
15. Information and statistics about the extent and workings of the market degraded.

a system of free availability or a prescription regime. But will it really be so easy to rid ourselves of a failed prohibition? A huge industry of prisons and treatment providers, lawyers and specialized police squads, and prosecutors will be feeding at the narco/prison trough. Instead of acceding to the calls for liberalization, these interested parties will constantly push for more – longer sentences, mandatory minimum jail terms, banning related activity like possessing paraphernalia. New drugs that come along will become fodder for their interest, their fetish to punish. They won't even have to work all that hard to make their case. Every drug-related tragedy will reinforce the perils of drugs in the public mind. How to avoid these tragedies? Reduce prevalence of use. How to reduce prevalence of use? Prohibition, more committed prohibition! The problems that will arise under prohibition will transmute into justifications for prohibition.[38] So even if my nightmare vision of greatly increased use and hundreds of thousands of Americans wasting in prison is unlikely, even if there is only a 10 percent chance of such an outcome, prohibition is too great a risk. Once the prohibition genie is out of the bottle, it cannot easily be put back – "and it is not a kindly genie."[39]

---

[38] The same dynamic has been observed with respect to the former gambling prohibition in the United States. Organized crime involvement with gambling was largely motivated by its illegality; nevertheless, the fact of Mafia involvement made prohibition seem all the more necessary. MacCoun and Reuter (2001, p. 133): "The prohibition [against gambling] was also sustained by the very problems that it generated." Similarly, estimates of the substantial costs of drug abuse that presently occur under a prohibitory regime often are transmuted into arguments for prohibition.

[39] Apologies to James Q. Wilson for purposely (mis)appropriating his genie line.

Even from the point of view of today, the irreversibility argument based on a worst-case scenario applies just as well to maintaining drug prohibition as it does to legalizing. For instance, the political instability and civil strife fostered by drug prohibition in several Latin American countries could grow worse and engulf the United States, too. Isn't that potential scenario sufficiently worrisome to make continued prohibition an irresponsible policy choice?

It is always tempting to make the claim that "the alternative I do not support is too risky and irrevocable for us to choose that alternative." But just because something is tempting doesn't make it right, as both opponents and proponents of drug prohibition should recognize.

U.S. ALCOHOL PROHIBITION, 1920–1933

National alcohol prohibition in the United States (1920–1933) has become nearly synonymous with policy failure, so much so that during the seventy-plus years subsequent to repeal there has been almost no sentiment for a return to Prohibition. The experience of Prohibition is generally mined today not so much for its relevance for contemporary alcohol policy but, rather, for the lessons that it holds for regulating currently illicit drugs such as marijuana, cocaine, and heroin. Would-be drug legalizers point to the shortcomings shared by alcohol and drug prohibition, most particularly, widespread evasion and corruption. Those who support the prohibitory regime for drugs, alternatively, suggest vast differences between drugs and alcohol, note the public health benefits that accrued from alcohol prohibition and emphasize the enormous social costs associated with consumption of legal alcohol today.

Bans on sales of alcohol have a long tradition on the territory of the United States. (Indeed, the recent seventy years of little prohibitory interest are outliers in a U.S. historical sense.) In 1735, the British Parliament prohibited the sale of rum in the colony of Georgia.[40] Beer and wine were encouraged as substitutes; nevertheless, rampant evasion led to a decline in enforcement, followed (in 1749) by repeal, a sequence destined to be much repeated. State-level attempts at prohibition cropped up during the first wave of the temperance movement, including the so-called Maine Laws that spread from Maine to twelve other states in the mid-nineteenth century[41] – recall that, in *On Liberty*, John Stuart Mill expressly attacked these statutes regulating self-regarding behavior. Again, evasion appears to have been rife, and, with one exception, the state laws were soon overturned by courts or repealed. Nevertheless, the prohibitory impulse was not extinguished, and in 1869, a new political entity, the National Prohibition Party, came into existence; its 1892 presidential candidate received

---

[40] See Barr (1999, pp. 40ff.) and National Commission on Marihuana and Drug Abuse.
[41] Merz (1931, p. 3).

270,710 votes, about 2.2 percent of the ballots cast.[42] A further, limited round of state-level prohibitions and local options for prohibition occurred during the 1880s.

When alcohol prohibition finally became the law of the land, however, the Prohibition Party was not a driving force. Rather, Prohibition was boosted by a confluence of factors, perhaps the most important of which was the activism of the Anti-Saloon League (ASL).[43] Founded in Ohio in 1893 (though with roots in Oberlin, Ohio, that dated from 1874), the ASL became a national organization in 1895. The league's construction on a single anti-alcohol dimension and cooperation with many Protestant churches, along with its massive publication and distribution of anti-alcohol materials, resulted in enormous political influence. The ASL endorsed candidates from any political party for local and state (and, later, national) elections, provided they were committed to its "dry" agenda. With significant sway over single-issue dry voters, these endorsements reduced the number of major party politicians willing to adopt a "wet" stance.

Why would a large group of people and resources coalesce around an organization formed in opposition to saloons? Much of the reason is that pre-Prohibition saloons differed significantly from modern bars or bars/restaurants. Saloons were all-purpose alcohol establishments, encompassing both on-site consumption and takeaway purchases. What they generally did not encompass was a welcoming environment for "respectable" women. Saloons were viewed, often rightly, as hotbeds of public nuisance; most notably, they were associated with gambling and prostitution, the toleration or encouragement of which were often conscious marketing elements for the saloons. (The ASL aimed its attack at the traffic in liquor, and not at the individual drinker.) Many saloons were decidedly odious, at least from the point of view of nonpatrons, and this impression was strengthened by the fact that saloons frequently were centers for local political activity of the disreputable, non-arm's-length variety. The flouting of the law by saloons was emphasized by one acute observer, looking back from the vantage point of 1931 when saloons had been closed for more than a decade:

> The trouble with the drink places was that they tried to think up cute ways of making a fool of the law instead of wisely endeavoring to keep up a semblance of decency and placate the noncustomers. In communities which attempted to enforce midnight closing they went in for double curtains and heavy blinds, so that when the place seemed dark from the outside it was very much illuminated

---

[42] National Commission on Marihuana and Drug Abuse. The Prohibition Party still exists, and thus is the oldest third party extant in the United States: see www.prohibition.org. For the 2.2 percent figure, see the Wikipedia entry on the 1892 election, at http://en.wikipedia.org/wiki/United_States_presidential_election_1892 (accessed January 28, 2007).

[43] Odegard (1928) and Kerr (1985) provide excellent histories of the Anti-Saloon League, and I draw upon them here.

and going full blast on the inside. Keeping open on Sundays and holidays, selling to minors, harboring outlaw elements, lining up voters who could be bought – these were some of the major offenses. . . .[44]

Its influence growing, the Anti-Saloon League in 1913 called for a constitutional amendment to institute a federal alcohol ban. Shortly thereafter, the outbreak of World War I converted workplace productivity into a national security issue; sobriety was considered to be a boon to productivity. Grain was needed to help feed a hungry world, so the use of potential food to produce alcoholic beverages was argued to be wasteful, a serious misalignment of priorities. (The "conserve food" argument was more rationale than reason, however; as famed criminal defense attorney Clarence Darrow observed, "The men who were responsible for [the wartime prohibition bill] were much more anxious to prohibit the use of liquor than they were to win the war."[45]) Anti-immigrant and wartime anti-German sentiment further promoted the fortunes of Prohibition, as Germans were seen as disproportionally represented among beer brewers and consumers of alcohol. These special conditions of wartime eventually led to a ban on manufacturing distilled spirits, followed by a measure that limited production of alcoholic beverages to those with an alcohol content no greater than 2.75 percent; ironically, this latter "wartime" measure did not actually take effect until seven months after the war was over.

Along with this war-era legislation, national Prohibition was preceded by higher alcohol taxes and several state-level alcohol bans. Further, the per capita consumption of alcohol in the US generally had been falling for some time prior to WWI (indeed, in 1915 per capita consumption was just over one-third of its circa 1830 peak[46]), so the "wet" viewpoint also was diluting. Already by 1913, a majority of the American population lived in areas that prohibited alcohol – though often the "prohibition" was packaged with numerous exceptions that made alcoholic beverages relatively easy to acquire and consume.[47] For instance, imports for personal use were legal in some dry states, and other states with alcohol prohibition permitted home-made wine.

Despite the long-term decline in alcohol consumption, a strict prohibition probably did not represent the majority viewpoint of US citizens; for instance, neither of the major political parties endorsed prohibition as part of their platforms – even in 1920, after Prohibition was the Constitutionally-sanctified law of the land.[48] There was never a nationwide vote on Prohibition; in Ohio, the only state that held a popular referendum on ratification of the federal

[44] Ade (1931, p. 23).
[45] Darrow (1960 [1932], p. 292). Darrow's evidence for his contention is that the "fanatical drys" were willing to stonewall the food conservation bill unless it contained a prohibition clause.
[46] Levine and Reinarman (1993, p. 167).
[47] National Commission on Marihuana and Drug Abuse. On the many exceptions built into state-level prohibitions, see Merz (1931, pp. 20ff.).
[48] Merz (1931, p. 72).

prohibition, the measure failed, even though a state-level prohibition had been adopted.[49] Urban areas in the northern United States were particularly unsympathetic to the Prohibition cause.

Following the ratification of the Eighteenth Amendment in 1919, Congress needed to formulate legislation to implement the national Prohibition. (The amendment referred to "intoxicating liquors ... for beverage purposes," prohibiting imports and exports, manufacture, sale, and transportation. The "beverage purposes" condition was necessary to exempt alcohol intended for industrial, medicinal, or sacramental use.) One possibility was that the wartime standard would be maintained, and hence that 2.75 percent beer would still be available. Alternatively, both beer and wine could have been exempt, if "intoxicating liquors" were deemed to refer only to distilled spirits. Congress chose a much stricter standard, however – the implementing legislation, known after the chair of the House Committee on the Judiciary as the Volstead Act, defined any product with an alcohol concentration above 0.5 percent (measured by volume) as an "intoxicating liquor." To protect homemade alcoholic cider, an exception was built into the Volstead Act (as it had been in the Maine Laws of the previous century) for the rustic fermenter "manufacturing nonintoxicating cider and fruit juices exclusively for use in his home," and this exception was later interpreted by the courts as applying to homemade wine.[50] While sale was prohibited, purchase, possession and consumption remained legal, so that the alcohol ban during Prohibition approximates what is referred to as "decriminalization" in today's drug policy debates.[51]

In evaluating the effects of Prohibition, perhaps the most important datum is the extent of alcohol consumption during Prohibition, relative to the pre-Prohibition period or the years following repeal. Unfortunately, one standard impact of banning (the sale of) a commodity is that information about consumption is degraded: people are generally not forthcoming about their illegal activity, and most alcohol consumption during Prohibition resulted from illegal production, transportation, and sale. Nevertheless, perhaps a very weak consensus might be along the lines suggested by economists Jeffrey Miron and Jeffrey Zweibel: the immediate impact of Prohibition was a 70 per cent fall in alcohol consumption; after that, consumption began to rise, and within a few

---

[49] Merz (1931, p. 44).   [50] Barr (1999, pp. 170–1, 178).

[51] While the Eighteenth Amendment made no reference to consumption, purchase, or possession of alcohol, the Volstead act (Title II, Section 3) did indicate that possession was illegal; see the text of the act in Merz (1931, p. 318). It appears that possession in your own home was legal, but carrying around alcohol, even in a hip flask, constituted transport and was hence illegal; see Behr (1997, pp. 83–4). As a practical matter, because search warrants were not issued for noncommercial home production, discreet in-house manufacture for home consumption typically would not generate trouble with the law. Many (but not all) prohibitionists did not agitate for rules against possession, as their general strategy was to demonize the traffic in liquor, not the individual drinker; see Kerr (1985, pp. 224–5).

years, had reached 70 per cent of pre-Prohibition levels.[52] There was a significant shift away from the consumption of beer to the consumption of wine and
hard liquor. Other unintended outcomes associated with Prohibition included
the growth of organized crime and a substitution to (then legal) marijuana and
(banned since 1914) narcotics.[53]

As alcohol remained an important ingredient in industrial processes, some
enforcement had to be aimed at preventing legal industrial alcohol from being
diverted for beverage purposes. This situation was not original to Prohibition,
however – industrial alcohol had been taxed more lightly than beverage alcohol
for years. To limit diversion, industrial alcohol was "denatured," that is, made
either unpalatable or outright toxic when consumed. (Denaturing industrial
alcohol continues to this day for the same tax enforcement purpose.[54]) Some
of this denatured alcohol, along with alcoholic beverages that were tainted for
other reasons, was consumed anyway: prohibitions undermine the usual mechanisms of quality control. At times the health results were devastating. In 1930,
consumption of an adulterated batch of "Jamaica Ginger," a high-proof beverage ostensibly sold as a medicine, was responsible for partially paralyzing some
50,000 Americans.[55]

Although evasion of the alcohol ban was widespread, it cannot be said that
Prohibition was a futile endeavor. It did appear, at least at first, to reduce alcohol consumption. (Perhaps similar reductions could have been brought about
by means short of a national ban, however. Recall, for instance, that alcohol
consumption generally had been falling for ninety years before Prohibition.)
In some small southern towns and other areas where it had significant public
support, Prohibition created a serious barrier to the acquisition of alcoholic
beverages. Even where alcohol remained readily available, the higher prices
tended to repress consumption by lower-income individuals.[56] Nevertheless, in
overall terms, extensive evasion and the concomitant corruption of officialdom

[52] Miron and Zweibel (1991); see Miron (1999b) for a different view of the effect of Prohibition on
alcohol consumption.

[53] On the stimulus to marijuana consumption provided by the Volstead Act, see the discussion in
Zimring and Hawkins (1992, pp. 70–1); see also Thornton (1991). The Harrison Act, which ushered
in the prohibition of opiates and cocaine, was passed in December 1914 but did not take effect until
March 1915.

[54] On denaturing and taxation, see the website of the Bureau of Alcohol, Tobacco and Firearms, at
www.atf.treas.gov/about/service/sda/ (accessed on August 6, 2003).

[55] Morgan (1982); see also Baum (2003). If jake was able to be manufactured and sold legally during
Prohibition, why would there be adulterated versions or any significant problems with quality
control? The reason lies in the desire of Prohibition enforcers to limit the size of the "for medicinal
purposes" loophole. To prevent beverage alcohol from being easily available through the "medicinal
purposes" dodge, regulations were enacted to make fluid extracts like jake unpalatable (in a manner
similar to the denaturing of alcohol intended for industrial purposes to preclude its diversion to
beverages). It was in an effort to skirt these subsidiary regulations, it seems, that led two shady
Boston brothers to adulterate their jake (Baum [2003]) and ultimately to paralyze thousands.

[56] See the estimates in Warburton (1932, pp. 233–7).

soon became apparent. Rather than being a solution to the crime issue – advocates referred to the elimination of "alcohol-related" crimes as one of the major gains that could be realized from Prohibition – the ban seemed to spread lawlessness.[57] Veritable armies of individuals took up the manufacture of alcohol: in 1928, more than 18,000 stills and more than 217,000 illicit fermenters were seized by federal prohibition agents.[58] By comparison, there were some 255,000 saloons in the United States in the early years of the twentieth century, and perhaps 170,000 on the eve of Prohibition.[59]

Prohibition can be viewed as a success in some dimensions beyond diminished consumption. First, it appears – from hospital data on cases of liver cirrhosis and other alcohol-related health phenomena – that illnesses associated with heavy drinking declined during Prohibition. (These inferences of lower alcohol-related morbidity are not automatic, as the recording of an illness as drinking related is influenced by social attitudes toward drinking, which can be shaped by the legal regime.) Second, the saloon, the institution so contemptible that the Anti-Saloon League formed to combat it long before the league supported a national alcohol ban, was effectively destroyed and did not return following Prohibition's own demise. (By separating on-site consumption from "package" sales to go, post-Prohibition did not see a revival of the typical pre-Prohibition saloon. Prohibition itself instigated the opening up of drinking establishments to women.) As with decreased consumption, the transformation of the saloon might have been accomplished with regulations less stringent than a ban.

Pro-Prohibition forces didn't simply give up when the widespread evasion became apparent. The standard battle cry of more enforcers and harsher punishments was raised right from the outset. Both of these policy changes were adopted, too. Total federal expenditures on Prohibition enforcement, net of fines and penalties collected, rose from less than 2.5 million dollars in 1920 to more that 38.6 million dollars in 1930.[60] The Jones Act in 1929 elevated the penalties for first-time alcohol violations by roughly an order of magnitude, to five years in prison and a $10,000 fine. In fiscal year 1921, federal prohibition agents arrested 34,175 individuals; in fiscal 1928, the corresponding figure was 75,307.[61] But the heightened enforcement did not translate into lower consumption.

Rampant circumvention of the alcohol ban, and its corollary effects, such as official corruption, eventually joined with the economic conditions of the Great Depression to sound the death knell for Prohibition.[62] Fiscal incentives, on the

---

[57] See Miron (1999a). [58] Merz (1931, p. 331).
[59] Barker (1905, p. 5) indicates that in 1903, there were an estimated 254,498 establishments selling liquor in the United States; Aaron and Musto (1981) provide the 170,000 figure for pre-Prohibition saloons.
[60] Warburton (1932, p. 246). [61] Merz (1931, pp. 330–1).
[62] See, e.g., Levine and Reinarman (1993, pp. 163–4).

part of both the government and leading businesspeople, were particularly influential. When an official ban is widely evaded, the government receives no (direct) tax revenue, while organized criminals and related lawbreakers collect the informal equivalent of a tax. (The government might receive tax revenues indirectly, in the form of bribes to enforcement agents, whose official salaries are then lower than they otherwise would be, in tacit recognition of their informal bonuses.) The argument for legalization and taxation becomes compelling once a banned vice activity becomes prevalent. (This is a pattern that has been observed with respect to gambling.) That alcohol abuse in the United States did not seem to be any lower than in other countries where alcohol was legal but taxed also added to the pressure for repeal. The income tax, legitimized by the Seventeenth Amendment (adopted in 1913), was becoming a nuisance to businesspeople, and they saw taxes on legal liquor as a way of offering a reprieve.[63] The influence of fiscal concerns on repeal is reflected in the fact that, to this day, federal alcohol laws are administered through the Department of the Treasury.[64]

Like its inception, the end of Prohibition was a gradual process, though its repeal on the precise date of December 5, 1933, might suggest otherwise. Per capita alcohol consumption had been increasing throughout Prohibition, after the initial decline. Beer with an alcohol content of no more than 3.2 percent was legalized earlier in 1933 by amending the Volstead Act. Many jurisdictions had given up on enforcing Prohibition long before its official repeal. New York and other states abandoned Prohibition enforcement by the mid-1920s, leaving the administration of the unpopular ban to the thinly staffed federal Bureau of Prohibition.

Repeal ended national prohibition, but by no means did it create an unfettered marketplace for alcohol. Rather, the Twenty-first Amendment explicitly granted the individual states the right to control alcohol as they saw fit. In general, two models for alcohol control were instituted based on guidelines developed in a 1933 report that had been drawn up under the sponsorship of John D. Rockefeller, Jr.[65] Some states chose to distribute packaged-to-go alcohol only through state-owned stores. The alternative model involved issuing licenses for privately owned liquor stores. Under both regimes, restaurants and bars needed to obtain liquor licenses in order to serve alcohol. Some states chose to continue with state-level prohibition – the last state to go wet for spirits was Mississippi in 1966[66] – and local options allowed municipalities or counties to remain dry even in states that permitted alcohol.

---

[63] National Commission on Marihuana and Drug Abuse.

[64] Federal prohibition enforcement was in the ambit of the Department of the Treasury (along with some necessary partners such as the Coast Guard) until 1930, when it was transferred (until its demise) to the Department of Justice; other alcohol tax and regulatory authority remained at Treasury, however. See www.atf.treas.gov/about/history.htm (accessed August 3, 2003).

[65] Levine and Reinarman (1993, pp. 174–6).   [66] Barr (1999, p. 250).

Box 4.3: *Clarence Darrow on Prohibition*

The Chicago-based criminal defense attorney Clarence Darrow was an outspoken opponent of national alcohol prohibition, even long before the Eighteenth Amendment was passed. Darrow continued to agitate against Prohibition during the 1920s and early 1930s, co-authoring a book in 1927 in response to a pro-Prohibition volume released a year earlier by the eminent Yale economist Irving Fisher.[a] In his memoirs, *The Story of My Life*, published in 1932, Darrow devotes two chapters to alcohol prohibition, and it is these that I draw upon here.

Darrow highlights the contradiction between the gluttony that he attributes to many temperance reformers and their stern warnings about touching even a drop of alcohol, even though

> There were always more graves filled from overeating than from over-drinking.... Puritanism has always associated pleasure with sin. To the real Puritan, life is a grim, depressing duty; this earth is nothing but a preparatory school for entering heaven. And to be happy in heaven, one must be unhappy here. So the old revivalist and temperance reformer had no difficulty in holding up the drunkard as a horrible example: Just see how happy and carefree and unmeddlesome he was; always so satisfied with his lot in life and willing that every one else should do as he liked; naturally there was something wrong with such a method of living. The glutton dragged himself to the meeting and shouted "Amen!" in the right places, a friend to heartburn but not to hiccough.... Devouring all the food that one could hold was praiseworthy. But drinking liquor, even one mouthful, was damnable.... It was on this popular foundation that prohibitionists organized their forces and waged the campaign to destroy the liberties of American citizens. It was on this foundation that they foisted upon the United States a reign of terror, intimidation, violence, and bigotry unprecedented in the modern world.[b]

A constitutional amendment was needed for the federal government to have the power to regulate alcohol. But that was all that was "needed," Darrow notes, for the amendment could simply have given the federal government that power (without specifying the nature of the regulation), and then Congress could have voted for national prohibition. Instead, the dry forces enshrined the policy, prohibition, into the Constitution, "intending thereby to make it impossible ever to permit the sale of intoxicating liquor in the United States."[c] As for the Eighteenth Amendment and its implementing measure, the Volstead Act, "If senators and representatives had voted as they drank, no such legislation would ever have disgraced America."[d]

Darrow condemns the methods taken to make Prohibition even remotely enforceable. That extraordinary enforcement measures were deemed necessary is evidence of the folly of criminalizing alcohol. "A small minority cannot nullify a law, but where a statute is considered tyrannical and unjust it always meets with protest. Refusal to be bound is such a protest. If protest is so great as to interfere with

(continued)

Box 4.3 *(continued)*

its enforcement by ordinary methods, it is plain that it has no place in the law in the land."[e] Prohibition enforcement often involved the use of lethal force: "If the prohibition law had been treated like any other act of Congress or State legislation it would have died long ago. No other statute is openly enforced with guns and revolvers. For no other minor offense can officers with impunity shoot down a human being in seeking to make an arrest."[f] Denaturing industrial alcohol to limit its diversion to drink presents Darrow with another example of enforcement run amok:

> So far as I know, no organization of human beings heretofore has coldly and deliberately advocated poisoning any one who might run counter to their will. The prohibitionists insist that alcohol sold for mechanical purposes and shipped broadcast over all America shall contain deadly poison. They advocate this, knowing that much of it is redistilled and used as a beverage, that many people might and do get it through accident and without any design to take intoxicants; and that, at best, or worst, to drink it is only a minor offense; yet men and women, who in ordinary life are kind and humane, are so obsessed by their delusions and so sure of their convictions, and so resentful of those who do not follow their dictates, that they are willing to condemn to blindness and death thousands of people, without arrest or indictment or trial, by putting poison into their drink. Heretofore such measures have not been resorted to against anything but rats and vermin, and many humane persons hesitate to do this.[g]

Alcohol prohibition exceeds the desirable limits of the criminal law. "Criminal statutes are very different from civil legislation. Punishment is inflicted on the theory that a right-thinking person could not commit the act without a feeling of guilt. No such feeling has ever been experienced with the taking of a drink of intoxicating liquor."[h] Nevertheless, "The Volstead Act in effect brands every one who takes a drink as a criminal, as a felon. It does this in spite of the fact that the greatest men of the world have always taken intoxicating drinks."[i] The world could profit from recognizing historical examples of the overreach of the criminal law: "Men were as sure that it was just to condemn heresy and witchcraft by death as their lineal descendants are sure of the righteousness of spreading poison broadcast to-day in the interest of the 'Noble Experiment' of prohibition."[j]

---

[a] Fisher's (1926) book is *Prohibition at Its Worst*; Darrow and Yarros (1927) countered with *The Prohibition Mania*. Fisher's book was secretly funded, in part, by the Anti-Saloon League, and the research for the book was prepared not by Fisher directly, but by the World League Against Alcoholism. Fisher also contributed his own funds to the publication of the volume; see Kerr (1985, p. 250).

[b] The quotations start from page 287 of Darrow (1932 [1960]). Obesity leads to more early deaths than alcohol in the modern United States, too.

[c] Darrow (1932 [1960], p. 293).   [d] Darrow (1932 [1960], p. 295).
[e] Darrow (1932 [1960], p. 296).   [f] Darrow (1932 [1960], p. 297).
[g] Darrow (1932 [1960], pp. 297–8).   [h] Darrow (1932 [1960], p. 296).
[i] Darrow (1932 [1960], p. 299).   [j] Darrow (1932 [1960], pp. 296–7).

The demise of Prohibition did not bring with it a surge in drinking: per capita alcohol consumption in 1935 was no higher than in 1930, though the movement away from spirits and toward beer was getting under way. Alcohol consumption began to rise slowly after 1935, attaining the pre–World War I level by 1970.[67]

Alcohol prohibition was part of the broader Progressive agenda, and the women's movement was an important component in both the narrow and broad programs. (The Eighteenth Amendment prohibiting alcohol was closely followed, in 1920, by the Nineteenth Amendment, which secured women's right to vote.) The connection is exemplified by the National Woman's Christian Temperance Union (WCTU), founded in 1874, which embraced a host of progressive causes, including an eight-hour workday.[68] While the WCTU devoted most of its energy to alcohol prohibition and women's suffrage, it also worked toward a national ban on cigarettes. The national cigarette ban did not get very far, but by 1922, fifteen states had passed laws prohibiting all cigarette sales, and twenty-one other states had considered such laws.[69] Enforcement tended to be soporific, however, and by 1927, these bans were relegated to the ashtray of history – or will we soon see a revival?

DRUG PROHIBITION AND POLICING

Drug prohibition in the United States has had a profound and baleful influence on policing. The source of the difficulties is that drug transactions are voluntary exchanges that in general do not generate victims motivated to register a complaint with the police or provide testimony against the transactors.[70] (Open-air drug markets do generate complaints from neighborhood residents, of course, as such markets constitute a public nuisance or worse. But the buyers and sellers themselves have no incentive to go to the police, and if the exchanges were to take place in a private setting and without extensive foot traffic, no one would be interested in notifying the local constabulary.)

The dearth of complaining victims means that whether the antidrug laws are enforced at all is a decision made by street-level officers. Traffickers involved in the illegal trade have strong incentives and ready cash to influence those decisions. As a result, vice prohibitions put unrealistic demands on police probity. A police officer can make thousands of dollars just by turning his head, and the exchanges that are thereby countenanced don't generate victims or 911 calls or trouble with the sergeant. It isn't a surprise that the temptation to be corrupted in this fashion has proven irresistible to some police – perhaps it is surprising

---

[67] Levine and Reinarman (1993, pp. 166–8).

[68] National Commission on Marihuana and Drug Abuse. The WCTU still exists; see www.wctu.org.

[69] On the state-level cigarette bans, see Alston, Dupré, and Nonnenmacher (2002).

[70] Barnett (1987) provides a good analysis of the implications of victimless crime prohibitions on the police, and I draw upon his analysis in this section.

that more cops do not give in to such inducements.[71] Sometimes, of course, the corruption moves from cases of omission (turning your head) to cases of commission (targeting a protected gang's rivals, robbing drug sellers, planting drugs on innocent individuals, privately appropriating cash found in drug raids, and so on).

The economist Robert Klitgaard has fashioned the following heuristic equation as a guide to the extent of corruption that will be seen in a government agency: Corruption = Monopoly + Discretion − Accountability.[72] The rationale underlying Klitgaard's qualitative encapsulation of the prevalence of corruption is as follows. It is hard to solicit a bribe for providing a nominally free service if there are hordes of other officials who also are available to provide the service: that is the sense behind the positive relationship between monopoly and corruption. If an official has no discretion, then a bribe cannot be used to influence his (dictated) action. An official endowed with some choice over his official actions will still find his ability to use his discretion in a corrupt manner limited by close supervision of his behavior. The less the accountability, the more dilatory the supervision, the greater the scope for corruption.

A vice prohibition promotes corruption primarily by boosting discretion: the police officer on the beat can decide, more or less independently, whether to arrest a drug offender. Crimes with actual victims who generate reports do not provide the same opportunities for corruption. The vicitimless nature of voluntary drug transactions also undermines accountability, as there is no one to complain to an officer's supervisor about the misuse of discretion. Corruption is held in check in the United States, however, even in the face of vice prohibitions, by competing law enforcement agencies.[73] The local police have to fear that internal affairs or state or federal police (or drug-law offenders willing to trade information for reduced sentences) will uncover their wrongdoing, and a single officer will generally not be in a position to market credible, twenty-four-hour protection to favored drug sellers. The monopoly power of any one officer or police force is incomplete, in vice prohibition as in other areas of law enforcement.

Discretion doesn't end at arrest. Prosecutors, judges, witnesses, and juries all have discretion, and they, too, might be tempted to sell their decisions. This is true in general, but again, the absence of harm to others in pure vice offenses puts the behavior of justice system officials under less scrutiny. Even if a prosecution is brought against a drug seller, the arresting officers often will be the only witnesses. They can alter their testimony, or suggest some

---

[71] There have been cases where corruption in vice control has appeared to be almost universal; see, for instance, the discussion of gambling enforcement by New York City police circa 1970 in the *Knapp Commission Report on Police Corruption* (1973).

[72] Klitgaard (1991, p. 225).

[73] This point is made by MacCoun and Reuter (2001, p. 119).

irregularities in the search and arrest that would be sufficient for charges to be dropped by the prosecutor or for the case to be dismissed by the judge.[74]

Perjured testimony by police to aid drug arrestees is certainly possible, but it seems that perjury in the name of law enforcement is even more common. Police are generally required to have a warrant or probable cause to search someone, but they might not always abide by that standard. There are now more than a million and a half arrests in the United States on drug possession charges each year, most of them involving small amounts of drugs. (And of course, there are millions of additional searches that do not yield any drugs or arrests.) How do police officers, generally operating without warrants, uncover so many folks possessing drugs? One way is through "consent searches," where suspects agree to be searched. But even setting consent searches aside, there are still boatloads of drug possession arrests annually. As Joseph McNamara, former police chief of Kansas City and San Jose, puts it, "The inescapable conclusion is that in hundreds of thousands of cases, police officers violated their oath to uphold the Constitution and often committed perjury so that the evidence would be admitted."[75] For instance, drug arrests often follow from situations where the police claim that the defendant dropped drugs when approached by an officer. Sometimes this is true, as many drug violators think that they might have less legal trouble if the drugs are not actually found on their person. But at other times, "dropsy testimony" is a cover-up that provides a rationale for what in reality constituted an illegal search.[76] The adoption of unconstitutional and illegal means to enforce drug laws is not a matter of a few bad cops; rather, it is built into the system.[77] How else can police effectively enforce laws that make drug possession illegal? "Drug law enforcement . . . is . . . plagued by a higher degree of lawlessness and corruption than any other area of law enforcement."[78]

Vice prohibitions not only undermine the integrity of police forces, they also put officers' lives at high risk. As vice transactions involve two volunteers, the main tools the police will have to enforce prohibitions are to engage in surveillance and to set up undercover buys or sales, conducted either by police or informers. Vice officers have to operate in a criminalized and well-armed sector and in a manner that will not reveal their identities as officers. This is a recipe for danger, and tragically, one that has led to many officer injuries and deaths; in recent years, on the order of one officer per month in the United States loses his or her life in a manner connected with drug prohibition. Alcohol

[74] See Barnett (1987, pp. 90–7) and Barnett (1994, pp. 2596–7).
[75] McNamara (2000, p. 125).
[76] See, e.g. Dershowitz (1994, pp. 233–6) and Kaplan (1983, pp. 96–7). Also on police perjury and vice prohibitions, see Simon and Burns (1997, pp. 168). On page 330, the same source notes: "A day in Western District courtroom saw enough perjury to make any lawyer think twice about asking anyone in a police uniform to take the oath."
[77] This inference can be drawn from various sources, including the *Knapp Commission Report on Police Corruption* (1973) and the Mollen Commission. See also Gray (1998, pp. 36–7).
[78] Blumenson and Nilsen (1998, p. 99, footnote with references omitted).

Prohibition faced an analogous problem: during its first decade, fifty-seven federal Prohibition agents were killed in the line of duty.[79] Vice enforcement also results in the death of civilians, both those engaging in vice crimes and nonparticipants: alcohol Prohibition's first ten years saw 144 civilians killed or fatally injured by Prohibition officers.[80]

The victimless nature of much drug-related crime means that the best evidence against a drug defendant will be the seized contraband. (Informants can be helpful, but they are problematic witnesses, as their testimony generally can be impugned by the fact that they are mired in illegal activities themselves and are receiving some benefit to induce their cooperation.) But small amounts of drugs often can be dumped or destroyed by those who anticipate a police search. As a result, anticipation must be kept to a minimum. Searches without probable cause, as noted, are one expedient. A second tactic is the "no-knock" raid, where, after obtaining the requisite type of search warrant, officers enter a home unannounced, to minimize the time available for a suspect to destroy the key evidence. Unfortunately, such raids are quite dangerous, both to the police and to residents. How would you react if suddenly, early in the morning, a group of armed men burst through your door? Nor do the police always break into the "right" house; even when police have the correct address, the intelligence that provided the search warrant necessary for the no-knock raid might be faulty. Horror stories of innocent (and not so innocent) citizens terrorized in such raids abound.[81]

In vice-heavy areas, drug prohibition not only undermines integrity and endangers police enforcers, but the negative effects also seem to seep out to other areas of policing. One source that provides deep insight into how drug prohibition affects policing is *The Corner: A Year in the Life of an Inner-City Neighborhood*, by David Simon and Edward Burns. *The Corner* follows activity around Fayette and Monroe, a drug-selling street corner in West Baltimore; one of the authors, Burns, is a former Baltimore police detective:

> ...on Fayette Street and a hundred other corners like it, there is nothing for a patrolman or plainsclothesman that is as easy, as guaranteed, and as profitable as a street-level drug arrest. With minimal probable cause, or none at all, any cop can ride into the circus tent, jack up a tout or a runner, grab a vial or two, and be assured of making that good overtime pay up at Wabash [the district courthouse]. In Baltimore, a cop doesn't even need to come up with a vial. He can simply charge a suspect with loitering in a drug-free zone, a city statute of improbable constitutionality that has exempted a good third of the inner city

[79] The Wickersham Report (1931; vol. 1, p. 152); the precise dates for which the figure (of fifty-seven agents killed in the line duty) was derived are January 16, 1920, to October 17, 1929.

[80] The Wickersham Report (1931; vol. 1, p. 169); the precise dates for which the figure of civilian deaths was derived are January 16, 1920, to October 14, 1929.

[81] See the compilation of Drug War Victims at http://blogs.salon.com/0002762/stories/2003/08/17/drugWarVictims.html (accessed November 8, 2003).

from the usual constraints of probable cause. In Baltimore if a man is standing in the 1800 block of Fayette Street – even if he lives in the 1800 block of Fayette Street – he is fodder for a street arrest.

As a result, police work in inner city Baltimore has been reduced to fish-in-a-barrel tactics, with the result that a generation of young officers has failed to learn investigation or procedure. Why bother to master the intricacies of probable cause when an anti-loitering law allows you to go into anyone's pockets? Why become adept at covert surveillance when you can just go down to any corner, line them up against the liquor store, and search to your heart's content? Why learn how to use, and not be used by, informants when information is so unnecessary to a street-level arrest? Why learn how to write a proper search warrant when you can make your court pay on the street, without ever having to worry about whether you're kicking in the right door? ...

Not surprisingly, as street-level drug arrests began to rise with the cocaine epidemic of the late 1980s, all other indicators of quality police work – and of a city's livability – began to fall in Baltimore.[82]

There's a sad irony that among the most prominent victims of drug prohibition are inner-city youths and police.[83] Prohibition makes it illegal to traffic in a commodity that many people want to consume. Then, a black market develops, primarily in neighborhoods where schools are low-quality and legal earning prospects are poor. The black markets are policed intermittently, and any young men who are arrested for selling the verboten commodity are labeled as "drug pushers"; they are sent to jail for a long term. Prohibition simultaneously sets up ongoing integrity tests for the police, too. Antidrug officers learn that their own efforts will not alter much of anything, that people will still buy and sell drugs irrespective of police efforts, and that the drug use in and of itself only directly harms the user. The officers also see that they can earn a lot of money by looking away at the appropriate times. Some of them do look away, and some of them get caught, and they are labeled "corrupt cops," and shipped off to prison, too. Meanwhile, the police, the drug sellers, and others in the neighborhood are subject to the lethal violence that frequently is employed to settle disputes in underground markets.

PROHIBITION AND INDIVIDUAL RIGHTS

Effectively enforcing a prohibition against drug possession demands tactics that put pressure on constitutional guarantees of freedom from unreasonable search and seizure. Even such questionable tactics often do not demonstrate effectiveness, creating renewed pressure for stricter legal measures that will

[82] Simon and Burns (1997, pp. 167–8).
[83] This paragraph and the next are drawn from my guest post, "Attractive Nuisance and Drug Laws," at the blog Overlawyered, July 24, 2004, http://www.overlawyered.com/2004/07/attractive_nuisance_and_drug_l.html (accessed March 4, 2007).

increase deterrence. For instance, drug sales are hard to prove in court – another consequence of the lack of a complaining witness. As a result, many drug sales charges result in convictions for drug possession under plea bargains. Substantial mandatory minimum sentences have been enacted, precluding judicial discretion in sentencing. The mandatory sentences are then used as a tool by prosecutors to provide incentives for the plea bargain, or to induce reluctant testimony by drug defendants against others involved in the trade. (Although judges can be constrained by the mandatory sentencing rules, prosecutors can still seek leniency for those who provide substantial assistance to cases against others charged with drug crimes.)

The sheer numbers of drug cases also induce prosecutors to employ significant amounts of plea bargaining, in a situation redolent of the years of alcohol prohibition. In 2001, there were over 32,000 new federal prosecutions for drug-related crimes, more than one-third of the overall caseload. The next largest category of federal defendants were the approximately 16,000 people charged with immigration crimes.[84]

Much of the war on drugs is fought on the nation's highways. Police commonly stop cars under some pretext, and then question the driver and visually scan the inside of the car, using a flashlight if it is nighttime. They might ask the driver and passengers to step out of the car. If they see something that they believe provides probable cause for a search, they may proceed to search the vehicle. If they have no grounds to establish probable cause, the police might request permission from the driver to search the car. The overwhelming number of drivers agree to this request for a warrantless search, many when they are carrying contraband! It seems that the circumstances make it difficult for motorists to say no – they might not even realize that the officer's request can be refused – or they might suspect, rightly, that refusal will be far from the end of the encounter.[85] A common police tactic for those who decline a consent search is to bring in a trained dog to sniff around, on, and under the car, as such intrusions currently do not require probable cause or a warrant. If the dog "alerts," that typically is taken as providing probable cause to conduct a search, even though the dogs (or their trainers and handlers) are frequently mistaken.[86] The Supreme Court has found the use of pretextual stops, visual scans, dogs, and "profiles" of likely drug carriers to be consistent with the Fourth Amendment, which guarantees the rights of individuals to be free of unreasonable searches and seizures. "It is no exaggeration to say that one of our most basic, traditional rules concerning police power – that police must have probable cause or reasonable suspicion of criminal activity in order to search

[84] See the TRAC Reports at http://trac.syr.edu/tracreports/crim/136/. By 2005, immigration cases exceeded drug cases, though there were still more than 30,000 federal drug prosecutions annually.
[85] On the extent to which ostensibly consensual searches can actually be perceived as coercive, see Nadler (2003).
[86] Bird (1996/1997).

or seize – has almost no application to citizens driving or riding in cars."[87] And for this erosion of constitutional rights, drug prohibition is largely to blame.

Drug-law enforcement has a hugely disparate impact on racial minorities, who use illegal drugs at about the same rate as whites. According to the Substance Abuse and Mental Health Services Administration, in 2005, the percentage of the U.S. adult population that had engaged in any illegal drug use over their lifetime was about 51 percent for whites, 47 percent for blacks, and 39 percent for Hispanics.[88] Nevertheless, the overwhelming majority of federal drug defendants are minorities, and the same is true in many state and municipal judicial systems, too. Writing in 1999 for the American Civil Liberties Union, law professor David Harris noted that: "Today, blacks constitute 13 percent of the country's drug users; 37 percent of those arrested on drug charges; 55 percent of those convicted; and 74 percent of all drug offenders sentenced to prison."[89] Traffic stops motivated by drug enforcement show similar imbalances. On I–95 in Maryland, drivers violating traffic laws were 74.7 percent white and 17.5 percent black, according to a survey conducted in mid-1996. Drivers who were stopped and searched on a corridor of I-95 north of Baltimore, however, between 1995 and mid-2000, were 59.7 percent black, though the searches of whites had a slightly greater incidence of yielding drugs than did the searches of blacks.[90]

CIVIL FORFEITURE

The Fourth Amendment is but one element of the Bill of Rights that has been attenuated by the war on drugs. The Fifth Amendment, which prohibits the government taking of property without due process of law, is another. Suspected drug offenders can be punished without going to the trouble of proving them guilty beyond a reasonable doubt before a jury of their peers. "Civil forfeiture" is the name of the legal process that has allowed this end run around the presumption of innocence. By instituting a civil as opposed to a criminal proceeding, the usual protections of criminal law, such as the right to avoid self-incrimination and the right to a lawyer, can be sidestepped.

The federal asset forfeiture system circa 1970–2000 worked something like this.[91] If "probable cause" could plausibly be asserted, the government could seize private property, such as homes, cash, or automobiles, that it claimed had been used or were intended to be used in a drug crime. These seizures could take place before any trial or conviction, or even without charges being filed. The dispossessed owner could then challenge the seizure in a court procedure. If he

---

[87] Harris (1998, p. 557, internal footnote omitted).

[88] See Table G.13 in Substance Abuse and Mental Health Services Administration (2006).

[89] Harris (1999, p. 7).   [90] Gross and Barnes (2002).

[91] Assets can also be forfeited through criminal convictions, of course. On the workings of civil asset forfeiture, see Blumenson and Nilsen (1998); Johnson (2001/2002); and Duffy (2001).

could show by a preponderance of the evidence that the government was wrong, he would get back his property, though often at substantial cost. The asset forfeiture tactic resulted in many homes and thousands of autos being seized because the owners (or others) allegedly used them to buy or sell small quantities of drugs.[92] These assets (or their value) were then made available to the law enforcers, creating an incentive to deploy police resources not where they were most needed but to where they would prove most lucrative.[93] Rather than seizing drugs before they are sold, for instance, forfeiture encourages police to seize the money received by sellers after the drug sales happen – the police force legally can keep most of the money, but none of the drugs. The incentive to plant a small amount of a drug to facilitate a forfeiture is also manifest.

Many completely innocent citizens have been victimized by asset forfeiture. Probable cause generally can be "established" with quite minimal evidence, such as a single tip from an anonymous informant. Or, an owner of an apartment building might forfeit the building if, unknown to the owner, one of the tenants is conducting drug sales. In fact, in most drug-law related asset forfeitures, no criminal charges are ever filed.[94] Yale Law Professor Steven Duke has identified a further impact of forfeiture laws:

> The forfeiture provisions are not only horribly unjust, they inflict great damage upon our inner cities. They encourage drug dealers and even drug users to invade the property of strangers rather than conducting their activities on their own premises, thus increasing the hazards of property ownership in poor neighborhoods, where owners can quickly lose everything to forfeiture. Bankers have few incentives to lend money on such property, for the bank itself can lose its security interest if forfeiture occurs.[95]

The federal civil asset forfeiture system was reformed in 2000.[96] When private residences are at issue, indigent defendants must be provided counsel, just as is required for criminal proceedings. The standard of proof that the government must meet to seize private assets has been raised, from "probable cause" to "a preponderance of the evidence." And the protections for innocent owners have been bolstered. The distribution of forfeited assets to police forces and the resulting distortions on the incentives of enforcers have not been altered, however. Whether the reforms will make for a fundamental shift toward a more just system remains to be seen.[97]

State and local government law enforcers also employ various types of asset forfeiture schemes. Not only drug crimes, but other vice-related offenses,

---

[92] Duke (2000, pp. 54ff.).   [93] Blumenson and Nilsen (1998).

[94] Duke (2000, p. 52).   [95] Duke (2000, p. 56).

[96] The discussion of the reformed civil asset forfeiture system is drawn from Johnson (2001/2002).

[97] Johnson (2001/2002) identifies three problems of the old system that are not solved by the reforms, including the inability of innocent heirs, spouses, and minor children to protect property transferred to them by an alleged drug malfeasor.

particularly prostitution, drunk driving, and gambling violations, can trigger the seizure (often before any finding of guilt) of cars, homes, money, and other property. The same sorts of incentives to skew law enforcement that exist at the federal level are reproduced by these statutes, too. Some states have responded with laws ensuring that seized assets are not transferred to the law enforcement agency. In the case of drugs, however, these restrictions can be avoided: by bringing federal agents in on a bust, federal asset seizure laws can be triggered, with the proceeds then shared with the state and local law enforcers. This sharing takes place even if state rules preclude law enforcement agencies from benefitting directly from seized assets. The federal rules permitting such transfers imply that states do not have budgetary control over their own law enforcement agencies.

To recapitulate, the policy dynamics within drug prohibition seem to work as follows: the dearth of victims or complaining witnesses necessitates questionable and sometimes illegal police tactics, as well as corruption. The continued failure of prohibition to display visible effectiveness in terms of reduced drug use leads to tougher sentencing provisions. The longer sentences interact with police and prosecutorial tactics, inducing informant testimony and plea bargains. Continued lack of success with ending drug use then leads to further legal changes to give the enforcement officials more tools (such as "drug free zones" or civil asset forfeiture), simultaneously emitting pressure for the slackening of constitutional protections against government intrusions. Where does this process stop? Here is a summary of the prohibitory dynamic, from *The Corner*:

> But these successes [in the drug war] aren't nearly enough, and when the rules of engagement get in the way of lasting victory, we simply change the rules, creating new tracts of federal statute, establishing strict mandatory punishments and unforgiving guidelines for sentencing, granting so much raw punitive power to U.S. prosecutors that federal judges around the country are left to grumble in legal journals about draconian and immoral sentencing laws. It used to be said that only in a police state could police work be made easy; yet for the sake of this war, we've gutted the Fourth Amendment, allowing race-based profiling and stop-and-frisk police tactics based on the most minimal probable cause. We've created civil forfeiture statutes that make it a game for government to take what it wants – houses, boats, planes, cars, cash – from anyone it targets without the necessity of criminal conviction. We've made mandatory drug testing a prerogative not only of parole and prohibition agents, but of any private employer in the nation. Most dramatic of all, perhaps, we have continued to escalate this war of occupation in our inner cities until more than half of the adult black male population in places like Baltimore are now, in some way, under the supervision of the criminal justice system.[98]

---

[98] Simon and Burns (1997, p. 475).

Box 4.4: *One forfeiture-related horror story*[a]

On October 2, 1992, at 8:35 in the morning, thirty law enforcement officers descended upon the home of Donald Scott on his 200-acre ranch in Malibu, California. The officers had obtained a search warrant based upon some evidence – extremely limited, contradictory, and misleading evidence, as it turned out – that marijuana was being cultivated on Scott's property. Scott and his wife were slow to the door, which was then broken open by the officers, who earlier had cut the padlock on the front gate to the property. Scott was holding a handgun when he met two officers. He was fired upon and killed. No marijuana was found under cultivation on his property, nor were any signs of cultivation (irrigation channels, marijuana stems and seeds) uncovered.

What prompted this rather massive effort to search the Scott ranch? (The ranch was subjected to earlier aerial surveillance, as well as other ground-based searches.) According to the Office of the District Attorney of Ventura County (where the ranch was located), the potential for the valuable ranch to be seized in the event of marijuana cultivation was part of the motivation for the raid. A property appraisal statement had been distributed to officers at an earlier briefing, along with the recent sale price of nearby property.

---

[a] Information on the Scott case comes from the "Report on the Death of Donald Scott," issued by the Ventura County, California, Office of the District Attorney, March 30, 1993 (www.fear.org/chron/scott.txt), and a related memo from the Deputy District Attorney, March 31, 1993 (www.fear.org/chron/denoce.txt).

THE BUDGETARY COSTS OF DRUG PROHIBITION

Negative impacts on police, policing, inner-city youths, and individual rights, are among the worst consequences of U.S. drug prohibition. But there are also direct monetary costs associated with criminalizing drugs. Drug squads, court time, interdiction efforts, and prison cells – all require expenditures, the majority of which would not be needed under most legal drug control regimes. (Legalization would entail new costs for such features as inspectors and tax collectors, however, as is now the case for alcohol and tobacco control.)

What are the budgetary costs of drug prohibition? This question is surprisingly difficult to answer, or at least interpreting any suggested answer requires some care. One issue is comparative: with what sort of regime is prohibition being compared? If the alternative to prohibition is government manufacture and subsidized monopoly distribution of drugs, then prohibition is likely to be less of a burden on the public fisc than nonprohibition. Second, there is no single "budget line" in federal or state budgets that encompasses anti-drug spending.

Total drug-related government spending goes well beyond enforcing prohibition, of course. In particular, public funds are aimed at prevention – such as anti-drug advertising campaigns – and at treatment for drug abusers, while research into treatment and prevention is publicly funded, too. The White House publishes a partial drug budget summary each year in which federal expenditures are delineated into prevention, treatment, and enforcement functions.[99] A supplementary delineation is into supply and demand-side programs, where antidrug enforcement is the chief supply-side measure. Expenditures for supply-side policies generally would not be incurred under any legalization alternative.

According to the White House summary, recommended federal funding for fiscal year 2007 comes to $12.7 billion, with more than 64 percent aimed at the supply side. (Surprisingly, supply-side policies seem to dominate drug policy budgets in Western Europe as well, even in the Netherlands.[100]) Costs of prosecuting and incarcerating federal drug offenders, however, are not included in the published figures. Boyum and Reuter (2005, p. 51) suggest that the annual cost for incarcerating the 70,000 federal drug law inmates in 2002 came to about $2.5 billion dollars: the majority of federal inmates are imprisoned for drug offenses. Miron (2003, p. 10) puts total U.S. federal supply-side antidrug expenditures at $13.6 billion for 2002.

State and local drug prohibition enforcement expenditures are harder still to estimate, but generally they are thought to exceed federal expenditures. State prison drug-law inmates outnumber federal inmates by more than 3-to-1.[101] Miron (2003, p. 12) places overall (federal, state, and local) drug enforcement expenditures, circa 2002, at about $33 billion, a figure that is in-line with other, independent estimates.[102] So drug prohibition spending costs each American citizen more than $100 annually.

Is $100 per year per citizen a lot of money or a little bit of money? If it is a lot, then on that basis alone, the war on drugs could violate robustness, by imposing too heavily upon all citizens, consumers, and nonconsumers alike. Although I think that most of our drug enforcement spending is unwise, I do not think that the amount of spending is itself to blame. Indeed, if drug prohibition is otherwise sensible, then even $200 or $300 per citizen per year ($60 or $90 billion overall) might be money well-spent. Relative to overall government spending, antidrug enforcement is not a major item. Annual U.S. federal government spending exceeds $2.7 trillion, while state and local spending exceeds $2.2 trillion; even $100 billion of drug enforcement expenditures would amount to less than 2.5 percent of overall government spending.[103] Current drug war spending, it seems to me, likewise is a minor concern when compared with

[99] The proposed budget for fiscal 2007 can be found at http://www.whitehousedrugpolicy.gov/publications/policy/07budget/budget07.pdf (accessed on November 25, 2006).
[100] Reuter (2006).   [101] See Boyum and Reuter (2005, pp. 51–5).
[102] *Informing America's Policy on Illegal Drugs: What We Don't Know Keeps Hurting Us* (2001, p. 1) reports that combined annual expenditures on drug enforcement from all jurisdictional levels came to more than $30 billion during the 1990s.
[103] See Table S-1 in the fiscal year 2007 federal budget, at http://www.gpoaccess.gov/usbudget/fy07/pdf/budget/tables.pdf (accessed November 25, 2006).

the nonbudgetary costs of prohibition, including the lives lost in drug-related violence or squandered in prison, and the civil liberties surrendered.

Although enforcement spending does not determine the overall desirability of the war on drugs, it does point to the scale of resources that would be released through drug legalization. These resources could then be put to use into establishing a regulatory apparatus for the legal distribution of drugs, and they could buy a gold-plated regulatory structure. Instead of $30 billion annually, the Occupational Safety and Health Administration, for instance, makes do on less than half a billion dollars per year, which itself is some five times the budget of the National Transportation Safety Board.

ZERO TOLERANCE[104]

The ineffectiveness of traditional policing methods in adequately controlling drug and other vice crimes has spurred the widespread adoption of "zero tolerance" policies. Although there is no precise definition of what constitutes a zero tolerance policy, legal regimes adopted in the name of zero tolerance tend to display certain common features. These features are consistent with the usual connotation of "zero tolerance," that of unbending rigor.

Regulatory regimes can be characterized by the standards of behavior that they call for, the nature and extent of enforcement of those standards, and the punishments imposed on those violators who are identified and apprehended.[105] Zero tolerance policies ratchet up strictness in all three dimensions: standards are raised, so behavior that was not transgressive before becomes redefined as an offense; more police officers or other enforcement resources are deployed to raise the probability that offenders are caught; and jail sentences, fines, or other punishments are enhanced. More cops and stiffer penalties are familiar components of any crackdown. The broadening of what constitutes an offense, however, is somewhat more surprising, though we have already seen one example in arrests for loitering in "drug-free zones." Schools seem particularly prone to designate offenses broadly when they adopt zero tolerance policies: aspirin becomes a forbidden drug, or a key chain becomes a weapon.

Zero tolerance was born of vice policy: the term seems to date from the early 1980s, when the U.S. Navy was looking to control drug use among its sailors. The National Drug Policy Board adopted a Zero Tolerance Program in 1988, which led to such measures as the seizure of a $2.5 million yacht because less than one-tenth of an ounce of marijuana was found on board.[106]

Zero tolerance policies are designed to work by increasing deterrence. If people know that impeccable behavior is expected, that failure to meet high

---

[104] This section is based upon chapter 3 ("Zero Tolerance") in Leitzel (2003).

[105] See Bardach (1989).

[106] Fred Strasser and Marcia Coyle, "Defendants Have Zero Tolerance for Forfeitures," *National Law Journal*, May 23, 1988. The yacht was later returned to its owner.

standards is likely to result in apprehension, and that the penalties imposed on violators are significant, then they will adjust their behavior to conform to the standards. Or at least that is the theory.

The problem is that the theory of zero tolerance is internally inconsistent for most adult, vice-related offenses. For the deterrence to work, you have to make it clear that you will actually be able to catch offenders and that you will be willing to punish them according to the zero tolerance standards. In other words, the threatened punishments must be credible. But for vice offenses, both the ability to uncover and the willingness to punish are hard to establish. Indeed, the "victimless" nature of vice crime undermines both components of credibility. The crimes are difficult to detect, and the willingness to impose harsh sentences for behavior that directly harms no one is frequently tepid or absent, despite the fiery rhetoric.

As a result, the adoption of a zero tolerance policy often sets a trap for enforcers. To try to establish credibility, they indulge in public proclamations of their commitment to the new policy. Then some minor or inadvertent "violation" comes to light, and the authorities can either destroy the hard-gained credibility of the policy by not implementing it or look foolish by harshly punishing some minor violation or even a clearly beneficial act. And the ridicule that attends meting out grossly disproportionate penalties itself harms the legitimacy of the enforcers and the credibility of the policy. Even when zero tolerance policies can be imposed with a strong dose of credibility – for instance, if mandatory drug testing is sure to uncover any violations – the credibility can come with a heavy price attached. You must still occasionally harshly punish people who haven't done much of anything wrong, and furthermore, you might induce behaviors that are even worse. Provoking marijuana smokers to switch to alcohol (or hallucinogens) to pass mandatory drug tests is probably not an improvement. Even when few people are punished, the price of a zero tolerance policy might be severe. Imagine a credible zero tolerance policy against speeding, tailgating, or changing lanes without signaling while driving. The entire driving experience would be incredibly nerve-racking; even well-intentioned people would have to watch over their every move with such assiduous care that their quality of life would be undermined. But to some extent this is what we have done to many teenagers, who have to ensure that they don't have an aspirin on hand, don't forget to wear their belt, don't forget one thousand other things that might trigger a zero tolerance "violation" and school suspension.

Zero tolerance reduces the discretion of enforcers: offenses that come to light under a zero tolerance regime have to be punished to the letter of the law. The lack of discretion frequently is viewed by enforcers as a benefit of the policy because the application of discretion undermines credibility and deterrence. Making the punishment automatic should reduce special pleading – what is the point of arguing with a machine? But the harsh penalties for minor crimes associated with zero tolerance often lead to significant lobbying as discretion, at some level, is almost always available. The unjust treatment of school kids caught in the vise of zero tolerance frequently prompts pressure campaigns by their parents and friends for some rationality in the disposition of their cases.

The discretion that necessarily remains under a zero tolerance regime can be exercised in a hidden way. Given a broad zero tolerance policy against drugs at school, teachers might choose not to notice the aspirin that falls out of the purse of an honor student. Even worse, hidden discretion can be used by enforcers to discriminate in socially undesirable ways, on the basis of race, for instance, and there is evidence that suspensions and expulsions under zero tolerance policies in U.S. schools are employed more aggressively against African American students. All enforcement regimes present opportunities for abusive discrimination, of course. What zero tolerance adds to the mix is enforcement against minor infractions that under standard disciplinary approaches might be entirely overlooked. Further, the heightened punishments attached to minor infractions increase the consequences of discriminatory enforcement.

The popularity of zero tolerance policies with respect to drug crimes is not that surprising, given the widespread moral condemnation of drugs. Once you define a commodity to be evil, there is no obvious constraint on measures that should be taken to combat consumption of the commodity. You will put people who use the commodity for their own pleasure in prison. You will make it illegal to manufacture paraphernalia that might be used in combination with the reviled commodity. You will force people to take tests revealing whether someone has used the commodity. You will put people in prison who distribute materials that can be used to confound your tests. You will withhold the commodity even from deathly ill people who find medical comfort from consumption of the commodity; indeed, you will put them in prison if they persist in seeking such illicit comfort. So the "raised" standards, expanded enforcement, and tougher penalties associated with zero tolerance policies begin to look natural, even desirable, when you are fighting an evil commodity.

THE BIRTH AND UNLAMENTED DEMISE OF ONE VICE PROHIBITION: THE MANN ACT[107]

In a tragedy of enormous proportions, the United States in the early years of the twentieth Century was at the mercy of organized gangs of "white slavers," men who would buy or kidnap, sell, and transport women for the purpose of coerced prostitution. No woman, married or unmarried, respectable or tawdry, was safe from the clutches of the traffickers in white slaves. Any civilized society would need to respond to such a fateful development, and the U.S. Congress

---

[107] This section relies very heavily on an excellent book by David Langum (1994), *Crossing over the Line: Legislating Morality and the Mann Act.*

Box 4.5: *Zero tolerance in Renaissance Vienna*

No more evasion.
– Shakespeare, *Measure for Measure*[a]

Although the "zero tolerance" label is of recent vintage, the sort of crackdowns that are adopted under this rubric have a long provenance. One early fictional account is provided, with characteristic insight, by William Shakespeare. In *Measure for Measure*, Shakespeare describes a zero tolerance policy adopted to combat vice in Renaissance Vienna. Shakespeare's drama develops around the same inherent contradiction that causes modern zero tolerance policies to beget controversy: the credibility necessary for zero tolerance to succeed is itself undermined by the implementation of the policy.

THE VIENNESE INCIDENT

The Duke of Vienna is reputed wise but lenient. The Duke's indulgence emasculates the strict laws governing vice in Vienna; debauchery runs rampant. As *Measure for Measure* opens, the Duke suddenly departs Vienna on a long, mysterious journey.

Angelo, a courtier, fills the Duke's place during the Duke's absence. Angelo is described as "a man whose blood / Is very snow-broth; one who never feels / The wanton stings and motions of the sense / But doth rebate and blunt his natural edge / With profits of mind, study and fast."[b] The puritanical Angelo dusts off statutes that had long been dormant, reinstituting enforcement of the harsh vice laws. Brothels are closed and bawds harassed, though those cases that fall to Angelo's assistant, Escalus, are still treated rather mercifully.

Mercy is not on offer for one unfortunate offender brought before Angelo. The gentleman Claudio is arrested for fornication, ostensibly a capital crime. Claudio's guilt is admitted and beyond question: his lover Juliet is obviously pregnant. The offense is only a technical one, however, in that Claudio and Juliet are engaged to be married; the official wedding ceremony merely had been postponed until a more propitious time was found to procure the dowry.

In the old regime, under the Duke, there would have been no penalty for this slight indiscretion. Far more egregious cases of fornication would have gone unpunished: "Ere he [the Duke] would have hanged a man for the getting a hundred bastards, he would have paid for the nursing a thousand."[c] But Angelo is determined to provide a warning to others, parading the arrested Claudio through the streets of Vienna before following the letter of the law by imposing the death penalty. Public opinion favors leniency for Claudio: "if myself might be his judge / He should receive his punishment in thanks,"[d] notes one observer. Claudio's sister, Isabella, a devout young woman on the verge of becoming a nun, regards her brother's fornication as a profound moral matter, though not a grievous offense – it could be remedied by a formal marriage. But Angelo refuses to "make a scarecrow of the law,"[e] and follows "close the rigour of the statute / To make him [Claudio] an example."[f]

(continued)

Box 4.5 *(continued)*

THE TRADE-OFFS INHERENT IN ZERO TOLERANCE

Angelo intends to alter the established course of justice by strictly enforcing the formal rules, but his zero tolerance policy fails to distinguish between relatively inconsequential offenses and more weighty infractions. Thus Claudio, honorable but perhaps o'erhasty, is treated as the most notorious of lechers. Claudio's case parallels typical modern-day zero tolerance horror stories, the good student suspended or expelled for some technical violation of the rules.[g]

The Viennese crackdown, again like many current variants, is aimed at relatively minor (and victimless) crimes that have become widespread and, to some extent, tolerated. At the time of the Duke's departure, there had been more than a decade of neglect of Vienna's antifornication laws. (Extremely serious crimes like murder are not the stuff of zero tolerance because statutes against serious crimes are not neglected.) Why suddenly enforce laws against minor crimes? The usual concern is that a lack of enforcement will lead, or, perhaps, already has led, to more and more offenses, until the situation becomes intolerable. In the case of lechery in Vienna, a friar notes, "It is too general a vice, and severity must cure it."[h] Zero tolerance policies don't claim that the punishment for a given offense provides justice in an isolated sense but, rather, that severe sanctions are needed to deter, to stem future offenses. Angelo cites the previous cascading of offenses in answering Isabella's plea for mercy: "Those many had not dar'd to do that evil / If the first that did th' edict infringe / Had answer'd for his deed."[i]

Zero tolerance policies can work well if their adoption actually deters most of the specified offenses and thereby prevents a spiral of violations. But if violations continue at a considerable level despite a zero tolerance policy, the social costs of the policy become enormous. The enhanced penalties for minor crimes increase the expense of adjudicating cases and punishing offenders, while courts and prisons become jammed. Even worse, if the infractions are relatively minor – like Claudio's – those jamming the courts and prisons are paying too heavy a price for their indiscretions.

The greater the belief among potential malefactors that the crackdown will indeed be implemented – that the authorities have both the capability and the intention to enforce stringently – the more successful a zero tolerance campaign will be. So enforcers take pains to market their new toughness, to make it clear that they mean business. By staking their reputations, enforcers like Angelo then have little choice but to actually follow through on the threatened punishments. Angelo argues to Isabella that his hands are tied, that he has no discretion, that even his own relatives would be punished so: "It is the law, not I condemn your brother."[j] But of course, it is not true that Angelo has no discretion, so Isabella's lobbying is not the equivalent of arguing with a machine.

The commitment to the rule creates a trap for enforcement authorities, who can neither punish nor excuse without serious consequences when faced with an inconsequential or inadvertent violation. And inconsequential violations of vice crimes are almost certain to arise: one character in *Measure for Measure*, speaking to a holy man, notes that lechery "is well allied; but it is impossible to extirp it quite, friar, till eating and drinking be put down."[k] (He also points to the stress zero tolerance brings even to those who are well intentioned, suggesting that he will have to avoid good food and drink, for sensual meals would induce his own lechery.)

So zero tolerance policies generally cannot eliminate offenses. Even worse, the similarity in penalties for minor and more serious offenses that accompanies zero tolerance reduces the incentive for offenders to temper the severity of their violations. Why not escalate the hallway shoving match into a full-fledged fight, if the first push merits the maximum punishment? Macbeth (OK, different play) understood that his previous ignoble deeds made it just as easy to continue in evil as to seek redemption, that he was "in blood / Stepp'd in so far, that, should [he] wade no more, / Returning were as tedious as go o'er."[l]

THE VIENNESE TWIST

So how does Shakespeare's zero tolerance policy end? The Duke's return to Vienna is almost as sudden as his departure. Isabella approaches the Duke, accusing Angelo of corruption and, more to the purpose, fornication! Isabella claims that Angelo agreed to pardon her brother Claudio if she yielded to Angelo's desires but that after she had performed her part of the bargain, Angelo reneged and had Claudio executed anyway.

Isabella's tale eventually leads to the emergence of the truth, which is more complicated still. Angelo proposed the bribe, and Isabella agreed – talk about hidden discretion by enforcers. The actual assignation, however, was conducted between an unsuspecting Angelo and another woman, Mariana, who had at one time been betrothed to Angelo. The fornication of Angelo, therefore, is in some respects parallel to that of Claudio.

There are further developments. First, Claudio had not been executed. The severed head previously presented to Angelo as evidence of execution was that of another prisoner who conveniently died of natural causes. Second, the substitution of Mariana for Isabella, as well as the prevention of Claudio's execution, had actually been directed by the supposedly absent Duke. In fact, the Duke had never even left Vienna. He had disguised himself as a friar and stage-managed the actions following Angelo's solicitation of a bribe from Isabella. Angelo's execution is rescinded, Angelo and Mariana are married, Claudio and Juliet likewise are headed for the altar – and the Duke hopes to persuade Isabella to forgo the nunnery and become his wife.

What prompted the Duke to act in so strange a manner? He recognizes that his failure to punish vice in the past was virtually equivalent to persuading his citizens to undertake vice offenses. "Sith 'twas my fault to give the people scope, / 'Twould be my tyranny to strike and gall them / For what I bid them do: for we bid this be done, / When evil deeds have their permissive pass, / And not the punishment."[m] The Duke somehow convinces himself that it would not be tyrannical to let his deputy punish evil in his stead. And in this belief, he might be right. The Duke's adoption of a zero tolerance policy would lack credibility, given his reputation for discretion and leniency, and credibility is necessary for such policies to succeed. A zero tolerance policy adopted by Angelo, whose own reputation is of a puritanical rigidity, would carry instant credibility. Nevertheless, Angelo's implementation of the crackdown is misguided. Even if a zero tolerance policy would restore morality to Vienna, the retroactive (and necessarily partial) imposition of the policy, for past offenses, is an injustice, and one that almost costs Claudio his life. Only the behind-the-scenes activity of the disguised Duke prevents the execution of someone who, at worst, is a minor transgressor.

Shakespeare's *Measure for Measure* reminds us that there are degrees of offending. A zero tolerance policy that eliminates discretion in enforcement is bound to catch up some offenders whose culpability is negligible. The problem will be magnified if the proscribed behavior is defined expansively: if forbidden drugs include aspirin, or if fornication includes all out-of-wedlock sexual relations. This is the source of the contradiction inherent in a zero tolerance policy: to be successful, to deter violations, the threat to punish all offenders must be credible. But when a minor or inadvertent offender is faced with a large, obviously disproportionate punishment, the enforcement regime will be perceived as unfair, and pressure rightly will be applied to soften the prescribed punishment. That is, the actual application of a zero tolerance policy tends to undermine the credibility that is necessary for the policy to be successful in the first place.

---

^a I. i. 50. The citations are to the Arden edition (Third Series) of *Measure for Measure*, Thomas Nelson & Sons Ltd., Walton-on Thames, 1998.

^b I. iv. 57.   ^c III. ii. 113.

^d I. iv. 27.   ^e II. i. 1.

^f I. iv. 67.

^g For some of these horror stories, see www.ztnightmares.com.

^h III. ii. 96. The friar, of course, is the supposedly absent Duke, in disguise.

ⁱ II. ii. 92.   ^j II. ii. 80.

^k III. ii. 98.

^l III. iv. 135, the Arden edition (Third Series) of *Macbeth*, Routledge, London 1995.

^m I. iii. 35.

---

did. In 1910, the Mann Act, officially entitled the "White-Slave Traffic Act," became the law of the land. The Mann Act made it illegal to transport women across state lines "for the purpose of prostitution or debauchery, or for any other immoral purpose. . . ." The state-line provision was necessary because the U.S. Constitution generally provides "police powers" to the states, not the federal government. The authority of the Mann Act therefore had to be based upon the federal jurisdiction over the regulation of interstate commerce.

This aggressive legislative response quickly eliminated the organized groups involved in the coerced transportation of women for the purposes of prostitution. The only catch was that, well, there were almost no such groups to begin with. Some percentage of prostitutes in the United States at the time (as now) could reasonably be described as being involuntarily pressed into the trade, but most prostitution was willful.[108] And slavery or kidnapping were illegal even before the Mann Act was adopted.

So the Mann Act was a solution to a much exaggerated problem. It might be thought that the law would then be repealed or be quickly forgotten, a dead letter, but that turned out to be far from the case. Even though the White-Slave Traffic Act was aimed at coerced commercial sex its language was actually rather broad: "for any other immoral purpose." With so little coerced interstate commercial sex to go after, the Mann Act became a tool used to prosecute voluntary commercial sex and even voluntary noncommercial sex. A Supreme Court decision in 1917 upheld the use of the Mann Act to prosecute two married men who in the midst of affairs with young women, crossed from California into Nevada. Thus freed of the requirement that prostitution and coercion be involved, prosecutors turned their attention primarily to private relationships: between 1917 and 1928, the bulk (about 70 percent) of Mann Act prosecutions were noncommercial, unrelated to prostitution.[109] So adult men (and, to a lesser extent, women) who were voluntarily engaged in nonmarital sex began to go to prison. Rich married men who were having affairs or who could be tempted into one became targets for extortionists, and jilted spouses of adulterers could use the threat of the Mann Act to drive better divorce settlements.

Fortunately, the moral panic eventually gave way to more pressing concerns, and by the end of the 1920s, most noncommercial Mann Act prosecutions came to an end, though the statute could still be trotted out to imprison suspected malfeasors who were proving hard to convict of actual crimes or to harass troublesome types who were (otherwise) fully law abiding.[110] For instance, Charlie Chaplin's radical politics contributed to an unsuccessful Mann Act prosecution against him in 1944.

It seems that no law is so bad that it doesn't have its defenders. So the Mann Act lived on, despite its manifest infringement upon liberty and the injustice with which it was applied:

One consequence of the enactment of the Mann Act was that it acquired a real constituency. The law became a symbolic statement of the preferred norm. Church groups and moralists approved the hegemonic statement of the superiority of their own values as shown in the repression of any other.[111]

Attempts to repeal the act, or to revise it to exclude noncommercial prosecutions, were derailed by pressure from morals and religious groups. The

[108] There is some controversy over the extent of coerced prostitution. Langum's (1994, p. 35) judgment appears to me to be about right: "There was indeed *some* coerced prostitution at the time of the white slave hysteria, but very little. Nor was there any syndicate or organization." By 1922, the attorney general took the position that there had been organized prostitution, but that Mann Act enforcement had succeeded in eliminating it; Langum (1994, p. 156).
[109] Langum (1994, p. 155). [110] Langum (1994, p. 161).
[111] Langum (1994, p. 174).

offensive title of "White-Slave Traffic Act" was excised in the late 1940s, however, even as the offensive legislation itself plodded along.

A little judicial activism helped take some of the fangs out of the Mann Act – much precedent was sidestepped in 1960 when a federal judge dismissed one noncommercial prosecution. The Department of Justice soon ceased almost all prosecutions of consensual, noncommercial Mann Act violations. In 1978, the act was revised to require a commercial or criminal purpose in its section relating to minors. Finally, in 1986, further revisions decriminalized what earlier would have been Mann Act violations for situations involving private, consensual, noncommercial sex.[112] Sentiment to revive the stricter legislation seems to be negligible.

PROHIBITION AND ROBUSTNESS

The robustness principle accepts that there are rational vice consumers and in part aims to make sure that policies are not too constraining upon their self-regarding choices. For most forms of private, adult vice, then, prohibition of consumption is not an acceptable policy. Nor would be prohibitions of other elements that are nearly requisite for consumption, such as possession, but also including production and possibly sale and purchase. (For some vice goods that can rather easily be produced at home – perhaps marijuana – robustness might not necessitate legal purchase and sale.) The cost-benefit-style comparisons discussed in this chapter, looking at the consequences of prohibition versus a legalized regime, support the same conclusion in the realm of alcohol and other drugs: regulate, but do not prohibit, recreational drug use by adults.

Even if the current U.S. drug prohibitions are maintained, policy can be pushed in the direction of robustness by decreasing the penalties for possession and relying more on education and treatment. Prohibition regimes that are less punitive in this sense are common in Europe; they seem to perform no less well in terms of limiting drug use, while offering reductions in some of the social costs of drug control and drug abuse.[113] Spain, Portugal, and the Netherlands have drug problems less severe than those in the United States, even though drug possession (including possession of heroin, cocaine, and Ecstasy) for personal use is de facto decriminalized in these countries. What is the United States buying with its costly purchase of 1.5 million drug possession arrests each year?

As with drug prohibition generally, justifications for the extreme punitiveness of U.S. drug control are not exactly thick on the ground, whereas treatment

---

[112] On the fading away of the most objectionable aspects of the Mann Act, see Langum (1994, pp. 234–5, 245, 249–52, 255).

[113] This is my reading of the evidence, informed in part by MacCoun and Reuter (2001); see, e.g., their summary propositions concerning the *elimination* of criminal sanctions for drug possession on page 326.

and prevention programs are constantly evaluated. Economist and drug policy expert Peter Reuter undertook one study to look at the effects of the focus on punishment within U.S. drug policy. Reuter sums up his view of the cost-benefit analysis of the strict enforcement of criminal controls on drug supply in these terms:[114] "A policy that puts so many young, poor minority men and boys in steel cages needs a strong justification in terms of reducing cocaine and heroin use in order to justify the inequity and inhumanity. That justification has not been provided." Further, some studies suggest that in terms of reducing use in the current U.S. setting, an additional dollar spent on drug treatment is much more beneficial than one spent on enforcement of prohibition.[115] Diversion of even felony nonviolent drug offenders from prison to treatment appears to be extremely cost-effective.[116]

So there are good reasons to think that a less-punitive drug regime would offer an improvement. But the robustness principle would go further, toward legal possession of personal use quantities of drugs – including drugs like cocaine and heroin, as well as marijuana. Such a reform would be a step toward making drug policy more akin to alcohol policy under Prohibition; currently, U.S. drug prohibition is much more severe than the national alcohol Prohibition of the 1920s. Decriminalization of possession alone is not an optimal policy, nor would such a step in isolation surely represent an improvement over the status quo. But decriminalization of possession for adult personal use is a necessary component of any rational drug control regime, as well as any policy consistent with robustness.

AN INTEMPERATE CONCLUSION

Would that I could conclude vice prohibitions, especially the drug war in the United States. In this war, the negative effects have been tremendous, with little or nothing gained in the form of lessened abuse. The costs of prohibition in terms of the quality of policing and the extent of individual liberty are particularly pernicious, though much less obvious than prohibition-induced violent crime. And it is always helpful to keep in mind the less than noble purpose served by this disastrous war: a "successful" war on drugs will make it a bit harder for some of our friends and neighbors to consume a substance that they desire to consume.

The robustness principle and the admittedly rough cost-benefit-style analysis contained in this chapter argue against drug prohibition, though they might argue for very strict controls. Even without a commitment to robustness, and

---

[114] Reuter (2001, p. 23).

[115] See, e.g., Rydall and Everingham (1994). But see also Manski, Pepper, and Petrie (2001, p. 244).

[116] "Study Finds Drug Treatment Is Cost-Effective Alternative to Prison." RTI International, News Release, February 3, 2006.

even if the cost-benefit analysis tipped the other way, I would have a hard time supporting a vice prohibition. Locking someone up because they use or possess a drug is a misuse of the criminal justice system – indeed, it is itself an injustice.[117] People should only be put in prison if they have done something that harms others, or if their behavior offers a significant risk of harming others. Possessing small amounts of some substance for the purpose of personal consumption (as opposed to sale, say), does not satisfy this criterion. From this perspective, responding to the Peter Reuter quote, I don't think that any reduction in heroin or cocaine use, no matter how substantial, can in itself serve as a justification for locking drug possessors in steel cages. We might identify similar social gains from locking up all males between the ages of 16 and 35, or from imprisoning all motorcyclists, but we generally cannot use the argument that "society will improve" as a rationale for putting in prison someone who has done nothing wrong.[118] An adult using a currently illegal drug in private is doing nothing wrong, even if such use is imprudent or foolish.

Many of the supporters of vice prohibition likewise do not seem to be moved by cost-benefit style-arguments, though they end up in the opposite camp. For them, as for William Bennett, drug use is immoral, and that is a feature that trumps any demonstrated net benefits from legalization. John Stuart Mill, at the beginning of his essay *The Subjection of Women*, noted the imperviousness to reason of policies fundamentally grounded in the passions:

> So long as an opinion is strongly rooted in the feelings, it gains rather than loses in stability by having a preponderating weight of argument against it. For if it were accepted as a result of argument, the refutation of the argument might shake the solidity of the conviction; but when it rests solely on feeling, the worse it fares in argumentative contest, the more persuaded its adherents are that their feeling must have some deeper ground, which the arguments do not reach; and while the feeling remains, it is always throwing up fresh intrenchments of argument to repair any breach made in the old.[119]

In Uzbekistan, billiards are prohibited; in Turkmenistan, opera and ballet are outlawed; and rock music has been banned in more than one Muslim society.[120] We tend to smile (when we are not horrified) at these odd prohibitions – but our prohibition of small-scale drug possession is no wiser, displays no less folly. It is largely a matter of numbers. Enough people enjoy alcohol that we accept the legality of this drug, though its use comes with severe social costs. Alcohol possession is not even criminalized in dry counties in the United

---

[117] This argument, i.e., that punishing drug users is unjust, is fully developed in Douglas Husak's excellent 2002 book, *Legalize This! The Case for Decriminalizing Drugs*.

[118] I feel as if I have seen a very similar point made elsewhere, but I cannot recall where; at any rate, it closely parallels arguments in Husak (2002) and Huemer (2004).

[119] Mill in Ryan (1997, p. 133).

[120] "Officials Rail against Vice, Ban Billiards," *Chicago Tribune*, October 3, 2002, p. 6.

States, just as possession was not criminalized during national Prohibition. But if you happen to enjoy and possess marijuana or heroin instead of alcohol, we, the tippling majority, will happily put you in prison for your effrontery. (And in Turkmenistan, if you happen to enjoy opera instead of soccer, we need not respect your preference.) The majority viewpoint is buttressed by being the status quo – it somehow seems natural that alcohol is legal and heroin is illegal, though at times in the past, in the not-even-all-that-distant past, alcohol was illegal and heroin was legal.[121] So as we see another poor user arrested for heroin possession, we tend not to question the basic premise, that a free society has the right (perhaps even the obligation) to label that person a criminal. We aren't even concerned that such an arrest might be unjust or unwise, but it is both.

VICE VERDICTS (II): ASSET FORFEITURE AND CRUEL BUT USUAL PUNISHMENT

Asset Forfeiture: *Bennis v. Michigan* (1996)[122]

John Bennis was uncharacteristically late coming home from work one night. His wife, Tina Bennis, called Missing Persons. But it soon emerged that instead of driving straight home, John had visited a prostitute and engaged in some extramarital activity in the car – and he managed to get arrested for his infidelity. The state of Michigan, home of the Bennises, doesn't think too highly of prostitution, having adopted a statute that empowers the state to seize and sell cars involved in such illicit assignations. So John and Tina's car was indeed seized.

It was the "Tina's" part that caused the Bennises's case to go to the Supreme Court of the United States in 1995. The car was jointly owned: that is, Tina had a half interest in the car. She hadn't done anything wrong, and yet the state of Michigan was taking away her ownership interest, without compensation. Doesn't such a taking violate the due process clause of the Fourteenth Amendment, the takings clause of the Fifth Amendment, or just general fairness? The U.S. Supreme Court, in a 5-4 decision, said that there was no constitutional problem with the uncompensated auto forfeiture, so Tina was out her half of the car. The court didn't resolve the fairness question.[123]

---

[121] For more on why drugs remain illegal, see the Vice Squad post from February 6, 2006; see also "Why Is Marijuana Illegal?" by Pete Guither of the drug policy blog Drug WarRant, at http://marijuana. drugwarrant.com (accessed March 5, 2007).

[122] 517 U.S. 1163 (1996).

[123] The opinion of the court, however, did address the argument that the forfeiture was unfair; it claimed that such an argument "has considerable appeal" in the abstract, but a combination of lower court discretion and the fact that even Ms. Bennis recognized the right of Michigan to forfeit the car (the issue of whether she should receive compensation being the point of contention) allowed the court to uphold the forfeiture. *Bennis v. Michigan* 517 U.S. 1163 (1996).

Justice John Paul Stevens penned a dissent, joined by Justices David Souter and Stephen Breyer, that looks at the historical rationale for various types of forfeitures, arguing that the Bennis case falls outside of the tradition of legitimate forfeitures. Justice Stevens directly addressed the fairness issue: "Fundamental fairness prohibits the punishment of innocent people." He would hold the forfeiture to be invalid for being in contravention of the due process clause of the Fourteenth Amendment – a position reached, on slightly different reasoning, by Justice Kennedy, too.

Cruel but Usual Punishment: *Harmelin v. Michigan* (1991)[124]

The state of Michigan did not have a death penalty when Mr. Harmelin was convicted, which perhaps is some comfort to him. He was found guilty of a particularly grievous crime, possession of more than 650 grams of cocaine (672 grams to be exact, about a pound and a half). He was not charged with the more serious offense, possession of a similar magnitude of coke with intent to distribute – apparently proving such intent in a court of law would not have been as easy as proving mere possession. Mr. Harmelin harbored no previous felony convictions in his background. Without a prior record, it might be possible for a liberal judge to let such an offender off with a light jail sentence, or perhaps avoid jail altogether. Fortunately, the laws of Michigan required of the judge that a mandatory sentence be imposed upon Mr. Harmelin: life in prison without the possibility of parole, the severest sanction this non-capital-punishment state had on offer.

Harmelin's appeal reached the U.S. Supreme Court. He argued that the sentence violated the Eighth Amendment's protection against cruel and unusual punishments, both because the sentence was significantly disproportionate to the crime and because the mandatory nature of the sentence did not allow mitigating factors, such as being a first-time offender, to be taken into account.[125] The court ruled against Mr. Harmelin: "Severe, mandatory penalties may be cruel, but they are not unusual in the constitutional sense, having been employed in various forms throughout our Nation's history."[126] Further, "a sentence which is not otherwise cruel and unusual" doesn't become so "simply because it is 'mandatory.'"

One reason that severe punishments are not unusual in vice cases is because they have been blessed by the Supreme Court in the past. In 1992, the court upheld a sentence of forty years for possession with intent to distribute nine ounces of marijuana.[127] In 1892, the Supreme Court heard the case of a legal

---

[124] 501 U.S. 957 (1991).

[125] Recall from the Vice Verdicts section following Chapter 2 that the Eighth Amendment's protection against cruel and unusual punishments was applied to state action via *Robinson v. California*, 370 U.S. 660 (1962).

[126] The Opinion of the Court (part IV), 501 U.S. 957 (1991), internal citation omitted.

[127] *Hutto v. Davis*, 454 U.S. 370 (1982).

liquor seller from New York state. He had sent small shipments of alcohol, collect on delivery, into the neighboring state of Vermont to satisfy some orders he had received. But Vermont had gone dry, and sales there were forbidden. Vermont decided that the sales had occurred not in New York, where they were legal, but in Vermont, where they were verboten, and the seller was duly sentenced to more than fifty-four years in prison at hard labor – a sentence that the Supreme Court left intact.[128]

A second reason that severe punishments are not unusual in vice crimes is because such crimes typically are victimless. Without an obvious victim who has been harmed in some manner, there is no clear benchmark available by which to judge the seriousness of a crime. Possession of cocaine, distribution of small amounts of alcohol to adults who ordered it – who can judge whether fifty-four years at hard labor is too severe a mandate, or if one week in prison is too severe? The penalty cannot be calibrated against the size of the offense when there is no direct harm involved. As a result, the extent to which such vice crimes are punished varies widely across time and place. During a drug scare, or in the midst of a moral panic, statutory penalties know no bounds. (In much of the world today, Mr. Harmelin's cocaine possession would be considered grounds for execution.) And at many other times and places, such vice-related activities are perfectly legal, even laudable.

---

[128] *O'Neil v. Vermont*, 144 U.S. 323 (1892). Admittedly, this case arose before it was settled that the Eighth Amendment applied to the states: an observation taken up by Justice Field in his powerful dissent. The lengthy prison sentence was only to go into effect if a fine and fees of more than $6,500 – a small fortune at the time – was not expeditiously remitted.

5

Taxation, Licensing, and Advertising Controls

If the argument of earlier chapters is correct, then prohibition backed by criminal penalties is generally an inappropriate approach to the regulation of adult vice activity. What are some potential alternatives? In this chapter, I examine policies less restrictive than prohibition that can contribute to workable and robust regulatory regimes.

THE POLICY HUCKSTER

Step right up, ladies and gentlemen. Concerned about violent crime? Unsafe sex practiced by teenagers? Suicide? Cancer? Yes, there are troubles aplenty out there, enough to lead to despair. But don't abandon hope, folks. All of your worries can be addressed through one simple policy, contained right here in this little bottle. Now I'll probably catch some flak from headquarters for telling you the secret ingredient, but what the heck, we're all friends, right? The key to solving your troubles lies in raising the excise tax on alcohol.

Don't believe me? Well, you don't have to take my word for it. The evidence is all laid out in the leading scientific journals in the world. Read them at your leisure, but the bottom line is that to relieve a vast variety of your social ills, higher alcohol taxes are just the ticket.

THE APPROPRIATE LEVEL FOR A "SIN TAX": THE CASE OF ALCOHOL

Hucksters don't always lie, even if they embellish the truth a bit. Alcohol taxation really does alleviate a variety of problems. But if prohibition is not a good idea, ever-rising vice taxes cannot be a good idea either because sufficiently high levels of taxes effectively reproduce a prohibition regime. A one-million-dollar excise tax per bottle of beer would drive all of the beer trade underground. At some point, "sin taxes" on vice become excessive. What is the amount of taxation that will allow us to best capture the many benefits that accrue from taxing vice, without bringing on the significant harms of prohibition?

First, taxes "work" as a vice policy measure by discouraging consumption; in turn, the reduced consumption should bring lower social costs associated with the taxed commodity. But not always: even for a substance as problematic

Table 5.1: *Some of the evidence*

Effect of higher alcohol prices or taxes	Source
Lower consumption of alcohol	Leung and Phelps (1993)
Reduced drinking by teenagers	Grossman et al. (1994)
Reduction in binge drinking	Sloan, Reilly, and Schenzler (1995)
Fewer automobile fatalities	Ruhm (1996)
Fewer industrial accidents	Ohsfeldt and Morrisey (1997)
Reduction in violent crime	Cook and Moore (1993b)
Reduction in family violence	Markowitz and Grossman (2000)
Reduction in suicide	Sloan, Reilly, and Schenzler (1994)
Reduction in cancer rates	Sloan, Reilly, and Schenzler (1994)
Reduction in sexually transmitted diseases	Chesson, Harrison, and Kassler (2000)
Reduction in cirrhosis mortality	Cook and Tauchen (1982)
Fewer school dropouts	Cook and Moore (1993a)
Higher grade-point averages	Williams, Powell, and Wechsler (2002)

[a] The sources presented here are not the only studies documenting many of these effects, of course, and not all research on these issues reaches identical conclusions.

as ethyl alcohol (ethanol, the potable variety of alcohol), it is not readily apparent that a higher tax (starting from a low level) will add to overall well-being. One problem is that the dissuaded consumption might be the portion that is not all that harmful either to the drinker or others, or perhaps the tax impedes positively constructive drinking. A higher alcohol tax might eliminate drinking by moderate users – and there are some potential health benefits to moderate ethanol consumption (at least for middle-aged people) – while having little influence on the behavior of heavy drinkers. Even if the "bad" type of consumption is reduced by a tax, the substitution problem still looms large: if heavy drinkers are not consuming as much alcohol, do they instead switch to consuming more ketchup or more cocaine? A tax-induced substitution from alcohol to cocaine is probably not nearly as desirable an outcome as is a substitution to ketchup consumption.

Alternatively, maybe a higher tax won't cause vice participants to cut back. The claim that higher taxes dissuade consumption relies upon two antecedent conditions holding: first, that higher taxes will result in higher retail prices; second, that higher prices will reduce consumption. A tax policy will founder if either of these two underlying premises proves faulty.

Higher taxes are very likely to generate higher final prices. The main potential exception to the obvious rule is that vice markets might not be competitive. (In a competitive market, suppliers are already earning the bare minimum, so any increased tax on production or sales has to be passed through, essentially penny for penny, to the final price paid by consumers.) Neither alcohol nor tobacco markets in the United States could be described as fully competitive – a handful of firms tend to dominate the marketplace – but excise tax increases, by and large, do seem to result in higher retail prices.[1] The departures from competitive conditions in the tobacco and alcohol markets, if anything, appear to result in more than 100 percent of excise tax increases being passed along to consumers.[2]

Do higher retail prices cause alcohol consumers to cut back? On average, yes. Study after study has shown that higher retail prices lead to lower consumption.[3] The details of the reduced consumption are more controversial. What percentage decrease in consumption will be induced by a 10 percent increase in the U.S. retail price? Typical figures from empirical studies suggest that the answer is about a 3 percent decline for beer, a 10 percent decline for wine, and a 15 percent decline for spirits.[4] (The finding that beer demand is least responsive to price changes, followed by wine and then spirits, is quite sturdy and is replicated in international data.[5]) But these estimates are rather uncertain, as is the extent to which the decline is shared by light, moderate, and heavy drinkers. Contrary, perhaps, to expectations, heavy drinkers do seem to imbibe less when faced with higher prices.[6]

Reductions in drinking or smoking from higher taxes take place along what economists refer to as the "intensive margin" – current drinkers and smokers cut back a bit – as well as along the "extensive margin"; some people quit entirely, while some previous abstainers, who might otherwise have started to smoke or drink, are bolstered in their forbearance. In this respect, teens behave like adults, in that they reduce their drinking and smoking when the relevant taxes rise.[7] In the case of tobacco, there even is evidence that teens tend to be more responsive than adults to tax changes.[8] Further, the discouragement of consumption brought about by higher taxes is long term: "persons who faced higher cigarette taxes as youths are less likely to smoke as adults...."[9]

Radically different mixes of costs and benefits arise from the consumption of alcohol (or some other vicious good) by different people in different settings. Possibilities to substitute among vices and between vicious and non-vicious consumption are myriad and hard to predict. And, as just noted, the details concerning the responsiveness of consumers to price changes are not well understood. An "optimal" vice tax, therefore, cannot be calculated with

---

[1] States that maintain retail alcohol monopolies set their own prices; in these states, raising the controlled price can play a role analogous to a higher tax. Once taxes become so high as to be prohibitive, further increases would be unlikely to influence the effective price, which is established on the black market.

[2] See, e.g., Young and Bielinska-Kwapisz (2002) and Chaloupka et al. (2000).

[3] Cook and Moore (2002).   [4] Leung and Phelps (1993).

[5] Clements, Yang, and Zheng (1997).

[6] Cook and Tauchen (1982) and Kenkel (1996); but, see Manning, Blumberg, and Moulton (1995), for conflicting evidence suggesting that heavy drinkers do not reduce their ethanol intake in response to higher prices.

[7] Cook and Moore (2002, pp. 124–5) and Chaloupka et al. (2000, p. 252).

[8] Chaloupka et al. (2000, p. 252).   [9] Gruber (2002, p. 158).

fine precision. Further, the determination of an appropriate tax rate for alcohol (or any other vice) depends upon a host of related laws. Some of these pertinent policies, such as the minimum drinking age or the regulatory apparatus associated with drunk driving, deal rather directly with alcohol. Others, such as rules that influence the price or availability of potential alcohol substitutes like marijuana, cocaine, or even household solvents, are further afield. Despite these minefields of complications, however, guidelines can be developed that provide some basis for thinking about appropriate levels for alcohol taxes and vice taxes more generally.

Externalities

An initial attempt at determining a desirable level of vice taxation involves looking at the external costs associated with vice consumption, that is, those costs that are imposed upon others beyond the vice producers and consumers themselves. The notion is that drinkers (and alcohol producers) should at least be expected to pay the full costs connected with their activity; otherwise, their decisions to drink, even if well-considered from their personal perspective, will lead to too much drinking from the point of view of society. (This is a situation we have to worry about with vice consumption but not ketchup consumption because there are not any significant external costs imposed by ketchup ingestion.) In the case of alcohol, the associated external costs include violent behavior, automobile crashes, and public nuisances (including noise and violence) in the vicinity of drinking establishments. Infants are harmed in utero by heavy maternal drinking during gestation.

Some of the difficulties of identifying an appropriate tax rate to "internalize" the externalities of alcohol are apparent. (Incidentally, referring to an externality correction as a "tax" is somewhat imprecise: it is an adjustment to eliminate an implicit subsidy and hence rectify a current market distortion, not a mechanism introducing a new distortion. Any negative connotations that might adhere to the term "tax" should not be brought to the consideration of such externality-offsetting price adjustments.) The connections between alcohol consumption and these external costs are not fixed in stone and universal. In some countries and locales, alcohol consumption is not readily associated with violence, though in the United States in general, it is.[10] More drinking doesn't always imply more alcohol-related externalities. Drunk driving can rise or fall, even if the amount of alcohol consumed stays the same, and the costs that impaired motorists impose upon others can be altered through automobile and highway design changes and by improvements in emergency medicine. The time, place, and manner of drinking are important determinants of the magnitude of alcohol-related problems. Drinking that occurs at home does not

---

[10] On differences in "drunken comportment" across societies, see MacAndrew and Edgerton (1969).

have the same propensity to result in public nuisance or drunk driving as does drinking at a bar. Binge drinking tends to be more troublesome than more gradual consumption, holding constant the total amount of alcohol consumed. And, of course, the external costs associated with drinking vary at the individual level – many drinkers pose no risk of harm to others, whereas some people quickly behave in highly problematic ways when under the influence.

In a world of full information and costless policy implementation, it might be possible to design a set of alcohol taxes that would be specific to each and every situation. Joe, a troublesome drunk, would see higher and higher taxes for each additional beer he consumes. Harry's nightly cordial relaxes him and makes him a more pleasant person to be around, with no offsetting costs: his dram might even be subsidized (i.e., have a negative "tax" imposed). Alcohol consumed at home would be taxed less stringently than alcohol consumed in public, except for Tom, because he is violent toward his family when drinking at home but on his best behavior when in social settings. Men might face higher alcohol taxes than do women because men are more likely to be violent or create public nuisances under the influence. Younger drinkers, too, might have to pay more, as they have a higher risk of being involved in drunk driving. For that matter, drivers might be presented with higher alcohol taxes than are public transit users. And so on.

But of course, such fine discriminations generally are not possible in the real world; not every alcohol purchase can be matched with the tax rate that fully accounts for the expected external costs associated with its consumption. Nevertheless, some distinctions are workable in practice. First, different types of alcohol can be taxed at different rates. Spirits can face one tax, wine a second, and beer a third: current U.S. alcohol taxation invokes these distinctions. (The term "wino" came into use because wine has traditionally faced lower taxes than beer and spirits, and thus poor alcoholics tended to consume wine, often fortified, high-alcohol-content wine, to satisfy their cravings.) Alcohol for on-site consumption can be taxed differently from alcohol sold for home consumption. Taxes can be based on the containers in which alcohol is sold: pitchers or kegs could be taxed more heavily than bottled beer. Problematic adult drinkers can face judicially imposed personal prohibitions on alcohol purchase or consumption: in a sense, an infinite tax. Even these types of tax differentials are limited by enforcement considerations – major differences in taxes between alcohol consumed on the seller's premises and alcohol consumed at home could eventually lead to "smuggling" of alcohol into public establishments – but many distinctions prove to be viable despite significant tax variation. Evidence is immediate in the case of public versus private alcohol, where market price differentials (not driven by taxes) can be enormous: a bottle of wine might cost a consumer three times as much at a restaurant as at a retail wine seller, and "smuggling" of wine into pricey, alcohol-selling restaurants is not a major issue.

The potential distinctions that can be made within an alcohol regulatory regime change over time. It may be that alcohol detection technology develops to the point that it becomes easy to erect barriers that apply only to people who have demonstrated that their alcohol consumption carries a significant risk of harm to others. If that is the case, then those individuals can be made to face a higher (explicit or implicit) price for alcohol than do others. The general tax on alcohol needn't be set in such a way as to try to offset vexatious behavior because the externalities are adequately handled by a separate policy. But if the troublesome folks cannot be screened from alcohol by other means, a higher tax applied to all drinkers might be called for. A similar issue presents itself with respect to the behaviors that generate external costs following drinking – becoming violent or driving under the influence, for instance. The external costs arising from drunk driving could with as much justice (and even more directly) be "attributed" to driving as to drinking – maybe we should tax the driving and not the drinking? After all, most drinkers do not drive under the influence, so why should they have to pay more for alcohol because of a few bad apples? If other methods of deterring drunk driving were inexpensive and potent enough – perhaps car ignitions that would automatically turn off when alcohol impairment is detected – then again, there would be no reason (in terms of externalities) to increase the alcohol tax to reduce drunk driving. The weaker the ability to stem drunk driving by other means, however, the stronger the rationale for taking the external costs of impaired driving into account when developing alcohol tax policy.[11]

Recognizing that there are limits to the size and type of distinctions that can be made, do current levels of alcohol taxation in the United States, on average, fully internalize the external costs associated with drinking? The research on this point is fairly conclusive: no. Alcohol is undertaxed, in the sense that (rational) drinkers do not face the full social costs associated with their activity. This undertaxation is largely because the high inflation years of the 1970s saw the real value of alcohol taxes tumble.

Excise taxes are typically expressed in terms of so many cents per proof gallon of alcohol (or per barrel, for beer). As prices in general rise, the significance of such a tax will decline, unless the tax per gallon is simultaneously increased. Legislated tax increases since the 1950s have not kept up with inflation, despite federal alcohol excise tax hikes in 1985 and 1991. The real tax rate on alcohol therefore has fallen, quite noticeably during the high-inflation 1970s.[12] In the case of beer, the federal tax rate was established at $10.50 per barrel in November 1951. By 2006, occasional legislated tax changes had

---

[11] See Chapter 5, "Preventive and Punitive Controls," in Leitzel (2003); for an alcohol-specific discussion, see Kenkel (1996).

[12] The 1985 excise tax hike applied only to distilled spirits. In 1955, there was an excise tax increase that applied only to champagnes, sparkling wines, and artificially carbonated wines. See Talley and Cashell (1999).

driven the nominal rate to $18 per barrel, or about a nickel per twelve-ounce
can of beer. But because of inflation over the previous half-century, this $18
per barrel in 2006 was much less significant than the $10.50 per barrel tax of
1951. Had the 1951 tax been indexed to inflation so that its real value would be
maintained over time, the tax in 2006 would have amounted to approximately
$80 per barrel. In other words, the 2006 federal excise tax for beer, adjusting
for inflation, was less than one-quarter of where it stood in 1951.[13]

Some of the sources of external costs from alcohol consumption have
already been mentioned: violence, auto wrecks, and public nuisances. Not all
of the costs that arise from these sources are external, however. When a drunk
driver crashes his car in his own driveway and no one else is involved, most of
the costs of that crash are internal – though there might be a public (or external) subsidy component to his auto insurance, his medical coverage, and even
his use of sick days from work.[14] Nevertheless, the chief source of external
costs associated with alcohol consumption is impaired driving. In the United
States in 2000, more than 13,000 traffic accident fatalities related to a legally
intoxicated individual and an additional 2,500 traffic deaths involved alcohol,
but at levels below the legal limit. All together, alcohol is involved in about
40 percent of fatal traffic accidents. Nonfatal, alcohol-involved traffic accidents number in the millions annually.[15] Of course, many of those killed and
injured in alcohol-involved accidents are the drinkers themselves, and hence
the cost of these injuries or deaths are not "external" (abstracting from the
public component of medical expenses). But some one-third of the deaths are
of nondrinking individuals.[16]

A host of further considerations arise in attempting to quantify the external
costs of alcohol usage. Are injuries to passengers who willingly get in a car
with a drunk driver considered to be external? Wouldn't some of the accidents that involve alcohol have occurred even if every participant had been
stone sober? Don't the police underestimate the extent of alcohol involvement
in accidents, particularly for nonfatal accidents with drivers who consumed

[13] See Talley and Cashell (1999), plus "Tax and Fee Rates" at www.atf.gov/alcohol/info/faq/subpages/
atftaxes.htm (accessed on November 16, 2005). The inflation adjustment uses the Consumer Price
Index, as available from the inflation calculator at the Department of Labor's webpage, http://stats.
bls.gov/bls/inflation.htm.

[14] An important conceptual issue is whether the costs imposed on a drinker's family are "internal" or
"external." To the extent that the drinker actually takes into account the welfare of his intimates
in his own decision making, some of those costs might already be internalized. For discussion
of this issue, see, e.g., Cook and Moore (2002, pp. 129–30). Long-term intrafamily violence and
fetal alcohol syndrome have such sufficiently severe consequences that the case that their costs are
internalized by the drinkers themselves is particularly hard to sustain.

[15] "The Economic Impact of Motor Vehicle Crashes 2000."

[16] Manning et al. (1989, p. 1608) note an estimate for 1985 that 7,400 out of 22,400 fatalities in
alcohol-related crashes were of people who had not been drinking. In the European Union, it is
estimated that 10,000 of 17,000 drunk-driving fatalities each year are of people other than the
drinking driver; Anderson and Baumberg (2006).

alcohol but are not legally drunk? Researchers are aware of these and many other complications and often have done what is possible to adjust for them. Early studies looking at the external costs of alcohol consumption in the United States "estimated that the prevailing alcohol tax rates in the mid-to late 1980's were about one-half of the amount necessary to make up the difference between private and full social costs of drinking. . . . "[17] More recent studies generally reach a similar conclusion: on the basis of externalities alone, current alcohol excise taxes in the United States are too low.[18]

Harms to self

The traditional economic approach to corrective taxation would identify externalities, adjust for them, and be done with it. Once rational, well-informed decision makers face the full range of costs and benefits, there is nothing more that policy can do to try to improve matters by influencing choices. But if decisions are not fully rational – perhaps they are time inconsistent or result from a hijacking of the brain's reward system by a stealthy chemical – then compensating for externalities alone might not be sufficient.

As with most of the traditional vices, there is ample reason to believe that dynamic inconsistency (and the regret about previous levels of consumption that is likely to accompany it) is at work with alcohol. An unfortunately commonplace occurrence is that a plan to have one or two drinks collapses into an evening of much more extensive consumption, followed by internal and perhaps external disapproval. A tax that discourages consumption by the overly indulgent, then, will be viewed by their more prudent, long-run selves as a good thing. (This is in contrast to standard rational consumers, who are not helped when the tax is raised on a good that they currently consume.) Of course, those consumers who are completely rational in their alcohol-related decisions generally will be harmed by a higher tax. But interestingly, not by much. That is, an increased tax on alcohol can be of significant benefit to those who face self-control problems, while imposing a very minor burden on others. It's even possible, because the alcohol tax will raise revenue so that other taxes can be lowered, that both the time inconsistent and the fully rational people will be made better off by a higher tax.[19]

In any event, "internalities" associated with a less than fully rational choice provide a case for taxing vice beyond what externality correction alone would call for. The case might not be that strong, and the size of an appropriate tax is hard to pinpoint. Nevertheless, when each year there are more than 2 million U.S. residents seeking treatment for their alcohol addictions – about 1

[17] Kenkel and Manning (1996, p. 236).
[18] See the discussion in Cook and Moore (2002); an exception is Heien (1995/1996).
[19] O'Donoghue and Rabin (2003).

percent of the adult population but only about 15 percent of those with drinking problems – and when millions of nonalcoholics occasionally behave, when they are the worse for drink, in ways that they later rue, the likelihood that some of these costs can be avoided through a higher tax on alcohol provides a further rationale, beyond externalities, for alcohol levies.[20]

Distributional considerations

In the United States, richer people tend to spend more on alcohol than do poorer people, though as you move up the income scale, alcohol consumption expenditures do not rise as fast as income. Therefore, poorer people generally spend a larger fraction of their income on alcohol than do richer people. Richer people also tend to buy more expensive alcohol, so ethanol consumption itself does not rise with income as quickly as does spending on alcohol. (Expenditures on tobacco products and lottery tickets in the United States are much more regressive than is alcohol spending; the absolute amount paid in taxes associated with these products is higher for poor people than for rich people.)

Excise taxes typically apply to the amount of alcohol, not to the value. This is appropriate, in that the harms from alcohol are generally associated with the quantity of ethanol consumed, not the expenditures on drinks. Proposals to raise alcohol taxes, therefore, are frequently criticized on the grounds that such taxes are regressive: poorer people on average devote a larger share of their income to alcohol taxes than do richer people. The observation is correct, but it is not a determinative argument against tax hikes. Alcohol expenditures, on average, are only about 2 percent of total consumer expenditures, with a tax component of perhaps one-quarter of alcohol spending.[21] More important than any single (and relatively small) tax is the overall fairness of the entire government tax and spending regime, which includes an income tax, of course, and public benefit programs. The alcohol tax can be set to provide the best alcohol policy, and then the income tax (and other measures) can be used to produce distributive justice. Employing economics terminology, there are two targets (or goals), fairness and alcohol control, but these are matched by at least two policy instruments, the income tax and alcohol excises, so there is no need to sacrifice one goal for the sake of the other.[22]

But it may be that this logic is not compelling; perhaps it is thought that we cannot trust the folks devising the income tax to ensure fairness, so that we

[20] In 2005, 15.4 million Americans aged 12 or above were classified as being alcohol dependent, with another 3.3 million dependent on alcohol as well as an illicit drug. About 2.8 million Americans received treatment for alcohol or alcohol as well as an illegal drug. See sections 7.1 and 7.2 of the 2005 National Survey on Drug Use & Health: National Results, Substance Abuse and Mental Health Services Administration, available at http://www.oas.samhsa.gov/nsduh/2k5nsduh/2k5results.htm#7.2 (accessed February 18, 2007).
[21] Cook and Moore (2002, p. 123); employers pay for about 20 percent of alcohol purchases.
[22] See Schelling (1984).

have to consider that issue directly with alcohol policy, too. There remain six issues worth noting. First, even for poor people, the percentage of their income spent on alcohol taxes is small.[23] Second, alcohol taxes can be earmarked for programs that disproportionally benefit poor people, such as publicly funded treatment for alcoholics.[24] Third, to the extent that the consumption of alcohol is not fully rational, our usual notions concerning the burden of tax payments are inapplicable. In particular, drinkers with self-control problems can be made better off (as judged by their own "long-term" preferences) through tax increases.[25] If troublesome drinkers who are induced to limit or give up drinking by a higher excise tax are disproportionally poor, then the "incidence" of the tax hike may not be regressive at all. Fourth, those who drink a lot also tend to be those who are most at risk from the alcohol-related misbehavior of others.[26] So once again, those who pay alcohol taxes are likely to be among the beneficiaries of the behavioral changes induced by higher taxes. Fifth, alcohol consumption among teens impedes their later earnings capacity when they are adults; a longer-term view of the distributional consequences of alcohol taxes, then, could yield a very different judgment than what would be forthcoming from an analysis of short-run tax incidence. Sixth, responsiveness to tax increases might be greater for poorer people than for richer people – this seems to be the case with tobacco, for instance.[27] With such differential responsiveness, an increase in an existing, regressive tax can lead to a lower overall level of regressivity: the cutback in consumption by poorer individuals, being greater than that of richer individuals, means that the proportion of income that poor people will spend on the sin tax will decline, relative to the proportion spent by richer people.

Taxes that correct for externalities provide improved incentives for rational alcohol consumers to engage in the "optimal" amount of drinking. But there will still be people hurt or killed through the alcohol-related behavior of others, and the taxes themselves do not compensate such victims. Compensation might be achieved through the tort system, but some injurers will lack the means or insurance to actually provide the requisite restitution. A portion of alcohol tax revenues could be designated for a victim's compensation fund that would

---

[23] Some people with low incomes are not poor; they are young people in nonpoor families or retirees with substantial savings. Taking these "life cycle" effects into account, alcohol taxes are slightly less regressive than they appear to be when measured against current income. See Lyon and Schwab (1995).

[24] Of course, the earmarking might largely serve as a symbolic gesture. Dollars are fungible, and general revenue funds that otherwise would have gone to treatment might be diverted to other programs. There is some evidence that this sort of diversion occurs for lottery revenues that are earmarked for certain sectors, such as education; see the 1999 National Gambling Impact Study Commission's report on lotteries.

[25] Gruber and Mullainathan (2002).

[26] See Rossow and Hauge (2004); this evidence is from Norway.

[27] Chaloupka et al. (2000, p. 258–9).

be used to recompense people injured by uninsured drunk drivers or other alcohol-related miscreants of limited means.

Revenue

Alcohol taxes have historically been important sources of public revenue, both in the United States and other countries. In the pre–World War I years, alcohol taxes accounted for roughly one-third of all U.S. federal revenues; likewise, the Soviet Union of the 1960s and 1970s collected about one-third of its tax revenue from alcohol.[28] Poorer countries tend to rely more heavily upon excise taxes on alcohol and other products such as tobacco and gasoline than do richer countries. As economies develop, then, the role of alcohol as a government revenue generator fades. Currently, federal alcohol excise taxes in the U.S. amount to less than 1 percent of national collections, while state alcohol excise taxes form about 1 percent of state receipts.

Most estimates of the responsiveness of alcohol purchases to price changes indicate that an increase in the alcohol excise tax would reduce consumption, but not by so much as to decrease tax payments. That is, in the United States, a legislated increase in the alcohol tax would, in all probability, lead to more government revenue.

A policy reform is not necessarily worth undertaking because it would raise government receipts. If the government is receiving more revenue, then some individuals are paying more taxes, and it is not clear that this transfer of funds is a good thing. But if there are other sound reasons to raise the alcohol excise tax – externality correction and Table 5.1 provide such reasons – then at least you don't have to worry that the higher tax will lead to a revenue loss for the government. Further, all taxes are imperfect, creating distortions and requiring resources for administration. To achieve a given level of government revenue, shifting somewhat away from an income tax, for example, to higher alcohol excises, is likely to improve the efficiency of the overall tax regime.[29]

Special taxes on alcohol that are adopted to reduce consumption (perhaps motivated by a desire to correct for externalities) might see their original purpose superseded. The fact that these taxes bring in revenues might induce the government to look for ways to increase those revenues – by selling more alcohol. The government could "promote" taxed alcohol sales, for instance, by being lax in other elements of the alcohol regulatory regime, whether it be in terms of licensing of sellers, opening hours, or advertising controls. Are there ways to ensure that governmental "addiction" to tax revenue does not lead to excessive promotion of alcohol use?

One potential restraint on the domination of alcohol policy by revenue considerations is the earmarking of alcohol tax receipts to a specific program. By

---

[28] Hamm (1995, pp. 95–6), and White (1996, p. 37).
[29] Sgontz (1993).

designating alcohol tax payments to a particular area, the widespread interest in general revenue collection becomes less of an influence upon alcohol policy – though of course the specified beneficiaries of the tied program might become advocates for measures that would increase alcohol sales. Further, the earmarked beneficiary cannot be a program that already receives significant funding, lest the tied alcohol tax funds just replace monies that otherwise would have come from general revenues. For that reason, states instituting lotteries occasionally earmark the profits to entirely new programs that therefore cannot see their "usual" state funding cut as their lottery proceeds mount. Alcohol tax revenues could be designated for prevention or treatment programs designed to reduce alcohol abuse or to compensate victims of alcohol-related misbehavior.

So earmarking alcohol taxes is one method to try to shield alcohol policy from the potentially perverse incentives that can be generated by significant tax revenues. Federalism provides a second method. In the United States, most elements of alcohol control policy occur at the municipal, state, or county level, so the revenue-raising ability of the federal excise tax should have little or no ability to undermine commitment to the more localized regulatory measures.

SIN TAXES AND JOHN STUART MILL

It might be argued that the government should not use tax (or other) policy to discriminate among goods. By this reasoning the government should establish a level playing field and enforce the rules, without attempting to influence consumer spending patterns. But recall that the part of any tax increase that simply accounts for externalities is not a case of the government discriminating against the taxed good; rather, correcting for externalities levels the playing field between the taxed good and other items of expenditure. And on the basis of externalities alone, it appears that U.S. alcohol taxes are currently too low, while the presence of internalities and tax revenue prospects provide additional rationales for a boost in the alcohol tax.

In Chapter 5 of *On Liberty*, John Stuart Mill struggles with whether the government should employ taxes to influence consumption patterns. After first suggesting that consumer choice should be left to personal judgment, Mill continues:

> But it must be remembered that taxation for fiscal purposes is absolutely inevitable; that in most countries it is necessary that a considerable part of that taxation should be indirect; that the State, therefore, cannot help imposing penalties, which to some persons may be prohibitory, on the use of some articles of consumption. It is hence the duty of the State to consider, in the imposition of taxes, what commodities the consumers can best spare; and *à fortiori*, to select in preference those of which it deems the use, beyond a very moderate quantity, to be positively injurious. Taxation, therefore, of stimulants, up to the point

which produces the largest amount of revenue (supposing that the State needs all the revenue which it yields) is not only admissible, but to be approved of.[30]

So Mill, it seems, whose "harm principle" puts no weight at all on internalities (harms to nonaddicted adult users themselves), would nevertheless support higher alcohol taxes in the United States.

Would it make sense to go beyond Mill to promote vice taxes even to the point wherein they decrease government revenue? Although this query does not have much current practical significance in the United States, given that taxes on most legal vices are well short of the Millian revenue-maximizing cutoff, the question helps to reveal the principles that should govern vice taxation. Recall that a commitment to robustness permits supra-Millian taxes to combat the potential irrationality exhibited by choices with respect to many vices. (I am assuming here that taxes to correct externalities alone are not so high as to decrease revenue – if they were so high, they should still be maintained, as these excises eliminate an existing implicit subsidy, and enhance, rather than detract from, the workings of rational choice in markets.) But recall one implication of the robustness principle, that vice control should aim to aid those with self-control problems, while not unduly inconveniencing those whose vice choices are fully rational. Extremely high taxes violate robustness by placing too great a burden upon fully rational consumption decisions. In many instances, such high taxes would not be expedient, either, as they would generate significant black-market activity for purposes of tax evasion.

The relevant constraint on alcohol taxes might not be externality correction or revenue maximization but simple administrative feasibility, especially in poorer countries. It might be easy to collect a small excise tax from a handful of manufacturing plants and at the border (for imports), while larger taxes would generate widespread smuggling and an underground trade. The level of taxation that is administratively sustainable also is likely to depend on the tax regime in nearby jurisdictions. A U.S. state with a very high excise tax on alcohol is better able to enforce its taxes if its neighboring states have similarly high excises.

The potential for smuggling is a problem that vice tax design must contend with. In rich, well-governed countries, however, high sin taxes and even substantial internal tax differentials can be maintained without fomenting widespread smuggling. On a global basis, despite huge price differentials and relative ease of transport, less than 10 percent of cigarettes are smuggled. In the United States, smuggling and cross-border shopping in cigarettes account for an even smaller portion of consumption.[31]

As long as they are administratively feasible and do not place extreme burdens upon rational consumers – and whether or not these two conditions are met

[30] Ryan (1997, p. 120), footnote omitted.
[31] See the discussion in Chaloupka, Wakefield, and Czart (2001, pp. 65–6).

Box 5.1: *Technological developments in alcohol control*

The largest source of external costs stemming from alcohol consumption is automobile accidents involving impaired drivers. In the United States, nearly 1.4 million people are arrested for drunk driving each year, and most (over 90 percent) of those who are driving when legally impaired do not get arrested.[a] How can alcohol-impaired motorists be kept off of the roads?

Numerous technologies in various stages of development are designed to prevent drunks from driving. Some are quite sophisticated, such as mechanisms that recognize erratic handling and shut down the car if the dangerous driving continues. (Such systems would operate irrespective of whether alcohol is the source of the hazardous driving.) Other approaches to keeping drunk people from operating automobiles are more basic. For instance, Saab is developing an ignition interlock system – the Alcokey – that would prevent someone from starting his or her car following a failed Breathalyzer test. The Alcokey works in concert with a standard remote door opener/theft prevention system.[b] After the driver pushes the usual unlock button, an astonishingly compact alcohol sensor carried on the key chain is activated. The driver blows into a small opening on the device, which gives the go-ahead if the measured blood alcohol content is sufficiently low; otherwise, the car will not start. The standard that must be achieved can be altered, depending, for instance, on the legal requirements in the jurisdiction in which the driver resides. One advantage of this proposed system relative to existing alternatives is that it is relatively cheap, around 250 euros. Another type of ignition interlock works similarly, though the breath tester is located within the car, and repeated tests can be called for at random intervals.

People concerned about their own drinking and driving might voluntarily acquire a Breathalyzer or install an ingnition interlock system.[c] Insurance companies might offer lower rates to insure drivers whose cars contain alcohol detection technology. By 2006, some 70,000 automobiles in the United States already had ignition interlocks, "most of them ordered by courts for repeat drunken-driving offenders."[d]

Drunk driving is only one source of external, alcohol-related costs. What about people who are violent or engage in sexual harassment when under the influence? How can they be prevented, not from drinking and driving, but simply from drinking in the first place?

Some people in the United States and elsewhere are enjoined from using alcohol as a condition of probation or pretrial release. The personal prohibition is hard to enforce, however. Standard approaches require the targeted individual to check in to a testing location twice a day or require him or her to be at home for regularly scheduled breath tests several times per day. Random checks are another alternative. These are resource-intensive enforcement mechanisms that would be hard to extend to all troublesome drinkers. But technology might be progressing to the point where it is possible to reliably track the drinking behavior of large numbers of people at relatively low cost. Alcohol Monitoring Systems, Inc., manufactures an eight-ounce ankle bracelet that tests alcohol concentration through ethanol that

(continued)

Box 5.1 *(continued)*

passes through the skin.[e] The bracelet measures and records alcohol consumption hourly, and once the bracelet is fitted, the tests do not require any active participation on the part of the wearer. Nor does the wearer have to be at a specific location for the measurement to take place, though at some point during the day (if daily tracking is warranted) proximity to a special modem is required for a wireless uploading of the measurement results. The bracelets are designed to detect and record attempts at tampering, too. The bracelet is already in use in some court systems. Although it's a better deal than jail, the bracelet is far from free: in Seneca County, Ohio, a 2004 report indicated that "The device would cost offenders a $100 refundable deposit, a $75 installation fee and $12 a day."[f] In-home Breathalyzers are slightly less expensive, though they do not offer the same disincentive to drink, as those tests are not conducted hourly. Skin sensor devices are being developed for automobile interlocks, too, to eliminate the relatively unwieldy Breathalyzer tests.[g]

These are just a few of the developments in monitoring and either preventing or deterring dangerous drunken behavior. As these technologies progress and become less expensive, their adoption will reduce drunk driving and other major externalities associated with alcohol consumption, perhaps justifying a lower excise tax.

---

[a] One study found that the probability of someone who is driving with a blood-alcohol content above the legal limit has a 2 percent chance of being arrested. See the Vice Squad post on January 1, 2007.

[b] From "Carpages," available at www.carpages.co.uk/saab/saab_unveils_lock_out_concept_22_06_04.asp?switched=onecho=303023026 (accessed July 24, 2004).

[c] See the Vice Squad post on February 21, 2007, about a personal Breathalyzer sold for $79.

[d] "Will all autos some day have Breathalyzers?" by Jayne O'Donnell, *USA Today*, April 24, 2006; available at www.usatoday.com/money/autos/2006-04-24-breathalyzer-usat_x. htm (accessed on April 28, 2006). See also the Vice Squad post from January 4, 2007.

[e] See www.alcoholmonitoring.com (accessed February 19, 2007).

[f] This description of the workings of the Alcokey is drawn from Matt Suman, "Device can remotely test, record alcohol use by offenders," Friday, April 09, 2004, Advertiser-Tribune. Com, Seneca County, Ohio; available at www.advertiser-tribune.com/news/story/049202004_new02scram0409.asp (accessed July 24, 2004). A later news story concerning Racine, Wisconsin, indicated a slightly lower price of $10 per day; see the Vice Squad post for May 2, 2004. South Dakota is another location that employs some alcohol bracelets; see the Vice Squad post from February 19, 2007.

[g] "Will all autos some day have Breathalyzers?" by Jayne O'Donnell, *USA Today*, April 24, 2006; available at www.usatoday.com/money/autos/2006-04-24-breathalyzer-usat_x. htm, visited on April 28, 2006.

---

is, of course, a matter of judgment – vice taxes that exceed revenue-maximizing rates might be desirable. Imagine a vice that brings with it no externalities, and where the demand for the vice is so price sensitive that any tax above the standard sales tax would lower the total amount of revenue collected. If there were large internalities associated with the consumption of that vice, a small excise tax could be very helpful in limiting those internalities, without being very imposing upon rational consumers of the vice or creating any difficulties in tax administration. Such an excise tax would then be consistent with robustness, even though it would exceed the Millian, revenue-maximizing level. Another factor that broadly supports vice taxation is that vice goods, as Adam Smith said of sugar, rum, and tobacco, "are commodities which are no where necessaries of life, which are become objects of almost universal consumption, and which are therefore extremely proper subjects of taxation."[32] Vice goods are forms of leisure spending. Income is taxed in most countries, providing a disincentive to work and an artificial stimulus to leisure. Economists, therefore, have long suggested that goods that are consumed in combination with leisure are "extremely proper subjects of taxation," in part because such taxes help to redress the excessive promotion of leisure brought about as a by-product of income taxation.

Efforts to change vice taxes can be highly controversial. But it should be kept in mind that, because of the manner in which U.S. alcohol excise taxes are stated ("cents per proof gallon"), they change of their own accord. That is, inflation eats away at the real value of taxes that are fixed in nominal terms. For this reason, there is much to be said for indexing excise taxes to the inflation rate, so that price-level changes alone don't alter the real burden of taxation.

Along with the indexation, current federal alcohol excise taxes in the United States could be doubled, without violating any principle of desirable vice policy. Indeed, a doubling of alcohol excises would almost surely move these duties closer to the elusive "optimal" rate, though the variance in individual state taxes might not make this assertion true throughout the nation. In real terms, doubled federal excises would (in the case of beer) put such taxes at approximately the same level that existed in 1973. (And such taxes were well administered at 1973 rates, that is, smuggling was a minor problem.) The doubling would probably still leave alcohol undertaxed, judged solely in terms of externalities. Internalities and revenue consequences would push for even higher levies. The doubling of the tax would meet with a host of consequences, almost all of them positive – as suggested by Table 5.1. So there is a strong case for doubling the federal alcohol excise tax in the United States.

SIN TAXES AS AN UNEASY HALFWAY HOUSE

Some observers view special taxes and other vice restrictions as steps on a slippery slope toward prohibition, and no doubt some of the supporters of such measures would be happy if public policy actually were to slide down that slope. It is true that drawing some sort of legal line (such as a significant but not prohibitive tax) and sticking with it is not an easy task with respect

---

[32] Smith (1976 [1776], vol. 2, p. 474). But between the first and second editions of *The Wealth of Nations*, Adam Smith removed a reference to beer as a necessity; Smith (1976 [1776], p. xx).

to traditional vices. The line, by the usual nature of rules, must be to some extent arbitrary. Further, no policy governing a legal vice will completely put to rest the standard $3\frac{1}{3}$ vice concerns: the consumption of vicious goods will continue to lead to various tragedies, whether they be drunk-driving deaths or alcoholism in the case of drinking, bankruptcy or embezzlement in the case of gambling, kids becoming nicotine addicts or people dying in accidental fires in the case of cigarettes, or other equally calamitous events.

When some high-profile vice-related tragedy occurs, there will be calls to tighten the regulatory regime. If the excise tax composes 30 percent of the retail price, why not raise it to compose 50 percent, or 60 percent? If the drunk-driving blood alcohol concentration standard is .10, why not make it .08, or .05, or set a legal standard of no detectable alcohol in the bloodstream of drivers?

Though regulatory line drawing is somewhat arbitrary in all areas of public policy, one of the distinguishing features of vice is that the benefits of the vicious activities are not accorded much weight, or are sometimes even ignored completely (or believed to be nonexistent). As suggested earlier, we could have fewer highway deaths if we instituted and enforced a national speed limit of thirty miles per hour. But there is no sentiment to do so, presumably because people recognize the benefits of more expeditious transport, and are, in essence, willing to accept more fatal accidents to procure those benefits – even though we rarely frame the question in those terms. (They would be even happier, of course, if they could have higher speeds with no increase in risk or expense, but generally that is not an available option.) The benefits to alcohol consumption or gambling, alternatively, can seem to many people not to be worth any increase in risk, any augmentation of social costs. For such people, any inexpensive restriction that holds a glimmer of hope for reducing the social costs of vice will look like a good idea.

That vice controls can cascade and possibly become overly restrictive does not imply that every attempt to strengthen them is misguided. I have argued that alcohol in the United States is undertaxed, and I believe that a significant increase in the federal alcohol excise would make for better policy. There is some risk that such a move will serve a neo-prohibitionist agenda, but the fact that an excise tax increase would be supported by those who would be willing to go much further in restricting alcohol, and perhaps even bolster their ranks, is to my mind insufficient rationale for foregoing the considerable benefits available from raising the federal excise tax.[33] Nevertheless, special (though nonprohibitive) taxation of a legal vice can be a hard-to-sustain policy, as there will be almost natural political forces pushing for tighter controls.

Taxation of a legal vice is an uneasy halfway house not only because of pressure to ratchet up the tax toward prohibition but also because of systematic pressures in the opposite direction. In particular, legal vice involves

---

[33] On mechanisms through which laws or policies might tumble down a slippery slope, see Volokh (2003).

producers (liquor manufacturers, cigarette companies, and so on) that control large resources and also maintain a substantial interest in seeing their sales expand. (This might be true of illegal vices, too, but in the United States, illegal manufacturers and traffickers do not seem to have the same influence on the political process as do the completely open lobbyists for legal vice industries.[34]) Increased sales can be achieved by liberalizing various regulations – on advertising, for instance – or even, more directly, by lowering existing taxes. Substantial vice interests will lobby intensely to further their concerns, including campaigning for a liberal (or specially protected) regulatory regime. Vice producers might be assisted in their efforts to increase vice consumption by the beneficiaries of earmarked tax revenues, who also might perceive a personal benefit from retailing more vice (though probably not in lowering excise tax rates).

The potential for legal vices to create a politically powerful constituency that might be able to prevent the adoption of strict regulations is one argument against drug legalization in the United States. Some commentators suggest that a legal but highly regulated regime for cocaine or marijuana is not politically sustainable: the drug manufacturers would be able to use their political influence to ensure that regulations over their activities would not be strict. One problem with this contention, however, is that controls over legal vices such as alcohol and cigarettes sometimes are quite strict – in the case of alcohol, many parts of the United States even remain "dry" – and further, such regulations often have been tightened. Tobacco has become much more heavily regulated in recent years, with controls over smoking in public, significantly higher taxes, and so on. Although it is true that vice producers are potent contributors to political campaigns, it is far from clear that their impact on the political process is different in kind or even degree from that of other moneyed interests. Of the approximately eighty industries and special interests tracked by the Center for Responsive Politics, the 1990 to 2006 political contributions of the alcohol (rank 34), tobacco (44), and gambling (38) industries put them in the middle of the pack, well behind pharmaceuticals (16), education (22), and autos (20).[35]

PROHIBITION PLUS TAXATION

High but nonprohibitive taxation of legal vices produces forces that push in both directions, toward more stringent and toward more liberal policy regimes. Taxation of *illegal* vices, perhaps surprisingly, has been both a common activity and one that also has proved hard to sustain. Though it sounds paradoxical, vice transactions have been both simultaneously banned and taxed.

---

[34] The "bootleggers and Baptists" theory of regulation, however, notes how both of these groups support laws prohibiting Sunday alcohol sales; see Yandle (1983).
[35] The industry contribution figures are available from http://www.opensecrets.org/industries/list. asp; the rankings are as of February 21, 2007.

After the Twenty-first Amendment ended national alcohol prohibition in the United States, many states maintained their own prohibitions. Mississippi prohibited anything stronger than 3.2 beer, but in the 1940s passed a tax on the illegal, stronger stuff.[36] (There was pre-Prohibition precedent: Iowa, a dry state, started to tax illegal alcohol sellers in 1894.[37]) Why would underground sellers pay the tax? Payment of the tax by bootleggers provided a license of sorts, an understanding that the law would largely wink at their activities. (Instead of remitting formal taxes, some sellers made informal payments to local constables.) In the mid-1960s, following a high-profile alcohol raid, a Mississippi judge ruled that the fact that taxes were being collected meant that liquor was de facto legal. The state legislature followed the judicial suggestion by converting the informal licensing system into a formal legality, so in 1966, Mississippi became the last U.S. state to repeal statewide alcohol prohibition.

Brothels became explicitly legal in Nevada along similar lines in the early 1970s. An illegal brothel owner was fined $1,000 per month for the previous three months that the brothel had been in business. He didn't go out of business but kept sending $1,000 per month to the relevant county authorities. Eventually, the county recognized that acceptance of these checks needed to be put on a legal basis. The state then passed a statute setting up the broad rules for legal brothels in those rural Nevada counties that were willing to host them.

Many states in the United States officially tax marijuana. These taxes have been implemented to give prosecutors another tool with which to suppress the trade in (and use of) marijuana. Few dealers pay the taxes – it seems that the limited purchases of "marijuana tax stamps" are dominated by stamp collectors – but these state governments should be careful if their goal is to heighten the suppression of marijuana. If more dealers begin to pay the tax, courts might again declare that prosecutions based on the de facto legal pot could not go forward. (As it stands now, it would be hard to use the tax laws to gain a second conviction against a pot dealer, anyway. Double jeopardy, being tried twice for the same crime, is forbidden by the U.S. Constitution. A federal court ruled a marijuana tax evasion prosecution conducted under Wisconsin's state laws illegitimate on double-jeopardy grounds in May 2004.[38])

Taxing an illegal vice good sometimes sets up conflict between various levels of government.[39] From the Civil War until national Prohibition, the federal government collected a sort of license fee from liquor manufacturers, wholesalers, and retailers. This fee was even collected from individuals who illegally sold liquor in dry states. Payment of the federal fee did not provide an exemption from state prohibition laws, but for many years, the existence of the

---

[36] For the story about the Mississippi tax and the ending of the state-level prohibition, see Barr (1999, pp. 250–2).

[37] Hamm (1995, p. 124).

[38] See the Vice Squad post of July 28, 2004.

[39] This paragraph is drawn from information in Chapter 3 in Hamm (1995, pp. 92–119).

tax did muddy the waters considerably about what alcohol-related behavior was legal. There was some question about whether payment of the federal tax could be used as evidence against an illegal seller in a dry state court, as such evidence might be a form of mandated (and hence unconstitutional) self-incrimination. Nor were federal revenue agents always willing to share their tax lists with state law enforcers. The federal government sometimes exacerbated tensions with local officials by auctioning off, in dry states, liquor seized from sellers who had not met their federal tax obligations – auctions that would have been illegal had anyone except a federal agent conducted them.

REPLACING A PROHIBITION WITH A TAX[40]

One way to reduce the consumption of some vice is to make it illegal, and to apply criminal penalties against manufacture, sale, purchase, possession, or other activities related to the vice. Another way to reduce the consumption of a vice is to keep it legal, but to tax it. Indeed, prohibition backed by criminal penalties can be viewed as a type of tax, though not one that relies primarily on monetary payments to the government.

That prohibition and taxation are both routes to reduced vice consumption raises the question whether it might be possible to eliminate the current vice prohibitions (on drugs or prostitution, say) and replace them with a tax. Might it even be possible to set the tax at such a level that there would be the same amount of vice consumption as with a prohibition?

Prohibition typically raises the nominal price paid by consumers for a good. The "full price" is even greater because purchasers also face some risk of being arrested or robbed during their black-market transaction or sold inferior or adulterated goods. Rephrasing the earlier query, would it be possible to determine this full, effective price and to choose a tax rate under legalization that would result in the same final price to consumers?

In theory, yes, this can be done, though in practice not with precision. (The lack of precision needn't be permanent: evidence that the legal tax over- or undershot the target could result in the appropriate adjustment.) The chief difficulty would occur if the prohibition has been effective in making the full price quite high. In that case, the "equivalent" tax (that would produce the same amount of consumption) would also have to be very high – and then the evasion of the prohibition might be reproduced under a legal regime by evasion of the tax. One lesson that might be drawn, then, is that it is easier to replace a prohibition with an equivalent tax when the prohibition is not very effective at reducing consumption – because the equivalent tax need not be so high that it becomes hard to control tax evasion.[41]

---

[40] This section draws heavily on a section with the same title in Chapter 2 of Leitzel (2003).

[41] One reason that it would not make sense to replace a prohibition against some crime that involves victims – murder or theft, say – with an "equivalent" tax is that those crimes do not represent voluntary exchanges. Even without any third-party involvement, the crime itself makes society worse

Replacing a prohibition with an "equivalent" tax does not mean that society should be indifferent between these two policy regimes. The tax is much less wasteful: the buyer pays the tax, and the government receives the revenue. But in the case of a prohibition, the high effective price paid by the buyer in terms of risk of arrest and violence in stealthy, black-market exchanges, does not result in revenue to the government. (And, of course, court cases and jail terms are quite costly both for the government and the vice producers and consumers.) Prohibition sets up a sort of clumsy tax, one that by and large does not raise revenue; rather, implementing and maintaining a prohibition tends to involve major expenses. Replacing a prohibition with an equivalent tax that does raise revenue is an improvement, substituting a relatively smooth tax for an extremely clumsy one.

So replacing a vice prohibition with an equivalent tax looks like a promising policy, especially if the prohibition is widely evaded. One complication, however, is that the effective price imposed by a prohibition varies among individuals. As opposed to the case with most legal goods, the full price of an illegal good involves substantial nonmonetary components. One such component takes the form of search costs, the time and trouble that must be taken to establish reliable connections between buyers and sellers. And a second such component is the risk of arrest and imprisonment. The costs imposed by the possibility of arrest tend to be greater for those who have more to lose from an arrest – in particular, those with good jobs and future prospects that would be compromised by a vice arrest or conviction.

Both search costs and arrest costs tend to make the effective price of a prohibited vice lower for poorer individuals than for richer individuals. As the illicit markets are predisposed to arise in low-income communities, people who live in those communities often have much better access to prohibited vice than do outsiders. (Indeed, better access than they have for many legal goods; even children in such neighborhoods might be able to purchase illicit drugs in the middle of the night.) As a result, a tax that maintains the effective price for poor people might lower the effective price for richer people following a vice legalization. For this reason, it might be desirable to "overtax" a newly legalized vice, to ensure that most potential consumers do not see a steep price decline with the onset of legalization.

A tax combined with other controls – perhaps state provision through monopoly stores, quantity limits, advertising regulations, information provision concerning potential harms, and so on – offers an attractive alternative to criminalization, particularly for those vices that are common despite the prohibition. The most harmful manifestations of vice consumption – especially those manifestations imposing a high risk of harm to others – can be targeted

---

off (else it could have been arranged voluntarily). So any "equivalent" tax would be prohibitive, and the perpetrator would have every incentive to evade it.

with specific bans or controls. That is, a well-designed tax and regulatory regime should be able to prevent a significant increase in consumption, while shifting the consumption that does take place to less socially costly varieties – and collecting tax revenue to boot. And of course, a tax-and-regulate approach can satisfy the robustness principle, while most vice prohibitions cannot.

The end of alcohol Prohibition is one instance in which a vice ban was successfully replaced with a regulatory scheme that included, in many U.S. states, high taxes. A similarly successful transition could be made in the case of currently illegal drugs: "drug control along the lines of alcohol control is a reasonable and practical policy option."[42] Licensing and advertising controls, as discussed below, are other elements of the regulatory apparatus that can be brought to bear on legal vices.

LICENSING

All places of public resort require the restraint of a police, and places of this kind [i. e., that sell "stimulants" such as alcohol] peculiarly, because offences against society are especially apt to originate there. It is, therefore, fit to confine the power of selling these commodities (at least for consumption on the spot) to persons of known or vouched-for respectability of conduct; to make such regulations respecting hours of opening and closing as may be requisite for public surveillance, and to withdraw the licence if breaches of the peace repeatedly take place through the connivance or incapacity of the keeper of the house, or if it becomes a rendezvous for concocting and preparing offences against the law.

John Stuart Mill, *On Liberty*[43]

A licensing system often forms part of the regulatory apparatus governing a legal vice. Licenses can be required of manufacturers, input suppliers, wholesalers, retailers, merchants, and consumers, or any combination of these participants in the trade. (Licensing of producers and importers is practically a necessity in facilitating the collection of an excise tax.[44]) Beyond identifying whom to license, the other key elements of licensing regimes are the criteria upon which licenses are granted, suspended, revoked, and reinstated.

Consider the licensing of sellers of alcohol or some other drug. What standards does an applicant for a license have to meet to be awarded a license? First, there might be a background check, to weed out, say, convicted felons or others who have given notice that they might not be all that scrupulous in obeying regulations. Second, there might be a license fee, not huge but not paltry, to ensure that every alcohol enthusiast doesn't find it in his interest to become a licensed dealer. One point of this fee, besides to cover the cost of

---

[42] Levine and Reinarman (1993, p. 181). Becker, Grossman, and Murphy (2004) provide a theoretical analysis, indicating that optimal taxation of a legal good, combined with black-market policing, often generates better outcomes than prohibition.

[43] Mill in Ryan (1997, p. 120).

[44] See, e.g., Sunley, Yurekli, and Chaloupka (2000, p. 416).

some of the alcohol control apparatus, is to restrict license awards to genuine sellers so that administrative resources will not be swamped by the necessity of overseeing thousands of extremely minor operations. The license fee also operates as a sort of bond, the returns to which will be forfeited by a seller whose malfeasance results in license revocation.

Once a license is obtained, how is a vice vendor expected to behave? Regulations can legitimately be adopted that aim to counter the $3\frac{1}{3}$ standard vice concerns, along with regulations aimed at easing enforcement of the primary rules. As is common in the case of alcohol, licensed sellers might have to respect minimum age requirements for buyers. They have to ensure that all of the requisite taxes are collected on sales. Hours of operation might be restricted, to reduce the possibility of public nuisance and to ease the policing requirements near vice outlets. Advertising or promotion controls might have to be complied with, and so on. In essence, a license holder agrees to act as the first level of enforcement for a potentially wide variety of vice-related regulations. Failure to perform this role in good faith would be sufficient for fines or license revocation.

The role of licensed sellers as regulation enforcers provides a case to directly restrict the number of licenses granted or to employ a substantial license fee to similarly limit, indirectly, the number of licensees. With such "artificial" restraints upon the issuing of licenses, a license becomes a more valuable asset to its holder: there is reduced competition among legitimate sellers, as there are fewer sellers, so higher profits will be available to license holders. With licenses highly valued, license holders will be reluctant to risk losing their license through inappropriate actions, including failure to enforce the various regulations governing vice sale and consumption. The knowledge that noncompliance puts at risk a valuable license spurs the enforcement effort of sellers, motivating a good deal of voluntary compliance with the rules. The scarcity of licenses provides a reward to good behavior on the part of sellers. Perhaps sticks can be used as well as carrots to provide motivation. If licenses are not particularly valuable, similar incentives could be established through fines for rule breaking; but it may be that, in practice, fines alone do not serve as substantial deterrents.[45]

A further rationale for limiting seller licenses might be that the scarcity of sellers serves to reduce consumption of the vice. Such a policy would be similar to using taxes to correct for "internalities," and it faces the same objection. Is it a legitimate government enterprise to direct consumption in one direction or another, once the regulatory regime has accounted for externalities, revenue considerations, and administrative concerns? Not surprisingly, John Stuart Mill

---

[45] Alternatively, if licenses are extremely valuable, regulatory authorities might grow reluctant to revoke a license for relatively minor violations, in which case the valuable license would no longer help to induce regulatory compliance.

would have no truck with such sumptuary policies: "The limitation in number, for instance, of beer and spirit houses, for the express purpose of rendering them more difficult of access, and diminishing the occasions of temptation, not only exposes all to an inconvenience because there are some by whom the facility would be abused, but is suited only to a state of society in which the labouring classes [i. e., the customers of taverns] are avowedly treated as children or savages, and placed under an education of restraint, to fit them for future admission to the privileges of freedom."[46] (Presumably the upper classes in Mill's time would consume their alcohol at home, and hence have no need of the taverns.) Mill would brook no inconveniencing of rational vice consumers to aid others with self-control problems. But the robustness principle provides a different approach: vice control should aim to assist those with self-control problems, while not *unduly* inconveniencing those whose vice choices are fully rational. This principle is not as averse to licensing restrictions for the purpose of limiting consumption. The trade-off between the interests of rational and less-than-rational vice consumers would permit some limitation of sales outlets, even beyond what would be called for to promote regulatory enforcement, as long as the inconveniencing of rational consumers was not severe. In practice, however, licensing restrictions are similar to taxes, in that typically there would be little or no need to go beyond Mill to combat internalities, once the other purposes for restricting licenses have been fully served.

LICENSING VICE CONSUMERS

Mandatory licenses could be applied to buyers as well as sellers. Buyer licenses are implicit in legal vices reserved for adults: those who meet the age requirement are licensed buyers, while the underage are not. But as we saw in Chapter 3, buyer licensing could be much more complex than a simple "old-enough?" inquiry, just as meeting the minimum age is only one of many requirements for acquiring a driver's or hunter's license. Vice license applicants might have to demonstrate familiarity with the harms associated with consumption, including the potential for addiction; knowledge of the regulatory restrictions could be required, too, following the model of those states that test driver's license applicants on their awareness of road rules and drunk driving laws. The license could allow purchases only up to some limit (per month or per year, say) – to help police any potential black market – and licensees themselves might choose a limit less than the maximum allowed by law, to help control their own consumption. The consumption licenses would only be valid for a year or two, though they could be renewed. Sellers again would provide the primary enforcement by checking all purchasers for valid licenses, just as alcohol and tobacco sellers currently require identification to ensure that the

---

[46] Mill in Ryan (1997, p. 120).

minimum purchase age requirement is met. (The sellers could even be limited to government-run outlets and perhaps those that only allow advance or mail-order purchases.) Vice-related malefactors would have their license to purchase temporarily or permanently revoked.[47] Insurance companies, employers, and prospective spouses could discriminate on the basis of license status.[48]

In the case of alcohol, some elements of a buyer's licensing system already are in place. First, there is the minimum age condition. Second, courts increasingly are imposing "no drinking" requirements on those found guilty of (or on pretrial release from) alcohol-related offenses. One could imagine going much further, by requiring an explicit alcohol consumption license for anyone who chooses to drink.[49]

Although a requirement that adult consumers of alcohol obtain a license does not violate the robustness principle, I suspect that there would be little to be gained by such a licensing system, especially if other elements of the control regime, including anti-drunk driver measures, work well. An alcohol licensing system for users sets up a fairly complex apparatus for the purpose of controlling a relative handful of people – and by itself it only prevents *purchases* of alcohol by nonlicense holders but does not prevent *consumption* if they manage to get hold of alcohol by other means. A workable policy that affected only those who are targeted by a personal alcohol ban would likely offer an improvement over a universal licensing regime, especially if the more discriminating policy controlled alcohol consumption as opposed to purchase. Improvements in technologies (such as the alcohol monitoring bracelet) that help keep problematic individuals from consuming alcohol make the rationale for a broader alcohol buyer licensing scheme less compelling. In the terminology of Mark Kleiman, explicit positive licenses – those that can only be required by jumping through various hoops – may not be necessary if negative licenses – revoking drinking privileges for those who misbehave under the influence – work well.

In evaluating the desirability of licensing consumers, it should be remembered that there are large numbers of regular alcohol users who are satisfied with their consumption and whose own satisfaction does not come at the expense of the quality of life of others. Tobacco is different in this regard: most regular smokers express a desire to quit, and many attempt to quit.[50] In terms of harms,

---

[47] Mark Kleiman spells out some of the issues with respect to alcohol buyer's licenses in a post on his blog; see "Taking the bottle away from dangerous drunks," March 20, 2004, available at www.markarkleiman.com/archives/policy_briefs_/2004/03/taking_the_bottle_away_from_dangerous_drunks.php (accessed on July 24, 2004).

[48] Whether it should be legal for employers to discriminate on the basis of off-the-job consumption of addictive drugs is a controversial question. Many states in the United States have laws that preclude such discrimination with respect to nonworking-hour use of alcohol and tobacco. At least in the early stages of a legalization of heroin or cocaine, it might be prudent not to extend such nondiscrimination laws to those newly legalized substances. On the other hand, nondiscrimination laws might be necessary for compliance with the robustness principle, if their absence imposes large costs upon rational drug users.

[49] Kleiman (2007) suggests alcohol licensing for consumers.

[50] U.S. Department of Health and Human Services (USDHHS) (2000).

the most important distinction in alcohol consumption is between bingeing and moderate consumption, whereas for cigarette consumption, the most important distinction is between abstinence (or occasional use) and regular use. These alcohol/tobacco differences could be reflected in the pricing of buyer licensing regimes, too.

Given the large number of satisfied and unproblematic regular consumers of alcohol, any explicit alcohol buyer's license regime should not involve a substantial fee for the license. A high license fee would violate the principle that rational vice consumers should not be unduly inconvenienced by regulations that might help bolster the self-control of others. Individual drinks, however, should still have a significant excise tax attached to combat externalities, including those associated with binge-drinking episodes. But in the case of cigarettes, an explicit buyer's licensing regime might with more reason involve a large license fee and low excise taxes per pack.[51] The current per pack taxes could even be lowered in such a way that a switch to a buyer licensing regime would lead to reduced overall expenditure on cigarettes by regular users. The notion is that the high license fee will help some regular users implement their intention to quit. It is likely that the decision to make a considerable payment for a cigarette license would be sufficiently momentous that many users would be given pause, in ways that do not occur with quotidian decisions to buy a pack. Those who choose not to quit would not be harmed, given that the per pack excise tax was lowered to the point that typical regular users would not spend more on cigarettes. (The lowered per pack price might tend to increase the consumption of those who continue to smoke. To combat that tendency, regulations could limit the number of packs that the license allows holders to purchase at the low excise tax price; purchases above that limit would involve higher taxes.) Taxed purchases of a small number of packs each month or year per adult might be allowed for people without a cigarette license, to allow experimentation and for the "benefit" of light smokers.[52]

Whereas the discussion of licensing has so far taken place primarily with respect to the legal drugs of alcohol and nicotine, both buyer and seller licensing are feasible approaches to the regulation of currently illegal drugs such as opiates and cocaine. For these drugs, advance purchase requirements and quantity limits would presumably play a prominent role, unlike the current regulation of alcohol and tobacco.

ADVERTISING

In the absence of any governmental or industry-imposed restrictions, legal vice goods tend to be heavily advertised. The marketing budget for alcohol manufacturers in the United States comes to more than $5 billion annually. Televised professional sports include about two alcohol ads per hour, a much

[51] Such a proposal is made by O'Donoghue and Rabin (2003).
[52] O'Donoghue and Rabin (2003) note this possibility.

Box 5.2: *Regulating a legal addictive drug: Nicotine*

The regulatory regime surrounding legal vices such as alcohol, tobacco, and gambling is enormously complex, and it should be. For centuries, these vices have
shown themselves to be problematic in ways that ketchup is not. Here is a synopsis
of the typical regulatory apparatus surrounding cigarettes (and some other tobacco
products) in the United States.

First, sellers are licensed. Excise taxes, sometimes at very high levels, are applied
by the federal government, individual states, and municipal authorities. There is a
minimum-age-for-purchase requirement, and financial pressure from Washington,
DC, has forced states both to adopt an age limit no lower than 18 and to devote
resources to enforcing the age control. Some localities have made possession of
cigarettes by minors illegal. Tobacco marketing is limited, in part voluntarily by sellers, but mostly owing to explicit regulations or as a response to potential tort liability.
For instance, federal law prohibits cigarette advertising on broadcast television or
radio. Free samples and tobacco branding of nontobacco products are restrained.
Controls aimed at limiting the exposure of minors to advertisements for tobacco
are particularly common. Consumption is forbidden by law in a variety of locales;
in some establishments where smoking is not forbidden, designated nonsmoking
areas are required. The government helps to superintend a vast education campaign
about the dangers of smoking, while promoting and subsidizing aids to smoking
cessation. Warning labels are required on packs of cigarettes, and similar cautions
are bundled, by law, with print advertisements undertaken by tobacco manufacturers. Research into the effects of cigarette use and various treatments is publicly
funded. The overall regulatory regime emanates from all levels of government, from
local by-laws to international treaties. Private regulation takes place as well, in the
forms of workplace smoking policies and insurance provisions regarding tobacco
use and treatments, for instance, along with philanthropic support for initiatives to
reduce smoking. Informal social norms also govern smoking behavior, although
these norms evolve in tandem with formal policies.[a] The main input into cigarettes,
tobacco, for decades was supported in price by the federal government, which also
implemented production quotas to limit the expense of the price support. Inspec-
tion, grading, and pesticide-testing services are still available from the Department
of Agriculture for tobacco crops. Diplomatic pressure has been applied by Washington on foreign countries to ease the penetration of their domestic markets by
U.S. cigarette firms.

In 1998, the major tobacco manufacturers settled a lawsuit that was brought by
the attorneys general of forty-six U.S. states. (The four excluded states came to
separate, similar deals.) This Master Settlement Agreement includes massive payments from the manufacturers to the states. The payments, slated to be perpetual,
are tied to the market shares of the manufacturers and should amount to more than
$200 billion by the year 2025. The tying of these settlement payments to future
sales makes them operate much like an excise tax, estimated to be on the order of 45
cents per pack.[b] As with explicit sin taxes, these large payments render the state a
sort of partner with the cigarette manufacturers and might compromise government

interest in reducing smoking. Beyond the large transfers to the states, the Master Settlement Agreement also includes a host of limitations on tobacco marketing. For instance, billboard ads are prohibited, as are the use of cartoon characters to promote cigarettes.

The general approach that the United States takes toward tobacco regulation, including excise taxes and marketing controls, is paralleled in many other countries. Though cigarette prices tend to be much lower in developing countries than in developed countries, excise taxes frequently are a high percentage of pretax prices, even in poor countries: more than 60 percent in Zambia and more than 130 percent in Mauritius, for instance.[c] Cigarettes tend to be the highest taxed of all customary goods. Minimum ages for purchasing cigarettes are common, too. Public smoking bans have been adopted in India, Ireland, and Italy and are spreading to the rest of the alphabet. Bhutan has gone further (too far, our robustness principle would suggest) by banning the sale of cigarettes.[d]

In February 2005, an international tobacco control treaty emanating from the World Health Organization (WHO) went into effect, following the ratification of the accord by forty nations. The terms of the treaty apply only to those signatory nations that ratify it, but the roster of signatories includes more than 100 countries, so it appears that soon its reach will be near global. The treaty, officially entitled the WHO Framework Convention on Tobacco Control, is the first international treaty formed under WHO auspices. The convention calls for taxes, indoor smoking limitations, large warning labels on tobacco products, prohibitions on sales to youths, and a comprehensive ban on tobacco advertising, to the extent that such policies are compatible with the constitutional principles of the signatory nations. Measures to try to prevent cross-jurisdiction smuggling of cigarettes also are endorsed. Furthermore, parties to the convention commit to protect their tobacco-related public health policies "from commercial and other vested interests of the tobacco industry in accordance with national law."[e]

This capsule summary of tobacco regulation indicates the complexity of the overall regulatory scheme. Public policy influences virtually every step leading to the smoking of a cigarette: manufacturing, marketing, selling, purchasing, consuming, and treatment are all subject to controls, with the interventions radiating from the highest to the lowest echelons of government. Similarly complex, multidimensional regulations will be required when the bans on currently illegal drugs such as cocaine, marijuana, and opiates are lifted.

The U.S.-style tobacco regulatory system is broadly consistent with the robustness principle. Minimum age requirements, seller licensing, marketing controls, antismoking campaigns, aids to cessation: none of these measures surely fall afoul of robustness, though they could if they were severe enough, if there were only one small licensed seller per state or if the minimum purchase age were 35. The elements of current policy that are most questionable from the point of view of the robustness principle are taxation and public smoking bans.

In most areas of the United States, cigarette taxes are tolerable, but in the highest tax locations, the burden upon smokers is too great, in my opinion, to be

(continued)

consistent with robustness. In New York City, a pack of cigarettes in the early part
of the twenty-first century retailed for around $7.50, with state and city taxes of
$3.00 per pack – on top of the federal excise and the Master Settlement Agreement
assessment.[f] Perhaps a rule of thumb for relatively cheap and repeatedly purchased
vice goods, such as a pack of cigarettes or a six pack of beer, is that taxes (beyond
those correcting for externalities) that more than double the retail price are suspect
from a robustness standpoint (and often from a tax administration standpoint as
well).

Indoor smoking bans imposed for buildings that people cannot easily avoid
entering, such as courthouses or state motor vehicle agencies, are probably consistent with robustness, as mentioned in Chapter 3. Nevertheless, setting aside a
smoking room often would represent a better compromise between the interests
of smokers and nonsmokers. Public smoking bans that extend to all restaurants
and bars violate robustness, in my judgment, by being too costly upon smokers.
(Recall from Chapter 3 my contention that mandated nonsmoking areas in bars and
restaurants are consistent with robustness.) Perhaps a desirable compromise would
be for restaurants to choose whether to acquire a special license (for a moderate
fee) to permit smoking on a portion of the premises, just as restaurants now choose
whether to acquire a liquor license.

[a] Nyborg and Rege (2003).   [b] Gruber (2002, p. 151).
[c] Viscusi (2003).
[d] A ban on cigarette sales would not violate the robustness principle if loose tobacco and papers
for hand-rolling cigarettes were readily available. In some high cigarette tax countries, hand-
rolled cigarettes form a major part of overall tobacco consumption.
[e] The quote is from Article 5, paragraph 3 of the convention, which is available at
www.who.int/tobacco/framework/en/ (accessed February 24, 2007).
[f] Fleenor (2003).

higher frequency than in typical programming.[53] Tobacco companies are major
advertisers, too. In the late 1990s, it was estimated that the production costs
for a pack of Marlboros came to 16 cents, with an additional 55 cents per
pack spent on promotion.[54] The broad scope of vice advertising subsumes
television commercials, layouts in national magazines, newspaper ads, event
sponsorship, and point-of-purchase marketing.

The long-term use of advertising by profit-motivated firms suggests that ads
raise the consumption of the promoted goods. By this reckoning, more beer
commercials lead to more beer quaffed, and more cigarette billboards lead
to more cigarettes smoked. Alcohol and tobacco manufacturers, along with
some researchers, frequently dispute this contention, however. They claim

[53] See the discussion in Agostinelli and Grube (2002), and Babor, Caetano, and Casswell et al. (2003,
p. 178).
[54] Slade (2001, p. 72).

that advertising boosts sales of specific brands but not aggregate consumption. Advertising expenditures, under this alternative view, re-allocate a fixed amount of consumption among the offerings of competing producers. Such a re-allocation might occur among varieties of similar products, too: wine advertising might raise the consumption of wine while lowering the consumption of hard liquor, for instance. One could even imagine a perverse effect, in which advertising reduces aggregate consumption because the costs of advertising lead to higher prices that dissuade potential vice buyers. (With no effect or a perverse effect on consumption from advertising, industry trade groups would seem to have an incentive to lobby for the imposition of an advertising ban.[55])

The empirical evidence about whether vice advertising raises vice consumption is mixed. Similarly, whether abusive consumption (alcoholism, for example) and harmful related activities (drunk driving) increase when vice is more strongly advertised remains unsettled. Underage consumers see many vice ads, and the possibility of a positive relationship between marketing and youth consumption and harmful behaviors is a particular concern. Exposure to advertising might influence perceptions of the extent of vice consumption by others; such overestimates of social norms can then feedback to individual decisions to engage in vice.[56] In the United States, for instance, college students typically overestimate the extent to which their peers drink alcohol. The provision of accurate information about drinking norms has become a common measure taken to combat binge drinking by young people.[57]

The uncertain connection between advertising and vice consumption is reflected in contradictory findings from studies of the impacts of advertising bans. Looking at wealthy country data, for instance, leads Saffer and Chaloupka (2000) to conclude that cigarette advertising bans result in a more than 7 percent decline in consumption, while Nelson (2003) finds no evidence from international data that advertising bans reduce smoking. Prohibitions on advertising that apply only to a subset of the main marketing channels are unlikely to have much impact on consumption, though presumably broader bans, those that include radio, television, newspaper, magazine, and billboard ads, as well as event sponsorship, hold more hope for restraining vice. One study of youth alcohol consumption in the United States found that a broad advertising ban could reduce drinking binges among young people by more than 40 percent.[58]

Marketing might serve the goal of harm reduction. If a vice good such as cigarettes involves a health risk, then manufacturers might be able to increase their market share if they design lower toxicity into their wares. For this strategy

---

[55] Will Baude suggested this to me.

[56] Babor, Caetano, and Casswell et al. (2003, p. 176).

[57] An early evaluation of "social norms marketing interventions" did not demonstrate effectiveness in reducing the alcohol use of college students, however; see Wechsler, Nelson, Lee et al. (2003).

[58] Saffer and Dave (2003).

to be profitable, however, manufacturers of a safer vice good need to be able to inform potential consumers about the improved safety features of their product. Marketing controls that prevent the dissemination of comparative health risks, then, might limit or eliminate the incentive of manufacturers to compete on the basis of safety. As a result, total vice-related harms might go up in the presence of a broad marketing ban, even if overall consumption falls.

Mandated health warnings are one type of marketing regulation that aims to enlist labeling and advertising into reducing harms. In the United States, cigarette packages and ads must contain health warnings, as must alcohol labels. Other countries, including Canada and Great Britain, prescribe much larger warnings and sometimes graphic images on cigarette packs, and some evidence indicates that the increased prominence adds to a warning's impact.[59] Counteradvertising, public service announcements or paid messages that warn against vice-related dangers, likewise can be employed to attempt to reduce the costs or prevalence of vice. (Counteradvertising can even be aimed at nonvice consumers, as in anti-drunk-driving ads that encourage friends to prevent their friends from driving drunk.) The impacts of alcohol and tobacco warning labels and counteradvertising do not appear to be large, but there is evidence that such measures have reduced some forms of costly consumption.[60] The ban on television advertising of cigarettes adopted by the United States in the early 1970s simultaneously ended the free provision (under the Federal Communications Commission's Fairness Doctrine) of antismoking ads; the prevalence of smoking increased after both types of televison messages were curtailed.

Most people who engage in legal vice are "satisfied customers." (This probably is the case for illegal vice, too.) They appreciate the opportunity to drink wine, for instance, or to spend a few hours in a casino. But, as noted earlier, there is a significant exception: cigarettes. Most adult smokers indicate that they want to quit. This situation renders cigarette marketing to be somewhat tricky. "The tobacco manufacturers face the unpleasant reality that most of their customers do not want to be their customers."[61] Policy can respond to widespread desires to quit by mandating that information on how to access help in quitting be included in every pack of cigarettes; this is a measure that has been adopted in Canada.[62]

Private codes of conduct tend to play a significant role in vice marketing controls. Distilled spirits producers in the United States have adopted elaborate rules that preclude ads in college newspapers, for instance. The beer and

---

[59] See "Graphic warnings on cigarette packs DO help smokers quit," News-Medical.Net, February 7, 2007, at www.news-medical.net/?id=21764 (accessed February 24, 2007).Graphic images on Canadian cigarette packs can be viewed at www.smoke-free.ca/warnings/Canada-warnings.htm (accessed February 24, 2007). Images on cigarette packs sold in Singapore are all but unbearable: http://www.smoke-free.ca/warnings/Singapore-warnings.htm.
[60] Agostinelli and Grube (2002).   [61] Slade (2001, p. 73).
[62] Slade (2001, p. 99).

wine industries have adopted separate codes aimed at limiting youth exposure to advertisements and reducing abusive alcohol consumption or related activities. One advantage of such industry codes is that they tend to be self-enforcing. If one producer airs an ad that violates the code, its competitors have an incentive to file a complaint – an approach to encouraging compliance that can be effective.[63] In the case of tobacco in the United States, the Master Settlement Agreement provides legal enforcement against violations of the agreed-upon marketing restrictions.

Industry-wide, voluntary vice marketing controls tend to conflict with antitrust laws, however. If all firms in the soft-drinks industry jointly agreed to eliminate advertising, they would save the massive amounts of money in their marketing budgets and possibly even increase their profits. In other words, advertising of existing products in mature industries shares many features of an arms race, and the participants might well prefer an arms-control treaty to unbridled competition. But such an agreement would violate antitrust laws, especially if the agreement also tried to limit the advertising of new entrants to the industry. The tobacco industry's Master Settlement Agreement might not survive an ongoing court challenge based upon the anticompetitive features of the accord.

Sometimes vice providers can find themselves in a bit of a dilemma over marketing controls. For instance, it is not uncommon for bars near college campuses to come under pressure from college and local officials to refrain from sponsoring happy hours or other low-priced drinks specials. Business imperatives might make any specific establishment unlikely to avoid such promotions, however, unless its competitors similarly desist. But any agreement among local bars to ban price cutting holds the potential to violate antitrust rules. This scenario played out in 2003 in Madison, Wisconsin, the home of the main campus of the University of Wisconsin. Local bars adopted a ban on weekend alcohol price promotions and shortly thereafter were sued (with the plaintiff in line to collect the triple damages that are provided for in private antitrust actions) for restraint of trade. The state lawsuit was eventually dismissed, though a similar federal case followed in its wake; whatever the final resolution, the episode indicates the difficult line that vice providers must tread when looking to limit marketing.[64]

The rationale for antitrust provisions is that the interests of consumers tend to be served through free competition. The externalities and internalities associated with the traditional vices, however, strongly call this rationale into question. The low prices and frequently intensive marketing that characterize vigorous competition in consumer goods, and are desirable in most circumstances,

[63] See the Vice Squad post from March 8, 2005.
[64] See www.overlawyered.com/2005/10/update_suing_madison_taverns_a.html (accessed February 24, 2007).

are less likely to conduce to the advantage of consumers as a whole when alcohol and tobacco are the commodities in question. So it might be sensible to relax standard antitrust rules in the case of vice goods; indeed, such relaxation might be a requirement of robustness.

COMMERCIAL SPEECH REGULATION IN THE UNITED STATES

Vice marketing controls exist at the edge of legality in a second, probably more important sense: government limits on vice advertising in the United States might be construed to conflict with free-speech provisions of the First Amendment. Can the government preclude a legal firm from advertising its wares in the manner that it chooses?

In the United States, advertising does not receive the highest level of First Amendment protection. Rather, "commercial speech" such as advertising can be regulated provided the provisions of a four-part legal test are met – a test that was developed in the 1980 case of *Central Hudson Gas & Electric Corporation v. Public Service Commission of New York* (commonly referred to as the *Central Hudson* case).[65] A regulation upon advertising is viewed as consistent with the First Amendment's freedom of speech provision either if (1) the advertising is for an illegal activity or is misleading; or, if the following three conditions hold: (2) the government has a substantial interest; (3) the regulation directly advances the asserted government interest; and (4) the regulation is not more extensive than necessary to serve the interest.[66] In recent years, the Supreme Court has overturned various laws curtailing alcohol, gambling, and tobacco advertising on the grounds that the restrictions did not satisfy one of the prongs (typically prongs 3 and 4) of the *Central Hudson* test. These decisions suggest that for legal vices, public controls over marketing are becoming harder to sustain. A hostile climate toward vice marketing restrictions signifies quite a revolution from the situation prevailing just a few decades ago, when advertising was not provided any First Amendment protection at all and hence could be subject to extensive regulations and bans.

The current direction of commercial speech regulation in the United States presents a substantial barrier to drug legalization. The first prong of *Central Hudson* makes it clear that banning the advertising of an illegal good, such as marijuana, is perfectly acceptable. If marijuana were to be legalized, however, the other elements of the *Central Hudson* test might necessitate nearly uncontrolled advertising. That is, the stronger the First Amendment protection for

[65] 447 U.S. 557 (1980).
[66] This approach to the constitutional jurisprudence surrounding commercial speech has its detractors – including Supreme Court Justice Clarence Thomas, who has made it clear many times that he believes that content-based restrictions on truthful commercial speech should receive the same "strict scrutiny" that the court would apply to restrictions on noncommercial speech.

commercial speech, the harder it becomes to establish a drug control regime (à la John Stuart Mill or the robustness principle) in which drugs are made legally available to adults but where the commercialization of drugs is limited. Even many supporters of drug legalization might have qualms if the only alternative to prohibition were a legal industry employing the full panoply of marketing strategies and promotions. Ironically, increased freedom for commercial speech can lead to less commercial speech, as goods for which advertising is a particular concern might find themselves – and their advertising – prohibited as a result.

THE *POSADAS* CASE: A WAY AHEAD?[67]

In 1986, the United States Supreme Court ruled on a case, *Posadas de Puerto Rico Associates v. Tourism Company*, that concerned limitations on casino advertising in Puerto Rico.[68] When the legislature of Puerto Rico legalized casino gambling in the late 1940s, it simultaneously prohibited advertising by the casinos directed toward residents of Puerto Rico. (Advertising aimed at foreign tourists was permitted.) By a 5-4 majority, the U.S. Supreme Court, employing the *Central Hudson* test, upheld the legitimacy of the advertising restrictions.[69] The majority opinion also argued that "the greater power to completely ban casino gambling necessarily includes the lesser power to ban advertising of casino gambling." This commonsense notion has attracted a good deal of critical commentary (including some from later opinions by Supreme Court justices) and, indeed, appears to fly in the face of the *Central Hudson* approach to regulating commercial speech.

In many circumstances, the existence of a "greater" power need not imply the existence of a "lesser" power. For instance, capital punishment for convicted murderers is constitutional in the United States, while the (arguably) lesser power of extreme torture is not constitutional. (That is, torture would be inconsistent with the Eighth Amendment's protection against cruel and unusual punishments.) But in terms of vice regulation, the power (if it exists) to ban one of the traditional vices probably should include the lesser power of legalizing the vice while controlling the advertising of the vice, as the *Posadas* case suggests for casino gambling. A legal-sales-but-controlled-advertising regime essentially consists of an offer from the government to license sellers, conditional on their willingness to refrain from specified types of advertising. The threat not to license the vices in the absence of ad controls is quite credible, in that

---

[67] This section draws heavily upon Berman (2002).
[68] 478 U.S. 328 (1986).
[69] The advertising restrictions that were upheld were not the full set adopted by the Puerto Rican legislature but a narrower version that had been constructed by Puerto Rican courts.

the traditional vices legally can be banned today and often have been banned in the past. (And, of course, many vice-related activities currently are prohibited in the United States.) Such conditional offers, therefore, have a strong claim for promoting both individual liberty and speech, relative to the alternative that would arise if such licenses were not available. A conditional license to sell ketchup only in the absence of advertising cannot similarly be argued to be speech-and-liberty enhancing – a threatened ban on ketchup is neither credible nor traditional. Therefore, a *Posadas*-like acceptance of the constitutionality of conditional vice licenses need not imply that the government can more generally confer benefits only if speech rights are waived.[70] The traditional vices have proved their exceptionalism from most other types of consumer goods and services over centuries, and it is appropriate that the legal regime recognize that exceptional history.

Antitrust law is meant to promote the interests of consumers. The First Amendment is intended to protect and promote speech. Nevertheless, applying standard antitrust and commercial speech legal doctrine in the vice domain is likely to harm consumers and to limit speech. In Chapter 8, a similar situation will be shown to exist in the area of free trade. The application of typical free trade principles to vice is likely to redound to the detriment of both vice policy and trade.

VICE VERDICTS (III): ADVERTISING

The power to regulate vice is generally a state and local matter in the United States. The main federal role is to control interstate aspects of vice and to try to create the legal space for efficacious state-level regulations. Just as the Twenty-first Amendment tries to protect dry states from liberal alcohol control policies in wetter neighbors, federal law seeks to limit the extent to which liberal vice policies in one state can undermine stricter controls in other states. Advertising is one aspect of vice that often holds interstate ramifications.

Gambling Advertising: *United States v. Edge Broadcasting Co.* (1993) and *Greater New Orleans Broadcasting Association, Inc., v. United States* (1999)

Federal lottery legislation attempts to insulate individual state decisions on lotteries by forbidding broadcasters in nonlottery states from airing lottery commercials sponsored by nearby states that do operate a lottery. Virginia has a state lottery and, in the 1990s, North Carolina did not. More than 90 percent of the listeners to a North Carolina–based (and licensed) radio station located

---

[70] The legal issues involved by conditional offers are examined thoroughly in Berman (2002).

near the Virginia border were residents of Virginia. This North Carolina radio station wanted to broadcast advertisements for Virginia's state lottery but was prevented from doing so by the federal law. The station asserted that the law violated its First Amendment and equal protection rights. In *United States v. Edge Broadcasting Co.*, the Supreme Court decided against the radio station, by applying the four-part test of *Central Hudson*.[71] In the *Edge* case, the Supreme Court overturned the opinion of lower courts, which had ruled that the government interest in shielding North Carolinians from the effects of Virginia's lottery was not directly advanced by the law and hence failed the third element of the four-part *Central Hudson* test.

In the 1999 case *Greater New Orleans Broadcasting Association, Inc., v. United States*, the Supreme Court employed similar reasoning in striking down the use of the same federal law (as was at issue and upheld in *Edge*) when applied to certain casino advertising. Radio and television broadcasts originating in the New Orleans area sometimes reach Arkansas and Texas. Private for-profit casinos are legal in Louisiana but not in Arkansas or Texas (though tribal casinos are legal in these locales). A Louisiana-based broadcaster can advertise state-run gambling even though the broadcast is heard in Texas (just as a Virginia radio station can advertise the Virginia state lottery even though some North Carolina listeners hear the ads). But the casinos concerned in *Greater New Orleans* were private, that is, not state run, and so the federal law barred their ads being broadcast into states that did not permit private casinos. (The Federal Communications Commission's interpretation of the federal law did not actually bar all casino ads; rather, the FCC permitted advertising that referred to the amenities of the casinos but not to the gambling itself.) "nongambling" states, nevertheless, could legally receive broadcasts of ads for state-owned casinos and lotteries from other states, tribal casinos, and nongaming aspects of private casinos. The Supreme Court ruled, therefore, that the third prong of *Central Hudson* was not being met by the extremely selective ad ban – the law and its accompanying FCC enforcement was "so pierced by exemptions and inconsistencies that the Government cannot hope to exonerate it." What government interest could be served by restricting such a narrow element of advertising (for private out-of-state casinos), when essentially identical ads (for Indian or state-run casinos) were widely available?

Alcohol and Tobacco Advertising: *44 Liquormart, Inc., v. Rhode Island* (1996) and *Lorillard Tobacco Co. v. Reilly* (2001)

In between *Edge* and *Greater New Orleans* was another interstate vice advertising case, *44 Liquormart, Inc., v. Rhode Island* (1996).[72] Rhode Island law prohibited price advertising by state-licensed alcohol vendors, even if those

---

[71] 509 U.S. 418 (1993).   [72] 517 U.S. 484 (1996).

advertisements were placed in other states where such ads were legal. A liquor
retailer near the border with Connecticut wanted to advertise prices in a Connecticut newspaper but was told that his Rhode Island liquor license would
be revoked if he did so. (The retailer, 44 Liquormart, first got in trouble for a
Rhode Island–based ad that hinted – only hinted! – at low liquor prices.) The
Rhode Island Supreme Court found against the retailer because the state had
a substantial interest in promoting temperance. Had the state shown that the
ad ban actually did promote temperance, à la the *Central Hudson* test? No,
but the retailer hadn't shown the contrary, and the Prohibition-ending Twenty-
first Amendment added validity to the state statute, according to the Rhode
Island Supreme Court. The U.S. Supreme Court felt differently, however. It
found that the advertising ban failed both the third and fourth prongs of the
Central Hudson test: aren't there ways of promoting temperance that do not
involve restrictions on speech? Further, the Supreme Court majority held that
"the Twenty-first Amendment does not qualify the constitutional prohibition
against laws abridging the freedom of speech embodied in the First Amendment," and it spoke on vice more broadly:

> Moreover, the scope of any "vice" exception to the protection afforded by the
> First Amendment would be difficult, if not impossible, to define. Almost any
> product that poses some threat to public health or public morals might reasonably
> be characterized by a state legislature as relating to "vice activity." Such char-
> acterization, however, is anomalous when applied to products such as alcoholic
> beverages, lottery tickets, or playing cards, that may be lawfully purchased on
> the open market. The recognition of such an exception would also have the unfor-
> tunate consequence of either allowing state legislatures to justify censorship by
> the simple expedient of placing the "vice" label on selected lawful activities, or
> requiring the federal courts to establish a federal common law of vice. For these
> reasons, a "vice" label that is unaccompanied by a corresponding prohibition
> against the commercial behavior at issue fails to provide a principled justification
> for the regulation of commercial speech about that activity.[73]

[One possible rejoinder, of course, is that other proclaimed vices are not quite
the same as alcohol, in that they do not have a specific provision (the Twenty-
first Amendment) of the highest law in the land giving states control over their
regulation. It's not a vice exception to the First Amendment, it's an alcohol
exception, and the exception, arguably, is (or was, until *44 Liquormart* was
decided) required by the Constitution.]

In January 1999, the attorney general of Massachusetts imposed new regulations on the advertising of cigarettes and other tobacco products. These
regulations included a ban on any outdoor advertising within 1,000 feet of
public playgrounds or elementary or secondary schools and a requirement that
"point-of-sale" advertisements be at least five feet off of the ground. Adopting

[73] 517 U.S. 484 (1996), internal case reference omitted.

these advertising regulations was a bit provocative, given the existence of a federal law, the Federal Cigarette Labeling and Advertising Act (FCLAA), which says that "No requirement or prohibition based on smoking and health shall be imposed under State law with respect to advertising or promotion of any cigarettes . . ."[74] The Supreme Court held that the two regulations previously mentioned (on outdoor advertising and height of point-of-sale ads) were preempted by the FCLAA, but the court also considered First (and Fourteenth) Amendment challenges of the new regulations as they applied to smokeless tobacco products and cigars (as these items are not covered by the FCLAA). Using *Central Hudson* once again, the court found (among other things) that the outdoor ad restrictions were too broad and hence failed the fourth prong of *Central Hudson*. The *Lorillard* opinion, like the *44 Liquormart* opinion, shows that fear that it might be difficult to limit the advertising of legal products in the United States is well-placed, at least if the court does not return to *Posadas*-style reasoning: "The First Amendment also constrains state efforts to limit advertising of tobacco products, because so long as the sale and use of tobacco is lawful for adults, the tobacco industry has a protected interest in communicating information about its products and adult customers have an interest in receiving that information."[75]

[74] This provision of the FCLAA is quoted in the court opinion, *Lorillard Tobacco Co. v. Reilly*, decided June 28, 2001.
[75] *Lorillard Tobacco Co. v. Reilly* (2001).

6

Commercial Sex

Sex is dangerous. Sex puts emotional and physical health at risk, sometimes with fatal consequences. Sex is potentially addictive. Even for nonaddicts sex is repeatedly "Past reason hunted," and after a successful chase, "Past reason hated."[1] Teens are particularly vulnerable to sex-related dangers. Third parties suffer from the sex (or the search for sex) of others, through noise and violence and public health care costs. In terms of each of the $3\frac{1}{3}$ standard vice concerns – kids, addicts, externalities, and harms to nonaddicted adult participants – sex fares poorly. Surely, if a new drug emerged with the same vice profile as sex, legislators would rush to ban it.[2]

But sex is popular, and so it remains legal for adults. Those types of sex that are less popular – homosexual relations, incest, bestiality – regularly are illegal. Commercial forms of sex, including prostitution, pornography, and exotic dancing, tend to be banned or strictly regulated, even in societies with relatively liberal rules governing sex.

The main focus of this chapter is the application of the robustness principle to the regulation of pornography and prostitution. Before looking at commercial sex, however, I note a few sexual issues involving kids and addicts, followed by an examination of sadomasochism, a variety of sex that underscores the potential for harms to befall nonaddicted adults.

KIDS

Teens and young adults seem to be more at risk than their elders for suffering undesirable consequences from sex. In the United States, infection rates for sexually transmitted diseases tend to be much higher for older teenagers and young adults than for their elders; nearly half of new HIV infections develop in the 15 to 24 age group.[3] Unintended pregnancies are more prevalent among

---

[1] Shakespeare, Sonnet CXXIX.

[2] Of course, many legislators rush to ban any new vice or new form of an old vice. Recent examples include alcohol inhalers and Internet gambling. See Vice Squad posts from September 21, 2003, and September 29, 2004.

[3] See CDC (2005) and the tables in the CDC's "STD Surveillance, 2004."

younger women.[4] Children face a greater risk of being victimized by sexual assault than adults.[5]

The special dangers that sex poses for the young, combined with other factors such as adult perceptions of youthful sexual innocence, motivate various public policies toward kids and sex. Laws regulate youth sex itself, the availability of contraceptives, the provision of information about sex and contraception, and abortion or other responses to unwanted pregnancy.

The main policy toward child sexual activity is prohibition. For kids, sex with others is forbidden. The age at which sex becomes unforbidden varies, though 16 is fairly typical.[6] In the United States, these laws often are not enforced aggressively when there is no coercion and the participants are of similar ages, though sex between older people and children is policed more strictly. Sometimes "Romeo and Juliet" laws formalize this distinction, by permitting sex between adolescents of similar ages, while criminalizing the behavior of an appreciably older person who engages in sex with an adolescent. Other dimensions upon which legal ages of consent might turn include whether the sex is heterosexual or homosexual, whether the participant is a male or a female, and whether the older participant holds some position of authority (e.g., teacher) vis-a-vis the younger partner.

The negative consequences of adolescent sex suggest that, for their own protection, kids should be informed of the dangers of sexual activity. Precisely when, where, and what they should be told, and the associated messages that the information sends about personal policies toward sex, are controversial in the United States – though much less so in Europe.[7] Ensuring that children understand the dangers of sex protects adults, too, given the standard externalities associated with disease transmission and publicly subsidized health care costs. Safeguarding of youth, internalities, and externalities all imply a public interest in seeing that sexual health issues are recognized by those who might be sexually active. But not everyone is comfortable with having such matters discussed in public schools nor in ensuring that contraceptives are easily available to teens.

A thorough discussion of the consequences of sexual activity should indicate that different types of practices entail different risks. Here, the usual harm reduction versus zero tolerance encounter takes place. Some people want to frame the discussion in "sex is risky, abstinence is safe" terms (the zero tolerance approach), while others want to indicate that sex with condoms is less risky than unprotected sex, though not as safe as abstinence. The "abstinence only" supporters are concerned that information about relative risks of different

[4] Henshaw (1998), as discussed in Grossman and Markowitz (2002).
[5] Schaffner (2005, p. 198).
[6] The internatonal AIDS charity AVERT provides a good discussion of ages of consent, at www.avert.org/ageconsent.htm (accessed on March 6, 2006).
[7] See Chapter 6, pp. 137–56, in Heins (2001).

forms of sex (or the provision of contraceptives) could lead to more adolescent sex – and perhaps more total harm, if the increased sex more than compensates for lower harms per sex act. The harm reduction discussion of relative risks is premised on the notion that many teens will have sex even if they are told not to; therefore, for their own protection, they should be informed of and given access to methods to lower the risks of sex. There is no definitive empirical resolution to this debate, nor need it be the case that any given approach is superior for children of all ages in all places at all times. Cross-country comparisons between continental Europe and the United States suggest, however, that there is much to be said for the harm reduction approach. Teen birth rates in the United States exceed those in every European country, and U.S. teens are profoundly ignorant about sexual health.[8] In surveys, more than a third of U.S. ninth to twelfth graders report sexual activity in the prior three months, with more than two-thirds of American women engaging in vaginal sex by the age of 18.[9] Programs that provide information about contraception and disease prevention to American teens have reduced risky sexual behaviors, without increasing sexual activity or accelerating sexual initiation.[10]

The standard policy toward commercial sex and kids parallels the policy toward adolescent private sexual behavior: prohibition. Underage prostitution and youth involvement in pornography production are illegal, and the ban generally is policed with vigilance. Consumption of commercial sex by the underaged – for example, purchase of pornography, attendance at live erotic acts, and the hiring of legal prostitutes – also is prohibited. Commercial sex activities, buying as well as selling, often involve higher ages of consent than does sex itself.

Censors routinely operate upon material aimed at children or youths to eliminate described or depicted sexual conduct. Nevertheless, there is surprisingly little evidence that kids actually suffer from exposure to pornography. We know that literature and film can be influential; whether sexually explicit literature or films viewed by teens are, on average, influential in a negative way, remains unknown, despite a proliferation of studies:

> But although social science has not proved any identifiable subject or medium to cause significant, predictable changes in children's attitudes or behavior, provocative ideas in art or entertainment do affect the human psyche in myriad ways. It is just that these effects cannot be quantified. They undoubtedly include, in some instances, persuasion, reflection, revulsion, catharsis, excitement, and mindless enjoyment. And, of course, imitation. An often cited example is the Bible: full of sex and violence, it has, not surprisingly, inspired psychotic acts as well as charitable ones.[11]

---

[8] Heins (2001, pp. 145, 148).

[9] See Table 4 in Mosher, Chandra, and Jones (2005, p. 22); see also "Effective Sex Education," at www.advocatesforyouth.org/publications/factsheet/fssexcur.pdf (accessed on April 12, 2006).

[10] See "Science and Success" at www.advocatesforyouth.org/programsthatwork/.

[11] Heins (2001, p. 11).

SEX ADDICTION

The notion that for some people sex can become a compulsion has gained currency within the past generation: the journal *Sexual Addiction & Compulsivity* debuted in 1994, some ten years after a U.S. national organization devoted to studying and treating sex addiction coalesced.[12] The American Psychological Association's *Diagnostic and Statistical Manual of Mental Disorders*, which provides diagnostic criteria for some vicious habits such as substance dependence and pathological gambling, does not yet include a separate category for sexual addiction, however, and the use of the terminology of addiction in application to sex remains highly contested.[13] In any event, compulsive behaviors that are associated with gambling or drug addictions have counterparts in the sexual realm.[14] People can become obsessed with sex and repeatedly pursue sexual adventures despite severe negative consequences. The relatively new phenomenon of internet pornography has taken the path trod by the introduction of many novel vices, that of stoking fixation, with family misery and breakup sometimes resulting from excessive devotion to cybersex.

Despite the similarities among sexual and other addictions, public discourse in the United States seems more open to frank talk about drugs, alcohol, and gambling pathologies than to sex obsession. Sex addicts are perhaps more private, more embarrassed, or less likely to be taken seriously than are those afflicted by the more established addictions. "Consequently, it is hard for those who have not personally experienced the pernicious destruction of unabated sexual appetite to appreciate the human dimension to a topic rife with misperception."[15] Patrick Carnes, the author of a 1983 book that first brought widespread attention to sexual addiction, felt compelled to change the book's title (to *Out of the Shadows*) shortly after it first appeared: "So much shame existed about the illness that readers found it difficult even to purchase the book with the title *The Sexual Addiction*."[16]

Public policy toward sex seems to be almost entirely unaffected by an interest in helping sex addicts. Sexual behaviors such as public exposure that are compulsive for some people are criminalized, but presumably the criminalization would remain even if there were no compulsive exhibitionists. Private responses to sex addiction have flourished in recent years, however. These responses include precommitment techniques as well as devices designed to bolster sexual self-control. For instance, a cybersex addict can download free software that keeps track of visits to "questionable" websites; then, every few weeks, the software e-mails a list of suspect surfing to someone the addict has

---

[12] Schneider (2004).

[13] The controversy over sex addiction is nicely described in a Wikipedia entry, at http://en.wikipedia.org/wiki/Sex_addiction (accessed March 27, 2006). The forthcoming fifth edition of the *Diagnostic and Statistical Manual* likely will devote more attention to sexual compulsions.

[14] Irons and Schneider (1996).   [15] Herring (2004, p. 40).

[16] Carnes (2001, p. ix). *Out of the Shadows* is subtitled *Understanding Sexual Addiction.*

designated as his "accountability partner."[17] With this software, your wife can be apprised of your Internet wanderings, and presumably your foreknowledge of her knowledge will increase your resolve to avoid pornographic sites or lead to dialogue if resolve proves wanting. Treatments for sex addicts, like vice addiction treatments more generally, often rely upon twelve-step-style protocols and are far from sure-fire cures. Therapy options, again as with other addictions, also are available for family members of sex addicts.[18]

The commercial components of the alcohol and gambling worlds sponsor efforts to reduce the social costs of the bad relationships some people develop with drinking or wagering. Alcohol is packaged with responsible drinking appeals, beer companies underwrite anti-drunk-driving advertisements, and casinos maintain lists of people who have volunteered to be kept off the premises. But the commercial sex world – the (legal) pornography and exotic dancing industries – does not yet engage in similar activities.[19] (This situation might reflect both the relative youth of the notion of sex addiction, as well as the traditional less than fully legitimate standing of the porn and strip club sectors.) Surely, some such private policies could be helpful and perhaps could even be mandated.[20] Voluntary consumer-initiated bans (where folks who recognize that they have self-control problems exclude themselves in advance) could be adopted both by live entertainment venues and Internet websites. For cybersex, links to commitment devices limiting access and treatment information could pop up after every hour logged into a porn site, or occasional cooling-off periods of five or ten minutes could be imposed. A legal requirement for adult sites to provide such links or brief cooling-off periods would satisfy robustness, by imposing but little on rational porn consumers while offering some aid to people battling addiction. Consumers themselves might try other types of precommitment by eschewing Internet access, by installing timers that limit Internet surfing hours, or by employing filters that screen out sexually explicit material. Live venues could allow patrons to establish binding time or budget limits, on a per visit, per week, or per month basis. The use of credit could be restricted both in the real and the virtual adult entertainment worlds.

From the point of view of vice purveyors, one of the advantages of focusing attention on the relatively small subset of vice afficionados who suffer from chronic self-control problems is that such attention tends to legitimize the vice more generally. The product or service is not evil; rather, there are

[17] xxxchurch.com visited on March 6, 2006; see the Vice Squad post from November 1, 2004.
[18] See, for instance, the "Groups and Meetings" webpage of the Society for the Advancement of Sexual Health, available at http://www.ncsac.org/addicts/addict_groups.aspx (accessed February 22, 2006).
[19] Herring (2004, pp. 40–1).
[20] The remainder of this paragraph draws on my guest post for the weblog Crescat Sententia on November 2, 2003; see http://www.crescatsententia.net/archives/2003_11_02.html (accessed on September 5, 2007).

some vulnerable people who are diseased, who are predisposed to having bad relationships with the product. Perhaps this is one reason why commercial sex suppliers have not been involved in anti-sex-addiction policy (whereas the alcohol industry is involved in fighting alcoholism). Sex is sufficiently popular that almost everyone already accepts the notion that adult sex is not evil, even though some folks develop an unhealthy fixation on sex. Alcohol, however, is viewed by much of society as inherently evil – a viewpoint that was an important factor in bringing on national alcohol Prohibition in the United States – and the demonization of some illegal drugs is still more extreme.

REGULATING SADOMASOCHISM[21]

Just about all sex involves risk, but not to the same degree. Some folks engage in sexual practices that are violent or otherwise dangerous and where the added risk is viewed as a desirable feature. The variety of such practices is extensive, including bondage, whipping, breath control, and body piercing. For the sake of convenience, though with some sacrifice in terms of precision, I will refer to all of these as sadomasochistic (S&M) practices.[22] The potential public interest in regulating sadomasochistic behavior primarily derives from the involvement of kids and from internalities, harms to participating adults.[23]

Protecting children almost necessitates that a legal age of consent be established – that is, with kid involvement, the government cannot rely solely upon private regulation of S&M. The usual choice is to adopt a general sexual age of consent, without detailed specifications of the sexual activities that are covered. S&M (to the extent that it is legal for adults) tends to be lumped together with other forms of noncommercial adolescent sexual activity when it comes to establishing a legal minimum age.

But it is at least theoretically possible that the government would want to base the age of consent on the precise sexual activity engaged in. Why not decide that a 17-year-old is legally capable of consenting to "standard" sexual activity but not to activities that involve the intentional infliction of extreme pain or the possibility of permanent scarring? S&M might be hard to define, but some rough idea of the risk of serious consequences, or the likelihood of long-term damage, associated with certain behaviors clearly is feasible – indeed,

---

[21] This section draws heavily from my comment (Leitzel 2006) on Eitmann (2006).

[22] One objection to the term "sadomasochism" stems from the notion that a sadist takes pleasure from giving pain to someone else; some practitioners would argue that the "dominant" partner takes pleasure from giving pleasure to someone else. See Welldon (2002, p. 5).

[23] Purported externalities are sometimes raised in discussions of regulating S&M. One such externality lies in the possibility that S&M practice (or depiction) contributes to the oppression of women, or even in nonconsensual violence directed toward them. A second externality might lie in the form of "notional damage" – the bare knowledge that others are engaged in S&M upsets some folks. On notional damage and the bare knowledge problem, see Kleiman (1992, Chapter 3) and Feinberg (1985, p. 60–71).

guides to containing S&M risks already are available for private purposes. Analogous guides could be adopted for public purposes, to regulate adolescent involvement in hazardous sexual practices.

Legal controls placed on adult S&M similarly must come to grips with the definitional issue of determining precisely (at least precisely enough to avoid invalidation of the controls on the grounds of vagueness) what acts to sanction, and how finely to distinguish among acts for varying regulatory scrutiny. A workable definition of, and fine distinctions among, the physical sadomasochistic acts themselves still will not provide a sufficient basis for legal controls. Rather, in most cases, consent will be the factor that differentiates a legal act of S&M from a sexual assault.

Of course, consent is the distinguishing feature between legal and illegal adult sex of the nonkinky, "vanilla" variety, too. And even in that context, it presents a host of difficulties, as the provision or nonprovision of consent typically occurs in the absence of nonparticipating witnesses. But consent is a more problematic issue with sadomasochism, in which a conflict can easily arise between the general consent of an individual to engage in an S&M "session" and consent to specific undertakings within that session.[24] Although consent is not unique to kinky sexual activity, the issue of the coverage of initial consent is compounded in the case of S&M: much S&M activity involves dominance submission or other role-playing in which a less than fully consensual pose is part of the point of the proceedings.

The potential murkiness of consent suggests that for those activities that are riskiest strong evidence of specific consent could be required: a dash of ex ante evidence gathering to minimize ex post disputation. But does that exhaust the public role? If adult S&M activity, though demonstrably consensual, is extremely risky, should there be stricter controls? After all, public regulation of risky adult voluntary activity occurs in many fields, such as workplace safety and consumer protection.

The robustness principle can provide some guidance. Certain sadomasochistic practices display features – a small risk of imposing severe injury or death, or current benefits paired with deferred costs – that do not always bring out the best in human decision making. Controls that offer some aid to folks for whom S&M decisions will be suboptimal, when viewed from the perspective of their own informed long-term interests, might be worth adopting, especially if those controls do not impose large costs upon practitioners whose S&M decisions are fully considered. For instance, a requirement that consent cannot be conferred for particularly risky practices, absent demonstration of an understanding of those risks, might make for advantageous policy. The inclusion of health warnings and safety information could be a condition for legal sales of

[24] See Santa Lucia (2005).

S&M equipment. Even training requirements for those who want to legally engage in breath restriction, or a mandated waiting period before any long-term body alteration receives license, are not precluded in principle – though they may well be ill-advised or even counterproductive in practice. The sort of barriers that should stand in the way of voluntary but extreme (and rare) S&M conduct, such as amputation or consensual homicide, would be sufficiently daunting as to be well approximated by a complete ban.[25]

Nevertheless, the personal and self-regarding nature of voluntary sexual practices, including S&M, lowers the desirable scope of public regulation relative to private regulation, especially for those practices that are not quite so extreme. S&M enthusiasts have developed, often through negative experiences, suggested codes of conduct, and the Internet has seen to their widespread distribution.[26] The dominant strain of private policy appears to be the "safe, sane, consensual" school, though an alternative (that, for instance, suggests that perfect safety is an illusion and that conceptions of "sanity" can differ) is "risk-aware consensual kink."[27] The publication and discussion of these codes and other S&M issues provide useful harm-reduction measures. A novice might be ignorant of the potentially fatal dangers of rapid overheating when wearing a hood or rubber mask over the head, but the Internet publicity given to a death that occurred under such circumstances furnishes a warning to those most likely to benefit from it.[28]

PORNOGRAPHY

The second half of the twentieth century witnessed a tremendous increase in the availability of pornography in the United States and elsewhere: Denmark became the first nation to legalize hard-core pornography in the late 1960s. Whether gay or straight, hard or soft, fetishistic or vanilla, every genre of pornography has flourished in recent decades.

Externalities associated with pornography consumption are speculative but are sometimes asserted to be vast: one suggestion, for instance, is that porn

---

[25] Perhaps interest in some forms of amputation is not all that rare. In 2006, three North Carolina men were charged with castrating six other men; presumably the castrations were fully consensual. (See "Gay Lovers Charged Over Videotaped Castrations," by Harry Mount, *The Daily Telegraph* [London] April 14, 2006.) Robustness suggests a policy regime that would require training of castrators and mandatory information provision and waiting periods for those seeking castration.

[26] Negative experiences are the source of laws in other settings, too; see Dershowitz (2004).

[27] Wikipedia is a good source of information and links concerning sadomasochism (for the moment, that is – the nature of wiki is that it could change from second to second); see http://en.wikipedia.org/wiki/Safe_sane_and_consensual and http://en.wikipedia.org/wiki/RACK (accessed on January 8, 2006).

[28] At http://gloriabrame.typepad.com/inside_the_mind_of_gloria/2005/12/scary_tragic_sm.html (accessed January 8, 2006).

creates an atmosphere hostile to women and enhances male sexual aggression and crime.[29] Confirmation that such effects exist in any significant manner would tie a huge external cost to porn. But so far there has been no compelling demonstration of the reality of these externalities – which is not to say that their existence has been disproved.[30] For a subset of the potential porn externalities, the evidence of the past few decades, and comparisons among countries, are encouraging. In many countries (including the United States), the prevalence of reported sex crimes has fallen during the porn explosion, and some cultures awash in porn (even violent porn), such as Japan, do not seem to exhibit higher levels of violence toward women as a result.[31]

Public vice manifestations provide another (related) rationale for regulation. In the case of pornography, however, the startling increase in availability has occurred in tandem with a privatization of consumption. In 1970, X-rated public theaters were almost the only available mode of widescale distribution of pornographic films. Since then, home viewing of adult material via video-cassettes and DVDs, cable and satellite television, and the Internet has replaced most public viewing. The Internet and pay-TV also have moved pornography sales out of bricks-and-mortar stores into the private domain. The remaining bricks-and-mortar porn purveyors, along with other public manifestations, remain an important lightening rod for community outcry over pornography. Broadcast pornography or indecency is a common source of public contention, for instance, largely because of the heightened potential that broadcast holds for reaching children.

Pornography is an aid to masturbation, and to some extent, the increased acceptance of pornography parallels the increased acceptance of masturbation. The demonization of masturbation has relented for various reasons, including the paucity of scientific evidence that anything short of compulsive masturbation is physically harmful. (Fantastically exaggerated claims to the contrary have held sway in the past.) Also, the advent of AIDS has put a premium upon safe sex, of which masturbation can be one form.

PORNOGRAPHY REGULATION IN THE UNITED STATES

The obscenity concerns of bygone days are the stuff of present laughter. Bowdlerized Shakespeare and the suppression of *Ulysses* are approaches to obscenity control that most Americans are happy to be quit with. In part, this reflects a general loosening of sexual mores. It also reflects the explosion of visual

---

[29] See, for example, Bartlett (1988) and the discussion of the harms of pornography in Posner (1992, pp. 365–74).

[30] See, for instance, the discussion in Heins (2001, pp. 242–53). Some recent analyses of U.S. data suggest that pornography might reduce sex crimes; see Wongsurawat (2006) and D'Amato (2006).

[31] Internal costs, those possible ill effects visited upon consumers themselves from occasional indulgence in pornography, seem to be generally of minor social concern, at least when viewed in isolation from any associated externalities.

media – photography, film, and television – to which the main thrust of cen-
sorial impulse in the West has been diverted.[32] Written or verbal descriptions
of sexual activity, in the absence of visuals, attract little regulatory attention,
unless those verbal descriptions are broadcast over radio or television or are
otherwise made available to kids.

By no means, however, does laissez-faire characterize the regulation of
pornography in the United States. People are in U.S. prisons in the twenty-first
century for distributing adult pornographic materials to other willing (perhaps even eager) adults. Further, there is no guarantee that the suppression
of pornography will not be stepped up; indeed, an intensification of antiporn
policing was a policy championed by President George W. Bush's attorneys
general, John Ashcroft and Alberto Gonzales. Current law does not preclude
(rather, it almost invites) a significant suppression of sexually related materials.
Communities in the United States possess the latent legal power to prohibit
the distribution of hard-core pornography and perhaps even of soft-core pub-
lications such as *Playboy*.

The claim that pornography could be banned in parts of the United States
might seem odd given the freedom of speech guaranteed by the First Amendment.[33] But Supreme Court decisions have carved out an obscenity exception
to free-speech protection. The exception is quite specific to "obscenity"; nonobscene sexually-explicit material cannot be banned.

So the crucial legal distinction concerns what subset of pornography is considered to be obscene and what subset is not obscene. The variety of sexual
material and behavior makes obvious dividing lines hard to discern. Obscenity potentially covers a vast expanse, from Boccacio's *Decameron* to *Playboy*
to homosexual sadomasochistic magazines to simulated rape movies. Nevertheless, a 1973 Supreme Court case, *Miller v. California*, attempts to provide
some guidance and supplies the legal standard for delineating obscenity in the
United States:

> A work may be subject to state regulation where that work, taken as a whole,
> appeals to the prurient interest in sex; portrays, in a patently offensive way, sexual
> conduct specifically defined by the applicable state law; and, taken as a whole,
> does not have serious literary, artistic, political, or scientific value.[34]

If these three conditions are not all met, a work is not obscene, and it cannot be
banned. Possession in your own home of material judged to be obscene cannot

---

[32] Coetzee (1996, p. x).

[33] Obscenity control potentially conflicts with rights beyond free speech. Some pornography might
be considered as having a medical use in sex therapy or couples counseling, or to be an element
of the free expression of a religion. India's restrictive anti-obscenity laws include an exception for
the explicit sex scenes that appear in the decorations of many temples.

[34] 413 U.S. 15 (1973); the quote comes from the syllabus to *Miller*. A "syllabus" of a Supreme Court
case is a sort of summary of the case prepared for the convenience of readers, though the syllabus
itself has no legal standing.

be criminalized, though production and distribution of that material can be outlawed. Possession of child pornography, in one's home or anywhere else, can be forbidden.[35]

The precise wording of the standard set forth in *Miller* has taken on an almost sacred significance in obscenity prosecutions. But the Delphic formulation remains obscure. What qualifies as "patently offensive" and to whom? What is a "prurient interest in sex"? According to the relevant definition from the online *Oxford English Dictionary* (www.oed.com), "prurient" means "Given to the indulgence of lewd ideas; impure-minded; characterized by lasciviousness of thought or mind." U.S. courts have approached "prurient" in varying ways, including distinguishing between a prurient interest and a "good, old fashioned, healthy" interest in sex.[36]

The first prong (prurient interest) and second prong (patent offensiveness) of the *Miller* test are required to be applied in light of "contemporary community standards." Therefore, a film can be legally obscene in one town and not legally obscene in a neighboring town. Although the legal standard of obscenity invokes a "community" that might be geographically quite restricted, obscenity regulations can be adopted at the state or federal level. As a result, obscenity prosecutors can forum-shop, choosing to pursue purveyors of pornography in the most puritanical community to which the porn can be arranged to be distributed. So producers or distributors of sexually explicit works, if they want to be certain of remaining at liberty, either must restrict their distribution to areas or states that they are assured are safe or limit their productions to material that will not be considered obscene by a jury in the community with the lowest threshold for obscenity in America.

The experience of a California couple who operated an Internet bulletin board advertising adult material illustrates the risk. Their bulletin board restricted access to its pornographic material by requiring an application, after which a password was provided. A U.S. postal inspector in Tennessee signed up under an alias, downloaded pornographic pictures, and ordered video tapes that were sent to him via a private package delivery service. The West-Coast couple was then charged and convicted in Tennessee of violating various federal obscenity statutes. The husband received a thirty-seven-month jail sentence, and the wife received thirty months.[37] The same pornographic material might not have been considered to be obscene under the "community standards" prevailing in California.

[35] Possession of adult porn in the home was decriminalized throughout the United States by *Stanley v. Georgia*, 394 U.S. 557 (1971); the Supreme Court declined to extend the decriminalization to the possession of child pornography in *Osborne v. Ohio*, 495 U.S. 103 (1990). Child pornography need not meet the *Miller* obscenity standards to be prohibited.

[36] See the post by Eugene Volokh at the weblog The Volokh Conspiracy on June 29, 2004; http://volokh.com/archives/archive_2004_06_28.shtml#1088523122. See also *Brockett v. Spokane Arcades, Inc.*, 472 U.S. 491 (1985).

[37] *U.S. v. Thomas*, 1996 FED App. 0032P (6th Circuit).

The "taken as a whole" clauses in the *Miller* formulation are more protective
of sexually explicit works than is "community standards." They suggest that
one short sexually explicit scene in a much longer film would be insufficient
to result in a ban on distribution of the film anywhere in the United States.
The "taken as a whole" provisions also intimate that the articles in *Playboy*
are a helpful or necessary component to its legal distribution, even if the frequent claim that no one reads the articles in *Playboy* is accurate. (My earlier
contention that communities in the United States might be able to ban *Playboy* requires that juries themselves not read much into the articles.) Further,
the third prong of *Miller* (sometimes nicknamed LAPS or SLAPS for Serious
Literary, Artistic, Political, Scientific value), as developed in some later cases,
does not include a community standards component.[38] If the avant-garde of
Tribeca or South Beach considers your work to have serious artistic merit, then
(presumably) your artistic or literary creation should be legal across the breadth
of the United States – though it probably would be imprudent for a producer
of sexually explicit material to rely upon the approval of a distant avant-garde
as guarantor of his or her immunity from an obscenity conviction.

BROADCAST AND INDECENCY

The legal standards in the United States for what words and images can be
transmitted over traditional broadcast radio and television are much stricter
than the obscenity criteria of the *Miller* test. Indecent material that falls short
of being obscene can be precluded from broadcast during hours in which children are likely to be in the audience; in practice, the Federal Communications
Commission bans indecent broadcasting between 6 a.m. and 10 p.m. What
warrants an indecency label? Patent offensiveness and contemporary community standards are once again part of the formulation, as described on the FCC's
webpage:

> The FCC has defined broadcast indecency as "language or material that, in
> context, depicts or describes, in terms patently offensive as measured by con-
> temporary community broadcast standards for the broadcast medium, sexual or
> excretory organs or activities." Indecent programming contains patently offen-
> sive sexual or excretory material that does not rise to the level of obscenity.[39]

Standard profanity qualifies as indecent, too. Sex, excrement, and dirty words
are the stuff of indecency: violent programming does not implicate FCC indecency regulation.

[38] *Pope v. Illinois*, 481 U.S. 497 (1987); see also Clyde DeWitt, "Jurors Appreciate Good Production
Values – Really," Adult Video News.com, October 1, 2005, at http://www.avn.com/index.php?
Primary_Navigation=Legal&Action=View_Article&Content_ID=242316 (accessed January 13,
2006).
[39] From the FCC's webpage on Obscene, Profane & Indecent Broadcasts, at http://www.fcc.gov/cgb/
consumerfacts/obscene.html (accessed on January 13, 2006.

The FCC's enforcement of its indecency provisions is complaint-driven. One lone but vocal malcontent, therefore, is in a position to have sanctions (including fines and license revocation) imposed upon a broadcaster, even if thousands of others in the audience are perfectly satisfied customers.[40] As a result, broadcasters cannot be certain that what they send over the airwaves will pass muster. Their dilemma is particularly acute when public and FCC sensibilities are suddenly raised as a result of a broadcast scandal, as occurred following the partially exposed breast of the singer Janet Jackson during a televised halftime performance at the 2004 Super Bowl. The FCC fined Super Bowl broadcaster CBS $550,000 for the brief transgression, while fear of fines cascaded throughout the broadcast industry. In the aftermath of the football kerfuffle, radio political talk-show host Rush Limbaugh found some of his verbiage censored by an Indianapolis radio station, sixty-six ABC affiliates chose not to air the violent and straight-talking movie *Saving Private Ryan*, and the media company Viacom (parent of CBS) paid $3.5 million to settle various other FCC indecency complaints. Months after the fact, incidentally, the chairman of the FCC declared that *Saving Private Ryan* was not indecent, though that judgment came too late for the thousands of viewers who had the replacement programming *Return to Mayberry* inflicted upon them. The chairman could just as easily have made the opposite decision and fined the broadcasters of *Saving Private Ryan:* in some markets where it aired the film garnered complaints. The stations that chose not to broadcast the war film, therefore, were not being oversensitive. Even a single mention of a profane word before 10 p.m. could result in a significant fine, and *Saving Private Ryan* contains many such mentions.

Nonbroadcast television – cable and satellite – is not governed by the FCC's indecency regulations, though programming is still subject to obscenity laws. Cable operators carrying channels devoted to indecent programming must scramble or otherwise block those channels for nonsubscribers. Since 2000, the FCC has mandated that every thirteen-inch or larger television sold in the United Stated be equipped with a V-chip that allows objectionable programming to be blocked. (The main concern at the time was with violent programming, which explains the "V.") V-chip filtering works for programming that carries a rating, which is standard for broadcast, cable, and satellite shows; parents can regulate the sensitivity of the filter and override the chip via a password when the kids are safely tucked away.

ROBUSTNESS AND PORNOGRAPHY

The standard sorts of considerations that robustness brings to vice policy apply to porn: there should be legal means for consuming porn, distribution must not

---

[40] See the Vice Squad post from May 14, 2004.

be regulated so strictly as to place a significant burden upon consumption, externalities as well as internalities in production and consumption can be addressed, and public manifestations legitimately can be controlled. Within the contours of these broad precepts, however, there is scope for a variety of regulatory regimes.

Public manifestations and broadcasting

Sexually explicit billboards can be banned from the side of public roads: such ads are too imposing, too costly to avoid, for those who wish to be free of them. (Similarly, the relatively new phenomenon of "dirty driving," where DVD players in cars show porn movies that can be viewed by pedestrians or travelers in other cars, legitimately can be controlled.) Alternate means of porn distribution are less public: even broadcast transmissions require a receiver, a radio or television, before a consumer can partake. But at the same time, radio and television are ubiquitous. In many countries it is very hard to lead a normal, day-to-day existence while being able to shield yourself or your children from exposure to what comes across the public airwaves. So regulations akin to the FCC's indecency standard are defensible for broadcast television and radio. In implementing such standards, however, better guidance and moderate fines would be helpful, so that intensive scrutiny need not constantly be applied by well-intentioned broadcasters wishing to remain within the regulations.

Even if indecency standards are not particularly effective at shielding kids from exposure to porn, or if successful shielding itself isn't very beneficial, the costs imposed by such broadcast indecency standards are low, and they have fallen considerably in recent decades. Adults interested in consuming "indecent" material between 6 a.m. and 10 p.m. now have available a variety of options that allow them to do so, from cable television to video on demand to satellite radio. It is perhaps ironic, given the increased permissiveness on the public airwaves, but the case for broadcast indecency standards is stronger today than it was in the 1950s. The relative ease with which those standards now can be avoided means that they are not very constraining, while the "environmental" exposure of kids to television and radio has increased. (U.S. Supreme Court Justice John Paul Stevens, in a 1978 case upholding the FCC's indecency regulations, suggested in a footnote that sufficient substitution possibilities for listening to profanity were available even in the mid-1970s: "Adults who feel the need may purchase tapes and records or go to theaters and nightclubs to hear these words."[41])

---

[41] From footnote 28 of *FCC v. Pacifica Foundation*, 438 U.S. 726 (1978); this is the case that arose from the radio broadcast of comedian George Carlin's routine concerning words that you can't say on television.

The necessity to subscribe and pay for cable and satellite services suggests a degree of attention and control that is well beyond that of simply owning a television or radio. Private policy, therefore, is likely to be more effective (than it is for broadcast television or radio) in protecting kids from offensive programming. The FCC's absence from the cable/satellite arena is sensible.

The penetration of cable and satellite television is quite extensive; more than 80 percent of U.S. households now subscribe to such services.[42] The argument for applying indecency standards to broadcast television and radio depends upon the ubiquity of these media, and the consequent difficulty of shielding kids and unwilling adults from environmental exposure, that which happens casually as they go about their daily lives. But if cable and satellite services are nearly as ubiquitous, then perhaps indecency standards should be extended to programming transmitted via these means.

The balancing notion that underlies the robustness principle provides a different perspective, however. It is precisely the ease of attaining indecent programming via cable or satellite that justifies the indecency ban on broadcast television. Without such alternatives (and *pace* Justice Stevens), the broadcast controls would impose fairly heavily upon those who enjoy something spicier than kid-friendly fare. Further, a cable or satellite subscription almost guarantees that programming options have been weighed. Subscribers are forced to consider alternative packages, and those viewers with the most interest in indecent programming can purchase it at a premium. Rules that require cable or satellite companies to provide a' la carte offerings, so that a customer who wants to receive Nickelodeon needn't also receive R-or X-rated material, can further ensure that only those who desire indecent programming purchase access to it.

If V-chips were expensive, then a mandate that all televisions be equipped with them would violate robustness, by imposing too severely upon rational viewers of "indecent" television.[43] A requirement that television manufacturers offer the option of an embedded V-chip would satisfy robustness, however. In practice, V-chip censoring seems to be unvalued by most television consumers. Parents typically monitor their children's viewing, but most do so without ever activating their V-chip.[44] Nevertheless, decentralizing indecency regulation via a V-chip has the advantage, relative to controlling the programming directly, of not inconveniencing those who are uninterested in filtering out indecency.

[42] Aline van Duyn, "Subscribers switch on to cable, satellite," May 6, 2005; see http://msnbc.msn.com/id/7762929/ (accessed February 7, 2006).
[43] As long as the option to acquire a V-chip is available, it is unclear what public interest is served by making V-chips mandatory – even if they are inexpensive. Thanks to Michael Alexeev for bringing this point to my attention.
[44] See Thomas Hazlett, "Requiem for the V-Chip," *Slate*, February 13, 2004; available at http://www.slate.com/id/2095396/ (visited January 14, 2006). Also, see Mike Himowitz, "Easy-to-use V-Chip keeps smut from kids," MiamiHerald.com, December 31, 2005; available at http://www.miami.com/mld/miamiherald/living/13514015.htm (accessed January 14, 2006).

Mandated provision of information about program content is one element of a robust regime that improves private decision making. The rating and warnings systems adopted by broadcasters empower parents to appropriately control the programming that reaches their children and themselves. Viewer discretion warnings placed on televised films in the 1980s reduced the number of children aged 2 to 11 in the audience, without affecting the number of older viewers.[45]

What would happen if there were no indecency controls on broadcast TV, and no mandates for V-chips or similar technologies? Parents likely would alter their families' relationship with radio and television. Pressure from the public at large would probably motivate (perhaps through legislation) owners of radios and televisions placed in public areas to ensure that they only tuned in to family fare, and frequent warnings of adult content might be required or voluntarily adopted by broadcasters. Private companies would offer filtering equipment to those customers who were interested in technological censoring. People who wanted to listen to their favorite shock jock in the morning would not have to subscribe to satellite radio. In short, there might be some difficulties with a transition into a world without FCC-style indecency regulation, but the final outcome does not look all that undesirable.[46] FCC indecency regulations are consistent with the robustness principle, but they do not appear to be a necessary feature of a regulatory regime that effectively addresses the $3\frac{1}{3}$ standard vice concerns.

Porn in private and in production

From the point of view of the harm or robustness principles, private consumption of even extreme hard-core adult pornography generally must be permitted. Sales would seem to be requisite for consumption to take place, so trade in such material must be allowed, too. Sellers can be regulated in such a manner, however, to hinder exposure of kids or unwilling adults to pornographic materials. For instance, zoning laws that restrict adult businesses to certain areas of town (such as red-light districts) do not run afoul of the robustness criterion.

This general acceptance of legal pornography need not extend to instances where in the pornography in question imposes significant harms in its production. The use of children in pornographic movies, for instance, is a form of child abuse that legitimately can be combated via prohibitions on sale and possession, along with the ban on production.

---

[45] Hamilton (1998, p. 303).

[46] Some countries have laxer standards for public displays of nudity, but there is little evidence that low standards are harmful. French children (or American children visiting Paris) do not seem to be damaged by the public depictions of nudity that appear on French billboards, though these advertisements go far beyond what is tolerated in the United States.

For adult porn performers, the potential public regulatory interest is less compelling than it is when underage actors are involved – less compelling but not completely negligible, given the possibility of internal and external costs associated with porn production.

Once produced, pornographic images can last indefinitely – that's a long time in which to regret a fleeting desire to be a porn star. A mandatory waiting period between the time a contract is entered into by a would-be porn actor and the production of the images might be helpful, where in the actor could back out of the deal with no penalties during the waiting period. Such a waiting period could apply to any first-time actor, or to any actor who is agreeing to a type of pornography unlike his or her previous work. (Nor would it violate the robustness principle for the waiting period to apply to all pornographic performances, as the "rational" performers could easily plan ahead.) The public interest in controlling the spread of sexually transmitted diseases would permit a mandate of safe sexual practices or up-to-the-minute health testing in the event that unsafe sexual practices were to be engaged in. Advances in HIV testing now allow cheap and accurate tests with results available in less than half an hour.[47] Further, the risks of commercial unprotected sex should be explained to and understood by the performers. Training and strong evidence of consent to specific acts might be required for sadomasochistic productions.[48]

One benefit of the near mainstreaming of much pornographic movie production in recent years (after decades in the shadows) has been improved private regulation. When porn movies are filmed in a semicriminalized underground, producers don't seem all that concerned with reducing internal and external costs imposed on actors and the public at large. But open, legitimate producers have a larger stake in not being perceived as irresponsible.[49] Major porn producers, including industry leaders Vivid and Wicked Pictures, abide by a code of conduct involving regular health testing. When an actor tested positive for HIV in April 2004, the major adult studios suspended production, and those performers who recently had been teamed with the affected actor were temporarily suspended from filming. Eventually five actors in total tested positive, but the quick voluntary response by most of the industry probably prevented a much more extensive HIV outbreak.[50] Nevertheless, the failure of most heterosexual porn producers to require condoms, even for types of sex most susceptible to HIV-transmission, adds to the danger of such outbreaks. Infected individuals are capable of transmitting HIV for a period of time before tests can indicate their HIV-positive status.[51] Given the potential externalities (spread of HIV beyond those who are involved in porn production), a legal requirement for condom use, especially for anal sex (which compared with

---

[47] See http://www.cdc.gov/hiv/rapid_testing/index.htm#overview (accessed February 4, 2006).
[48] See Leitzel (2006).   [49] Hawkins and Zimring (1988, pp. 200–3).
[50] See the Vice Squad post from May 11, 2004.   [51] CDC (2005).

oral and vaginal sex is more conducive to spreading HIV), would be consistent with the robustness principle.

Not only are aboveground porn producers concerned with their image, they also are susceptible to government regulation in ways that underground producers are not. In the wake of the 2004 HIV outbreak, the Division of Occupational Safety and Health of California's Department of Industrial Relations issued citations to two porn industry employers for not meeting health and safety standards.[52]

Private regulation could become much more expansive in the porn industry. Sharon Mitchell, the founder of the Adult Industry Medical Health Care Foundation, which among other activities administers health exams to actors in the porn industry, has suggested that a "seal of approval" be developed and awarded to films that are made using safe workplace and health practices.[53] Mainstream hotel chains and cable companies could then be encouraged to show only films awarded the seal of approval, providing the financial incentive to filmmakers to employ the safe procedures.

The promotion of private regulation via pressure on "legitimate" elements of the trade can be further extended. As long as legal and not-too-onerous channels of distribution remain for those so inclined, private individuals could use the threat of boycott to pressure stores not to carry (or at least not to feature) exceptionally hard-core DVDs, for instance; companies that advertise in porn magazines could similarly be pressed to avoid some of the most extreme material. Hawkins and Zimring (1988, p. 208) suggest a role for "negative endorsement," a sort of flip side to a seal of approval, where a respected panel might identify and call for a boycott of particularly egregious productions.

Boycotts aimed at moving the distribution of extreme pornography away from mainstream retailers might be desirable, a sort of private implementation of zoning. Entreating others to avoid such porn, letting your own views be known – these are perfectly appropriate actions. But boycotts go too far, I maintain, if their aim is to eliminate the consumption (or production) of porn by other adults who desire access to pornography. If successful, such boycotts go beyond entreaty and enter the world of command. And even though boycotts are private policies, not government policies, they can still violate the robustness principle when they impose potentially significant costs upon rational porn consumers.

PROSTITUTION[54]

Berkeley, California, is justly renowned for its liberal approach to social issues. In November 2004, a Berkeley ballot referendum specified that prostitution

---

[52] CDC (2005).   [53] See the Vice Squad post from May 11, 2004.

[54] Two articles by Weitzer (1999 and 2000) provide excellent analysis of U.S. prostitution policies, and I draw upon them considerably in this section.

enforcement should receive the lowest priority from the police and that the
city council should petition the state government to legalize prostitution. The
proposal was resoundingly defeated, with 63.9 percent opposed and only 36.1
percent in favor.[55]

Even a Berkeley-residing proponent of legal prostitution might have voted
against this measure, of course, because of its local nature and its lack of
accompanying regulations. If Berkeley became the only safe haven for streetwalking in the area, and a well-publicized one at that, then both sex workers
and johns would flood to Berkeley, from the Bay Area and beyond. With
streetwalking unregulated but de facto legal, the public nuisance and other
social costs accompanying such uncontrolled prostitution would render many
Berkeley streets unfit for activities other than commercial sex. A statewide
liberalization might have more appeal, by reducing the incentive for regional
vice tourism, though residents of other states and nations would still be drawn
into California by the prospect of legal prostitution. (Such vice tourism might
be a positive development, of course, if the legalized prostitution market were
effectively regulated to minimize the $3\frac{1}{3}$ standard vice concerns.)

Probably few other urban areas in the United States would have mustered
anywhere near the one-out-of-three support that the Berkeley referendum attracted. For many decades now, criminalization has been the standard approach
to urban prostitution in the United States.[56] Other countries have taken different paths, including legalization of some forms of prostitution. Whether the
regulatory regime is centered on criminalization, however, the outdoor urban
sex trade tends to be subjected to a sort of formal or informal zoning: red-light
districts, essentially. Within the relevant zones, some types of prostitution are
legal or semitolerated (though subjected to periodic crackdowns), while outside
the zone, prohibition is maintained.

The discussion here will be framed around the dominant type of prostitution, involving female prostitutes and male clients. With respect to clients, this
framing accords well with reality, as the overwhelming majority of patrons of
prostitutes are men. The supply side of prostitution, however, includes a significant minority of males and transgendered individuals.[57] Nonetheless, despite
the "male client–female provider" framing, the approach generally applies to
other varieties of prostitution.

Most prostitutes in the United States are not streetwalkers, but most arrests of
prostitutes are of streetwalkers, a pattern that is replicated elsewhere. This arrest
configuration partly reflects the fact that the public nature of streetwalking eases
the job of the police. Focusing enforcement on streetwalking, while turning a
near blind eye to call girl activity, also suggests that the greater public concern

---

[55] See the November 4, 2004, Vice Squad post.   [56] Weitzer (2000, p. 159).

[57] Cooke and Sontag (2005, p. 470).

is not so much with commercial sex but rather with certain unseemly public manifestations of commercial sex. In some countries, such as Canada and Britain, prostitution per se is not illegal, but solicitation is illegal. In these countries, call girls can conduct business within the law, but streetwalkers and operators of escort agencies that employ call girls remain subject to arrest.

Those unseemly public manifestations associated with street prostitution can go beyond the indecorous to the dangerous. Areas with rampant street-walking often are marked by pavements littered with used condoms and hypo-dermic needles.[58] The sexual activity might take place in semipublic fashion. Prostitutes might proposition unwitting passersby, and women or teenage girls passing through the neighborhood might be propositioned by johns. Traffic might be reduced to a standstill as prospective customers crawl along the streets in their cars to arrange a deal. The red-light district approach to pros-titution control in some measure arose to ensure that these sorts of behaviors do not take place in respectable parts of town.

Harms to the participants themselves probably constitute larger costs asso-ciated with prostitution than do externalities, at least under U.S. style crimi-nalization and policing. For consumers, the prospect of being the victim of a robbery or of acquiring a disease must be contended with. Prostitutes face the possibility of being robbed, beaten, or raped, as well as contracting an STD; abuse at the hands of customers, pimps, and police is a particularly frequent occurrence among urban streetwalkers.[59]

The costs of the lack of safety fostered by the criminalization of prostitu-tion are enormous: "prostitution is one of the most dangerous professions."[60] In recent years, there have been fourteen murders of prostitutes along U.S. Interstate 40, and a Seattle-area serial killer murdered forty-eight prostitutes over a twenty-one-year period. The killer's statement as part of his guilty plea makes for chilling reading, including this excerpt: "I also picked prostitutes as victims because they were easy to pick up without being noticed. I knew they would not be reported missing right away, and might never be reported missing. I picked prostitutes because I thought I could kill as many of them as I wanted without getting caught."[61]

Both johns and prostitutes – primarily prostitutes – risk arrest, of course. Hardly a week goes by in the United States without a person of some local

---

[58] Weitzer (2000, pp. 166ff.) offers an accounting of the social effects of street prostitution.

[59] There is an externality element to the spread of any infectious disease, as increased prevalence puts nonparticipants at higher risk.

[60] Sanders (2005, p. 73).

[61] From page 7 of Statement on Plea of Guilty, available at http://metrokc.gov/kcsc/docs/statement_of_defendant.pdf, visited February 21, 2006. On the I-40 cases, see, e.g., "Truck Stop Prostitute Killings," MyEyewitnessnews.com (Memphis), at http://www.myeyewitnessnews.com/news/local/story.aspx?content_id=CA8C80C3-4E94-456D-845C-81D6AD11831E (accessed on February 21, 2006).

standing – a principal, teacher, or minister, for example – being arrested for a prostitution-related offense. Typical consequences of the arrest are public embarrassment and job loss, all for behavior that in much of the world is completely legal and of no public concern.

Many localities have chosen to take extraordinary measures to try to assure that arrestees are publicly embarrassed. Such measures take the form of direct publicity or of arranging antiprostitution policing in such a way that the local media serve as enthusiastic partners. The direct methods include posting the pictures of prostitution arrestees on police websites, on local billboards, or even on special television programming. The indirect methods involve tipping off the media to sting operations so that their cameras are on the scene or conducting arrests and bookings in such a public manner as to ensure coverage.[62]

An interest in reducing the internal and external harms associated with prostitution would seem to favor a legal and regulated commercial sex industry and for making any remaining illegal segments of the sex market as small as possible, while promoting the safety of participants. In theory, a legal commercial sex sector could take most of the trade off the street, customers and workers could meet in safe environments, condom use could be mandated, and screens for STDs could be put in place. Underage patrons and prostitutes would remain barred from participation, but health and alternative employment services would readily be available to illegal as well as legal prostitutes. Many nations have adopted variations of such a regulatory scheme, which was made even more attractive following the advent of the AIDS pandemic.

THE ROBUSTNESS PRINCIPLE AND PROSTITUTION

The harm reduction strategy of legal, regulated prostitution also is consistent with the robustness principle. Indeed, robustness requires that some avenues of adult prostitution be legally available. If such non-burdensome legal prostitution channels exist, significant penalties legitimately could be imposed upon johns who patronize the informal sector.

The rationality concern with respect to adult participants largely comes down to whether prostitutes are well-informed and farsighted about the consequences of entering into the commercial sex trade. In some poor countries or neighborhoods, both prostitutes and their customers might be ignorant about sexually transmitted diseases, including hepatitis C and AIDS:

> In India, knowledge about HIV is still scant and incomplete. In a 2001 national
> behavioural study of nearly 85 000 people, only 75% of respondents had heard
> of AIDS and awareness was particularly low among rural women in Bihar,
> Gujarat and West Bengal. Less than 33% of all respondents had heard of sexually

---

[62] See the November 14, 2003, Vice Squad post on the doings in Maricopa County, Arizona.

transmitted infections and only 21% were aware of the links between sexually transmitted infections and HIV.[63]

Measures to help those who are not fully cognizant of the consequences of prostitution would include informing people about potential repercussions of entering into prostitution; policies also could involve efforts to lower the negative effects of remaining in sex work and to ease exit from the trade. These harm reduction measures reduce the average costs of prostitution, while legality itself promotes exit. Under prohibition, prostitutes can rack up a slew of arrests and convictions that make it difficult for them to find other types of work. Legality eliminates those arrests, diminishing an important barrier to employment outside of the commercial sex sector. (Legality does not fully eradicate barriers to employment in nonsex sectors because some of the impediments arise from social stigma, not law; workers in legal pornography production, for instance, typically have trouble moving outside of the porn industry. High pay for some sex workers also can lead to a lifestyle that cannot be maintained cheaply, again contributing to some inertia within sex work.[64]) But robustness might require additional, positive steps to help those who feel trapped in the prostitution (and frequently drug-using) lifestyle. Subsidized counseling services, safety tips, alcohol and drug treatment, financial advice, and training opportunities might be further steps toward ensuring that those who engage in prostitution are clear-sighted and possess options. As in the case of pornography, mandated waiting periods before someone can embark on a legal prostitution career also might be desirable.

While a robustness approach precludes the criminalization of prostitution, public manifestations such as streetwalking can be regulated or prohibited. Activities related to the commercialization of sex can be controlled or banned, as long as those bans are not too costly upon rational prostitutes and their customers. Thus attempts to eliminate pimping via prohibitions on "living off the proceeds of prostitution" are not clear violations of the robustness principle. Such bans, however, need not be helpful to prostitutes, who might want to outsource their marketing activities, for instance. Prohibitions on living off the proceeds also can make it hard for prostitutes to maintain standard relationships with partners or roommates, as people with such an affiliation could risk arrest. Safety can be promoted when two or three prostitutes share a workplace or live together while conducting their business from their home; nevertheless, this arrangement is illegal in some countries in which prostitution per se is not criminalized.[65] Bans on pimping or living off the proceeds might violate robustness

---

[63] UNAIDS (2004, p. 27).

[64] See, for instance, Abbott (2000, p. 33) and Barton (2006, pp. 89–90).

[65] In early 2006, Britain announced its intention to tolerate (though not officially legalize) such minibrothels. See "Britain Cracks Down on Prostitution," by Mark Rice-Oxley, *Christian Science Monitor*, January 31, 2006; available at http://www.csmonitor.com/2006/0131/p07s02-woeu.htm (accessed March 7, 2006).

if in practice they impose these sorts of significant costs upon prostitutes: the issue is one of expedience rather than principle, and there is no reason to think that the best approach is the same in all locales.

There are various feminist perspectives with respect to prostitution.[66] One shared policy prescription is that prostitutes should be in no danger of incurring criminal penalties from plying their trade. In this regard, the feminist perspectives cohere with both harm reduction and robustness. A major element of contention within feminist thought, however, is whether the customers, the johns, should similarly be protected against arrest. Sweden has chosen to decriminalize sales of sex, while maintaining a ban on purchases. This reverses what often has been standard practice, to arrest prostitutes while giving a pass to johns.

Criminalizing one side of a market does not necessarily make the market safer for those on the other side. Exchanges remain subject to the usual black-market problems of largely being beyond regulation and involve uncertain and at times violent contract enforcement. (Legalizing the behavior of sellers does make it easier for them to approach the police when they are victimized; a policy of no adverse ramifications from approaching the police also can be introduced when sales are illegal, however.) Johns who are placed at greater risk of arrest become interested in negotiating their deals less publicly and more quickly, alterations which do not conduce to the safety of streetwalkers.[67] Further, for women who are engaging in prostitution against their will, johns sometimes serve to communicate their plight to authorities, a communication made less likely when patronizing a prostitute is illegal. One-sided enforcement aimed at johns, therefore, not only fails to satisfy the robustness principle, it also might fail to serve the goal of reducing harms to prostitutes.[68]

Many public health or harm reduction approaches to prostitution suggest that legalization be combined with mandatory STD testing. Positive tests for HIV typically would result in a ban from the trade, with penalties applied for any future prostitution convictions. Positive tests for other STDs might be met by temporary bans until the tests are negative.

Given the potential internal and external costs associated with the spread of STDs, mandatory testing is consistent with the robustness principle. Whether mandatory testing actually serves the goal of harm reduction is debatable, however.[69] Short of abstinence, the best defense against STD transmission is condom use. The commitment to condom use might be undermined by mandatory STD testing. For instance, johns might feel protected by the tests (which are imperfect, of course) and lobby more ardently for sex without a condom. The imposition of mandatory tests might push more of the trade into the illegal

---

[66] See, e.g., Bingham (1998).　　　　　　[67] Sanders (2005, pp. 95, 98).
[68] On one-sided enforcement, see Lott and Roberts (1989).
[69] See Monet (2004) and Jürgens (2001).

sector, where a variety of harms are more likely.[70] Further, sex workers already are often extremely careful about safe sex, perhaps more so than the johns or many sexually active individuals who do not operate as prostitutes; indeed, one role played by sex workers is to convey information about disease transmission to their clients.[71] Prostitutes in Nevada's legal rural-county brothels – where condom use is required – have lower STD infection rates than does the female population at-large.[72]

SHAME, VICE, AND THE LAW

Public embarrassment can be an unavoidable consequence of a prostitution arrest, but most urban misdemeanor arrests generate no publicity, limiting the amount of attached stigma. The exceptional methods that many jurisdictions use to maximize embarrassment for alleged prostitution offenders often are aimed at arrestees who have never been convicted of any crime and hence are still entitled to a presumption of innocence. The measures sometimes are adopted and supported quite openly as means to *punish* arrestees – though the U.S. Constitution requires that punishment take place following the due process of law. Stigma-generating publicity might serve as an effective deterrent, of course, but so might all other sorts of extraconstitutional policing. Like the civil asset forfeitures discussed in Chapter 4 – forfeitures themselves are widely used for antiprostitution policing in the United States – abnormal attempts to enlist shame into the costs imposed on arrestees should not be tolerated. (For those *convicted* of prostitution crimes, this due process objection does not apply, of course.) Another curious feature of shaming publicity is that these methods seem to be most popular with prostitution offenses and drunk driving, as well as for those convicted of sex crimes. People arrested for robbery generally do not have to fear that their photograph will appear on a local billboard or police website.

The uncertain association of selling or purchasing sex with any sort of "inherent" or generalized criminality lies at the heart of the shaming approach. Johns and prostitutes often are just regular folks who actually will be shamed by having their photos circulated in the case of an arrest.[73] Robbers tend to be less in thrall to the norms of mainstream society, so there is little deterrence value in a publicity threat.

Re-education camps are another technique used in antiprostitution enforcement. Some localities in the United States and abroad sentence convicted johns (perhaps in lieu of a permanent criminal record) to attend a class where they are

---

[70] One of the undesirable outcomes associated with the criminalization of solicitation (and prostitution more generally) is that condom possession becomes evidence of criminal behavior. As a result, prostitutes are less likely to carry and use condoms where prostitution is criminalized.

[71] Sanders (2005, pp. 153–4). [72] Snadowsky (2005, p. 228).

[73] See Weitzer (1999, p. 96).

lectured about the dire consequences that arise from their interest in purchasing sex.[74] The classes are thus similar to traffic school, though more ideologically charged. Reckless driving is dangerous to others and illegal everywhere. Purchasing sex is legal in many places and is far from universally condemned as causing harm to the prostitutes or to women more generally. A convicted john might well respond, that perhaps it is your laws, and not my desires, that are the main source of the costs imposed upon prostitutes. Should legislators be required to attend classes on the harms of vice prohibitions?

THE INTERACTION BETWEEN LEGAL AND ILLEGAL PROSTITUTION

One of the chief dilemmas of prostitution control concerns the relationship between legal and illegal or formal and informal varieties. In the case of alcohol, legalization with modest taxation and enforcement in developed countries goes a long way toward eliminating the black market. Most beverage alcohol consumed in the United States is completely legitimate, despite a mass of regulation and significant taxation. But in the case of prostitution, the ability of the legal sector to outcompete the illegal sector is much less obvious. Indeed, it may be the case that a legal sector serves as a spur to illegal prostitution.

Consider a delineated red-light district in which regulated brothel prostitution is legal. This district will attract men interested in purchasing sex. A streetwalker, therefore, might find that her best opportunity for attracting customers will exist in this neighborhood. She might be able to meet prospective clients before they enter a legal brothel or undersell her regulated (and perhaps taxed) counterparts. Or an informal, occasional prostitute desirous of making some quick cash might also suspect that the brothel zone (or just outside it) is her best bet for making connections. Underage or HIV-positive prostitutes or undocumented residents, none of whom would be able to work in the legal sector, will be drawn to the neighborhood. Johns might prefer the informal version, even in the absence of a price differential, if picking up a streetwalker is less publicly visible or more exciting than walking into a licensed brothel. Johns who intend to be violent or engage in other criminal behavior also will seek out the informal market.

Even long-term, legally eligible prostitutes might have considerable incentive to avoid the formal sector. First, they might find the various regulations to be overly onerous and intrusive. Second, working in a legal brothel might involve adhering to a whole set of rules imposed not by the state but by the brothel operators, and these rules, too, might be perceived as unduly burdensome. For instance, brothel management might fire a prostitute who regularly

---

[74] See, e.g., Weitzer (2000, pp. 171–2), and Monto (2000, pp. 69–71).

refuses to service certain clients. Brothels also have been known to use dra-
conian measures to limit the nonworking time activities of their employees,
in part to try to prevent outside meetings between prostitutes and clients that
are arranged to avoid sharing the fee with the brothel. (Sometimes restrictions
on the movements of prostitutes are imposed informally by localities, as conditions of brothel licensing.[75]) Perhaps most daunting is the necessity to have
one's name added to some official register of prostitutes, especially in the
absence of guarantees that the list will remain confidential.

Does it have to be this way in an urban setting, that a regulated commercial
sex sector cannot outcompete, and might even pave the way for, a parallel,
unregulated sector? Perhaps not. To the extent that the legal and illegal sectors
do seem to go together in many places, the correlation might simply reflect
the fact that countries or cities that provide legal prostitution tend to be fairly
tolerant of illegal prostitution, too. But the parallel, informal sector presents a
serious challenge to legal and regulated prostitution. One possibility is to try to
move the legal brothels to areas that are a bit out of town, so that the condensed
array of streets and traffic that promote streetwalking are not available. Of
course, if the brothel zones are too remote, then they will not be competitive
with the informal trade in more urbanized areas. Another possibility is to try
to ease safe connections with call girls, again to try to limit the market for
informal street trade. Further, if there are nonburdensome legal prostitution
channels available, significant penalties could be imposed upon johns who
patronize the informal sector.[76]

Indoor prostitution, even when it is not legal, tends to involve much
lower levels of violence than does streetwalking.[77] Prostitutes who work
indoors needn't work alone, and they have a wider array of strategies at
their disposal to limit negative encounters – including a longer time period
available in which to screen the clientele. Within a criminalized regulatory
regime, then, there remain good reasons to be relatively tolerant toward indoor
work.[78]

The comparative safety of indoor prostitution, however, might largely arise
because of the typical criminalization of streetwalking. A legal zone for streetwalking, along with a safe parking area in which sex acts can be undertaken
and health services provided, could greatly increase the safety of streetwalking,
too.[79] Even when streetwalking remains illegal, the enormous costs associated
with violence and STDs in this sector argue for measures to render street

[75] Hausbeck and Brents (2000, pp. 229–32).
[76] A similar suggestion is made by Snadowsky (2005).
[77] See, e.g., Sanders (2005).
[78] Weitzer (1999) argues for a dual approach that would focus enforcement at street prostitution while
liberalizing the treatment of indoor prostitution.
[79] See the discussion of legal streetwalking in Wotton (2005).

prostitution as safe as possible. Illegality of streetwalking also contributes to the sorts of police corruption and abuse that are familiar from drug prohibition.[80]

COERCION AND TRAFFICKING

The robustness approach assumes, of course, that becoming or remaining a prostitute can be a free and rational adult choice. Not everyone accepts this premise. The United Nations, which promulgates a strong antitrafficking agenda, seems to be of the mind that no well-informed person would consent to being trafficked for commercial sex activities: "Victims often consent to the initial stage of trafficking because they are misled or deceived by traffickers."[81] The U.S. State Department declares that "Prostitution is inherently harmful."[82]

The misleading and coercive techniques that the UN warns of occur quite frequently. Women trafficked across national boundaries are particularly vulnerable; they can have their passports taken and will not feel free (or be free) to go to the police to report any abuse – and such women are frequently beaten and raped. The victims might fear retribution against themselves or their families from organized criminal traffickers, and their own illegal presence or activities inside a foreign country might make them fear the police, too. Language barriers also can impede attempts by foreign women to seek help. Many countries, including the United States, have instituted special visa programs to allow trafficked women to temporarily (and perhaps permanently) remain in the country if they provide evidence against their traffickers, but the threat of reprisals remains. Many of the problems associated with trafficked illegal migrants and forced laborers are similar whether or not they are trafficked for the purposes of commercial sex. Most forced laborers in the United States are not involved in the sex industry, though that sector apparently contains more coerced workers than any other single industry.[83]

That abusive trafficking exists should not obscure the fact that many women who move to cities from rural areas, or are trafficked abroad, understand the nature of their commitment. (Once again, however, general consent to become a commercial sex worker does not imply specific consent to later abusive

---

[80] See, in general, the eighth volume (2005) of the journal *Research in Sex Work*; this volume is devoted to prostitution and policing.

[81] From the UN's FAQ at http://www.unodc.org/unodc/en/trafficking_victim_consents.html; visited on February 4, 2006. Later in the same FAQ appears an estimate of annual trafficking into the US: "A recent CIA report estimated that between 45,000 to 50,000 women and children are brought to the United States every year under false pretenses and are forced to work as prostitutes, abused labourers or servants."

[82] "The Link between Prostitution and Sex Trafficking," U.S. Department of State, Bureau of Public Affairs, Washington, DC, November 24, 2004; available at http://www.state.gov/r/pa/ei/rls/38790.htm (accessed March 7, 2006).

[83] "Hidden Slaves: Forced Labor in the United States," 2005.

Box 6.1: *Nevada's legal brothels*[a]

Since the early 1970s, rural counties in Nevada have had the option of permitting legal brothels. Many do so. Nevada requires legal brothel prostitutes to obtain a health card, which is issued to female applicants who are 18 or older and who are not infected with a sexually transmitted disease. After securing employment, prostitutes must undergo weekly health checks, with tests for syphilis and HIV conducted monthly. Brothels are required to post notices indicating that condom use is mandatory. The counties (or incorporated areas within them) apply a variety of regulations in conjunction with the state-level controls. For instance, most counties do not allow women under the age of 21 to work as prostitutes. Counties often receive considerable revenue from registered brothels and charges for the work cards they require of prostitutes, but the brothels do not pay state taxes.

Nevada brothels face various controls over advertising. Signs on the ranch property, though perhaps visible from afar, are permitted. (The brothels are known as "ranches.") Advertising brothels in counties that do not permit them is prohibited by state law. As a result, alternative methods of publicity are used: cab drivers who deliver clients typically receive a cut for providing some word of mouth advertising.[b] Nor can the brothels place help-wanted ads or otherwise openly advertise for prostitutes, as such efforts would put ranch owners and managers at risk of arrest for pandering. These advertising controls might not meet constitutional muster, though Nevada brothel owners tend to recognize that they are operating in an industry that is barely tolerated – a court challenge to the regulations, even if successful, could well result in the imposition of statewide prohibition of prostitution.[bb] Their marginal status has led the brothels to attempt a tactic that is almost unheard of in other industries: they asked the state to impose a tax upon them. The state legislature refused the offer in April 2005, being unwilling to grant further imprimatur to legal prostitution.[c]

Nevada's legal brothels do not solve the usual urban prostitution problems, in part because they are not permitted in the counties that contain Nevada's two largest cities, Las Vegas and Reno.[d] Casino interests are said to be major opponents of legal prostitution for those cities, presumably because they view legal prostitution as competing with their own entertainment offerings. Both Las Vegas and Reno, however, apparently host thriving illegal sex markets, and in 2003, the mayor of Las Vegas suggested that legalization might be worth pursuing.[e]

In terms of harm reduction, Nevada's rural brothels appear to be quite successful. With few exceptions, underage girls have been kept from working in the brothels, violence against the workers is rare, safe sex is practiced, and the spread of disease has been minimized. Writing in 2001, Dr. Alexa Albert noted: "Since March 1986, when the state's Bureau of Disease Control and Intervention Services began requiring brothel prostitutes to undergo monthly HIV tests, over 42,500 such tests have been conducted, and no licensed prostitute has ever tested positive."[f]

(continued)

Box 6.1 *(continued)*

The legal brothels in Nevada currently only extend to female prostitutes servicing male clients. Brothels staffed by men or by transgendered individuals, pitched at either a female clientele or a male clientele, have been proposed but not opened. Nor do I know of such brothels in other locales – for example, Australia, New Zealand, Netherlands, Turkey, Germany, and Switzerland – that allow legal brothel prostitution. How much of this vacuum is due to the commercial shortcomings of such establishments and how much is due to social and political reluctance to license nontraditional brothels is hard to disentangle, but surely the political reluctance is a salient component, even in locations where traditional brothels are legal. (Escort services are widely available for nontraditional forms of prostitution.) An antiprostitution advocate in Nevada once applied for a license for a male homosexual brothel, in the apparent hope of undermining the legal regime for all types of establishments.[g]

---

[a] This section relies significantly upon Albert (2001) and Hausbeck and Brents (2001); see also my review of the Albert book in the *Journal of Policy Analysis and Management* 21(2): 311–4, Spring 2002.

[b] Albert (2001).

[bb] Update: A federal court found the state advertising controls unconstitutional in July 2007.

[c] See the April 15, 2005, Vice Squad post. One brothel owner has taken on a much higher-profile approach, which has included having a cable TV documentary series filmed at his ranch. See "Nevada Gives Legalised Prostitution Uneasy Embrace," by Adam Tanner, Reuters UK, February 14, 2006, at http://today.reuters.co.uk/news/newsArticle.aspx?type=worldNews& storyID=2006-02-14T011522Z_01_N08357784_RTRUKOC_0_UK-LIFE-PROSTITUTION. xml&archived=False (accessed on February 21, 2006).

[d] Weitzer (2000).   [e] See the Vice Squad post for October 31, 2003.

[f] Albert (2001, pp. 173–4), footnote omitted. The claim of no positive HIV-tests was reiterated in early 2006 by George Flint, a longtime lobbyist for Nevada brothels. See "Nevada Gives Legalised Prostitution Uneasy Embrace," by Adam Tanner, Reuters UK, February 14, 2006, at http://today.reuters.co.uk/news/newsArticle.aspx?type=worldNews&storyID=2006-02-14T 01-1522Z_01_N08357784_RTRUKOC_0_UK-LIFE-PROSTITUTION.xml&archived=False (accessed on February 21, 2006).

[g] See the Wikipedia entry on "Prostitution in Nevada" at en.wikipedia.org/wiki/Prostitution_ in_Nevada (accessed March 7, 2006).

---

practices.) Some entry into prostitution, including transborder prostitution, is consensual. Nevertheless, public discussion frequently confounds coerced and uncoerced sex work, adult and underage trafficking, and migrant sex workers with migrant labor in nonsex industries.[84] These conflations are dangerous because broad anti-trafficking rules can themselves be quite exploitative and coercive when practiced upon voluntary sex workers.[85]

---

[84] See Weitzer (2004) and Chapkis (2005).

[85] See some of the information available at the Network of Sex Work Projects homepage, http://www. nswp.org (accessed March 7, 2006), including their submission to the Senate Legal and Constitutional Legislation Committee of the Australian Parliament, at http://www.nswp.org/pdf/AU-TRAFFICK-NSWP.PDF.

Even if one favors the complete abolition of prostitution and trafficking, equating all trafficking with coercion likely will prove counterproductive, a case of letting the best (zero trafficking) be the enemy of the good (minimized coercion in trafficking). The sorts of approaches that are needed to reduce the two types of trafficking, coercive and noncoercive, are different. Coercive trafficking can be attacked by ensuring that information is available, that commercial sex workers can operate in a legal environment, and that women (and their families) can be protected from reprisals should they go to the police. The noncoercive variety does not involve obvious victims, and hence the best interventions entail promoting alternative types of employment and ensuring access to occupations in other sectors.

The choices of sex workers, like those of all of us, do not always fall neatly into the categories "coerced" or "noncoerced." People with a plethora of desirable options, however, will not choose to become street prostitutes. Rather, such prostitutes generally operate under a slew of disadvantages, including poor education, low earnings, alcohol and drug addiction (sometimes pressed upon them by those who want to encourage their prostitution), mental disorders, and violent relationships. Even when street workers are not victims of traffickers or pressured by pimps, their circumstances merit social attention. Compounding their troubles through arrests and fines – the payment of which drives them into more active engagement in the trade – seems to combine ineffectiveness with inhumanity.

A TABLE IN LIEU OF CONCLUSIONS

As in many other areas of vice policy, there are no simple solutions to the issues posed by pornography and prostitution. Nor is it easy to feel fully comfortable with any commercial sex regulatory regime. Our lack of knowledge of "best practice" in obscenity and prostitution control, along with the diversity of local conditions, suggests that there is much to be said for local experimentation.

The robustness principle cannot characterize best practice, but it can eliminate from consideration some policy regimes, including those that are insufficiently mindful of internalities and externalities, as well as those that impose too heavily upon rational, adult participants. And as the robustness criterion applies at the level of policy regimes, individual measures cannot be judged in isolation against the robustness standard. With these qualifications in mind, let me conclude this chapter by offering a capsule summary of some commercial sex policies that do not run counter to the robustness criterion. (A subset of these policies is already in place in the United States and elsewhere.) The table somewhat arbitrarily categorizes policies in relation to the standard vice concern – kids, addicts, externalities, or harms to nonaddicted adult participants – that they primarily address.

Table 6.1: *Pornography and prostitution policy screened
through the robustness principle*

Public concern	An array of robust policy responses
Kids	Prohibition on kids working in porn or prostitution, with penalties applied to the employers or clients of kids. Production and possession of child pornography banned. Information provision to older teens concerning risks of commercial sex. Bans on advertising of porn and prostitution in media with significant kid exposure. Prohibition of purchase of porn or sex by kids, and a ban on underage attendance at live erotic shows, with licensing of sellers to help enforce the bans.
Addicts	Porn websites and live commercial sex venues such as strip clubs offer voluntary opt-out arrangements. Adult websites periodically provide timed pop-ups or brief time-outs and links to addiction help sites. Live venues offer voluntary time, budget, or credit constraints. Information provision about sex addiction and treatment options for both addicts and family members. Public funding for trials and evaluation of policy interventions and treatment programs.
Externalities	Indecent broadcasting and sexually explicit public displays regulated or banned, though nonbroadcast transmission legal. Advertising of porn and prostitution restricted. Porn limited to adult-only areas of shops. Licensing of prostitutes, health tests, and condom use required. Zoning of legal prostitution and other commercial sex venues. Penalties imposed upon prostitution participants operating outside of the formal sector.
"Internal" Costs	Waiting period prior to porn performance or sex work. Explicit, detailed consent required for particularly risky behaviors. Information provision concerning dangers of commercial sex, and for consumers, information dissemination concerning compulsive sexual behavior. Counseling and health services made available for sex workers, including information on employment alternatives and alcohol and drug treatment. Moderate "sin" taxes imposed, along with advertising restrictions. Intoxicated participants barred.

VICE VERDICTS (IV): NUDE DANCING AND SODOMY

Nude Dancing: *Barnes v. Glen Theatre, Inc.* (1991), and *Erie v. Pap's A. M.* (2000)[86]

If you want to dance nude in the privacy of your own home, among adult friends and relatives, then you have my blessing; more important, you have the government's blessing. If you want to operate a club open to the public (adults

[86] This section derives from some Vice Squad posts from late May 2004.

only, of course) in which some of your employees dance nude, however, things get a bit more complicated – the extent of their constitutional rights to dance undraped may depend on the federal court district in which your establishment resides. The reason that the constraints on regulating nude dancing are not more uniform is that the Supreme Court decisions that are the basis for the rules have not provided authoritative majority opinions.

You might ask what the Constitution has to do with nude dancing. You would not be alone. Justice Antonin Scalia essentially asks that question in his concurring opinion in *Barnes v. Glen Theatre*, answering that a general law regulating nude dancing concerns conduct, not expression, and thus "is not subject to First Amendment scrutiny at all."[87] But the Supreme Court as a whole (including the other eight justices in *Barnes*) has long held that nude dancing is expressive conduct (like flag burning, in that respect) and hence is entitled to free speech guardianship – though erotic dancing "falls only within the outer ambit of the First Amendment's protection."[88] As a result, strip clubs cannot simply be banned by a municipality. But such venues can be regulated, and the court frequently has become the arbiter of how severe the regulations can become. Once granting nude dancing the status of symbolic speech, the Supreme Court takes the approach that it has developed toward regulations over other forms of symbolic speech – and, in particular, draft-card burning – and applies that approach to nude dancing regulations.

In 1988, the state of Indiana enacted a law that banned complete nudity in public places, including adult entertainment establishments. An Indiana corporation whose business included nude peep shows sued the state, claiming that the public nudity prohibition violated the First Amendment. Thus was born the case that became *Barnes v. Glen Theatre*.

Chief Justice William Rehnquist wrote the plurality opinion for *Barnes*, though the Chief Justice was joined only by Justices Sandra Day O'Connor and Anthony Kennedy. In the draft-card case from 1968, the court ruled that the nonspeech component of "symbolic speech" or "expressive conduct" can at times be regulated, even if that regulation simultaneously imposes some incidental burden on the speech component of the conduct.[89] A four-prong test is used to determine if the regulation is justified. Among the conditions that a regulation of this type must meet to not fall afoul of the First Amendment is that the regulation must further a substantial government interest, where the interest is unrelated to the suppression of free expression, and the incidental burden on speech must be as small as possibly can be achieved when trying to advance that substantial government interest. The *Barnes* plurality determined that "protecting societal order and morality" was substantial government interest enough,

---

[87] *Barnes v. Glen Theatre*, 501 U.S. 560 (1991).
[88] Justice O'Connor opinion, *Erie v. Pap's A. M.*, 529 U.S. 277 (2000).
[89] *United States v. O'Brien*, 391 U.S. 367 (1968).

even though there was no direct evidence that protecting order and morality was the goal behind the Indiana statute. Further, the opinion claimed, this "interest is unrelated to the suppression of free expression." The "expression" that is part of nude dancing is eroticism, presumably, and eroticism, even erotic dancing, was still permitted by the statute – it was only completely nude erotic dancing, along with all other forms of public nudity, that was suppressed. As for whether the burden on speech is the unavoidable minimum needed to promote morality, the Rehnquist opinion summarily (and knowingly punnily?) disposed of that issue: " . . . Indiana's requirement that the dancers wear at least pasties and G-strings is modest, and the bare minimum necessary to achieve the state's purpose." Therefore, the court held that Indiana's statute forbidding public nudity, even in adult entertainment establishments, was not in violation of the First Amendment.

Justice David Souter wrote a separate concurring opinion. Rather than relying upon the promotion of order and morality as constituting the public's stake justifying regulation, Justice Souter called upon " . . . the State's substantial interest in combating the secondary effects of adult entertainment establishments. . . . " The secondary effects that Souter identified, which were noted by Indiana's lawyers, were prostitution, sexual assault, and other criminal activities. (As the dissent recognized, if these harms are the source of concern, then it would seem that there are ways of dealing with them that do not require the suppression of the expressive conduct of nude dancing.) The Souter opinion proved to be influential in later cases.

The four dissenters did not believe that the prohibition was unrelated to the expressive conduct, as required by the four-prong test. "Since the State permits the dancers to perform if they wear pasties and G-strings, but forbids nude dancing, it is precisely because of the distinctive, expressive content of the nude dancing performances at issue in this case that the State seeks to apply the statutory prohibition." If nude dancing conveys a message that differs significantly from non-nude dancing, then under U.S. constitutional law nude dancing could not be prohibited, as regulations that are aimed at specific messages must still leave open ample channels of communication.

The four-prong test (from the draft-card case) that the Supreme Court applied in *Barnes* is only appropriate if the restriction under review is "content neutral." (This is the point with which the *Barnes* dissenters took issue.) If the restriction is content-based (for instance, applies on the basis of what is being said as opposed to the time, place, and manner in which it is expressed), then a more demanding test is appropriate. Specifically, the Supreme Court looks at content-based restrictions with "strict scrutiny." A regulation can survive strict scrutiny only if it serves a compelling government interest and does so through means that are narrowly tailored to minimize the amount of speech that is affected.

A subsequent Pennsylvania court, faced with an ordinance very similar to the Indiana statute under contention in *Barnes*, felt that, except for the issue of whether nude dancing receives any First Amendment protection (it does), the four separate opinions in *Barnes* provided little clear precedent on other questions. The Pennsylvania court decided that its public nudity ordinance was content-based and unconstitutional under the strict scrutiny standard. The Supreme Court disagreed that the control was content-based, in *Erie v. Pap's A. M.* (2000).[90] Further, a plurality of justices justified their conclusion that the ordinance was content neutral by adopting the "secondary effects" approach that Justice Souter had employed in *Barnes*: the state's interest in reducing these harms "is unrelated to the suppression of the erotic message conveyed by nude dancing." But with four separate opinions again generated, *Erie* has not significantly cleared up the tangle of nude dancing jurisprudence. Even the strip club that lost the *Erie* case wound up a winner: the Pennsylvania ordinance eventually was overturned for being inconsistent with the Pennsylvania state constitution.[91]

Recall that the Twenty-first Amendment, which brought an end to alcohol Prohibition, did not legalize alcohol manufacturing, distribution, and sales; rather, it gave the power to regulate alcohol to the individual states. For this reason, a state regulation that controls nude dancing only in establishments in which alcohol is sold had, at least until recently, an additional basis for surviving Supreme Court review. The ability of the Twenty-first Amendment to trump other constitutional provisions has been impaired by *44 Liquormart v. Rhode Island* (1996), however, as discussed in Vice Verdicts III.[92] Nevertheless, use of liquor ordinances to control erotic dancing remains popular, and some strip club owners eschew alcohol sales, in favor of bring-your-own rules, to avoid the regulations.

Municipalities and states continue to adopt all sorts of directives that apply to adult establishments, including distance requirements between dancers and patrons, bans on nudity, bans on tipping, and so on. The constitutional status of these rules currently is rather confused. Although the Supreme Court claims that nude dancing receives some First Amendment protection, courts tend to apply their "tests" in ways that are unfavorable to nude dancing, even when it seems that the obvious application of the test would lead in the other direction – though the outcomes of cases have varied across federal court districts.[93] This variance is the basis for my earlier assertion that your right to operate a private club with nude dancing to some extent depends on the federal district in which you reside.

---

[90] 529 U.S. 277 (2000).   [91] Adler (2006, p. 110n).

[92] 517 U.S. 484 (1996).

[93] For critiques of the current situation, see Bruning (2000) and Doviak and Scamby (2000).

Sodomy: *Bowers v. Hardwick* (1986) and *Lawrence v. Texas* (2003)

Michael Hardwick was peacefully at home, engaging in an act of homosexual fellatio, when a police officer unexpectedly intruded.[94] The officer's mission was vice related: he was serving an arrest warrant on Hardwick for a previous incident of public drinking. In serving the warrant, the officer stumbled upon Mr. Hardwick's intimate behavior and a second vice-related charge emerged: Hardwick and his companion were arrested forthwith under a Georgia state law that barred sodomy, which in Georgia was defined to include both oral and anal intercourse. (Actually, there was still more to Michael Hardwick's rapidly deteriorating day, a marijuana possession charge stemming from a small amount of pot in the bedroom; no gambling offenses, apparently.) The district attorney elected not to pursue the matter, but Michael Hardwick wasn't done. As a practicing homosexual, Hardwick intended to continue in his lawbreaking; he felt himself to be in imminent danger of arrest under the terms of the antisodomy statute and its accompanying administration. Hardwick therefore challenged the constitutionality of the Georgia statute in federal court. A court of appeals agreed that the Georgia law violated the Ninth Amendment ("The enumeration in the Constitution of certain rights shall not be construed to deny or disparage others retained by the people.") and the due process clause of the Fourteenth Amendment ("... nor shall any State deprive any person of life, liberty, or property, without due process of law. ... ").

In a 5-4 decision, the Supreme Court begged to differ with the appeals court and Mr. Hardwick.[95] The opinion of the court, authored by Justice Byron White, noted that the due process provisions of the Fifth and Fourteenth Amendments had been found, in the past, "to have a substantive content, subsuming rights that to a great extent are immune from federal or state regulation or proscription."[96] Not just any old right received this substantive due process protection, however. Rather, to be in the protected pantheon, a right had to be fundamental, and the rights of homosexuals to engage in sodomy didn't meet this very high standard, according to the court.

Hardwick had further contended that even if there is no fundamental right to sodomy, laws require a rational basis. What is the rational basis here? Presumably, so his claim went, that the majority of the Georgia electorate thinks homosexual sodomy is immoral. (While the law as written did not single out homosexual sodomy, heterosexual violations were not pursued by enforcers – for that matter, adult homosexual violations typically were not pursued either.) Is that rational basis enough? The court thought so: "The law ... is constantly based on notions of morality, and if all laws representing essentially moral

[94] Beyond the Supreme Court report itself – *Bowers v. Hardwick*, 478 U.S. 186 (1986) – I am drawing upon the account in Posner (1992, pp. 341ff.).

[95] *Bowers v. Hardwick*, 478 U.S. 186 (1986).

[96] *Bowers v. Hardwick*, 478 U.S. 186 (1986), opinion of the court.

choices are to be invalidated under the Due Process Clause, the courts will be very busy indeed."[97]

Justice Harry Blackmun authored a dissenting opinion that was joined by three other justices: "The Court claims that its decision today merely refuses to recognize a fundamental right to engage in homosexual sodomy; what the Court really has refused to recognize is the fundamental interest all individuals have in controlling the nature of their intimate associations with others." Striking a Millian note, Blackmun continued: "This case involves no real interference with the rights of others, for the mere knowledge that other individuals do not adhere to one's value system cannot be a legally cognizable interest, let alone an interest that can justify invading the houses, hearts, and minds of citizens who choose to live their lives differently."[98]

If you think *Bowers* pretty much exhausts the potential cases arising from police barging into someone's home while homosexual sodomy is taking place, *Lawrence v. Texas* (2003) will disabuse you of that notion.[99] Called to an apartment building under false pretenses, Houston police entered the residence of John Geddes Lawrence, who was engaged in a sexual act with another male. The two adult men "were arrested, held in custody over night, and charged and convicted before a Justice of the Peace."[100] Unlike the Georgia statute, the Texas law criminalized sodomy only if the participants were of the same sex.

In agreeing to hear the *Lawrence* case, the Supreme Court decided to have another look at the *Bowers* decision: "We conclude that the [*Lawrence*] case should be resolved by determining whether the petitioners were free as adults to engage in the private conduct in the exercise of their liberty under the Due Process Clause of the Fourteenth Amendment to the Constitution."[101] This time, the court came to a different conclusion: "The statutes do seek to control a personal relationship that, whether or not entitled to formal recognition in the law, is within the liberty of persons to choose without being punished as criminals." It wasn't just that the world had changed since *Bowers*; rather, the *Lawrence* majority held that the court had previously erred: "*Bowers* was not correct when it was decided, and it is not correct today. It ought not to remain binding precedent. *Bowers* v. *Hardwick* should be and now is overruled."[102]

---

[97] *Bowers v. Hardwick*, 478 U.S. 186 (1986), opinion of the court.

[98] *Bowers v. Hardwick*, 478 U.S. 186 (1986), dissenting opinion of Justice Blackmun, internal case citation omitted.

[99] This section draws heavily upon a Vice Squad post from October 5, 2003.

[100] *Lawrence v. Texas*, 539 U.S. 558 (2003), opinion of the court.

[101] *Lawrence v. Texas*, 539 U.S. 558 (2003), opinion of the court.

[102] *Lawrence v. Texas*, 539 U.S. 558 (2003), opinion of the court. The Justices split 6-3 on *Lawrence*, but only four other Justices joined Justice Kennedy's opinion for the Court; Justice O'Connor, who had voted with the majority in *Bowers*, agreed with the *Lawrence* result but wrote a separate opinion based on the equal protection clause of the Fourteenth Amendment.

What about the traditional social disapproval of homosexuality? Well, first, the *Lawrence* court noted that the legal prohibition of homosexuality wasn't all that traditional to begin with: old laws were aimed at nonprocreative sex more generally, whereas laws aimed specifically at homosexual sodomy were primarily a product of the previous fifty years. Further, the social disapproval was dissipating, as reflected by the fact that many states had repealed their antisodomy laws in recent years. Of course, there has been (and still is) a good deal of moral condemnation of homosexual behavior: "The condemnation has been shaped by religious beliefs, conceptions of right and acceptable behavior, and respect for the traditional family. For many persons these are not trivial concerns but profound and deep convictions accepted as ethical and moral principles to which they aspire and which thus determine the course of their lives. These considerations do not answer the question before us, however. The issue is whether the majority may use the power of the State to enforce these views on the whole society through operation of the criminal law."[103] And, quoting the dissent of Justice Stevens from the *Bowers* case, "... the fact that the governing majority in a State has traditionally viewed a particular practice as immoral is not a sufficient reason for upholding a law prohibiting the practice...."[104]

Of the Stevens quote, a dissenting Justice Scalia claimed: "This effectively decrees the end of all morals legislation."[105] It is not clear why the failure of a sufficient condition to hold implies that the result cannot hold; nevertheless, it does look as if some morals legislation is in constitutional trouble, especially laws regulating sexual acts conducted in private between consenting adults.

Does the *Lawrence* decision pave the way for a constitutional decriminalization of adult drug use in one's private residence (or for that matter, engaging in other prohibited, noncommercial vices)? It is unlikely that the court would take that step anytime in the foreseeable future, but certainly some of the arguments from the court's opinion apply almost as directly to drug use as they do to sodomy.

Earlier, in his dissent in *Bowers*, Justice Blackmun explained why a ruling in favor of Michael Hardwick would not establish a principle that would also require the freedom to use drugs. Drugs are not victimless, he argued; rather, they are "inherently dangerous." (Blackmun classifies drugs with weapons in this regard.) But drugs pretty much are victimless, at least in the same sense that homosexual acts are – nonconsenting others are not directly harmed. Any other definition of "victimless" would seem to fall victim to the notion that, given the prospect of sexually transmitted diseases, sex is less victimless than marijuana use.

---

[103] *Lawrence v. Texas*, 539 U.S. 558 (2003), opinion of the court.
[104] *Lawrence v. Texas*, 539 U.S. 558 (2003), opinion of the court.
[105] *Lawrence v. Texas*, 539 U.S. 558 (2003), dissenting opinion of Justice Scalia.

In determining the consequences of *Lawrence* down the road, the key question, presumably, is where the line will be drawn on what behavior is protected by the liberty interest associated with the due process clause of the Fourteenth Amendment. The opinion of the Court in *Lawrence* (and much of Justice Blackmun's dissent in *Bowers*) could be characterized, without much exaggeration, as saying that for noncommercial, consensual, adult, victimless activity that occurs in the privacy of the home, society will eschew the use of the criminal law. Society need not grant such behavior any other imprimatur. The activity can be punished in public manifestations, certain privileges can be withheld on the basis of the activity, negative consequences can be brought to bear even if a person so much as talks about the activity in public (as in the U.S. military's "don't ask, don't tell" policy toward homosexuality). But society will not throw you in jail because of such private conduct alone. That is, the *Lawrence* court, especially in matters of sexual intimacy, is close to enunciating as a constitutional standard a doctrine we have seen before: John Stuart Mill's harm principle.

7

Internet and Vice

Extensive sleuthing has yielded results: I can now verify that a dedicated web surfer endowed with extreme perseverance will manage to ferret out websites on which gambling can be conducted. Pornography, too, might be viewable upon the web for someone able to devote many hours to the quest. Other vice-related goods and activities that maybe, just maybe, are available online include tobacco, alcohol, prescription drugs, and escorts.

OK, I overplayed the sarcasm. Vice is not only easy to find on the web, it is difficult to avoid. Vice constitutes a major component of the Internet, and the spread of the web, a spread itself fueled by vice, has greatly altered the environment in which vice-related decisions take place. Most obviously, the Internet has eased access to a wide range of vice goods. People who enjoy playing slot machines previously might have had to drive hundreds of miles to a casino to indulge their passion. Now, in much of the world, virtual slot machines can be cyber-accessed at home. Purchasing wines from small, distant vineyards was difficult two decades ago. Now, in some U.S. states, oenophiles can quickly order over the web and have delivered to their door their preferred vintages. Not only does the web improve access to many vice goods, it also makes information (not always reliable, of course) about vice easy to come by. If you want to learn about poker or opium or Australian brothels, the Internet offers myriad opportunities.

These types of conveniences are similar whether it is wine or books or sweatshirts that are purchased or researched over the web. But the relative privacy and anonymity of the Internet is particularly important for reducing the discomfiture or shame that often accompany vice acquisition. There is no chance of running into your boss when visiting a porn site on the web (from your home computer, at least) and no need to deal with a salesclerk at a pharmacy when purchasing Viagra or condoms over the Internet. As a result, the informal social control exercised by the fear of embarrassment when obtaining some vice-related article can be eliminated when vicious behavior is Internet based.[1]

---

[1] Benkler (1999). "The Internet" itself consists of many components, including World Wide Web, Usenet, and e-mail. For some regulatory purposes, these different components should be treated differently; see Wu (1999).

The web-based privatization of vice may lower the average social harms attached to each vicious incident. Many of the external costs of vice (like nuisance problems) tend to be associated with public manifestations such as solicitation for prostitution. Even someone unalterably opposed to vice might view the Internet as a positive development, if the reduced "per unit" social costs outweigh the increased consumption of vice. In other words, Internet provision serves as a harm reduction measure for some varieties of vice.

The convenience and privacy of the web applies to vice producers as well as to consumers. Almost anyone with a computer and a hookup can become a purveyor of pornography and potentially reach a large audience. Connections between buyers and sellers of drugs or prostitution can be established over the web in relative privacy, at low cost, and with some degree of anonymity. Like-minded individuals can find each other and combine in ways that would have been nearly inconceivable in the pre-web world. For instance, fantasy sports leagues, which are statistics intensive and require a collection of fans to operate, have mushroomed thanks to the web, while simultaneously raising questions about whether they constitute illegal gambling.[2]

Most fantasy sports enthusiasts do not have to hide their passion. The same cannot be said of other "secret deviants," those whose vice interests carry significant social disapproval.[3] Secret deviants who require accomplices face the profound problem of locating a coterie of like-minded folks without simultaneously broadcasting their own identity to others – relatives, bosses, pastors – who might not take too well to knowledge of their kink. The web's combination of global reach, search capabilities, and substantial (albeit imperfect) anonymity is a major boon to secret deviants – and by happy symbiosis, a major boon to deviance researchers, too, who now possess a new tool for gauging the practices and prevalence of secret deviancy.

VICE AND THE WEB

The Internet is near-ubiquitous and becoming more so, available in public locales such as libraries, airports, coffee shops, schools, and walking down the street. The convenience, pervasiveness, and privacy of web-based vice present a problem for those who want to shield kids from vicious exposure or for those who want to regulate adult access to vice. Preexisting controls tend not to translate readily to the virtual environment: the situation is rather the opposite. A bricks-and-mortar X-rated movie theater might screen its customers to ensure an adults-only clientele. In the absence of new policies or regulations, however, the theater's web-based counterpart will be available to viewers of all ages.

---

[2] Thompson (2001).

[3] This brief discussion of secret deviancy is based on Leitzel (2006).

New regulations designed with the Internet in mind might not be all that effective, either. One complication is that webpage providers and consumers frequently live in different jurisdictions; people in Illinois easily can access content emanating from another state or another country. It might be hard as a technical matter to ensure that websites located elsewhere conform to regulations that Illinois chooses to adopt. Even if the technical obstacles can be overcome, there are thorny legal questions dealing with the limits of jurisdiction. An attempt by Illinois to claim control over servers based abroad is a recipe for conflict, as is extraterritorial web regulation more generally. Could legal U.S. Internet pornography purveyors run the risk of being prosecuted by "conservative" regimes such as those in Singapore or Iran?

An early international skirmish took place in May 2000, when France forced Yahoo! to preclude access by French residents to auctions of Nazi memorabilia. Yahoo! had already removed such auctions from its French servers, but auctions of Nazi memorabilia were available from the U.S. servers, and in the United States, such auctions are perfectly legal. So the court order required Yahoo! either to block France-based web surfers from Yahoo!'s U.S. sites or to remove the auctions from U.S. servers.[4] Facing the possibility that assets it owned in France would be seized if it failed to comply, Yahoo! voluntarily relinquished the auctions from its sites worldwide. But first, Yahoo! filed a suit in a U.S. Federal court seeking to make the French judgment unenforceable in the United States, as a violation of Yahoo!'s First Amendment rights. A U.S. appeals court eventually ordered the case returned to the district court for dismissal, on the grounds that (given Yahoo!'s removal of the auctions) there was no judicable controversy. Simultaneously, however, the appeals court ruled that U.S. courts did have jurisdiction to hear such a case, even though the French court had minimal contacts in the United States. The decision, therefore, heralds more jurisdictional conflicts ahead over internet content.[5]

FILTERING WEB CONTENT

Age and geographical controls can be placed at different points along the web, on the content provider, various intermediaries, the end user, or some combination.[6] Individual computers could have filters installed to weed out objectionable content. Such filters (placed voluntarily or mandated) could be employed in conjunction with a rating system (also voluntary or compulsory) for adult

---

[4] During the course of the proceedings, it was learned that French visitors to Yahoo!'s auctions were actually accessing pages contained on servers in Sweden, not in the United States; see Goldsmith and Wu (2006, p. 7).

[5] See "The Law, Borders and the Internet," by Michael Geist, BBC News, January 24, 2006, available at http://news.bbc.co.uk/1/hi/technology/4641244.stm (accessed February 24, 2006).

[6] Goldsmith and Wu (2006, pp. 65–85).

content on websites. Of course, some adult-oriented web sites (particularly those located outside of the relevant legal jurisdiction) might eschew rating systems, though perhaps the computer-specific filters could be configured to obstruct access to such sites.

Current filters suffer from problems of both under- and overinclusiveness.[7] Text is easier to screen than photos, so X-rated pictures can get by many filters if the photos lack suggestive, accompanying text. The desire to screen pornographic material also lends itself to overreach by filters, by screening-out sites dealing with breast cancer, for instance. Filters are more appropriate for computers used by young children than those for older adolescents, who are more likely to be constrained by the overreaching. But the older teens also are more likely to be able to evade the censoring, being generally more adept at using computers than are the adults who are nominally in charge.

The advantage of filtering or other supervision on a computer-by-computer basis is that these regulatory approaches do not impose any costs upon those who prefer unexpurgated access to the web. An alternative (or complementary) strategy is to regulate content providers. Individual websites can furnish, voluntarily or in compliance with laws, geographical or age filtering on their end. For instance, adult website operators can easily and without direct charge obtain software that will block access by users who do not have an adult personal identification number (PIN), although there is some technical burden in arranging content behind the appropriate filters. The acquisition of a PIN by adult users is rather inexpensive, too, though there is no shortage of free pornographic content available to all visitors on the web.[8]

Geographical filtering can take place without the user even being aware of it, through software connected to websites. The filtering employs Internet protocol addresses and information about transmission paths to yield a good but still imperfect estimate of users' geographical locations.[9] (International travelers notice that the content and language of ads are different when they are away from home, even at their otherwise native-language websites.) Web surfers from jurisdictions that preclude access to such a filtered site then can be prevented from connecting to the content. Internet users located in the Netherlands, for instance, where web gambling is limited to the state-monopoly provider, are blocked from British cybergambling sites, and French visitors could be kept away from Nazi memorabilia auctions available to U.S. patrons. Intranational or even intraneighborhood controls are another possibility: for

---

[7] For an early review of Internet filters, see the feature report, dated March 2001, available at Consumer Reports Online, www.consumerreports.org.

[8] MasterStats.com tracks the number of visitors to many adult websites, including free sites; see http://erotic.masterstats.com/Free (accessed on February 13, 2006).

[9] See "Geolocation: Don't Fence Web In," *Wired News*, July 13, 2004, at http://www.wired.com/news/infostructure/0,64178-0.html (accessed February 13, 2006).

instance, online gambling could be legal when conducted from home but illegal when undertaken from an Internet café. Sophisticated and motivated users generally can find means to evade geographical controls, however.

Current technological constraints on web regulations undoubtedly will prove ephemeral. Age and geographical filtering of Internet material has improved markedly over time.[10] For content providers, highly reliable geographical and age screening holds the promise of being serviceable at relatively low cost now or in the near future. Of course, methods to evade filters or other restraints might also improve over time; whether the Internet will be harder or easier to regulate ten years from now is far from certain. And while an advance in geographical filtering could help enforce varying national or state laws, there is the significant downside that governments might employ such technology to keep out any information that they find inconvenient. Already substantial blocking of web content at the national level occurs in countries such as China and Iran.

Other levels at which web-based communication can be controlled include intermediaries such as Internet service providers (ISPs), webpage content hosts, and search engines. Sites that store and disseminate content posted by users could be made legally accountable to ensure that the information is not impermissible. ISPs and search engines could be required to filter objectionable content, perhaps where what qualifies as "objectionable" depends on the age and geographical location of the user, which would then have to be ascertained. The filtering could be initiated by the government, under a "takedown" regime: after authorities identify illegal sites, ISPs would be required to block access.[11] More indirect approaches also can be employed to separate web surfers from taboo content. Search engines could be precluded from accepting advertising for adult sites or cybercasinos; credit card companies and other payment facilitators can be pressured to deny their services to unsuitable web locales, such as porn sites that have not implemented age checks.

Police and other enforcement agents are relatively unprepared to regulate cybervice,[12] while some preexisting controls (such as the antigambling Federal Interstate Wire Act[13]) over vice-related activity are medium-specific. New laws and new types of enforcement might be necessary to regulate vice on the web effectively. These new rules will have to meet the standards imposed by existing legal constraints, such as, in the United States, the First and Fourth

---

[10] Much of the information concerning age and geographical controls is drawn from Goldsmith and Sykes (2001, pp. 809–12).

[11] See Mann and Belzley (2005), which also identifies and examines "hot list" and tort remedy regimes.

[12] Keller (1999, p. 1606) disagrees: "... investigative techniques do not appear to have lagged behind in cybervice." He cites, among other evidence, a 1995 FBI cyber-sting operation aimed at child pornographers.

[13] 18 U.S.C. §1084.

Amendments. The precise translation of these legal constraints into cyberspace, however, is itself an uncertain matter.

In some respects, the web is easier to police than the nonvirtual world. Despite the web's potential for promoting anonymous dealings, Internet communications leave electronic trails, so online activities often can be traced. Further, any vice-related website that can be found by customers also can be accessed by enforcement agents.

The remainder of this chapter will look at regulating Internet vice of two varieties – gambling and prostitution – while the appended Vice Verdicts section recounts the evolution of federal Internet pornography controls in the United States.

GAMBLING

Access to legal (nonvirtual) gambling has accelerated in recent decades, particularly in the United States. Lotteries, effectively forbidden during the twentieth century until 1964, spread rapidly in the 1970s and 1980s, and now more than forty states offer lotteries.[14] Casino betting, spurred in part by legislation in 1988 that codified the rights of Native American tribes, also skyrocketed; by the end of the century, more than half of the U.S. states housed legal casinos, whereas only a quarter-century earlier, Nevada was the sole state offering casino gambling. Developments in many other countries also tended towards liberalization of gambling, as exemplified by the introduction of the British National Lottery in 1994 and the expansion of casino gambling in Australia, Canada, South Africa, and many parts of Asia.[15] Some Soviet bloc successor states have become inundated with gambling venues.

The benefits of gambling take the usual form of satisfying the desires of consumers, just like the benefits associated with other forms of entertainment or consumption goods.[16] The familiar issue of the rationality of choices with respect to gambling might call these putative benefits into question, of course. Other advantages often are claimed for legal gambling, though these are still less certain. Tax revenues can be raised through lotteries or casino taxes; such revenues primarily represent a transfer of resources from players to the government, and not, strictly speaking, a social benefit of gambling.[17] Casinos might provide economic stimulus, though much of the economic activity spurred by

---

[14] Walker (1998, p. 360).   [15] Eadington (1999, p. 177) and Walker (1998).

[16] This point often is overlooked in cost-benefit assessments of gambling. A notable exception is *Australia's Gambling Industries* (1999), an accounting of the positive and negative dimensions of gambling in Australia.

[17] If gambling taxes correct for externalities or internalities, or if gambling tax revenues allow for reductions in other taxes that are more distortionary, then there might be some social gain associated with gambling taxes; see Chapter 5.

a casino comes at the expense of other entertainment options.[18] But again, the chief social gain from expanded gambling opportunities is the increased satisfaction of consumers.

With respect to the tax revenues and economic development associated with a casino, the benefits to a locality will depend upon the extent to which the clientele is itself local. Even if tax revenues are a transfer when considered in toto, from the point of view of a neighborhood, they represent a benefit if the bettors live outside the jurisdiction. (Of course, the consumption benefits of gambling also will accrue to these outsiders.) Likewise, if casino gamblers are tourists who otherwise would not have visited the area, their spending does not come at the expense of other local businesses. Depressed areas are more likely to gain from new gambling ventures. If the workers at a casino would otherwise have been unemployed, their gambling jobs do not necessarily make it harder for other local firms to hire.

The traditional suppression of gambling is not solely a reflection of a moral view that money should be earned through hard work. Rather, there is a wide range of costs – the $3\frac{1}{3}$ standard vice concerns, essentially – connected to gambling: underage participants, problem or less than fully rational consumers, and public nuisances. Negative personal consequences of gambling include suicide, divorce, unemployment, bankruptcy, and arrest: gambling is implicated in crimes such as credit card fraud or embezzlement.[19] Wagering commonly has been associated with organized crime, though that association may primarily be an artifact of the regulatory structure surrounding betting operations.[20] Gambling interests can threaten the integrity of sporting events, as attested to by many scandals over the years, from baseball's 1919 World Series to 1990s match fixing in international cricket.

The American Psychiatric Association has adopted ten problem gambling criteria (such as "chasing losses" and withdrawal symptoms), classifying as pathological any gambler who exhibits five or more of these characteristics. Some 2.5 million American adults are considered pathological gamblers, with another 3 million classified as problem gamblers.[21] Problem or pathological gambling in the United States is estimated to cost some $5 billion per year, excluding "lifetime" costs such as those associated with divorce and

---

[18] "Gambling Impact and Behavior Study," 1999.

[19] "Gambling Impact and Behavior Study," 1999.

[20] The reputation of the gambling industry in Nevada began to improve after the 1969 Corporate Gaming Act permitted publicly traded companies to acquire casino licenses, providing access to equity markets and the participation of well-known, legitimate corporations. See Eadington (1999, p. 175).

[21] "Gambling Impact and Behavior Study," 1999. The researchers responsible for the "Gambling Impact and Behavior Study" identify as a problem gambler someone who exhibits three or four of the American Psychiatric Association's criteria, while someone who meets one or two of the criteria is "at-risk."

bankruptcy.[22] Sixteen- and 17-year- olds appear to be more at-risk for gambling problems than are adults, though the amounts of money involved in youth gambling are smaller.[23] Although problem gamblers compose only a small percentage of the population, they tend to wager a lot, of course; hence, as with other vices, those whose self-control is most questionable form a commercially desirable clientele. For instance, in Australia, a government review of gambling indicated that about 2.1 percent of the population could be classified as problem gamblers, but they accounted for approximately one-third of the take of the gambling industry.[24] On average, poor people gamble much more intensively than richer people, as a percentage of their income. In the case of lottery tickets, even the absolute amount of money spent by poorer people tends to exceed that of richer people.[25]

Varieties of gambling are sometimes classified as either "soft" or "hard," based upon their propensity to lead to compulsive play. Convenience, time between rounds of bets, payoff structures, and other features of a wager all influence the extent of reinforcement, and these features are susceptible to regulation. Occasional (once or twice per week, say) lotteries are among the softest form of gambling.[26] Instant win tickets available from accessible locations are much harder, as immediate repeat play can be encouraged. Likewise, electronic games that allow for fast, repeated play, especially when conveniently available and capable of accepting banknotes, tend to the hard side of the gambling continuum: some slot machines are capable of nearly 1,000 plays per hour.[27] For most people, casino table games are somewhat softer than electronic games. Internet day trading on the stock market presents a rather hard gambling environment. Nevertheless, securities trading simultaneously provides the positive externality of improving the valuation of firms and hence the allocation of capital; typically such gambling has not met with the same moral or legal condemnation that accompanies other forms of betting, despite the compulsive behavior displayed by some day traders.

People seem to find intermittent reward schemes to be particularly motivating: if things always turn out good (or if things always turn out bad), there's little reason to put forth any effort. But lots of negative feedback combined with occasional, random positive reward, can be quite reinforcing, as we "search"

---

[22] "Gambling Impact and Behavior Study," 1999.

[23] "Gambling Impact and Behavior Study," 1999. On youth gambling more generally, see Derevensky and Gupta (2000).

[24] *Australia's Gambling Industries* (1999).   [25] Walker (1998).

[26] Nevertheless, even lotteries display a highly skewed structure of ticket purchases, with the majority of tickets purchased by just a small percentage of the population; see Walker (1998).

[27] Eggert (2004, p. 277). Dowling, Smith, and Thomas (2005), however, argue that the empirical record does not support the view that electronic gaming machines are particularly likely to stoke addictive play. They also review evidence indicating that banknote acceptors significantly increase the amount gambled in an electronic gaming machine.

for what we can do to reproduce the good outcome.[28] Such an intermittent reward system has been brought to a state of near perfection by the designers of slot machines, who are quite adept at incentivizing gamblers to have one more spin, again and again.[29] The payout rates, visuals, sound effects, and other design features of gaming machines have become very sophisticated in keeping gamblers playing. For instance, some slots are designed to give the impression of a "near miss," where two of the requisite three bars appear and the third reel almost lands on a bar, too. But the notion of a near miss in slots is a fiction – there is only a win or a loss, predetermined (in the recent generations of computer chip-driven machines) before any symbols appear on the win line. What appears to be a near miss in the standard display is no closer to a win than a miss that appears to be not near at all. Once the bet has been placed and the (pseudo-) random number generator in the computer chip has done its work, the machine could simply display your winnings – usually zero, or if you are lucky, some positive number – from that bet. But such an unadorned display is not nearly as conducive to repeated play as is the screening of virtual wheels spinning and wins and near misses animated by bars and fruits falling into place.

Compulsive players are not alone in the questionable rationality of their gambling behavior: many nonaddicts can scarcely be credited with informed consumption of gambling products. The extent of misperception about gambling probabilities and about the performance of an individual gambler is mind-boggling. With respect to probabilities, people seem to have a hard time accepting that repeated plays of slot machines or lottery drawings effectively are independent of each other. For instance, many gamblers seem to believe that the chances that they will win in a given play of a slot machine increase if they have been playing for awhile and have not won. Likewise, lottery players often believe that their usual number is more likely to come up if it has not won recently. Simultaneously, many gamblers seem to hold an almost opposite bias, that a slot machine or even lottery outlet is "hot," offering temporary conditions of improved winning chances.[30] The attribution of personal control over essentially random events is a common gambling fallacy.

The 1999 "Gambling Impact and Behavior Study" in the United States, prepared for the National Gambling Impact Study Commission, uncovered some amazing information on the extent to which people seem to be misinformed about their past gambling performance. Lottery losses are underestimated by players by 80 percent. Casino gamblers collectively claimed to have won some $8 billion during the course of one year, though they in fact lost $20 billion.

---

[28] Carnwath and Smith (2002, p. 108).

[29] See Vice Squad posts from May 9, 2004; May 15, 2004; May 17, 2004; September 8, 2004; and February 3, 2005.

[30] On hot lottery stores, see Guryan and Kearney (2005).

Even in zero-sum private card games, for every person who recalls having lost the last time he played, three report that they went home winners.[31]

Neurochemistry plays a key role in gambling addictions, as with other compulsive disorders.[32] Pathological gamblers seem to differ from other people with respect to serotonin, dopamine, and endorphin functioning. Neurochemical influences on problem gambling are particularly apparent in recent evidence that drugs given to combat Parkinson's disease have the potential side effect of inducing pathological gambling in people who never before experienced gambling problems. And as with drug addicts, problem gamblers often suffer from other mental ailments, such as depression or bipolar disorder.

INTERNET GAMBLING

More than a thousand gambling sites are now available on the web, providing all types of action: lotteries, sports betting, poker among human competitors, video poker, slot machines, and other casino-style games. Typically, a bettor opens an account with the operator, funding it with a credit card, wire transfer, e-cash, or some other means. In the case of casino-style sites, software might have to be downloaded before gambling can commence. Winnings are credited to the account and can be transferred to the bettor in a variety of ways. Many gambling websites impose weekly or monthly betting limits and allow users to choose daily budget constraints.[33]

Internet betting can increase the consumption of gambling and hence consumer satisfaction. Internet gambling makes betting more accessible, and perhaps provides a more wholesome environment than casinos or betting shops – no undesirables lurking about, no waitstaff proffering free drinks.[34] Poker players can find others on the web who share their skill level and monetary means. The proximity of family members to home computers might temper compulsive gambling tendencies. Internet gambling might produce advantageous spillovers for other virtual sectors: lucrative commercial opportunities associated with Internet gambling (and pornography) help drive computer graphics, network, and e-commerce development.[35] Advertising by online casinos can raise revenue for nongambling web content providers. Licensing fees and income taxes for operators of Internet gambling sites and taxes on income can bring in significant funds for governments.

---

[31] "Gambling Impact and Behavior Study" (1999). Of course, it is mathematically possible that three out of four card players were winners during their last meeting – one unlucky or untalented participant ends up subsidizing the rest – but given the general overoptimism about past gambling outcomes, it seems more likely that only about half the players go home a winner.

[32] This paragraph draws upon Grant (2005a) and Grant (2005b).

[33] On the mechanics of Internet gambling, see Olson (1999) or Schwarz (1999). For one person's online experience, see Stevenson (1999); this article appeared in Microsoft's online magazine, Slate.com, which at the time frequently featured banner advertisements for Internet gambling sites.

[34] Bell (1998).   [35] Bell (1998).

Much more attention has been focused on the potential social costs than on the benefits of the rise of Internet gambling, however. The ease, privacy, and anonymity of Internet play might facilitate addiction, while increasing access to betting for those who already are addicted. Delays (sometimes of more than a month) in receiving winnings after a bettor "cashes out" can tempt gamblers to play again from their account during the interim. Physical proximity to a casino has been associated with marked increases in problem and pathological gambling[36] – and it is conceivable, even likely, that convenient virtual casinos will have a similar effect.

Sports betting, which traditionally is suppressed or subject to strict controls in the United States, has flourished on the web, while being transformed into a much "harder" style of gambling. (Sports betting, unlike cybercasino play, allows the gambler to be certain whether or not he has actually won his bet – which is no guarantee of being paid but does eliminate one dimension of trust that is otherwise requisite to entice gamblers online.) The web (and interactive television) opens up myriad in-game betting opportunities, so that what previously consisted of a simple pregame wager on a sporting event has been converted into the possibility of a near continuous series of wagers on micro-aspects of the contest.

A problem gambler, operating from his home, might have more difficulty finding help or for help to find him. Internet gambling might be particularly susceptible to underage play. Fraud on the part of game operators or players is another potential concern, as are other crimes such as money laundering.[37] Finally, the economic benefits that are sometimes claimed for neighborhoods with actual casinos would seem largely to be missing if local residents are engaged in gambling from their living rooms. And not just their living rooms: Internet gambling using mobile phones is a growth industry in the wireless world.

INTERNET GAMBLING REGULATION IN THE UNITED STATES

The legal status of online gaming in the United States is unsettled. Existing federal antigambling legislation appears to prohibit Internet gambling sites from locating domestically. Foreign-based sites that allow access for American gamblers probably also are violating U.S. law, though there are jurisdictional

---

[36] "Gambling Impact and Behavior Study," 1999.

[37] An international organization, the Financial Action Task Force on money laundering, has implicated internet casinos in money laundering. See FATF-XII (2001). In the Soviet Union, curiously, the lottery was frequently employed as a device for laundering substantial sums of rubles that were not acquired legally. Second economy operators would purchase winning lottery tickets, at a premium, to make their gains appear to be fortuitous. See Malyshev (1987). Finally, money laundering is a relatively recent crime, and in the absence of global drug prohibition, laws against money laundering would be deprived of much of their rationale.

complications, and enforcement often would be impractical.[38] The main federal antigambling statute, the 1961 Interstate Wire Act, applies only to providers (not consumers) of gambling services, those "engaged in the business of betting or wagering." In March 1998, the U.S. Department of Justice charged owners of offshore sports gambling sites under the Wire Act, and convictions have been obtained.

U.S. law governing web gambling is murky because the existing federal statutes (such as the Wire Act) do not specifically mention the Internet, or are only concerned with some forms of gambling: the Wire Act refers specifically to betting on "any sporting event or contest," so its relevance to casino-type games is suspect. (It could be argued, though unconvincingly, that the relevance of the Wire Act might be reduced further as wireless Internet connections become more popular.) Federal laws are sufficiently dense and voluminous, however, that prosecutors need not rely upon the Wire Act to charge Internet gambling entrepreneurs, nor need they restrict their attention to those "engaged in the business of betting or wagering."[39] For instance, anti–money laundering laws, not the Wire Act, were used in May 2006, to bring charges against two individuals who operated a licensed gambling website from Antigua. The situation is further complicated by Native American tribes, which are exempt from federal gambling statutes for sports betting, bingo, and lotteries. Whether tribes can legally offer online gambling of this nature is unclear.

The legal situation for U.S. consumers who gamble on foreign-based websites is similarly elaborate. Some states have explicitly forbidden Internet gambling, while attorney general opinions in other states claim illegality under preexisting laws.[40] Federal law speaks less directly to the consumption of gambling, but it is possible that engaging in Internet gambling is illegal throughout the United States – indeed, that is the position of the Department of Justice.[41] Nevertheless, until 2006 U.S.-based gamblers probably provided a majority of global internet gambling revenues, and most U.S. online gamblers believe that their activity is legal.[42] (Almost no Internet gamblers in the United States have been the subject of federal or state prosecution for their consumption of web gambling.) In many other countries, online gambling is perfectly legitimate, and some nations, most prominently in Latin America and the Caribbean, host and license Internet gambling sites.

In response to the exponential rise in legal gambling, the U.S. Congress created the National Gambling Impact Study Commission (NGISC) in 1996. In June, 1999, the commission made available its final report, which included

[38] See, for instance, Olson (1999).
[39] Another alternative is the Travel Act (18 U.S.C. §1952), which includes a criminalization of interstate or foreign travel for illegal commerce; see, e.g., Masoud (2004, pp. 998–9).
[40] Olson (1999, p. 3).   [41] Schwarz (1999).
[42] "Illegal Internet Gambling Soars in the US," by OUT-LAW.com, May 10, 2006; available at www.theregister.co.uk/2006/05/10/internet_gambling_soars/ (accessed May 10, 2006).

a recommendation for a "pause" in the expansion of gambling. The pause was suggested to allow time for assessing the impact of the recent growth.

One area of such recent growth is the Internet, and the NGISC recommendations include a prohibition on Internet gambling. Of course, web betting may already be illegal; nevertheless, Congress has on multiple occasions taken up legislation to institute an explicit federal ban on both the production and consumption of Internet gambling – so far without success. And while Internet gambling has grown significantly, web activity remains a small part of the overall gambling industry. In late 2003, a Gallup poll indicated that approximately 1 percent of Americans had gambled over the Internet in the previous year, in contrast to the nearly 50 percent who played the lottery and the 30 percent who visited a casino.[43]

Although new federal legislation aimed directly at Internet gambling has yet to bear fruit, the United States has been more successful at using legal measures to influence the behavior of gambling intermediaries. Credit cards are a convenient method for Internet gamblers to stock their web accounts, but this method is no longer convenient for Americans. Credit card companies first became loath to deal with gambling sites because state laws render gambling debts unenforceable. So if someone charged a significant sum to a web casino and then didn't pay the credit card company, the company probably lacked recourse. Once this possibility became salient, most U.S.-issued credit cards (including all American Express and Discover cards) removed themselves from the Internet gambling game.

The nonenforceability of gambling debts was a minor problem for payment intermediaries relative to another potential legal tangle of a criminal nature. If Internet gambling is illegal, as the U.S. Department of Justice claims, then a payment service that deals with web gambling sites puts itself, perhaps, at risk of being charged with a federal offense for conveying funds derived from criminal activity. In 2003, the online funds transfer service PayPal paid $10 million to settle a Department of Justice complaint that its dealings with online casinos were illegal.[44] So even in the absence of a new law – as recommended by the NGISC – the most convenient payment methods for Internet gambling were rendered inaccessible for Americans.

The new law eventually arrived, however. In October 2006, the United States adopted legislation that aimed to cripple Internet gambling by attacking payment intermediaries.[45] The most popular payment service at the time was Neteller, which had blossomed as credit card companies and PayPal withdrew from the field. Neteller's initial response to the new U.S. law was to continue

---

[43] See Kearney (2005, p. 36).

[44] See "PayPal Settles over Gambling Transfers," by Declan McCullagh, CNET News.com, July 25, 2003. Available at http://news.com.com/2100-1017-3-5055237.html (accessed February 28, 2006).

[45] This paragraph follows the Vice Squad post of January 18, 2007.

to serve the U.S. market, at least until the Treasury Department unveiled its enforcement plan, due by July 10, 2007. The arrest of two of Neteller's founders in January 2007, however, hastened its move to cut the e-gambling link of U.S. residents, including almost half a million U.S. customers who were active in Neteller during the fourth quarter of 2006. Other "e-wallet" firms remain active, but the effective closure of Neteller and other payment intermediaries to Americans resulted in a major disruption in Internet gambling.

Those who provide advertising for gambling websites also are at risk of a criminal prosecution, on the grounds that they are aiding and abetting a criminal enterprise. In 2004, both Yahoo! and Google stopped accepting such ads, and federal marshals seized $3.2 million from Discovery Communications, the owner of television's Travel Channel. The money represented a payment for televison ads on the Travel Channel from a Costa Rica–based cybercasino. So mainstream media, including mainstream web-based media, have been pressured in the United States to avoid Internet gambling ads. Nevertheless, there is a case to be made that, except for the provision of sports betting (covered by the Wire Act), other forms of web gambling are not illegal under U.S. federal law; hence, advertising those forms of gambling cannot be banned under the Supreme Court's current approach to commercial speech protection.[46]

Internet gambling sites located outside of the United States are not necessarily unregulated. Some countries require licensed sites to post bonds and meet other standards of probity. Meanwhile, Internet gambling firms are adopting their own industry regulations. International organizations such as the Canadian-based Internet Gaming Council (IGC) and London's e-Commerce Online Gaming Regulation and Assurance (eCOGRA) have developed extensive codes of conduct, which include such issues as limiting access to minors, promoting truth in advertising, and providing dispute resolution mechanisms.[47] Many Internet gambling sites are members of the IGC or eCOGRA and committed to the corresponding conduct code.

ROBUSTNESS AND INTERNET GAMBLING

Robustness requires that the regulatory stance taken toward Internet gambling work pretty well when everyone is informed and rational, and also work pretty well when a fair coterie of folks are confused or pathological gamblers. Working well involves effective control over the $3^1/_3$ standard vice concerns.

For those who can access bricks-and-mortar gambling relatively easily, it is not clear that robustness necessitates legal access to Internet gambling: the issue turns, in part, on the extent to which terrestrial gambling is an adequate substitute for virtual gaming. If the two forms of gambling are not close substitutes, then robustness implies that adult gamblers cannot be prohibited from

---

[46] The case is well-developed in Frese (2005).   [47] See www.igcouncil.org and www.ecogra.com.

web-based wagering; otherwise, the costs imposed upon rational gamblers would be meaningful, as such bettors lack a legal close substitute. For adults who do not live near a bricks-and-mortar casino, therefore, robustness requires legal access to web gambling. Another relevant issue is that any ban on Internet gambling is likely to be quite leaky, and by keeping web gambling criminalized and hence unregulated, the harms imposed upon compulsive gamblers will be raised. If that is the case, then robustness demands a legal, regulated regime for web gambling even in jurisdictions with nonvirtual casinos, so that gambling policy works acceptably in the face of significant irrationality among players.

Both harm reduction and robustness concerns suggest that legal, regulated online gambling constitutes a desirable policy option – paralleling the conclusion reached in the previous chapter concerning prostitution.[48] A regulated industry could ensure that the games are legitimate, and minimum payouts could be legislated. Periodic and unannounced audits of gambling software could be instituted, as is done for some land-based casinos. Information about odds could be prominently displayed. Unusual betting patterns, such as might arise if a sporting contest is fixed, can be identified and traced more readily in a legal, regulated environment.

Robustness requires that a regulatory environment work pretty well when many people are ill-informed or irrational in their gambling-related choices. Mandated disclosure of odds is helpful in overcoming some forms of ignorance. Net monetary positions could be displayed hourly, weekly, monthly, and annually to help combat the common problem of underestimation of losses. But beyond making sure that odds and losses are posted in a noticeable and easy-to-understand fashion, there is much to be said for a broader educational campaign about gambling and probabilities. Further, gambling advertising could be restricted to avoid promulgating common myths and misperceptions. Current gambling regulations in the United States are woefully inadequate in ensuring that players are well-informed. The effective price of a play of a slot machine can vary by a factor of ten, even among the machines within a single casino, but players are not apprised of these prices.[49] Eggert (2004) calls for "truth in gaming" legislation modeled after truth in lending laws: some such mandate, which would ensure that effective prices are communicated, appears to be a requirement for a robust gambling policy regime.

Age restrictions might serve to screen out most would-be underage gamblers. In registering on a cybercasino, players have to provide identity information (name, address, date of birth, e-mail address, and so on) that can be cross-checked with credit card or other financial information.[50] (Credit card

---

[48] See the discussion in Lang (2002).

[49] Eggert (2004, p. 237) notes that the price of a slot machine wager can vary up to a factor of 60.

[50] This paragraph draws upon "IGC Submission to the UK Gambling Commission," 26 January 2006, available at www.igcouncil.org/press.php?id=297 (accessed February 23, 2006).

possession itself is unreliable as an age check. Most states in the United States require casino gamblers to be 21-years-old, whereas many older teenagers have credit cards.[51]) Payouts of large winnings can be scrutinized carefully and withheld if it is determined that the winner is a minor, reducing the financial lure of Internet gambling to kids. Even gambling websites that don't involve money (that is, players participate only for fun or to practice) can be forced to preclude youth access, and advertising in outlets with a large youth clientele can be banned.

Anytime, anywhere access to Internet wagering presents an enormous temptation to problem gamblers, of course. At the same time, the Internet offers some resources that can provide assistance. The anonymity of the Internet might make it less threatening for problem gamblers to seek help. Help itself can be a click away, through links to such sites as www.gamblersanonymous.org. Licensing requirements for gambling websites could be required to make provision for such links or other aids for problem gamblers. Among such aids could be weekly or monthly betting limits or provisions for a gambler to take simple steps that would serve to preclude his or her own future access to gambling sites. Cybercasinos also could be required to provide methods for voluntary time limits to be enforced. Further, tracking software could identify patterns of gambling that suggest compulsion – a technological innovation that also could be employed in bricks-and-mortar casinos. When problem gambling is suggested by the software, information about help could be made available, the betting could temporarily be suspended, betting limits could be lowered, or the allowable rate of play reduced. One difficult issue, for both land-based and virtual casinos, is what actions to take when friends or family of an adult gambler, but not the gambler himself, ask to have the gambler excluded from gambling venues. (Similar thorny problems with "interventions" plague addiction treatment clinics for alcoholics or other substance abusers.)

Some existing regulations over land-based casinos could be applied to Internet casinos. For instance, Britain allows bettors at land-based casinos to fund their play with debit cards but not credit cards. Perhaps the credit card restriction will be extended to British-based Internet casinos, and a similar extension could be made of limits on bet sizes.

Preexisting forms of gambling, including lotteries and land-based casinos and their associated state tax revenues, might be threatened by the competition from untaxed, offshore online gambling.[52] Payout rates at popular web gambling sites seem to exceed those of land-based casinos, perhaps due both to lower operating costs (including lower taxes) and more competition in virtual

---

[51] See I. Nelson Rose, Gambling and the Law®: Minimum Legal Age to Place a Bet," at www. gamblingandthelaw.com/agechart.html (accessed on February 15, 2006). Professor Rose is a leading researcher concerning the legal environment surrounding gambling.

[52] Alternatively, these different forms of gambling might prove to be complementary.

gambling.[53] The desire to maintain "traditional" gambling tax revenues could eventually lead to pressure to legalize, regulate, and tax online gaming, especially if the negative consequences of gambling are being borne by the relevant jurisdiction, anyway.[54] Supporters of online gaming note that it bears a family resemblance to day trading on the stock market, which has also been associated with addiction in some investors, so a legal outlet for web-based "betting" will be available in any case.

The current de facto regulatory regime governing cyberbetting in the United States features a few elements that are consistent with robustness. For instance, strict advertising controls and the suppression of convenient payment methods put some barriers in the path to initiation into online gambling. These barriers are real but not all that costly for dedicated bettors to overcome – as robustness would require in not significantly burdening rational players. (Whether the October 2006 legislation that prompted the withdrawal of Neteller from the US web gambling market will make access overly cumbersome remains unknown.) Competition and licensing requirements in jurisdictions hosting servers have pushed major gambling sites toward fair practices and codes of conduct that also offer some help to problem gamblers. No doubt in a fully legal and regulated regime safeguards for problem gamblers and shielding of minors could be strengthened. Nevertheless, as long as adult U.S. online bettors have nothing to fear from the law and can access cybercasinos without too much effort, on many dimensions, the current regulatory approach comports with robustness. The chief drawbacks are the inadequate protection offered to pathological gamblers and the limited vigilance given to effectively screening out underaged players, along with the lack of efforts to counter widespread misunderstandings of probabilistic events.

Robustness is consistent with much greater exertions to restrict ill-informed and pathological gambling, both on the Internet and in land-based casinos. For instance, adult gamblers could be required to first acquire a license. A condition of the granting of the license might be the passing of a test indicating that the consumer is free from common misperceptions about statistical dependence, hot machines, and the like. A slot machine, real or virtual, might be required to shut down temporarily after 500 plays, with a ten-minute break period built-in. In the case of land-based casinos, the machine could provide the gambler with a three digit code. Between ten and fifteen minutes later, if the gambler chooses to resume play, the code first would have to be reproduced; once fifteen minutes elapse, the machine becomes available to any casino visitor. In other words, the previous gambler enjoys a five minute window in which to reestablish usage rights. Machines that directly operate on banknotes through a note acceptor could be regulated or banned. Many other variants of controls can be imagined, of course, and undoubtedly some will prove ineffective or not

---

[53] Morse (2006).   [54] Bell (1998).

worth the burdens imposed upon bettors. But a wide assortment of low-cost policies aimed at problem or misguided gambling seems worth trying, at least on an experimental basis.

BRITAIN AND GAMBLING: TOWARD ROBUSTNESS

Various forms of legal, regulated gambling are available in Britain. A National Lottery was introduced in 1994, and shortly thereafter drawings were expanded from once per week to twice per week; later, scratch-off cards for play anytime were made available. Small stakes "fruit machines" appear in many bars and arcades. Casinos can operate, though they cannot advertise; they are limited in size, and credit cannot be made available to bettors. (The regulation of casinos in Britain is currently undergoing revision; see below.) A person cannot just walk in off the street and start gambling at a casino. Rather, individuals must apply for membership in the casino, which only can be granted after a twenty-four-hour waiting period. With respect to the Internet, British citizens legally can gamble from their homes.

Sports wagering has long been popular in Britain, with high-street betting parlors operated by leading firms like Ladbrokes and William Hill legal since 1961. Their operations have expanded to the Internet. "The world bets with British bookies. Ladbrokes has 13 foreign-language websites. William Hill has online clients in 197 countries."[55]

As of early 2007, Internet casino-style gambling sites still were not located in Britain. Shares of major companies that operate such sites, however, are traded on London financial markets. In 2005, PartyGaming, a preeminent Internet gambling company based in Gibraltar, launched a successful initial public offering on the London Stock Exchange. PartyGaming went on to post profits of more than $290 million in 2005, with 84 percent of its nearly $1 billion in revenue coming from bettors located in the United States[56] – bettors who are behaving illegally, according to the U.S. Department of Justice.

The last few decades, then, have seen a gambling regulatory regime in Britain that possesses many marks of robustness: legal access to gambling, but advertising and credit controls that offer some protection to potential problem gamblers. (Nevertheless, more can be done in a relatively low-cost way to help gambling addicts.) Internet penetration and the popularity and seeming success of less-constrained casinos in other locales threaten the preexisting balance, however. As a result, a liberalizing reformulation of U.K. gambling laws was adopted in 2005, with implementation generally scheduled for 2007. Many new casino licenses will become available, including one for a large,

---

[55] "A Nation of Gamblers? You Bet," by Simon Kuper, *Financial Times*, April 22, 2006.
[56] See, e.g., "PartyPoker Boss to Fold His Hand," at http://www.online-casinos.com/news/news1811.asp (accessed March 1, 2006).

Las Vegas–style establishment. The ban on casino advertising will be lifted, as will be the requirement that would-be bettors wait twenty-four hours before they are admitted to a casino at which they seek membership. The 2005 legal changes also establish a procedure whereby cybercasinos can be licensed and regulated by the British government. The hope is that the system will ensure that licensed online casinos meet high standards of quality and combat underage and problem gambling.[57] For instance, self-exclusion options must be available to bettors, and operators must themselves take the initiative to exclude gamblers who show signs of problem gambling. Online casinos must make it clear to gamblers how much time and money they have invested into their play. Odds and the house edge also must be prominently displayed.

The British regulatory approach to Internet gambling is likely to pressure the prohibitory stance of other nations such as the United States. If the British experiment with a seemingly robust gambling regulatory regime succeeds in keeping the costs of problem gambling and underage access under control – as it has in the past for land-based gambling – the United Kingdom will offer a safe Internet gambling experience, while collecting tax on the business. Given that many people in the United States and elsewhere are likely to gamble on the web despite legal prohibitions, the rationale for maintaining bans upon Internet gambling will erode in the face of a proven, workable legal alternative.[58]

PROSTITUTION AND THE WEB

Sexual activities on the Internet run the gamut from the benign (dating services) to the decidedly less benign (information concerning opportunities for sex tourism involving minors, or solicitation of live sex acts with underage participants). Of course, dating services and sex tourism would exist with or without the web; nevertheless, the effects wrought on some sex-related behavior, including prostitution, by the Internet have been profound.

Commercial sex workers can employ the web in various ways. They can advertise over the web, they can screen clients via e-mail, and e-cash services can be used to receive payments.[59] Webcams can be employed to broadcast live shows, perhaps "directed" by online viewers.

Whether to advertise over the web and how to advertise if a web presence is desired have become major issues for many prostitutes. A website, ostensibly

---

[57] See http://www.culture.gov.uk/ROLE/gambling_review.html. A draft version of the gambling "License Conditions and Codes of Practice" was made available in March, 2006.

[58] In 2001, Australia set up an unusual Internet gambling regulatory scheme. Australian regulators license domestic-based providers of Internet gambling, while preventing the licensed sites from serving Australian patrons.

[59] A good description of cyberhooking appears in Goodell (2001).

Box 7.1: *Web poker*

The early years of the twenty-first century brought an explosion in poker playing in general and web poker in particular. Television coverage of poker, specifically that of the Texas Hold 'Em variety, helped to promote the game. The televised versions reveal to viewers all players' card holdings, rendering strategies and likely results discernible. Both TV and web sites allow novices to hone their skills without embarrassment and even without risking any money. But lots of money is risked on Internet poker, as much as a quarter of a billion dollars a day, by players who at a given moment can number more than 100,000.[a] Poker afficionados operate more than 150 blogs, full of tips, warnings, and analysis of recent play.[b]

The poker boom is not without its problems, of course. The Internet version can entice some people to engage in long, all-night sessions, compromising their other duties and interests as well as their financial resources. Web poker holds particular appeal for young people, such as college students, who generally are age-excluded from land-based casinos and extremely comfortable with Internet activity. They come to web gambling at a time when they have little experience with lives not closely supervised by adults. Further, they might be especially at risk of delusions about the income-earning potential of card games. Winners are happy to proclaim (and exaggerate) their fortune whereas those who lose money tend not to be very vocal.[c] Live sessions offer more in the way of sociability: some parents of teens living at home view poker games to be relatively salubrious weekend entertainments for their kids when compared with many of the alternatives.[d] Nevertheless, when in-person poker games become well-organized and publicized or involve high stakes they also can attract the attention of law enforcement.

Despite the risks and highly negative consequences for some players, the rapid rise of poker, like gambling more generally, seems to have been accomplished rather smoothly. Poker might even promote a more sophisticated approach to probabilistic events outside of the gambling arena. Modes of thought encouraged by poker, including the recognition that your play in one hand will influence how others play against you in future hands and that the choice to fold immediately often is best, might improve decision making in daily life.[e]

Computer programs ("robots" or "bots") have been developed to play Internet poker, and their quality is such that soon they might be as talented as any human opponent. Once robots become sufficiently sophisticated and available, online poker will lose its appeal to humans. Unless a player could be assured that her opponents were not bots, she might be unwilling to risk money on such a tilted playing field: what had been a form of gambling entertainment would become a mere donation. So the boost that computer technology has given to poker via the Internet might be taken away by further advances in computing – though live venues might fend off the robot invasion for somewhat longer.[f]

---

[a] "The Poker Machine," by Tim Harford, *Financial Times*, pp. W1–W2, May 6–7, 2006. PartyPoker.com is said to have 80,000 players at one time; see "Online Poker: Going All-in

(continued)

Box 7.1 *(continued)*

---

to Expose the Internet's Billion-Dollar Bet," by David Silverberg, DigitalJournal.com, May 5, 2006. The website www.pokerpulse.com tracks the number of players in a 24-hour period and the amounts at stake. In mid-2006, more than 120,000 players were online. Participation in web poker undoubtedly took a large hit in the aftermath of Neteller's abandonment of the U.S. market in January 2007.

[b] On March 3, 2006, I counted 164 poker-related blogs linked at *All In* magazine's blog, www.allinmag.com/blogs.php.

[c] See "Internet Poker a Powerful Draw," by Alan Greenberg, courant.com (*Hartford Courant*), May 7, 2006.

[d] See the Vice Squad post from October 1, 2004.

[e] On poker skills that might prove useful in other environments, see Parke, Griffiths, and Parke (2005).

[f] "The Poker Machine," by Tim Harford, *Financial Times*, pp. W1–W2, May 6–7, 2006.

---

offering escort services, allows a prostitute to reach a wide audience. In jurisdictions without legal prostitution, such websites greatly decrease the costs of establishing a connection: many potential clients would be at a loss (or perhaps too scared) to search out and approach prostitutes in another fashion. The web allows call girls to market directly, cutting out intermediaries: webpage designers and hosting services substitute for some of the services otherwise provided by pimps or madams.

Client screening is considerably enhanced via the Internet. An exchange of e-mail with clients tends to increase sex worker safety, as e-mail communications can be traced and clients generally realize that they cannot rely upon anonymity in the event of trouble or a dispute. Additional information about clients can be solicited and verified before any move to face-to-face encounters. That clients understand that their name and workplace or home address are known to the sex worker (and potentially her working partners) helps to counter any design that they otherwise might harbor to engage in theft, rape, or other violence. The meetings themselves can be arranged to take place in secure settings. Certainly relative to streetwalking, where client screening tends to occur within a matter of seconds, Internet connections are a much safer alternative for sex workers. As with call girl operations generally, the public nuisance associated with Internet-based prostitution also is minimal relative to streetwalking.

Nevertheless, the very reach of the Internet makes some prostitutes reluctant to initiate a web presence.[60] Even where prostitution is legal, prostitutes often try to hide their profession from certain people in their personal and social lives. To do this effectively, to lower the risk that their work lives and personal lives will overlap in a deleterious or emotionally wrenching fashion, prostitutes have to control the extent of their exposure as sex workers. Posting a webpage

---

[60] This paragraph draws on Chapter 7 ("Secrets and Lies") of Sanders (2005, pp. 116–37).

offering escort services, particularly if a recognizable photo is included, makes geographical and temporal control of exposure impossible.

The anonymity available to johns posting on the web provides an opportunity for unconstrained speech that can have external effects, as when a client "advertises" a prostitute without her permission. Before the web, few men would be willing or able to address a large audience in detail about their contemporaneous experiences with a prostitute, but now, thanks in part to the anonymity and reach offered by the Internet, some men are both willing and able. For those intending exploitation of women or children, the Internet can be a useful tool in finding and disseminating information.[61]

Internet postings by johns are not always undesired by commercial sex workers, however. Many escort sites offer ratings pages where (purported) customers leave comments on the quality of recent encounters, sometimes with lurid details included. Independent websites offering reviews have sprung up, and occasionally the prostitutes themselves participate, perhaps to challenge a negative review. The norms and expectations of appropriate john behavior also can be communicated using the web. Prostitutes use the web to spread warnings among themselves about dangerous customers.[62]

The possibility of anonymous blogging opens up yet another Internet-connected realm where information (as always, of variable quality) about prostitution can be transmitted. A few sex workers have become pseudonymous bloggers. One (purported) British call girl possessed of a particularly engaging prose style, who writes under the nom de plume Belle de Jour, won the *Guardian* newspaper's Best Written Blog award of 2003. Belle went on to publish two books and to a provide a regular column for another British daily.

ROBUSTNESS AND INTERNET PROSTITUTION

Most policy issues concerning web-based prostitution parallel those discussed in Chapter 6 for nonvirtual commercial sex. Robustness necessitates the availability of some legal channels for adult prostitution. Internet-mediated prostitution tends to involve lower social costs than other forms of prostitution. Therefore, legal web-based prostitution services would generally be a desirable element in a robust (or a harm-reducing) policy regime.

Beyond legality, effective approaches toward externalities for web-based prostitution again should be similar to those toward other sorts of prostitution; a safe-sex mandate likely forms part of any robust policy regime. Information provision and aid for those who wish to exit from prostitution help to allay (though not solve, of course) rationality concerns. In addition, self-exclusion

---

[61] See, e.g., Hughes (2000) and Plasencia (2000).
[62] The noncommercial dating scene has a somewhat similar webpage at DontDateHimGirl.com.

devices for customers could be employed for web-based prostitution, as with web-based pornography and gambling.

Children should be shielded from web-based prostitution, both on the demand side and the supply side. A requirement that commercial sex websites be available only behind an adults-only screen can go a long way to keeping kids away from such sites. Any commercial sex worker or establishment that knowingly allows underage patronage could be prosecuted.

Things are trickier with respect to kids as purveyors of prostitution-like services. Of course the underage can be forbidden from participating in commercial sex work, and their customers can be penalized. But how to draw the line about what sort of behavior qualifies as commercial sex? What if a 16-year old woman poses on her webcam (available to paying subscribers only, say) in a bikini? Should her behavior, or the behavior of her customers, be legal? What if she does not offer subscriptions but sets up a gift registry so that her web visitors voluntarily can send her expensive presents? What if they accompany their donation with a suggestion of other articles of attire that she might model for them? These questions about regulating the underage largely fall outside the purview of the robustness principle. Nevertheless, they reinforce, at a minimum, the desirability of adult oversight of the web behavior of teenagers.

CONCLUSIONS

The Internet makes vice harder – more costly – to control.[63] All else equal, then, we would expect that an appropriate policy response to the development of the web would be a loosening of vice regulations. The British gambling regulatory reforms appear to be of this nature.

But all else is not equal, of course. Along with a rise in the cost of control has come whole new subgenres of vice, including Internet porn and cybercasinos. These virtual vice variants present novel arrays of benefits and dangers, so that determining whether they are worth regulating more or less strictly than traditional vice requires an empirical, case-by-case analysis. Certainly the dangers to kids and addicts from Internet-based vice must be addressed. As in traditional vice arenas, however, robust regulatory regimes that confront these concerns can be formulated, without placing substantial impediments in the way of adult access to virtual vice.

The influence of the Internet on vice extends well beyond the regulatory climate. Particularly important is how the web alters the informational

---

[63] Some commentators have argued that attempts to regulate the web are so costly that they are effectively futile; see, e.g., Johnson and Post (1996) and Bell (1999); for critiques and evidence against the futility claims, see Lessig (1999) and Goldsmith (1998).

environment for vice. The profusion of web-based vice-related material offers an opportunity to improve vice policy, both terrestrial and virtual.

Much vice behavior is hidden by design; further, most people do not use cocaine, buy or sell sex, or engage in extreme sadomasochistic activities – many versions of vice are both secretive and minority interests. These conditions imply that the prevalence of vice is difficult to gauge, and for people who themselves are not practitioners, reliable information about a given vice might be hard to come by. In the past, this paucity of generally available information has put a premium upon the research of ethnographers who have immersed themselves in vicious subcultures. But ethnographers are necessarily limited to studying a slice of society that is geographically and temporally confined, making it hard to assess the generality of their findings. A policy maker committed to understanding the extent and nature of vicious behavior, therefore, encountered daunting obstacles to becoming well-informed. As a result, vice policy often has been formulated by individuals who are not particularly knowledgeable about the vice in question. When it comes to vice, however, lack of knowledge by policy makers does not imply lack of hostility; indeed, the opposite reaction seems more likely.

Thanks to the Internet, deviant subcultures are no longer so opaque, and the intermediation of ethnographers no longer so requisite.[64] Vice producers and consumers themselves can and do tell their stories and register their opinions. Information about vice is available like never before. Extreme views toward vice, such as claims that all prostitution is exploitation, or that virtually all prostitution is uncoerced, become less sustainable in this environment.

There is no guarantee that more information about vice will lead to reduced hostility or better legislation from policy makers. Nevertheless, the many articulate, reasoned voices from the prostitution world, the gambling world, or the sadomasochism world that can be accessed on the web are a resource that previous generations of policy makers (and researchers) did not readily have available. Those voices will likely be heard and wield some beneficent influence in future debates over the regulation of vice.

VICE VERDICTS (V): PORNOGRAPHY AND THE INTERNET

The U.S. Congress has been attempting to limit or outlaw pornography on the web in the service of protecting the underage. So far, these efforts have not met with much success in surviving constitutional challenges. Congress also has tried, with more success, to require public libraries to block web-based pornographic material.

---

[64] This discussion draws upon Leitzel (2006).

CIPA: *US, et al. v. American Library Association, et al.* (2003)[65]

A lack of Internet access puts enormous amounts of information out of reach. Public libraries, therefore, have been assiduous in trying to secure and augment Internet access for their patrons. Of course, the material that the Internet makes available ranges over the full spectrum, from the most detailed, prosaic data to the most lurid photographs and films, including some which might be prohibited in the United States as "obscenity." Sometimes kids (and adults, too) in public libraries access the lurid material, often purposely. Sometimes they even leave it on the screen so that the next user is involuntarily exposed to indecent images.

The specter of such questionable use of public Internet connections brought a federal response. The U.S. Congress passed the Children's Internet Protection Act (CIPA) in December 2000. Most public libraries in the United States receive federal funds earmarked to help them establish and maintain Internet access. CIPA requires public libraries that receive such federal funding to install filters on all of their computers connected to the Internet.

The constitutionality of CIPA was challenged by the American Library Association and a long list of fellow plaintiffs, including two candidates for Congress whose websites were blocked by filtering software. An injunction prevented the implementation of CIPA until the case had run its course. On June 23, 2003, the Supreme Court (in a 6-3 decision) upheld the constitutionality of CIPA, overturning the earlier ruling of a U.S. District Court. Chief Justice William Rehnquist authored the plurality opinion, joined by Justices Sandra Day O'Connor, Antonin Scalia, and Clarence Thomas. Justices Anthony Kennedy and Stephen Breyer agreed with the outcome, though each provided a separate concurring opinion.

The Rehnquist opinion argues that the free speech issues at stake in CIPA are minimal: "A library's decision to use filtering software is a collection decision, not a restraint on private speech."[66] Further, the law allows librarians to disable the filtering software if an adult makes a request consistent with "bona fide research or other lawful purposes." CIPA, according to the plurality opinion, does not violate free-speech protections, while it promotes the realization of Congress's legitimate purpose of limiting the manner in which federally authorized spending is undertaken.

Both sides of the court recognize the fallibility of filtering software. Current incarnations of such software vastly overexclude material, precluding access to unobjectionable, nonobscene sites. (Filters also allow some pornography to

---

[65] This discussion is based primarily on the case itself, *US et al. v. American Library Association, Inc., et al.*, 539 U.S. 194 (2003). See also Steve Chapman, "The Internet Law That No One Missed," *Chicago Tribune*, June 26, 2003, p. 27, and the inimitable Dahlia Lithwick's report on the oral arguments before the Supreme Court in *Slate*, at http://slate.msn.com/id/2079701.

[66] Opinion of Chief Justice Rehnquist, 539 U.S. 194 (2003, p. 12, fn. 4).

pass unmolested, especially as most filters primarily rely upon text and have no reliable way to judge the content of photographs.) In his dissent, Justice John Paul Stevens argues that "a statutory blunderbuss that mandates this vast amount of 'overblocking' abridges the freedom of speech protected by the First Amendment."[67] That the filters could be removed upon request does not vacate the free speech concerns of Justice Stevens in part because a user doesn't know precisely what is blocked in advance. CIPA also requires that every Internet-enabled computer in a library be filtered, even if the purchase of only one of the computers had been federally subsidized and even if the computer is solely for the use of library staff. "This Court should not permit federal funds to be used to enforce this kind of broad restriction of First Amendment rights, particularly when such a restriction is unnecessary to accomplish Congress' stated goal." Justice Stevens noted that in the absence of the CIPA requirement, only 7 percent of surveyed libraries indicated that they dealt with the problem of adolescent access to Internet pornography by installing filters on all computers.

Justice David Souter's dissenting opinion, joined by Justice Ruth Bader Ginsburg, observes that the disabling of the filters upon request is not automatic – the statute only states that librarians "may" unblock when a request is received. Justice Souter further takes issue with the plurality's claim that CIPA involves not censorship, but a "collection decision" akin to that of which books to purchase:

> ... In the instance of the Internet, what the library acquires is electronic access, and the choice to block is a choice to limit access that has already been acquired. Thus, deciding against buying a book means there is no book (unless a loan can be obtained), but blocking the Internet is merely blocking access purchased in its entirety and subject to unblocking if the librarian agrees. The proper analogy therefore is not to passing up a book that might have been bought; it is either to buying a book and then keeping it from adults lacking an acceptable "purpose," or to buying an encyclopedia and then cutting out pages with anything thought to be unsuitable for all adults.

CIPA's litigation history may well not end with the Supreme Court decision of 2003. In that case, CIPA was challenged as unconstitutional on its face, and the court ruled against such a challenge. The implementation of CIPA, however, could result in further lawsuits, especially if adults are denied relatively swift and painless unblocking.

If the unblocking is quick and painless, then CIPA comports with the robustness principle: it imposes few costs upon rational adult users, while offering some hope of reducing youth access. Nevertheless, CIPA is a perfect example of legislation that should never have been adopted, under the old adage "don't

---

[67] Dissenting opinion of Justice Stevens, 59 U.S. 194 (2003, p. 3).

make a federal case out of it."[68] The 93 percent of libraries that previously chose otherwise now have no choice, absent the loss of what for many are significant funds, to install filters on all of their computers attached to the web. And for what gain? As Internet access expands, fewer and fewer adolescents will need to rely on public libraries if they choose to procure pornography. And for those whose search for Internet porn is limited to public settings, librarians had already implemented policies to control such behavior. But now we are saddled with a federal rule that ultimately will have essentially no impact on adolescent exposure to pornography but will inconvenience thousands of library Internet users, whom, among other things, might be prevented (temporarily) from accessing the Supreme Court's decision in *U.S. v. American Library Association* (2003).

CDA and COPA: *Reno v. ACLU* (1997) and *Ashcroft v. ACLU* (2004)[69]

Recall that the Supreme Court distinguishes between obscene material and indecent material. Obscene productions lie outside of the free speech provisions of the First Amendment; indecent sexually explicit matter receives some First Amendment protection.

Constitutional protection of indecent material depends on the medium by which it is conveyed. Unseemly (though not necessarily legally obscene) matter can be regulated if it is transmitted via traditional broadcasting. The Communications Decency Act (CDA: Title V of the Telecommunications Act of 1996) was aimed at extending to the Internet this regulatory power over indecency, for the purpose of preventing minors from procuring lewd material online. In *Reno v. ACLU*, the Supreme Court, in a 7-2 decision, found the content-based restrictions of the CDA on speech vague and overbroad, and part of the act, therefore, unconstitutional on First Amendment grounds. The court thought that the CDA would chill protected speech on the Internet. For example, a community organization's web-based discussion of safer sex using street slang to reach teens might violate the CDA.

Congress responded to the invalidation of the CDA by passing the Child Online Protection Act (COPA), which follows the FCC's broadcast indecency definition by appropriating much of the language from the *Miller v. California* case.[70] For instance, under COPA, the targeted productions, taken as a whole, must lack serious artistic, literary, scientific, or political value "for minors," and "contemporary community standards" are to be employed by juries in determining whether material is harmful to minors. By tracking closely the FCC's formulation, Congress was trying to ensure that the COPA ban would

---

[68] This claim is congruent with the views expressed by columnist Steve Chapman in "The Internet Law That No One Missed," *Chicago Tribune*, June 26, 2003, p. 27.

[69] *Reno v. ACLU*, 52 U.S. 844 (1997) and *Ashcroft v. ACLU*, 542 U.S. 656 (2004).

[70] The FCC's indecency standard for broadcast media received Supreme Court imprimatur in *FCC v. Pacifica Foundation*, 438 U.S. 726 (1978).

not be overly (i.e., unconstitutionally) broad, even though it applies to material that is not legally obscene. In addition, COPA (unlike the CDA) pertained only to communications intended for commercial purposes, which currently receive a lower level of First Amendment protection than some other types of communications, such as political speech – those straight-talking safe-sex websites would not fall afoul of COPA. Further, again unlike the CDA, which arguably applied to all Internet communications, including e-mail and chat room messages, COPA restricted itself to webpage communications. COPA did not seek to ban "harmful to minors" material; rather, it required that commercial porn purveyors, and any other commercial site that includes material that might be found to meet the "harmful to minors" specifications, place their material behind some sort of age check or credit card screen.

A preliminary injunction by a district court prevented enforcement of COPA, based on the notion that the plaintiffs opposed to COPA would be likely to prevail on their argument that less restrictive alternatives to the COPA controls were available. Subsequent appellate and Supreme Court litigation has been concerned with the appropriateness of this district court grant of a preliminary injunction. The Third Circuit Court of Appeals initially upheld the injunction but on different grounds, ruling that the community standards provision was overbroad for regulating Internet communications. (One fear was that given the borderless nature of the web every community would be held to the standards of the most puritanical.) In May 2002, the U.S. Supreme Court disagreed with the Third Circuit, claiming that COPA's reliance on community standards by itself did not meet the "overbroad" test that would render COPA unconstitutional on First Amendment grounds. The Supreme Court kept the injunction in place, however, while sending the case back to the Third Circuit for a thorough hearing on COPA's constitutionality that would go beyond the "community standards" issue. In March 2003, the Third Circuit again found COPA to be unconstitutional, for an array of reasons. For instance, according to the Third Circuit, the restrictions on speech contained in COPA are not narrowly tailored to achieve the government's purpose of preventing harm to minors from exposure to indecent materials, nor does COPA employ the least restrictive means of achieving this purpose.

Upon appeal of this (second) decision to the Supreme Court, the majority upheld the Third District's affirmation of the district court's preliminary injunction because content-based speech restrictions are presumptively invalid. Once contested, the government has the burden of overcoming that presumption, in part by showing that there do not exist plausible alternatives that serve the same end while simultaneously being less restrictive upon speech. The government failed to make such a showing, and therefore, the court ruled, the district court did not abuse its discretion when it issued the preliminary injunction.

The main regulatory alternative considered by the district court in making its decision was software that blocks or filters objectionable material, and here lies the chief connection between the jurisprudence of COPA and of CIPA, the library case. The CIPA ruling helps to establish the viability of a filtering alternative. For COPA, the court proceeded as follows. Perhaps it might be argued that filters are not really a plausible alternative because the government cannot order people to use filters on their home computers, but (perhaps) the government can order commercial porn websites to set up an age check or credit card screen. According to the majority opinion, "That argument carries little weight, because Congress undoubtedly may act to encourage the use of filters. We have held [in the CIPA case] that Congress can give strong incentives to schools and libraries to use them." Further, "COPA presumes that parents lack the ability, not the will, to monitor what their children see. By enacting programs to promote use of filtering software, Congress could give parents that ability without subjecting protected speech to severe penalties."

A second rationale for preferring the less-restrictive filter alternative comes from a government commission that issued a report in 2002 on controlling Internet porn – and the commission, which itself was established via COPA, found that filters were more effective than age-verification requirements. Nevertheless, the commission's report stresses adult responsibility in teaching and supervising children, instead of mechanically relying upon filtering software.[71]

Justice Stevens's concurring opinion (joined by Justice Ginsburg), backs up the appeals court reasoning from the first time that the Supreme Court took on this case, that the "community standards" approach alone leads to unconstitutionality:

> I continue to believe that the Government may not penalize speakers for making available to the general World Wide Web audience that which the least tolerant communities in America deem unfit for their children's consumption, cf. Reno v. American Civil Liberties Union, 521 U.S. 844, 878 (1997), and consider that principle a sufficient basis for deciding this case.

The Stevens concurrence also takes aim at the contention that COPA really isn't all that constraining:

> I wish to underscore just how restrictive COPA is. COPA is a content-based restraint on the dissemination of constitutionally protected speech. It enforces its prohibitions by way of the criminal law, threatening noncompliant Web speakers with a fine of as much as $50,000, and a term of imprisonment as long as six months, for each offense. 47 U. S. C. §231(a). Speakers who "intentionally" violate COPA are punishable by a fine of up to $50,000 for each day of the violation. Ibid. And because implementation of the various adult-verification mechanisms described in the statute provides only an affirmative defense, §231(c)(1), even full compliance with COPA cannot guarantee freedom from prosecution. Speakers who dutifully place their content behind age screens may nevertheless find themselves in court, forced to prove the lawfulness of their speech on pain of criminal conviction.

---

[71] http://www4.nationalacademies.org/onpi/webextra.nsf/web/porn?OpenDocument .

In terms of the consistency of COPA with the robustness principle, the issue turns on implementation. If compliant website operators were to face the specter raised by Justice Stevens of being haled to a criminal court, then COPA impinges too deeply on adult providers of indecent material. An amended version of COPA that precluded charges against commercial sites employing an approved and inexpensive age-verification system, however, could serve as one element within a robust regulatory regime. (The idea is that employing an approved screen would create a safe harbor against prosecution.) Robustness requires that compliance with the age check mandate be not very onerous for adult web surfers, too. Even if such an amended COPA is robust, however, it may not be necessary or even desirable: parental oversight and filtering may well dominate COPA in terms of public policy toward Internet porn. But a COPA-like age-check system can be one component of an overall policy that shields kids from indecent material without imposing significant costs upon adult web users.

Justice Breyer's dissent identifies a possible perverse impact of the Court's COPA decision, namely, that the failure to uphold COPA will lead to more restriction on speech, not less, if current obscenity laws are enforced more strictly when a COPA-like mechanism for shielding kids from smut is not available. This concern parallels that identified in Chapter 5: applying standard free-speech legal doctrine in the vice domain holds the potential to limit speech. In the following chapter, a similar perverse impact is argued to apply at the intersection of vice and free trade.

The second Supreme Court decision concerning COPA did not end the statute's judicial journey; it merely kept in place the preliminary injunction preventing the enforcement of COPA. A full hearing on he constitutionality of COPA still had to take place at the district court level. The district court issued its opinion in March 2007, striking down COPA as inconsistent with the First and Fifth amendments to the Constitution.[72]

One important element in the district court's reasoning is the notion that filters installed on individual computers (or through Internet portals such as AOL) are quite effective at screening kids from adult content. Filtering technology made vast strides in the previous five years. Another element is that age verification (via credit cards or otherwise), which would have been required of commercial adult-oriented websites under the terms of COPA, is not yet at the same level of reliability, and such barriers are costly for websites or web surfers to implement and maintain.

COPA is a content-based restriction on legal speech and as such is subject to strict scrutiny by the courts. COPA can only be upheld, therefore, if it is narrowly tailored to achieve the compelling government interest of keeping kids away from Internet porn and if there do not exist alternatives, less restrictive

---

[72] The opinion is available at www.cdt.org/speech/copa/20070322copa.pdf; see the Vice Squad post from March 24, 2007.

upon speech, that similarly serve the government interest. The district court ruled that the United States had not shown that other alternatives are less effective than COPA; because COPA would not apply to foreign-based websites, there is a strong case to be made that filters are more effective than COPA at shielding kids from Internet pornography. The court also ruled that COPA's restrictions are not narrowly tailored, and that its provisions are unconstitutionally vague and overbroad, too.

8

Free Trade and Federalism

The Internet demonstrates how cross-jurisdictional exchange of ideas, services, and goods threatens preexisting vice regulations. Exchange, however, is vital for raising living standards and fostering economic growth. As a result, there is a longstanding conflict between vice control and commitments to open trade, between the fundamental principle of market freedom and the desirability of vice policy exceptionalism. Vice-related problems perceived to stem from trade policy will generate political reactions: if free trade extends to vice goods, and social problems mount in the face of the unfettered trade, then a free-trade policy becomes decidedly less appealing.

Alternatively, it might be a liberal vice policy that proves unsustainable in the face of a free trade mandate. In other words, the impossibility of providing special restrictions upon trade in legal vice might lead to a world of near or total prohibition. If the only available vice policy options are (1) the ketchup alternative, that is, legal vice with no vice-specific restrictions or (2) illegal or intensely regulated vice (the current heroin control regime, perhaps), then it might be that polities find themselves choosing the second option. Alcohol, cigarettes, and other vice goods are not ordinary commodities like ketchup, and public policy should respond to the special issues presented by such goods.[1] Allowing free trade to overrule vice controls, requiring that alcohol be treated identically to ketchup as components of commerce, holds dangers for vice policy as well as for free trade.

The nineteenth Century Opium Wars between Great Britain and China provide an extreme case of the conflict between vice control and trade openness. In these contests, British military power forced a reluctant China to open its markets both generally and also specifically to smuggled (and eventually legal) imports of Indian-produced opium. In U.S. history, alcohol has been the primary (and ongoing) source of trade–versus–vice-control conflicts; similar vice/trade struggles are now taking place inside the European Union and the World Trade Organization.

---

[1] Babor, Caetano, and Casswell et al. (2003) is titled *Alcohol: No Ordinary Commodity*.

Box 8.1: *The Opium Wars*[a]

Two popular psychoactive drugs precipitated the altercations that became known as the Opium Wars. The first is caffeine in the form of tea. The second, of course, is opium.

The East India Company was granted a monopoly right to import tea into Britain. And import it did, thousands of tons of Chinese tea per year. In 1776, Adam Smith noted that tea "was a drug very little used in Europe before the middle of the last century. At present the value of the tea annually imported by the English East India Company, for the use of their own countrymen, amounts to more than a million and a half [pounds] a year; and even this is not enough; a great deal more being constantly smuggled into the country...."[b] The tax on tea formed a major element in the finances of the British crown.[c]

Britain paid for the tons of Chinese tea primarily in silver, but it was looking for a cheaper alternative. Unfortunately, the Chinese were not particularly interested in the majority of manufactured goods that Britain could offer. But a new opportunity began to present itself late in the eighteenth century. The demand for opium expanded, and the East India Company had a ready supply available in India.

The medical use of opium had been established in both Britain and China for some time. By the end of the eighteenth century, however, the recreational consumption of opium was growing, and so were addiction-related problems. In Britain, opium "inebriates" primarily used laudanum, Thomas De Quincey's preferred potation. In China, the relatively new technique of smoking opium, which permitted quick transmission of the drug to the brain, became the favored form of recreational opium consumption. Responding to the increased recreational drug use, the Chinese emperor in 1799 prohibited the importation and smoking of opium.[d]

The East India Company nominally complied with the emperor's edict, but in practice, it connived in the smuggling of opium into China. Nevertheless, the company exercised monopoly control over the Indian opium supplies, keeping quantities limited and prices high. In this instance, monopoly probably served the interests of vice control, by slowing down the spread of opium to China. In the first two decades of the nineteenth century, Chinese opium smoking was primarily an upper-class pursuit, as high prices kept the drug from being easily accessible to people of modest means.

The East India Company's control over opium supplies was not absolute, so the high monopoly prices proved unsustainable in the face of competitors, including American and Portuguese opium traders. After 1819, the East India Company endeavored to supply enough opium to drive the price sufficiently low to dissuade would-be competitors.[e] As a result, opium imports into China rose.

Further spurs to the opium trade were in the offing. The supply of opium to China was not the only monopoly that the East India Company would see threatened. In 1833, Parliament eliminated the legal monopoly the company had enjoyed for British trade with China:

With China open to all comers, within a year the amount of tea imported into Britain quadrupled. The trade in opium to pay for all this tea also dramatically increased. In 1830, eighteen thousand chests of opium were imported [into China] from India. Three years later, the number of chests had soared to thirty thousand.[f]

All of these opium imports were officially illegal. The Chinese stepped up efforts to suppress the opium business, including their own limited internal production, significant internal commerce, and the foreign imports. When opium importation continued, China subjected Britain to a general trade embargo, thereby hindering the lucrative tea exports. During the crackdown, in an effort to save the tea trade, British-owned opium was surrendered to the Chinese authorities, who destroyed it.

In trying to normalize the trade situation while ending opium smuggling, Chinese authorities required traders to sign pledges to refrain from trading opium and to be subject to Chinese jurisdiction. British traders were unwilling to make this pledge, in part because of the severity of Chinese punishments, and they left the sole-permitted trading post of Canton to live offshore or in Macao.[g] The importance of jurisdiction to both sides was brought home in July 1839, when off-duty British sailors killed a Chinese man on the mainland. The Chinese demanded that the murderer – it is not clear who that was, as the victim was beaten by a mob – be handed over for punishment, but the British organized their own shipboard trial instead, which resulted in some convictions for minor charges; prison terms, supposed to be served in England, were never enforced because of the lack of authority of the makeshift court.

Skirmishes ensued and tensions increased, and when war broke out in earnest, superior British military technology forced a treaty (1842) on China that opened up trade, paid compensation for the destroyed opium, and guaranteed the rights of accused British subjects to avoid Chinese jurisdiction. The follow-up war of 1856–1860, which involved French forces as well, again ended in favor of the foreigners, with treaties that further opened trade – and legalized opium imports into China. "Opium importation increased from fifty-eight thousand chests in 1859 to 105,000 chests in 1879."[h]

---

[a] This section relies heavily upon Beeching (1975) and Hanes and Sanello (2005), as well as various Wikipedia entries: http://en.wikipedia.org/wiki/Opium_Wars, http://en.wikipedia.org/wiki/First_Opium_War, and http://en.wikipedia.org/wiki/Second_Opium_War.

[b] Smith (1976 [1776] , vol. 1, pp. 227–8). Smith (1976 [1776], vol. 2, p. 407) also notes that in Holland consumers have to purchase a license to drink tea.

[c] Beeching (1975, p. 29).

[d] Beeching (1975, p. 25); opium importation had been forbidden previously, but the smuggling continued without much hindrance.

[e] Beeching (1975, p. 34).   [f] Hanes and Sanello (2005, p. 24).

[g] The remainder of this paragraph relies heavily on Beeching (1975, pp. 87–9).

[h] Hanes and Sanello (2005, p. 293).

PRE-PROHIBITION: U.S. INTERSTATE ALCOHOL TRAFFICKING[2]

If Mississippi tried to enact tariffs on farm products entering from other states, it could not do so, because the Constitution gives the federal Congress, and not the individual states, the right to regulate interstate commerce. Federal control of interstate commerce has been interpreted by the Supreme Court to imply that state efforts to establish discriminatory control over markets generally are forbidden, even in cases where the federal power has not been exercised. The notion that unused congressional power to regulate interstate commerce precludes state incursions is known as the "dormant commerce clause": the default presumption given no federal action is that Congress intends unrestricted trade. States retain the "police power" to issue regulations concerning the health and safety effects of exchange, but such regulations cannot discriminate between goods originating in-state and goods from other states. As a result of this constitutional prohibition against state-level protectionism, the United States established a huge free-trade area within its borders, a development that has been credited with spurring protracted American economic success.

Alcohol has long posed a challenge to this commitment to free trade. Before the national alcohol Prohibition of the 1920s, individual states in the United States adopted widely divergent alcohol control measures, from extremely wet to bone dry. States with strict alcohol controls were faced with the problem that alcohol obtained more cheaply or more readily in neighboring states could be "imported." On a broad enough scale, such imports would render a state ban on alcohol sales to be ineffective to the point of futility. But could a dry state deter its residents from crossing into neighboring states and returning with booze, or obstruct out-of-state alcohol manufacturers from delivering their wares to the ostensibly dry region? Policies and court judgments made at the federal level determined the extent to which an individual state could enforce its alcohol regulations on actors temporarily or permanently beyond its borders.

In 1890, the Supreme Court decided that alcohol shipped in its "original packaging" could not be prevented from being imported into dry states and sold; nor could special taxes on such imports be applied.[3] The original packaging indicated that the alcohol was still within the stream of interstate commerce and hence the commerce clause applied.

Soon after the Supreme Court ruling, quasi-legal sales of liquor in dry states mushroomed.[4] The original packaging of liquor took on smaller dimensions, such that beer or whiskey could be sold by the bottle. Saloons even sprang up in dry states; as long as the customer purchased the alcohol in the original

---

[2] This section draws heavily upon Hamm (1995).
[3] *Leisy v. Hardin*, 135 U.S. 100 (1890); Hamm (1995, pp. 68–9).
[4] Hamm (1995, pp. 70–1).

container and opened it himself, how could he be stopped from drinking or sharing his beverage? So the Supreme Court essentially overruled the alcohol policy of dry states.

But the Supreme Court could itself be overruled, or at least circumvented. The dormant commerce clause only applies when Congress has not spoken on an issue of internal trade. The dismay among dry constituencies provoked by the Supreme Court decision led Congress to act, by expressly authorizing the several states to regulate their own alcohol imports. Within four months of the court ruling, Congress eliminated the "original packaging" exception through legislation known as the Wilson Act. States once again could govern or prohibit liquor as they pleased, as long as they treated in-state and out-of-state alcohol evenhandedly. What states still could not do was hinder alcohol that was in interstate commerce by, for instance, seizing all unlicensed alcohol shipments the moment that they crossed into the state. (Alcohol has industrial, medical, and religious uses, so dry states still licensed some imports.) This limitation opened up channels for collect-on-delivery (COD) shipments of alcohol to thrive. In operation, the Wilson Act gave scope to dry states to ban alcohol for resale, the commercial component of the industry, but not to prevent individual imbibing. A drinker could order beer to be sent COD and pick up his package (in the original container) at the warehouse of the express carrier.

This compromise contained some advantages. First, it accorded with the expressed aim of many temperance activists, that their target was not the individual drinker but rather the trade in alcohol. And determined drinkers in dry areas had less reason to forcefully oppose prohibition, given that its restrictions were not overly constraining.[5] At the same time, the COD trade allowed some commercial activity to take place under the guise of shipments for personal consumption.

Eventually, states began to take additional measures to restrict COD and other means of delivering alcohol. First in 1909 and more comprehensively in 1913, the federal government lent its support to these efforts. The 1913 legislation, which became known as the Webb-Kenyon Act, closed the obvious loopholes through which commercial alcohol moved relatively unencumbered into dry areas. After Webb-Kenyon, states were in a much better position to enforce their own alcohol policies, no matter how strict: a dry state no longer had to worry that interstate deliveries would openly undermine its ban. Large shipments of alcohol could be seized in dry jurisdictions, and in the extreme case, as in desert-dry West Virginia, even small-scale imports for personal use could be curtailed.[6] But soon this long-evolved, patchwork system, one that smoothed coexistence between wet and dry states, gave way to national Prohibition.

---

[5] Hamm (1995, p. 182). [6] Hamm (1995, pp. 224–5).

POST-PROHIBITION: U.S. INTERNET WINE SALES

Nearly fourteen years later, Prohibition itself gave way, when the Twenty-first Amendment granted sovereignty over alcohol policy to individual states. The second section of that amendment reads: "The transportation or importation into any State, Territory, or possession of the United States for delivery or use therein of intoxicating liquors, in violation of the laws thereof, is hereby prohibited." Control of its own imports allows a dry state to maintain its strict policies even though bordering states implement more lax alcohol regulations. The Twenty-first Amendment looks to avoid the sort of state-federal wrangling that characterized pre-1913 alcohol regulation, as the Webb-Kenyon Act hoped to do in the brief interim between 1913 and Prohibition, by putting the several states in charge.

The Twenty-first Amendment appears to give states carte blanche in designing their alcohol "import" policy. But can states discriminate against out-of-state producers? Could a state, for instance, ban imports of alcohol from other states and abroad, while licensing in-state producers?

In 2005, the extent of the reach of the Twenty-first Amendment was tested in a Supreme Court case involving interstate sales of wine, sometimes conducted over the Internet. Many U.S. states do not permit direct shipment of wine to consumers; rather, wine deliveries must go to licensed wholesalers or retailers. Before the 2005 case, other states openly discriminated against out-of-state wineries, in the following sense: state residents could receive direct wine shipments from in-state wineries, but not from out-of-state wineries. Such state laws present a conflict between two established principles: first, states do not have the authority to regulate commerce in a manner that discriminates against out-of-state producers or distributors; second, states can control imports of alcohol into their borders.

The Supreme Court decided, by a 5-4 vote, in favor of the dormant commerce clause: states can enact whatever regulations that they desire over alcohol distribution, but those regulations must be applied evenhandedly to in-state and out-of-state producers or distributors.[7] The court's decision does not directly limit the restrictiveness of any state's alcohol policy. The dormant commerce clause trumps some specific, discriminatory alcohol controls, but not an overall alcohol policy. The potential conflict between trade and vice policy is managed in Webb-Kenyon–like fashion.[8] The aftermath of the 2005 ruling indicates that the decision is not a clear victory for those who favor liberal alcohol control regimes: some states began to investigate extending to in-state wineries the

---

[7] Presumably, there are other constraints on the alcohol policies a state could choose, beyond the commerce clause's imposition of evenhanded treatment of out-of-state producers; for instance, an alcohol policy could not discriminate on the basis of religion. See Zwyicki (2004) for substantial background and analysis of the interstate wine case.

[8] See the Vice Squad post from May 19, 2005.

more stringent regulations that they previously applied only to out-of-state producers.[9]

ALCOHOL IN THE EUROPEAN UNION

Somewhat parallel developments in European alcohol regulation are afoot. The European Union (EU) is committed to the free movement of goods and people within its borders, which have been expanding rapidly, as more nations, including many from the former Soviet bloc, join the EU. The EU is establishing within Europe a free-trade zone similar to that among the U.S. states.

In recent years, alcohol control regimes have varied considerably within Europe. Some EU countries feature high taxes and state monopolies for retail trade in alcohol, while others impose minimal taxes and fewer controls. How will the EU handle the formation and expansion of a U.S.-style free-trade zone with respect to alcohol? Will countries continue to be able to design and implement their own alcohol policies or will centralized rules trump individual member-country controls? As in the United States, there is a potential European conflict between "federal" and "state" powers with respect to alcohol policy.

If it so chooses, a country within the EU can maintain high taxes for retail alcohol sales and apply those taxes to commercial imports, too. The strain on the system has to do not with commercial transactions but, rather, with imports of alcohol for personal use (as opposed to imports intended for resale by wholesalers or restaurants, say). An EU citizen traveling from France to Britain can bring lightly taxed wine from France with her, but how much wine can she bring? Until recently, this decision has been left to individual members of the EU, and countries such as Sweden and Finland preserved strict limits. In 2004, however, the EU adopted a rule permitting unlimited imports of alcohol, provided the booze genuinely is destined for personal use (which includes being served to hundreds of guest at a wedding, for instance). Individual EU member countries can no longer limit travelers to bringing in only a case or two of alcohol (though large consignments might require the presentation of reliable evidence that the imports truly are intended for personal use). The EU currently operates without the equivalent of the United States pre-Prohibition Webb-Kenyon Act, in that personal use imports cannot be constrained unilaterally by individual states.

These EU rules have put tremendous pressure on traditionally high alcohol-taxing countries, and on Finland and Sweden in particular. In the case of Finland, the most significant event was the accession of Estonia to the EU at the beginning of May 2004. Estonia is quite close to parts of Finland, and for

---

[9] See the Vice Squad post by Michael Alexeev on May 29, 2005, available at http://vicesquad. blogspot.com/2005_05_01_vicesquad_archive.html#111739443268835276 (accessed on November 16, 2005).

years has been a popular destination for Finns wanting to purchase alcohol at prices much lower than those featured at Finland's state-run liquor stores. The amounts of alcohol that Finns could bring back with them from Estonia previously were limited; however, those limits would disappear following Estonia's EU accession, given EU policy permitting unconstrained intraunion transport of alcohol for personal use. Finland came to the conclusion that its high taxes would not be sustainable once Estonia joined the EU: few Finns would bother to purchase their alcohol at high prices in Finland if the same brands were available in unlimited quantities at a much cheaper price via a quick jaunt to Tallinn. To try to forestall the threatened wave of Estonian imports, Finland cut back its alcohol taxes by an average of some 30 to 40 percent, a few months before Estonia's EU membership.

Sweden, like Finland, operates a state monopoly alcohol retailer and traditionally imposes high taxes. It is similarly exposed to the EU's liberal alcohol policy, as many Swedes can travel to Germany or other cheaper alcohol countries and bring back those now unlimited amounts of alcohol for personal use. Unlike Finland, however, Sweden elected to remain steadfast with its high alcohol taxes, though a surge in personal imports was forcing it to reconsider its lofty levies. As the Swedish prime minister noted when he expressed his own support for reduced domestic alcohol excises, for the substantial number of Swedes who purchase alcoholic beverages abroad, lower taxes are already a reality.[10] In August 2004, a Swedish government commission recommended a 40 percent cut in alcohol taxes, though two-and-a-half years later this measure still had not been adopted.

As during the pre-Prohibition era in dry U.S. states, deliveries of lightly taxed alcohol from elsewhere ostensibly for personal consumption emerged as a serious source of contention in Sweden. In recent years, Swedes have been ordering alcohol over the Internet from low-tax EU states, bypassing the state retail monopoly and its significant excise taxes. Swedish customs confiscated such deliveries when it could — 100,000 liters were seized in the first quarter of 2006 – under the claim that such deliveries were illegal.[11] The sellers and buyers disagreed with that claim and in June 2007, the European Court of Justice found against the Swedish alcohol policy arguing that the prohibition on personel imports was aimed more at protecting the monopoly provider then public health. Nevertheless, such imports will still be liable for Swedish alcohol excise taxes.[12]

Despite the initially different policy responses – Finland reduced its alcohol taxes, while Sweden did not – the results emanating from the liberalized EU

---

[10] See the Vice Squad post from August 9, 2004.

[11] "Record Booze Seizures By Swedish Customs," *The Local*, April 13, 2006, at www.thelocal.se/article.php?ID = 3552&date = 0060413 (accessed on April 28, 2006).

[12] See the Vice Squad post from June 9, 2007.

rules were similar in the two Scandinavian countries. Both Finland and Sweden saw a huge influx of imports for personal use. Swedish state alcohol store sales fell precipitously, along with alcohol tax collections. Of the alcohol consumed in Sweden, more is purchased abroad than is bought from the domestic state stores. In Finland, the lowered taxes led to an increase in state store sales, but tax revenues nevertheless dropped off because the sales increases were not sufficient to overcome the lower tax rates. There were reports of increased alcohol-related problems and deaths in Finland following the implementation of the tax decrease.[13] Sweden had its own new alcohol problems. For instance, the 500 million cans of German beer imported each year for personal consumption are having an environmental impact. Sweden applies a deposit system to encourage return of containers purchased in Sweden. Beverages purchased abroad, like the German beers, are outside the system, and so their containers tend to be discarded.[14] Finland and Sweden both support a rise in the EU-mandated minimum tax on spirits and beer, which, by raising alcohol prices in other EU countries, would dampen the incentive for Swedes and Finns to engage in personal importing. Nearby but non-EU member Norway also supports higher alcohol taxes in the EU, for the same purpose of discouraging low-priced imports.

If it were easy to control "imports," then allowing each separate member of a trade federation to choose its own alcohol taxes, without any "federal" mandate, would be desirable. But it may be that imports cannot be controlled in the absence of intense policing that would undermine the intended ease to engage in trade. If that is the case, then large alcohol tax differentials cannot be maintained among members of a free-trade area. At that point, federal rules cannot help but to take sides, to ease the path of low-tax or high-tax areas. A centralized minimum tax (as is required by the EU and collected at the federal level in the United States) helps those member states that want to see high alcohol prices but might overshoot the desired tax level of low-tax members. The Finnish-led attempt to raise the EU minimum alcohol tax in 2006 foundered when major beer producers such as Germany and the Czech Republic sought exemptions for beer, while wine-producing countries looked for similar special treatment.

Interstate sale of wine to households in the United States and personal alcohol imports in the EU present some common tensions. In particular, the commitments to free trade in both the United States and the EU are currently running up against "state"-level alcohol controls, and free trade, it seems, is beginning to get the better of the conflict. In other words, with respect to trade policy, there is growing pressure to treat alcohol as just another commodity, like, well, ketchup. As noted, such an approach presents dangers both for free

---

[13] See the Vice Squad posts from February 26, 2005, and February 19, 2007.
[14] "Sweden Wants Germany to Fix Mess," Sveriges Radio, April 25, 2006; available at www.sr.se.

trade and for alcohol. If a free-trade zone in Europe means that Sweden must tolerate a huge increase in drunken violence or alcohol-related crashes, it is likely that Swedes will rethink the relative advantages of free trade or of legal alcohol.

OTHER VICES IN THE EU: CANNABIS, SNUS, AND GAMBLING

Free-trade principles do not always prevail over local vice control, either in the United States or the EU. The approach of the EU toward cannabis is instructive in this regard. Of course, marijuana currently is illegal in all EU countries, but the Netherlands tolerates open sales and consumption in licensed coffeehouses. How does the EU's free-trade conviction play out with respect to the Netherlands and marijuana? Instead of smoothing trade, the EU exhorts the Netherlands to constrain trade in marijuana. As the EU cannot force the Netherlands to shut the coffee shops, it has instead mounted pressure to ensure that the relatively liberal Dutch policy does not undermine the stricter controls of neighbors – pressure that even has taken the form of calls upon the Netherlands to confine coffee shop sales of marijuana to the residents of the Netherlands.

Free trade is not allowed to trump EU vice policy in another case, that of "snus," a smokeless form of tobacco placed in the mouth. Snus is legal and popular in Sweden, where its use has probably played an important role in making the Swedish male death rate from lung cancer the lowest such rate in Europe. Snus appears to be much less harmful than smoking – which is not to say that it is perfectly safe – and thus inducing current cigarette smokers to convert to snus would probably result in significant health benefits.[15] Nevertheless, snus is banned throughout the rest of the EU; the Swedes negotiated an exception from the snus ban when they joined the union in 1995. (Snus, incidentally, also is popular in Norway, which is not a member of the EU. Public smoking bans adopted in recent years have probably contributed to increased snus use in both Sweden and Norway.)

A leading Swedish manufacturer brought a court challenge to the EU's snus ban. After all, cigarettes are legitimate items of intra-EU commerce, and in most respects, snus represents a healthier alternative to cigarettes (and presents no fire risk, either). Nevertheless, the EU rejected the legal challenge and maintained its snus ban, despite its usual commitment to free intraunion trade.

Although cannabis and snus are largely suppressed within the EU, another vice, gambling (particularly remote gambling), meets with widely varying regulatory approaches. To this point, the EU accepts nonuniformity across member

---

[15] According to Waldemar Ingdahl, writing in the online TCS Daily, "Statistically, the average life span of smokers is eight years shorter than for non-smokers, but for users of smokeless tobacco it is just 15 days shorter." "No Illusions," May 31, 2006, at www.tcsdaily.com/article.aspx?id=053106C.

states in gambling regulations. Nations can choose their overall gambling policy, and gambling is excluded from ongoing attempts to offer greater intraunion
competition in the provision of services. The difficulty, as with interstate alcohol in the United States, arises when an EU member's gambling policy is not
evenhanded in dealing with in-country and foreign (but EU member-based)
providers. For instance, some EU member states allow their residents to bet on
sports, even over the Internet, though only via an in-state monopoly provider.
Countries also place controls on the advertising of foreign gambling services,
while simultaneously aggressively promoting their own national lotteries. Both
of these practices are likely to contravene EU rules and are under challenge.

So federal or international commitments to free trade can sometimes undermine an individual state's vice controls, while broad commitments to high
taxes or bans can cramp an individual state's more liberalized approach. These
tensions can be sufficiently great as to threaten a country's continued participation in transnational arrangements. A small but telling case along these lines
developed in early 2006.[16] Aaland is a Swedish-speaking, semiautonomous,
demilitarized archipelago that is part of Finland. Finland is an EU member
and as Finnish territory, Aaland likewise is within the EU. Ferries registered
in Aaland have traditionally permitted on-board sales of snus. But snus is
banned in the European Union, except in Sweden, so the EU wanted the snus
sales on the Aaland ferries to cease. In the subsequent court case, Aaland was
represented by Finland. Aaland residents feared that this might not be high-
quality representation, however, as Finland actually sided with the EU, not with
Aaland, in the snus controversy. In part because of the need to rely upon such
ineffective counsel, Aaland raised the possibility of leaving the EU. In May
2006, the European Court of Justice ruled that Finland needed to terminate
the snus sales. Aaland has complied and not followed through on its threat to
leave the EU. But owners of Aaland-registered ferries are not pleased to see
their Swedish-registered cousins legally selling snus in runs between Finland
and Sweden.[17] (They can take some comfort, however, in the fact that Sweden-
Finland ferries that stop in Aaland are allowed tax-free sales of legal goods, as
its autonomous position has exempted Aaland from EU rules on value-added
taxes.)

The EU's contrasting policies with respect to alcohol, cannabis, snus, and
gambling suggest that tensions between free trade and vice policies are not
resolved based upon some general principles but, rather, on expedience or the
extent to which the good in question is favored or disfavored at the federal level.
Alcohol and cigarettes receive nearly the full free-trade blessing. Gambling

---

[16] See the Vice Squad post from February 7, 2006.

[17] Incidentally, mischievous Aaland is an outpost for another frequently suppressed vice: the islands
license Internet gambling servers. EU member state Malta also has emerged as a leading provider
of remote gambling.

is permitted some significant departures from open competition. Snus, safer than either alcohol or cigarettes, is not tolerated in most of the EU, whereas the current treatment (and, perhaps, the safety) of cannabis is similar to that of snus.

THE WORLD TRADE ORGANIZATION AND INTERNET GAMBLING

For a while it looked like a David versus Goliath tale, until a late-round comeback by Goliath. The arena was the World Trade Organization (WTO). The part of David was played by the twin-island nations of Antigua and Barbuda; the United States stood in for Goliath. The contention, improbably enough, concerned Internet gambling, and the battle played out in 2004 and beyond.

At the time the dispute arose, Antigua and Barbuda served as home to approximately 70,000 people and 30 Internet casinos. U.S. federal law appears to make illegal the provision of at least some forms of Internet gambling, particularly sports betting. Nevertheless, many types of gambling, both land-based and internet-conducted, are legal and widely available in the United States: even sports betting is legal in Nevada. So it looks as if the United States favors domestic gambling providers over foreign-based cybercasinos, a practice that runs counter to the usual WTO nondiscrimination precept. The initial decision in the dispute by a WTO panel in March 2004, sided with Antigua and Barbuda; almost on cue, some U.S. congressional representatives suggested that the United States would leave the WTO before being forced to liberalize Internet gambling rules.[18] The final WTO ruling, although technically a split decision, largely accepted the U.S. position. The major U.S. federal laws at issue, it was ruled, fell within a capacious exception to the nondiscriminatory principle: they were viewed as being necessary to protect public morals or to maintain public order.[19] (An obvious rejoinder to this reasoning is that the widespread availability of other forms of gambling renders moot the morals claim.)

The part of the decision that favored Antigua concerned Internet betting on horse racing, which is permitted in some states. Furthermore, a federal U.S. law explicitly makes such activity legal in states that license horse racing. But the United States still wants to prevent Antigua-based Internet wagering sites from legally offering betting on horse races to U.S.-based customers and is stalling the required adjustment in U.S. laws. The betting revenue and tax collections provide an incentive for the United States to discriminate against foreign competition, but these are the types of parochial concerns that WTO directives are designed to override. In this sense, the Antigua-U.S. Internet gambling

[18] See the Vice Squad post from March 28, 2004.
[19] See the Vice Squad post from April 9, 2005.

Box 8.2: *Native American Vice Suppliers*

In both the United States and Canada, federalism is complicated by Native American lands that traditionally are not governed by the same set of laws as are other territories. In the United States, federal law pertaining to Native American tribes generally exempts reservations from state laws, absent explicit federal legislation to the contrary. Such explicit legislation subjects Native Americans in many states to the criminal laws of their state, and some states also have been granted partial jurisdiction over Indian civil matters. At the same time, earnings made on reservations by Indians are outside the purview of state income taxes. In terms of the Constitution's commerce clause, Native American nations are treated like other sovereign governments: Congress is provided the authority to regulate commerce "with foreign Nations, and among the several states, and with the Indian Tribes."[a]

These legal exceptions potentially provide reservations or lands held in trust for Indian nations with competitive advantages in producing vice goods. For instance, sales of cigarettes on reservations, or conducted over the Internet from servers located on reservation property, might not be subject to the full panoply of state taxes. Gambling operations that would be suppressed outside of reservations might be allowable on reservation land. As a result, reservations in North America have become home to myriad gambling and other vice ventures, and greatly raise the monetary stakes over the legal recognition of a Native American tribe. Until recently, the largest casino in the world is a Native American casino located within Connecticut, and the Kahnawake Mohawk Reserve in Quebec hosts hundreds of Internet gambling websites.[b]

The opening of Native American lands to gambling in the United States started decades ago, when some tribes asserted their authority to operate gambling operations in contravention to state laws that perhaps were inapplicable to them.[c] The tribes' activities received federal blessing through various court decisions that recognized the civil (as opposed to criminal) nature of most gambling regulation. To clarify the situation, the federal government passed the Indian Gaming Regulatory Act (IGRA) in 1988. This legislation allows tribes to conduct gaming operations if similar gaming operations are legal elsewhere within the state. The similarities need not be all that substantial, however. For instance, if a charity could be state-licensed to run an occasional "casino night" fund-raiser, then casino games might be deemed to be permissible in that state; hence, reservations within the state could operate casinos. By such means, more than twenty states have come to house tribal casinos, though many of these states had little in the way of such operations before the IGRA. The growth of the Native American casino industry, in turn, increased pressure in nearby states or jurisdictions with stricter gambling controls to expand legal gambling. If their residents were gambling anyway, the temptation to grab a share of the significant tax revenues that gambling can generate becomes harder to resist.

(continued)

Box 8.2 *(continued)*

Technological change has combined with legal imprecision to give even more of a boost to tribal gambling. As with casinos, tribes can operate bingo parlors if the state in which they reside permits gambling through bingo – and almost all states permit charitable bingo.[d] What characterizes "bingo"? Definitions vary from state to state, with many jurisdictions offering no definition at all. Even when elements of the game are legally specified, such as the drawing of balls at random and the filling out of cards, it turns out that electronic gaming machines that look and feel like traditional slot machines can be designed in a manner consistent with the definition. That is, states with recognized federal tribes that permit legal bingo also must allow "bingo halls" that are essentially slot-machine parlors on Native American reservations.

The observation that economically underdeveloped areas are best positioned to benefit from expanded legal gambling is fully borne out in the case of tribal casinos. Native Americans in the United States have the highest poverty and unemployment rates among all ethnic groups, along with similarly high rates of alcoholism and other markers of social distress.[e] Tribes that have opened casinos, however, have seen large increases in tribal revenues and employment, on average, with those gambling venues located near major metropolitan areas securing the bulk of the gains.[f] Further, employment increases and health improvements seem to spill over into surrounding communities. Bankruptcy and some crimes, however, tend to increase in regions that host Native American casinos.

Under the terms of IGRA, states and tribes must come to an agreement about the type and extent of gambling permitted and how proceeds from the gambling are shared. (Remittances from tribes to the state are not taxes, as the state has no taxing power over Indian nations; in general, the payments are made in exchange for commitments by the state to limit gambling competition.) Agreements on revenue sharing are featured in tribal-state dealings over tobacco sales, too. Tribes have maintained in the past that such sales are free of state taxes, even if the purchasers are not members of the tribe. Such a tax exemption provides a huge competitive advantage to tribal sellers, while undermining state tobacco tax revenues. Not surprisingly, states have been reluctant to accept the contention that tribal sales are not taxable by the state, and in cases beginning in 1976, the U.S. Supreme Court agreed: reservation tobacco sales to buyers who are not Indian residents of the reservation require that the applicable state taxes be collected.[g]

The law is clear, then, with respect to state taxes on tribal tobacco sales. Enforcing the law is another matter entirely. Intratribal sales are exempt from state duties, a legal channel that opens the way for low-cost tax evasion on sales to outsiders. States generally take a pragmatic approach toward resolving this issue, negotiating compacts with tribes such that, for instance, 25 percent of the usual duties are collected and transferred for all reservation-based tobacco sales.[h] Nonreservation tobacco retailers and the jurisdictions that tax them often lobby for more intensive collection efforts to be mounted against their Native American competitors.[i]

Internet sites offer the possibility of sales to people in another state – how will the buyer's state even know that the transfer took place, and hence be in a position to collect the sales and excise taxes that legally apply to such transfers? This is an issue that extends beyond tribal commerce, and in the form of mail-order sales, long predates the Internet. The federal government passed a law in 1949 requiring tobacco sellers shipping to nondealers to keep track of names, addresses, and quantities shipped.[j] These records can then be used to send tax invoices to the purchasers. In the early 2000s, pressures on Internet sellers to maintain such records increased, and cigarette-buying residents of many states were shocked by receiving significant bills, sometimes in the thousands of dollars, for unpaid tobacco taxes from e-purchases made years previously. A smoker might well not have known that her web-based cigarette acquisitions had evaded legally required taxes.

The increased efforts to enforce taxes imposed on Internet tobacco sales by no means fully closed off access to tax-evading Internet sales, however, so states looked for complementary policies. Here, they could draw upon their previous efforts to repress interstate alcohol transfers and remote gambling by targeting vice intermediaries. Credit card companies and major shippers, consequently, have been persuaded not to lend their services to internet tobacco retailers.[k]

---

[a] The U.S. Constitution, Article I, Section 8, paragraph 3.

[b] On the Kahnawake Mohawk Reserve, see "Online Poker: Going All-in to Expose the Internet's Billion-Dollar Bet," by David Silverberg, DigitalJournal.com, May 5, 2006.

[c] Evans and Topoleski (2002) offer a helpful summary of the legal events that led to expanded Native American gambling.

[d] Information in this paragraph is drawn from Lester (2005).

[e] See Chapter 6 of the National Gambling Impact Study Commission Report (1999).

[f] This and subsequent claims about the impact of Native American casinos are from Evans and Topoleski (2002); see also Chapter 6 of the National Gambling Impact Study Commission Report (1999).

[g] *Moe v. Confederated Salish & Kootenai Tribes of the Flathead Reservation*, 425 U.S. 463 (1976); see the discussion in Frickey (2005, pp. 455–6).

[h] These are the terms of the agreement between Oklahoma and the Choctaw, Seminole, and Chickasaw nations.

[i] See, e.g., "County Files Suit to Force Tax Collection From Indians," *Newsday*, May 16, 2006.

[j] See Graff (2006, p. 382).   [k] Graff (2006, p. 387).

---

dispute is nearly identical to the intra-EU contention over remote gambling providers.

As in the Internet wine case, the WTO ruling need not undermine a state's overall policy on Internet horse race betting; it only requires a state's chosen policy to be evenhanded in application to in-state and out-of-state producers. In both instances, however, as well as in the EU, the preexisting discriminatory approach is defensible. Allowing (perhaps a handful) of in-state producers to operate under liberalized vice rules is a form of licensing – and restricting the number of licenses in an effort to reduce vice consumption is consistent with a robust policy approach. Perhaps it is best if the licensing restriction is simply numeric, where in-state and out-of-state producers can bid on an even footing for the limited number of licenses. But allowing free-trade commitments to overturn an existing implicit, geographically based licensing regime presents the possibility that, in the short run, there will be no effective constraint on the granting of licenses. Any resulting increase in vice-related problems could provoke a vice prohibition, or a step back from free trade, as opposed to paving the way for the implementation of a theoretically pure, evenhanded but numerically restricted, licensing system.

GLOBAL GOVERNANCE: THE UNITED NATIONS DRUG CONVENTIONS[20]

In 1961, following precedents that stretched back to the League of Nations, the United Nations adopted the Single Convention on Narcotic Drugs to help coordinate international actions against drug abuse. Adult recreational use of addictive drugs is not tolerated under the terms of the Single Convention: drug "use" and "possession" are listed alongside various manufacturing and commercial activities that require criminalization.[21] Simultaneously, protections are offered for drug use intended for medical and scientific purposes. The UN's International Narcotics Control Board (INCB) oversees the production and distribution of the legal component of the trade, those (otherwise illegal) drugs that are designated for legitimate scientific and medical uses.

The Single Convention sets up a system of "scheduling" of drugs, where the requisite control regime is stricter for drugs placed in the more problematic schedules. Many nations around the world, including the United States and the United Kingdom, have adopted a similar scheduling apparatus. One feature of this approach is that drugs can be scheduled without new legislation being passed. In the case of the UN's Single Convention, a recommendation by the World Health Organization can be the initial basis for adding a drug to the internationally controlled list – a list that now includes more than 110 drugs.[22]

The Single Convention was amended in 1971, in part to allow signatory countries to employ treatment programs in place of criminal penalties for drug users. The toleration of cannabis use and small sales in the Netherlands is technically in compliance with the Single Convention: the Netherlands criminalizes possession and sale of cannabis, as is necessitated, but it chooses not to enforce those laws. The Single Convention does not address the extent of enforcement required for rules criminalizing possession or sale.

Two other UN conventions are aimed directly at illegal drugs. The 1971 Convention on Psychotropic Substances extends international controls to

---

[20] The text of the conventions can be found at www.unodc.org/unodc/es/drug_and_crime_conventions. html.

[21] See Article 4c of the Single Convention on Narcotic Drugs, 1961, United Nations. Available at http://www.incb.org/pdf/e/conv/convention_1961_en.pdf (accessed November 26, 2006). Traditional drug uses, such as coca leaf chewing in the Andes, were to be eliminated within twenty-five years of the convention coming into force; see Article 49.

[22] The current list of internationally controlled drugs can be found at http://www.incb.org/pdf/ e/list/46thedition.pdf (accessed November 26, 2006).

hallucinogens such as LSD. The 1988 Convention against the Illicit Traffic in Narcotic Drugs and Psychotropic Substances provides ammunition against drug traffickers by requiring anti–money laundering efforts, asset forfeiture, control of precursor chemicals, and extradition of alleged drug commerce offenders; it also reiterates the necessity of criminalization of drug possession (the language in the Single Convention on this point being somewhat ambiguous). Each of the conventions has been adopted on a global scale, by more than 175 parties, with the INCB overseeing implementation. Certain provisions in the conventions conflict with constitutional rights guaranteed in some signatory nations. For instance, the 1988 convention seeks to criminalize incitement to use drugs, which would constitute an infringement on free-speech rights guaranteed by the First Amendment to the U.S. Constitution. Anticipating such potential conflicts, the conventions frequently employ language indicating that their terms apply only to the extent that they are consistent with national constitutional principles and legal norms. The international conventions establish minimum antidrug regimes. Nations can enact even more restrictive drug policies if they choose.

The international drug control regime organized around the UN conventions, to the extent that it criminalizes drug possession, clearly violates the robustness precept. Further, it tends to promote a prohibitionist standpoint, even embracing the chimera of eradication of recreational drug use. In 1998, the UN's General Assembly committed itself to "eliminating or reducing significantly the illicit cultivation of the coca bush, the cannabis plant and the opium poppy by the year 2008," under their special session rubric: "A drug free world – We can do it."[23] The very name of one of the main UN departments charged with drug issues, the Office on Drugs and Crime, indicates the depth of the commitment to prohibition. There is no UN Office on Alcohol and Crime, or Tobacco and Crime.

The INCB repeatedly has taken a harsh prohibitionist stance, even in areas outside its formal authority. Swiss heroin maintenance experiments, Dutch cannabis policy, Australian safe injection rooms, Canadian medical marijuana – all have attracted opposition from the INCB.[24] An unlikely coalition of countries generally presses for maintaining a strict approach to the international drug control regime; the hardliners include the United States, Sweden, Japan, Arab nations, and nations of the former Soviet Union.[25]

Countries experimenting with liberalized drug policies generally can do so without directly contravening their international commitments. First, the Dutch option is available, in which criminalization statutes remain on the books but

[23] From the General Assembly's Political Declaration S-20/2, available at www.unodc.org/unodc/en/resolution_1998-06-10_1.html (accessed on July 3, 2006); see also http://www.drugpolicy.org/global/ungass/ (accessed November 24, 2006).

[24] See MacCoun and Reuter (2001, pp. 248, 293–4), and Fazey (2003, p. 167).

[25] Fazey (2003, p. 160).

their enforcement is neglected. (Toleration of cultivation of "the opium poppy, the coca bush or the cannabis plant" probably would violate Article 22 of the Single Convention, however.) Second, any use of drugs that plausibly can be described as medical, as in heroin maintenance, is not ruled out by the UN conventions.[26] Nevertheless, sufficiently liberal drug regulations would be at least arguably inconsistent with the current international system and are surely inconsistent with its prohibitionist flavor. Full legalization, even of cannabis, will require either reformation or disregard of the UN agreements – a path that robustness recommends, too.

WHY VICE SHOULD WIN . . . AND WHY THE VICTORY MUST BE LIMITED

The fact that alcohol, tobacco, gambling, drugs, and other traditional vices have been problematic for hundreds of years is strong evidence that these are not ordinary commodities. Any standard liberal policy orientation, whether toward free trade, free speech (advertising), or free competition (antitrust), comes under significant pressure when faced with these troubling habit-forming goods. To insist on one-size-fits-all policies, applicable to ketchup and alcohol alike, is apt to produce outcomes that are sufficiently undesirable that liberalism in general might be discredited, or motivate a policy shift to strikingly illiberal policies (such as prohibition) targeted specifically at the vicious goods or activities. Vice should operate as an exception – a limited exception, but a clear one – from many of our more general policy doctrines. So federal rules, such as those in the United States and the EU, should not necessitate that all localities adhere to standard commitments to free trade, free commercial speech, and free competition, in the case of vice goods. The laudable ends that generally are served by those commitments to freedom are not similarly served in their application to vice.

Recall that in *44 Liquormart, Inc., v. Rhode Island* (1996), the majority opinion of the U.S. Supreme Court warned against vice exceptionalism. Permitting a vice exception to free speech, the court noted, might allow "state legislatures to justify censorship by the simple expedient of placing the 'vice' label on selected lawful activities. . . ."[27] Given the variety of activities that have been banned over the years due to their supposed viciousness, this warning is well taken. But previous overreach is no reason not to recognize what centuries of experience have taught, that the traditional vices are particularly troublesome: so troublesome that they justify some retreat from our usual devotion to free speech, free competition, and free speech. The failure to take such a strategic retreat would likely end up curtailing more freedom, by making the

[26] Fazey (2003, p. 161).   [27] 517 U.S. 484 (1996).

vice good illegal. The Supreme Court was suggesting as much: the justices were not condemning vice exceptionalism but only vice exceptionalism for "lawful activities." In practice, the question often will amount to whether the exception is made by banning the vice good (and its advertising and trade, of course) or by allowing the vice while controlling competition, trade, and advertising.

Vice policy exceptionalism is all but inevitable. The only issue is what form it will take. Robustness argues that vice should be a differently treated legal activity, while prohibitionists prefer to make vice exceptional via illegality. Assume that the robustness approach wins out. Can we be certain that the vice exception won't be extended to all goods and services that meet with official displeasure, hollowing out overall commitments to free speech, trade, and competition? No. The robustness principle still leaves us vulnerable to such an unfortunate turn of events – but it mitigates the associated damages. As long as governments abide by robustness in regulating vicious goods, the costs that they can impose by expanding the scope of proclaimed vice will be limited. Advertising of a supposed vice might be banned, but the activity itself cannot be banned, nor can private (noncommercial) speech that encourages vice participation. Poor vice policy will still be poor policy, but robustness rules out the worst policies: it is a sort of harm reduction measure against overreaching legislation. The same cannot be said for vice exceptionalism in the form of prohibition.

Within a federal system, then, the center's role should be to insist upon robustness, whether the "center" is taken to be a national government or the international community in the form of UN conventions. Given this constraint, individual states and localities can and should be encouraged to choose their own policies, with an additional federal mandate being to limit the extent that one locality's policies can undermine those of a neighbor.[28] Local vice policies legitimately could depart from standard commitments to free commercial speech, free competition, or free trade. Such departures might be a welcome feature. It's hard to know – and the fact that it is hard to know is more reason for the center to insist only upon robust policy regimes and not upon any specific element of vice regulation. Perhaps policy experiments over the years will eventually reveal that certain vice policies generally dominate others, even if "optimal" control regimes are time and place specific. If so, these proven successes need not be federally mandated, as informed localities can judge such policy dominance for themselves and respond appropriately. The desirability of encouraging vice policy experiments suggests one final federal role:

---

[28] It might not be possible to protect low-tax jurisdictions from high-tax neighbors within a free-trade area; in that case, the federal role might include forging some compromise, perhaps in the form of a minimum tax mandate or the imposition of a federal tax.

serving as a collector and clearinghouse for information over the experiences of various states and localities in regulating vice.

VICE VERDICTS VI: MEDICAL MARIJUANA

Gonzales v. Raich (2005)[29]

The federal government in the United States prohibits the possession of marijuana. Marijuana is classified as a so-called Schedule 1 drug, meaning that it has a high potential for abuse and no accepted medical use. This classification is itself quite suspect, as marijuana seems to relieve medical symptoms for a variety of ailments, including the nausea associated with chemotherapy, and marijuana is part of the legal pharmacopeia in other countries.[30] Further, from the mid-1970s through the early 1990s, U.S. federal authorities provided medicinal marijuana to a handful of approved patients. (The program was then terminated, though some of the original participants to this day receive legal pot from the federal government.)

Some states agree with the previous position of the federal government and have legalized, to the extent that they can, medical marijuana. The extent to which a state can legalize medical marijuana in the face of a national ban presents an ongoing federalism dilemma. Can a person who has a marijuana prescription endorsed by her state of residence be prosecuted by federal authorities for marijuana possession? The answer that the Supreme Court gave to this question in 2005, by a 6-3 margin, was "yes."

The Constitution's commerce clause once again provides the framework for the case. The federal government lacks the power to ban marijuana directly, so it has chosen to institute its ban through the guise of regulating interstate commerce. (Earlier federal controls on drugs were based on the taxation authority, but now they reside within the interstate commerce domain.) The main respondents in *Gonzales v. Raich* are two California women who also are longtime users of physician-recommended medical marijuana. They ingest locally cultivated marijuana, neither commercially traded nor transported across state borders. The patients contend, therefore, that the U.S. Congress's commerce clause power does not extend to prohibiting possession of their noncommercial, noninterstate marijuana. Following a 1942 case concerned with acreage restrictions on wheat and on-farm consumption, the *Gonzales v. Raich* Court reiterates that "Congress can regulate purely intrastate activity that is not itself 'commercial,' in that it is not produced for sale, if it concludes that failure to regulate that class of activity would undercut the regulation of the interstate market in that commodity."[31]

---

[29] 545 U.S. 1 (2005).
[30] See e.g., Shapiro (2001) and Joy, Watson, and Benson (1999).
[31] Opinion of the court, *Gonzales v. Raich* (2005).

So the medical marijuana patients can only procure their medicine at the peril of prison. Justice Clarence Thomas begins his dissent forcefully:

> Respondents Diane Monson and Angel Raich use marijuana that has never been bought or sold, that has never crossed state lines, and that has no demonstrable effect on the national market for marijuana. If Congress can regulate this under the Commerce Clause, then it can regulate virtually anything – and the Federal Government is no longer one of limited and enumerated powers.[32]

The majority opinion suggests an alternative for Ms. Monson and Ms. Raich through "the democratic process, in which the voices of voters allied with these respondents may one day be heard in the halls of Congress." That California voters (and residents of many other states) already side with the respondents in making medical marijuana legally obtainable is currently of no avail at the federal level.

---

[32] Justice Thomas, dissenting, *Gonzales v. Raich* (2005).

Conclusions

Dost thou think because thou art virtuous, there shall be no more cakes and ale?
– Shakespeare, *Twelfth Night*

A ROBUST APPROACH TO A NEW VICE

Imagine that a new vice were to descend upon us. Maybe it is an innovative drug, a sexual practice, a form of wagering, or some exotic combination that targets all of our vulnerabilities simultaneously. OK, let's make it a drug. Call it "Cake."[1] Cake consumption is a thoroughgoing (though imaginary) vice, one that people find quite pleasurable. Along with the delights of Cake come the usual $3\frac{1}{3}$ standard vice concerns of kids, addicts, externalities, and harms to nonaddicted adult users.

What sort of regulatory structure should be applied to Cake? The preceding chapters have argued that we should use the robustness principle as our guide toward appropriate vice policy and hence toward Cake control. The robustness principle states that a vice regulatory regime should work well irrespective of the precise extent of rationality or addiction reflected in vicious decision making. Policies that offer assistance to addicts or to those confronting self-management shortcomings can be (perhaps must be) part of a robust package, as long as such policies do not impose too profoundly upon rational adult consumers. Application of the robustness criterion is not automatic, as it requires judgments about, for instance, the extent to which adult decisions can be constrained in the interests of protecting children, and at what point a control becomes too burdensome upon rational adult vice participants.

Nevertheless, the general guideposts toward robust regulatory regimes developed in Chapter 3 will apply to Cake. There must be legal means available for adults to consume Cake, even for recreational purposes: adults can have their Cake and eat it, too. But those legal channels of availability can be

---

[1] In the late 1990s, the British comic Chris Morris, on the television show *Brass Eye*, asked British politicians and celebrities if they would comment on the epidemic of the new (and imaginary) East European drug "Cake." Morris managed to convince several of them, on camera, to condemn this terrible new drug, and a question was raised in Parliament concerning Cake. See http://en.wikipedia.org/wiki/Brass_Eye (accessed February 9, 2007). The *Brass Eye* "Cake" episode television clips are available on YouTube at http://youtube.com/watch?v=goGxUxKZdHk (accessed February 9, 2007).

quite constrained. Cake consumers and sellers might be required to acquire licenses, to agree to quantity limits, to arrange purchases in advance, and to pay significant Cake taxes. Public Cake use can be forbidden, advertising can be controlled or eliminated, warnings disseminated, and transfer of Cake to children can be prohibited.

More information about the potential benefits and harms of Cake is required to move beyond the general guideposts, to determine the desirability of specific regulations. Perhaps Cake is as wholesome and safe as, say, ballroom dancing. Or maybe Cake is more like crack cocaine. A vice with the characteristics of crack merits stronger regulation than one with the characteristics of ballroom dancing.[2] As Cake is a new vice, there might not be much reliable information about the consequences, particularly the long-term consequences, of Cake use. There will be even less information available about how those consequences will vary with alternative regulatory structures.

The usual temporal profile of recreational drugs, where current pleasure is paired with future pain, tends to impart a positive bias to the reputation of new drugs. When drugs are new, there are no long-term consumers who already are paying those eventual costs; simultaneously, there are many novice consumers who are enjoying themselves but who have yet to foot the bill. A sample of drug users, then, will give an overly optimistic picture of the qualities of a newly introduced drug.[3] Further, the rapid introduction of a new vice into societies with no previous experiences with the vice in question often has led to enormous upheaval; distilled alcohol has been a recurrent example. So the novelty of Cake suggests a conservative implementation of a robust regulatory regime at first, one that aims to dissuade or slow down Cake use. What information that is available about Cake can be disseminated, along with warnings of the typically overly optimistic perceptions of new drugs. Further research on the health consequences and addictive potential of Cake can be procured as part of the robust control strategy. A gradual familiarization with Cake also would provide scope for informal social controls to develop – controls that might be decisive in limiting the negative consequences of Cake. Finally, different jurisdictions could choose different robust regimes toward Cake, and these policy experiments would allow for successful policies to be mimicked, and unsuccessful policies jettisoned, as experience grows.

A ROBUST CONCLUSION

Cake consumption was stipulated to be a vice but given that Cake is new, how would we be certain of its vicious character? More generally, even if the

---

[2] A quick search on the web reveals that injuries related to ballroom dancing are common and that many people refer to their interest in ballroom dancing as an addiction; see, for example, www.ballroomdangers.com.

[3] Kleiman (1992, p. 43) and Courtwright (2001, p. 83).

robustness principle is accepted as a guide to vice control, there still remains the question considered in the Introduction: what qualifies as a vice? No doubt there would be substantial agreement that the traditional trouble spots would be widely regarded as potentially vicious: alcohol, tobacco, opiates, cocaine, wagering, prostitution, and pornography. Newer drugs that spark costly dependencies in many users, such as methamphetamine, also would qualify, but who is to judge about completely innovative and unfamiliar pleasures such as Cake? Nor is novelty the only dimension that complicates the attribution of vice. The consumption of substances such as fatty foods, participation in activities such as video gaming or helmetless motorcycle riding – these, too, are difficult to categorize. Are these self-regarding behaviors vicious, and hence potentially best controlled with robust regulatory regimes?

Properties to look for in delineating viciousness include the propensity toward costly compulsive behavior and the fostering of intemperance even among the nonaddicted. (These properties are not fully inherent in a good or activity, of course. Among other things, they depend upon the regulatory regime, the social setting, and individual inclinations.) The lure to intemperance perhaps can best be gauged by the extent to which individuals themselves seek out self-control devices. For instance, do people often adopt rules along the lines of "keep no ice cream (or Cake) in the house" or "limit internet surfing to two hours per day"? Under this approach, fatty foods qualify for the vice label. Not only do many people choose to limit their access to potato chips or ice cream, some obese individuals adopt radical commitment devices such as stomach reduction operations.

Sugar easily could be regarded as an addictive drug.[4] Our evolutionary past featured a struggle for adequate nutrition; we therefore developed a taste (favorable for reproduction) for high-calorie (but often unavailable) foods containing sugar or fat. Fortunately, most of the world has moved to a calorie-rich environment. While this development has been an enormous boon to people in general, it does present enhanced dangers that the taste for high-calorie products that served us so well in the past now leads to overconsumption. Abundant refined sugar, like cocaine and morphine, satisfies the condition in the definition of addiction provided by Jon Elster: "addiction results when the reward system of the brain is hijacked by chemical substances that played no role in its evolution."[5] So special policies concerning information disclosure, marketing restrictions, and taxes are defensible and consistent with robustness in the case of sugary or fatty foods.

---

[4] Further, sugar has been important in spreading the use of other drugs, including alcohol, tobacco, and caffeine. See Courtwright (2001, pp. 27–30).

[5] Elster (1999c, p. 53). Sugar presumably did play a role in the evolution of the brain's reward system, but that role was premised on a sugar-scarce environment.

Once again, defensible does not imply desirable, however. The prospect of thousands of product-specific food taxes finely tuned to caloric or fat content smacks of extreme social engineering — even ketchup might not be exempt! But encouraging jurisdictions to decide these matters for themselves, within the bounds of robustness, is the best way to determine the policies that are most and least appropriate.[6]

As for motorcycle helmets and other safety measures, the addiction markers for vice generally do not apply.[7] People might enjoy riding a motorcycle without a helmet, but rarely or never would this preference be characterized as an addiction. Self-control devices, such as a personal rule that requires helmet wearing or storing the helmet on the bike, might be applied in this realm, however. Nevertheless, it would probably stretch the notion of vice too far to include helmetless motorcycle riding within the category of vicious behaviors. But again, going a "vice too far" is not that costly an error if the robustness principle is respected. Moderate encouragement to helmet wearing would then be acceptable. Perhaps those who wanted to ride without a helmet would have to pay a slightly higher license fee. The fee differential could not be substantial, however, in a robust regime, as it might be a perfectly informed and rational decision to ride a bike without a helmet. Robustness limits the damage from both ill-advised vice policies and expansive demarcations of vice: that is its chief virtue.

[6] See Chapter 8.
[7] On motorcycles, drugs, and consumer protection laws, see Bakalar and Grinspoon (1984, pp. 17f).

Appendix: A Few Vice-Related Statistics

Table A.1: *Estimated totals of top 7 arrest offenses, plus gambling and prostitution arrests, United States, 2005*

Type of arrest	Number of arrests
Total arrests	14,094,186
Drug abuse violations	1,846,351
Driving under the influence	1,371,919
Simple assaults	1,301,392
Larceny/theft	1,146,696
Disorderly conduct	678,231
Liquor laws	597,838
Drunkenness	556,167
Prostitution and commercialized vice	84,891
Gambling	11,180

Note: Many or most of the disorderly conduct arrests are alcohol related, too, leaving alcohol and drugs as the impetus for five of the top seven arrest categories.

Source: FBI, *Uniform Crime Reports*: *Crime in the United States 2005* http://www.fbi.gov/ucr/05cius/data/table_29.html.

Table A.2: *Number of arrests, by drug type, selected years, US 1982–2005*

	Heroin/cocaine	Marijuana	Synthetic drugs	Other
2005	557,600	786,500	88,600	411,700
2004	530,700	771,600	89,000	356,100
2003	508,500	755,200	77,200	339,000
2002	463,200	697,100	67,700	307,800
2001	520,500	723,600	65,100	277,700
1994	636,500	481,100	23,000	210,800
1990	591,600	326,900	22,900	148,200
1982	112,900	455,600	24,800	82,900

Note: In 2005, 81.7 percent of drug arrests were for possession; in the case of marijuana, over 88 percent of the 2005 arrests were for possession (as opposed to sale/manufacturing).

The 2005 figures do not add to the total reported in Table 1 due to rounding.

In combination, Germany, France, the United Kingdom, Italy, and Spain have a population about equal to that of the United States, approximately 300 million people. In 2003, the approximately 720,000 drug law offenses recorded in those five countries were less than half of the U.S. total; marijuana arrests in the United States exceeded all recorded drug offenses in those countries.

Sources: FBI, *Uniform Crime Reports: Crime in the United States*, annual, www.ojp.usdoj.gov/bjs/dcf/ tables/drugtype.htm, www.fbi.gov/ucr/05cius/arrests/index.html, and (for Europe) http://statso6.emcdda.europa.eu/en/elements/dlotabo1a-en.html.

Table A.3: *U.S. Drug Enforcement Agency drug seizures, selected years*

Calender Year	Cocaine (kg)	Heroin (kg)	Marijuana (kg)	Methamphetamine (kg)	Hallucinogens dosage units
2006	69,826	805	322,438	1,711	4,606,277
2005	118,311	640	283,344	2,161	8,881,321
2004	117,854	672	265,813	1,659	2,261,706
2003	73,725	795	254,196	1,678	2,878,594
2002	63,640	710	238,024	1,353	11,661,157
2001	59,430	753	271,849	1,634	13,755,390
1994	75,051	491	157,181	768	1,366,817
1990	57,031	535	127,792	272	2,826,966
1986	29,389	421	491,831	234.5	4,146,329

Source: DEA (STRIDE)
Drug Enforcement Agency Website, http://www.usdoj.gov/dea/statistics.html#arrests (February 20, 2007).

Table A.4: *Economic impact of major health problems, United States, circa 1998*

Type of problem	Annual cost (billions)	Prevalence (millions)	Annual cost per prevalent case (per person)
Pathology/problem gambling	$5	5.4	$900
Drug abuse	$110	6.7	$10,000
Alcohol abuse	$166	13.8	$7,000
Mental illness	$105	44	$2,300
Stroke	$30	3	$10,000
Heart disease	$125	21	$6,000
Diabetes	$92	15.5	$5,800
Motor vehicle crashes	$71	19	$3,600
Smoking	$72	46	$1,500

Source: Table 20, Report to the National Gambling Impact Study Commission, http://www.norc. uchicago.edu/new/pdf/3.pdf (1999).

Table A.5: *U.S. gross gaming revenue*

Year	Total Commercial Casino	Total gaming
1995	$16.0	$45.1
1996	$17.1	$47.9
1997	$18.2	$50.9
1998	$19.7	$54.9
1999	22.2	$58.2
2000	24.3[a]	$61.4
2001	$25.7[a]	$63.3
2002	$26.5[a]	$68.7
2003	$27.02[a]	$72.87
2004	$28.93	$78.6
2005	$30.29	Pending

Note: All amounts in billions.

[a] Amount does not include deepwater cruise ships, cruises-to-nowhere, or noncasino devises.

Sources: American Gaming Association, Christiansen Capital Advisors LLC.

This table is taken verbatim from the American Gaming Association website, at www.americangaming.org/Industry/factsheets/statistics_detail.cfv?id=8 (accessed February 27, 2007). Gross gaming revenue is the net take of the provider from gambling, that is, the amount wagered minus the winnings of customers. Total gaming "includes pari-mutuel wagering, lotteries, casinos, legal bookmaking, charitable gaming and bingo, Indian reservations and card rooms."

Table A.6: *Types of illicit drug use in lifetime and past year, among persons aged 12 or older: percentages, United States, 2004*

	Lifetime	Past year
Illicit drug[a]	45.8	14.5
Marijuana and hashish	40.2	10.6
Cocaine	14.2	2.4
Crack	3.3	0.5
Heroin	1.3	0.2
Hallucinogens	14.3	1.6
Inhalants	9.5	0.9
Nonmedical use of psycotherapeutics[b]	20.0	6.1
Pain relievers	13.2	4.7
Tranquilizers	8.3	2.1
Stimulants	8.3	1.2
Methamphetamine	4.9	0.6
Sedatives	4.1	0.3
Illicit drug other than marijuana	29.4	8.2

[a] "Illicit drug" includes marijuana/hashish, cocaine (including crack), heroin, hallucinogens, inhalants, or prescription-type psychotherapeutics used nonmedically. "Illicit drugs other than marijuana" includes cocaine (including crack), heroin, hallucinogens, inhalants, or prescription-type psychotherapeutics used nonmedically.

[b] Nonmedical use of prescription-type pain relievers, tranquilizers, stimulants, or sedatives; does not include over-the-counter drugs.

Source: Substance Abuse and Mental Health Services Administration (2005); www.oas.samhsa.gov/NSDUH/2k4nsduh/2k4tabs/Sect1peTabs1to66.htm#tab1.1b

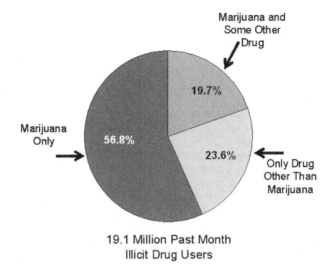

**19.1 Million Past Month
Illicit Drug Users**

Figure A.1. Types of drugs used by past month illicit drug users aged 12 or older: 2004

- Among persons aged 12 or older, the overall rate of past month marijuana use was about the same in 2004 (6.1 percent) as it was in 2003 (6.2 percent) and 2002 (6.2 percent).
- In 2004, an estimated 2.0 million persons (0.8 percent) were current cocaine users; of these, 467,000 used crack during the same time period (0.2 percent). Hallucinogens were used by 929,000 persons (0.4 percent). There were an estimated 166,000 current heroin users (0.1 percent). All of these estimates are similar to estimates for 2003.

Source: The figure and text above are taken from Figure 2.1 in Substance Abuse and Mental Health Services Administration (2005); www.oas.samhsa.gov/nsduh/2k4nsduh/2k4results/2k4Results.htm#fig2.1.

Table A.7: *Tobacco product and alcohol use in lifetime and past year, among persons aged 12 or older: percentages, United States, 2004*

	Lifetime	Past Year
Tobacco product[a]	71.4	34.5
Cigarettes	67.3	29.1
Smokeless tobacco	18.6	4.1
Cigars	36.3	10.8
Pipe tobacco	16.4	N/A
Alcohol	82.4	65.1

[a] Tobacco products include cigarettes, smokeless tobacco (i.e., chewing tobacco or snuff), cigars, or pipe tobacco. Tobacco product use in the past year excludes past year pipe tobacco use but includes past month pipe tobacco use.

Source: Substance Abuse and Mental Health Services Administration (2005); www.oas.samhsa.gov/NSDUH/2k4nsduh/2k4tabs/Sect2peTabs1to57.htm#tab2.1b

Table A.8: *Received substance use treatment in the past
year, 12 and older, United States, 2004*

Illicit drug[a]	2,192,000
Alcohol	2,658,000
Both illicit drug and alcohol	1,467,000
Illicit drug or alcohol[b]	3,791,000

Note: "Received Substance Use Treatment" refers to treatment
received to reduce or stop illicit drug or alcohol use, or for medical
problems associated with illicit drug or alcohol use. It includes
treatment received at any location, such as a hospital, a rehabilitation
facility (inpatient or outpatient), mental health center, emergency
room, private doctor's office, self-help group, or prison/jail.
[a] "Illicit drug" include marijuana/hashish, cocaine (including crack),
    heroin, hallucinogens, inhalants, or prescription-type
    psychotherapeutics used nonmedically.
[b] Estimates include persons who received treatment specifically for
    illicit drugs or alcohol, as well as persons who received treatment but
    did not specify for what substance(s).
Source: Substance Abuse and Mental Health Services Administration
(2005); www.oas.samhsa.gov/NSDUH/2k4nsduh/2k4tabs/
Sect5peTabs1to99.htm#tab5.38a.

Table A.9: *U.S. federal excise tax
collections, fiscal year 2006, approximate*

Total alcohol	$9.18 billion
Distilled spirits	$4.63 billion
Wine	$0.83 billion
Beer	$3.71 billion
Tobacco	$7.70 billion

Source: Alcohol and Tobacco Tax and Trade Bureau,
Statistical Release, Fourth Quarter 2006, available at
www.ttb.gov/tax_audit/tax_collections.shtml.

References

Aaron, Paul, and David Musto. "Temperance and Prohibition in America: A Historical Overview." In Mark H. Moore and Dean R. Gerstein, eds., *Alcohol and Public Policy: Beyond the Shadow of Prohibition*. Washington, DC: National Academy Press, 1981.

Abbott, Sharon A. "Motivations for Pursuing an Acting Career in Pornography." Chapter 2, pp. 17–34, in Ronald Weitzer, ed., *Sex For Sale: Prostitution, Pornography, and the Sex Industry*. New York: Routledge, 2000.

Ade, George. *The Old-Time Saloon*. New York: Ray Long and Richard R. Smith, 1931.

Adler, Amy. "Girls! Girls! Girls!: The Supreme Court Confronts the G-String." New York University School of Law, Public Law and Legal Theory Research Paper Series, Working Paper No. 06-01, January 2006.

Agostinelli, Gina, and Joel W. Grube. "Alcohol Counter-advertising and the Media." National Institute on Alcohol Abuse and Alcoholism, Bethesda, Maryland, August 2002.

Ainslie, George. "The Intuitive Explanation of Passionate Mistakes and Why It's Not Adequate." In Jon Elster, ed., *Addiction: Entries and Exits*. New York: Russell Sage Foundation, 1999.

Ainslie, George. *Picoeconomics: The Strategic Interaction of Successive Motivational States Within the Person*. Cambridge: Cambridge University Press, 1992.

Albert, Alexa. *Brothel. Mustang Ranch and Its Women*. New York: Random House, 2001.

Alston, Lee J., Ruth Dupré, and Tomas Nonnenmacher. "Social Reformers and Regulation: The Prohibition of Cigarettes in the United States and Canada." *Explorations in Economic History* 39: 425–445, 2002.

Anastasio, Michael. "The Enforceability of Internet Gambling Debts: Laws, Policies, and Causes of Action." *Virginia Journal of Law and Technology* 6, Spring 2001. Available at www.vjolt.net/vol6/issue1/v6i1a06-Anastasio.html.

Anderson, Peter, and Ben Baumberg. "Alcohol in Europe – A Public Health Perspective." Report for the European Commission, Institute of Alcohol Studies, UK, June 2006.

Aristotle. *Nicomachean Ethics*. In *The Works of Aristotle*, Great Books of the Western World. Chicago: Encyclopedia Britannica, Inc., 1952.

Australia's Gambling Industries. Final Report, Summary. Productivity Commission, Report No. 10, November 26, 1999. Available at www.pc.gov.au/inquiry/gambling/finalreport/summary.pdf.

Babor, Thomas, Raul Caetano, Sally Casswell, et al. *Alcohol: No Ordinary Commodity*. Oxford: Oxford University Press, 2003.

Bakalar, James B., and Lester Grinspoon. *Drug Control in a Free Society*. Cambridge: Cambridge University Press, 1984.

Baldino, Rachel Green. *Welcome to Methadonia: A Social Worker's Candid Account of Life in a Methadone Clinic*. Harrisburg, PA: White Hat Communications, 2000.

Bardach, E. "Social Regulation as a Generic Policy Instrument." In L. M. Salamon and M. S. Lund, eds., *Beyond Privatization: The Tools of Government Action*. Washington, DC: Urban Institute Press, 1989.

Barker, John Marshall. *The Saloon Problem and Social Reform*. Boston: Everett Press, 1905.

Barnett, Randy E. "Bad Trip: Drug Prohibition and the Weakness of Public Policy." *Yale Law Journal* 103: 2593–2630, 1994.

Barnett, Randy E. "Curing the Drug-Law Addiction." In Ronald Hamowy, ed., *Dealing with Drugs: Consequences of Government Control*. Lexington, MA: Lexington Books, 1987.

Barr, Andrew. *Drink: A Social History of America*. New York: Carroll & Graf, 1999.

Bartlett, Katharine T. "Porno-Symbolism: A Response to Professor McConahay." *Law and Contemporary Problems* 51: 71–77, Winter 1988.

Barton, Bernadette. *Stripped: Inside the Lives of Exotic Dancers*. New York: New York University Press, 2006.

Baum, Dan. "Jake Leg." *The New Yorker*, September 15, 2003.

Becker, Gary S., Michael Grossman, and Kevin M. Murphy. "The Economic Theory of Illegal Goods: The Case of Drugs." National Bureau of Economic Research Working Paper No. 10976, December 2004.

———. "Rational Addiction and the Effect of Price on Consumption." *AEA Papers and Proceedings* 81: 237–241, 1991.

Becker, Gary S., and Casey B. Mulligan. "The Endogenous Determination of Time Preference." *Quarterly Journal of Economics* 112 (3): 729–758, August 1997.

Becker, Gary S., and Kevin M. Murphy. "A Theory of Rational Addiction." *Journal of Political Economy* 96: 675–700, 1988.

Beeching, Jack. *The Chinese Opium Wars*. New York: Harcourt Brace Jovanovich, 1975.

Behr, Edward. *Prohibition. The 13 Years That Changed America*. London: BBC Books, 1997.

Bell, Tom W. "Internet Gambling. Popular, Inexorable, and (Eventually) Legal." *Policy Analysis*, No. 336, March 8, 1999.

———. "Internet Gambling: Prohibition v. Legalization." Testimony before the National Gambling Impact Study Commission, Chicago, May 21, 1998. Available at www.cato.org/testimony/ct-tb052198.html.

Benkler, Yochai. "Net Regulation: Taking Stock and Looking Forward." *Colorado Law Review* 71: 1203–1261, 2000.

Bennett, William. "Should Drugs Be Legalized?" *Reader's Digest*, March 1990. Reprinted in Schaler (1998, pp. 63–7).

Berman, Mitchell N. "Commercial Speech and the Unconstitutional Conditions Doctrine: A Second Look at 'The Greater Includes the Lesser.'" *Vanderbilt Law Review* 55 (3): 693–796, April 2002.

Bernheim, B. Douglas, and Antonio Rangel. "Addiction and Cue-Conditioned Cognitive Processes." *American Economic Review* 94 (5): 1558–1590, December 2004.

Bingham, Nicole. "Nevada Sex Trade: A Gamble for the Workers." *Yale Journal of Law and Feminism* 10: 69–99, 1998.

Bird, Robert C. "An Examination of the Training and Reliability of the Narcotics Detection Dog." *Kentucky Law Journal* 85: 405–433, Winter 1996/1997.

Blum, Kenneth, John G. Cull, Eric R. Braverman, and David E. Comings. "Reward Deficiency Syndrome." *American Scientist*, March–April 1996.

Blumenson, Eric, and Eva Nilsen. "Policing for Profit: The Drug War's Hidden Economic Agenda." *University of Chicago Law Review* 65: 35–114, Winter 1998.

Bogus, Carl T. "Gun Litigation and Societal Values." *Connecticut Law Review* 32: 1353–1378, Summer 2000.

Bonnie, Richard J. "Addiction and Responsibility." *Social Research* 68 (3): 813–834, Fall 2001.

Boyum, David. "The Distributive Politics of Drug Policy." *Drug Policy Analysis Bulletin*, No. 4, February 1998. Available at www.fas.org/drugs/issue4.htm#politics.

Boyum, David, and Peter Reuter. *An Analytic Assessment of U.S. Drug Policy*. Washington, DC: AEI Press, 2005.

Braun, Norman, and Paolo Vanini. "On Habits and Addictions." *Journal of Institutional and Theoretical Economics* 159 (4): 603–626, 2003.

Bruning, Kevin R. "Note: Nudity and Alcohol: Morality Lies in Public Discussion." *Stetson Law Review* 29: 775–810, Winter 2000.

Camerer, Colin, Samuel Issacharoff, George Loewenstein, Ted O'Donoghue, and Matthew Rabin. "Regulation for Conservatives: Behavioral Economics and the Case for 'Asymmetric Paternalism.'" *University of Pennsylvania Law Review*, June 2003.

Carnes, Patrick. *Out of the Shadows. Understanding Sexual Addiction*, third edition. Center City, MN: Hazelden, 2001.

Carnwath, Tom, and Ian Smith. *Heroin Century*. London: Routledge, 2002.

Carter, Derrick Augustus. "Bifurcations of Consciousness: The Elimination of the Self-induced Intoxication Excuse." *Missouri Law Review* 64: 383–436, Spring 1999.

Caulkins, Jonathan P. "Zero-Tolerance Policies: Do They Inhibit or Stimulate Illicit Drug Consumption?" *Management Science* 39: 458–476, 1993.

Centers for Disease Control and Prevention. "Trends in Reportable Sexually Transmitted Diseases in the United States, 2004," November 2005.

Centers for Disease Control and Prevention. "HIV Transmission in the Adult Film Industry – Los Angeles, California, 2004." *Morbidity and Mortality Weekly* 54 (37): 923–926, September 23, 2005.

Centers for Disease Control and Prevention. "STD Surveillance, 2004." Available at www.cdc.gov/std/stats04/toc2004.htm.

Chaloupka, F. J., T. W. Hu, K. F. Warner, R. Jacobs., A. Yurekli. "The Taxation of Tobacco Products." Chapter 10, pp. 238–72, in Prabhat Jha and Frank J. Chaloupka, eds., *Tobacco Control in Developing Countries*. Oxford: Oxford University Press, 2000.

Chaloupka, Frank J., Melanie Wakefield, and Christina Czart. "Taxing Tobacco: The Impact of Tobacco Taxes on Cigarette Smoking and Other Tobacco Use." Chapter 3, pp. 39–71, in Robert L. Rabin and Stephen D. Sugarman, eds., *Regulating Tobacco*. Oxford: Oxford University Press, 2001.

Chapkis, Wendy. "Soft Glove, Punishing Fist: The Trafficking Victims Protection Act of 2000." Chapter 4, pp. 51–66, in Elizabeth Bernstein and Laurie Schaffner, eds., *Regulating Sex: The Politics of Intimacy and Identity*. New York and London: Routledge, 2005.

Chesson, Harrell, Paul Harrison, and William J. Kassler. "Sex under the Influence: The Effect of Alcohol Policy on Sexually Transmitted Disease Rates in the U.S." *Journal of Law and Economics* 39 (1): 215–238, April 2000.

Cleland, John. *Memoirs of a Woman of Pleasure*. Peter Sabor, ed. Oxford: Oxford University Press, 1985 [1748/9].

Clements, K. W., W. Yang, and S. W. Zheng. "Is Utility Additive? The Case of Alcohol." *Applied Economics* 29 (9): 1163–1167, 1997.

Clotfelter, Charles T., and Philip J. Cook. *Selling Hope: State Lotteries in America*. Cambridge, MA: Harvard University Press, 1989.

Coetzee, J. M. *Giving Offense. Essays on Censorship*. Chicago: University of Chicago Press, 1996.

Conlin, Michael, Stacy Dickert-Conlin, and John Pepper. "The Effect of Alcohol Prohibition on Illicit Drug Related Crimes: An Unintended Consequence of Regulation." Mimeo, Syracuse University, 2001.

Cook, Philip J., and James A. Leitzel. "Perversity, Futility, Jeopardy: An Economic Analysis of the Attack on Gun Control." *Law and Contemporary Problems* 59: 91–118, Winter 1996.

Cook, Philip J., and Michael J. Moore. "The Economics of Alcohol Abuse and Alcohol-Control Policies." *Health Affairs* 21 (2): 120–133, 2002.

———. "Drinking and Schooling." *Journal of Health Economics* 12 (4): 411–429, 1993a.

———. "Economic Perspectives on Reducing Alcohol-Related Violence." In S. E. Martin, ed., *Alcohol and Interpersonal Violence: Fostering Multidisciplinary Prespectives*. National Institute on Alcohol Abuse and Alcoholism Research Monograph No. 24, NIH Publication Number 93-3496, Bethesda, MD, 1993b.

Cook, Philip J., and George Tauchen. "The Effect of Liquor Taxes on Heavy Drinking." *Bell Journal of Economics* 13 (2): 379–390, 1982.

Cooke, Jacqueline, and Melissa L. Sontag. "Prostitution." *Georgetown Journal of Gender and the Law* 6: 459–490, 2005.

Courtwright, David T. *Forces of Habit: Drugs and the Making of the Modern World*. Cambridge, MA: Harvard University Press, 2001.

———. "Should We Legalize Drugs? History Answers... No." *American Heritage*, February–March 1993. Reprinted in Schaler (1998, pp. 83–91).

———. *Dark Paradise: Opiate Addiction in America Before 1940*. Cambridge, MA: Harvard University Press, 1982.

Cowan, Richard. "How the Narcs Created Crack." *National Review*, December 5, 1986, pp. 30–1.

D'Amato, Anthony. "Porn Up, Rape Down." Northwestern Public Law Research Paper No. 913013, June 23, 2006. Available at http://ssrn.com/abstract = 913013.

Darrow, Clarence. *The Story of My Life*. New York: Charles Scribner's Sons, 1932 [1960].

Darrow, Clarence, and Victor S. Yarrows. *The Prohibition Mania*. New York: Boni and Liveright, 1927.

De Quincey, Thomas. *Confessions of an English Opium Eater*. Althea Hayter, ed. London: Penguin Books, 1986 [1821].

Derevensky, Jeffrey L., and Rina Gupta. "Youth Gambling: A Clinical and Research Perspective." *Egambling*, No. 2, August 2000. Available at www.camh.net/egambling/issue2/feature/.

Dershowitz, Alan M. *Rights from Wrongs: A Secular Theory of the Origin of Rights*. New York: Basic Books, 2004.

———. *The Abuse Excuse*. Boston: Little, Brown, 1994.

Dever, Vincent M. "Aquinas on the Practice of Prostitution." *Essays in Medieval Studies* 13: 39–50, 1996.

Diagnostic and Statistical Manual of Mental Disorders. fourth edition. Washington, DC: American Psychiatric Association, 1994.

Dispelling the Myths about Addiction: Strategies to Increase Understanding and Strengthen Research. Washington, DC: National Academy Press, 1997.

Doblin, Richard, and Mark A. R. Kleiman. "Marijuana as Antiemetic Medicine: A Survey of Oncologists' Experiences and Attitudes." *Journal of Clinical Oncology* 9: 1314–1319, 1991.

Doviak, Jenna, and Gina Scamby. "Casenote: Table Dancing around the First Amendment: The Constitutionality of Distance Requirements in *Colacurio v. City of Kent*." *Villanova Sports and Entertainment Law Journal* 7: 151–180, 2000.

Dowling, Nicki, David Smith, and Trang Thomas. "Electronic Gaming Machines: Are They the 'Crack-Cocaine' of Gambling?" *Addiction* 100: 33–45, 2005.

Dressler, Joshua. "Propter Honoris Respectum: Kent Greenawalt, Criminal Responsibility, and the Supreme Court: How a Moderate Scholar Can Appear Immoderate Thirty Years Later." *Notre Dame Law Review* 74: 1507–1532, June 1999.

Duffy, Michael J. "A Drug War Funded with Drug Money: The Federal Civil Forfeiture Statute and Federalism." *Suffolk University Law Review* 34: 511–540, 2001.

Duke, Steven. "The Drug War and the Constitution." In Timothy Lynch, ed., *After Prohibition: An Adult Approach to Drug Policies in the 21st Century*. Washington, DC: Cato Institute, 2000.

Dworkin, Gerald. *The Theory and Practice of Autonomy*. Cambridge: Cambridge University Press, 1988.

———. "Paternalism." In Richard A. Wasserstrom, ed., *Morality and the Law*. Belmont, CA: Wadsworth, 1971.

Eadington, William R. "The Economics of Casino Gambling." *Journal of Economic Perspectives* 13: 173–192, Summer 1999.

"The Economic Impact of Motor Vehicle Crashes 2000. Washington, DC: National Highway Traffic Safety Administration, May 2002.

Eggert, Kurt. "Truth in Gaming: Toward Consumer Protection in the Gambling Industry." *Maryland Law Review* 63: 217–286, 2004.

Eitmann, Nicole. "On Sadomasochism: Taxonomies and Language." *Carceral Notebooks* 2, 2006.

Elster, Jon. "Emotion and Addiction: Neurobiology, Culture, and Choice." In Jon Elster, ed., *Addiction: Entries and Exits*. New York: Russell Sage Foundation, 1999a.

———. "Introduction." In Jon Elster, ed., *Addiction: Entries and Exits*. New York: Russell Sage Foundation, 1999b.

———. *Strong Feelings*. Cambridge: MIT Press, 1999c.

Emmett, Gary A. "What Happened to the 'Crack Babies'?" FAS Drug Policy Analysis Bulletin, No. 4, February 1998. Available at http://fas.org/drugs/issue4.htm#babies (accessed May 29, 2004).

Evans, William N., and Julie H. Topoleski. "The Social and Economic Impact of Native American Casinos." National Bureau of Economic Research Working Paper No. 9198 September 2002.

FATF-XII. Report on Money Laundering Typologies 2000–2001. Financial Action Task Force on Money Laundering, February 1, 2001. Available from www.fatf-gafi.org/dataoecd/29/36/34038090.pdf.

Fazey, Cindy S. J. "The Commission on Narcotic Drugs and the United Nations International Drug Control Programme: Politics, Policies and Prospect for Change." *International Journal of Drug Policy* 14: 155–169, 2003.

Feinberg, Joel. *Harm to Self*. Vol. 3 of *The Moral Limits of the Criminal Law*. New York: Oxford University Press, 1986.

Fingarette, Herbert. *Heavy Drinking. The Myth of Alcoholism as a Disease*. Berkeley: University of California Press, 1988.

Fischer, Irving. *Prohibition at Its Worst*. New York: Macmillan, 1926.

Fleenor, Patrick. "Cigarette Taxes, Black Markets, and Crime: Lessons From New York's 50-Year Losing Battle." *Policy Analysis*, No. 468, February 6, 2003.

Frese, Megan E. "Rolling the Dice: Are Online Gambling Advertisers 'Aiding and Abetting' Criminal Activity or Exercising First Amendment-Protected Commercial Speech?" *Fordham Intellectual Property, Media & Entertainment Law Journal* 15: 547–622, Winter 2005.

Frickey, Philip P. "(Native) American Exceptionalism in Federal Public Law." *Harvard Law Review* 119: 431–490, December 2005.

Gambetta, Diego. *The Sicilian Mafia*. Cambridge, MA: Harvard University Press, 1994.

"Gambling Impact and Behavior Study." National Opinion Research Center at the University of Chicago, March 18, 1999. Available at www.norc.uchicago.edu/new/gamb-fin.htm.

Gardner, Eliot L. "The Neurobiology and Genetics of Addiction: Implications of the 'Reward Deficiency Syndrome' for Therapeutic Strategies in Chemical Dependency." In Jon Elster, ed., *Addiction: Entries and Exits*. New York: Russell Sage Foundation, 1999.

Godwin, Michael. "Prostitution and the Internet: Interview with Mike Godwin." February 1, 1995. Available at http://www.bayswan.org/EFF.html.

Goldsmith, Jack L. "Against Cyberanarchy." *University of Chicago Law Review* 65: 1199–1250, Autumn 1998.

Goldsmith, Jack L., and Alan O. Sykes. "The Internet and the Dormant Commerce Clause." *Yale Law Journal* 110: 785–828, March 2001.

Goldsmith, Jack, and Tim Wu. *Who Controls the Internet? Illusions of a Borderless World*. New York: Oxford University Press, 2006.

Goldstein, Avram. *Addiction: From Biology to Drug Policy*, second edition. Oxford: Oxford University Press, 2001.

Goodell, Jeff. "How to Run a Successful Silicon Valley Business." *The New York Times Magazine*, April 8, 2001, pp. 52–4.

Graff, Samantha K. "State Taxation of Online Tobacco Sales: Circumventing the Archaic Bright Line Penned By Quill." *Florida Law Review* 58: 375–424, April 2006.

Grampp, William D. "What Did Smith Mean by the Invisible Hand?" *Journal of Political Economy* 108 (3): 441–465, 2000.

Grant, Jon. "The Neurobiology of Pathological Gambling," with Alex Blaszczynski presiding. Proceedings of the 19th annual conference on prevention, research, and treatment of problem gambling, June 23–25, 2005, New Orleans. *Journal of Gambling Issues*, No. 15, December 2005a.

Grant, Jon. "Pharmacological Approaches," with Ken Winters presiding. Proceedings of the 19th annual conference on prevention, research, and treatment of problem gambling, June 23–25, 2005, New Orleans. *Journal of Gambling Issues*, No. 15, December 2005b.

Gray, Mike. *Drug Crazy: How We Got into This Mess and How We Can Get Out*. New York: Random House, 1998.

Griffiths, R. R., W. A., Richards, U., McCann, and R. Jess. "Psilocybin Can Occasion Mystical Experiences Having Substantial and Sustained Personal Meaning and Spiritual Significance." *Psychopharmacology* 187: 268–283, 2006.

Gross, Samuel R., and Katherine Y. Barnes. "Road Work: Racial Profiling and Drug Interdiction on the Highway." *Michigan Law Review* 101 (3): 651–754, December 2002.

Grossman, Michael. "The Economic Approach to Addictive Behavior." Chapter 10 in M. Tommasi and K. Ierulli, eds., *The New Economics of Human Behavior*. Cambridge: Cambridge University Press, 1995.

Grossman, Michael, and Sara Markowitz. "I Did What Last Night?!!! Adolescent Risky Sexual Behaviors and Substance Use." National Bureau of Economic Research Working Paper No. 9244, October 2002.

Grossman, Michael, Frank J. Chaloupka, Henry Saffer, and Adit Laixuthai. "Alcohol Price Policy and Youths: A Summary of Economic Research." *Journal of Research on Adolescence* 4 (2): 347–364, 1994.

Gruber, Jonathan. "The Economics of Tobacco Regulation." *Health Affairs* 21 (2): 146–162, March/April 2002.

———. "Tobacco at the Crossroads: The Past and Future of Smoking Regulation in the United States." *Journal of Economic Perspectives* 15 (2): 193–212, Spring 2001.

Gruber, Jonathan, and Botond Köszegi. "Is Addiction 'Rational'? Theory and Evidence." National Bureau of Economic Research Working Paper No. 7507, January 2000.

Gruber, Jonathan, and Sendhil Mullainathan. "Do Cigarette Taxes Make Smokers Happier?" NBER Working Paper No. 8872, April 2002.

Guryan, Jonathan, and Melissa S. Kearney. "Lucky Stores, Gambling, and Addiction: Empirical Evidence from State Lottery Sales." NBER Working Paper No. 11287, May 2005.

Hamilton, James T. *Channeling Violence. The Economic Market for Violent Television Programming*. Princeton, NJ: Princeton University Press, 1998.

Hamm, Richard F. *Shaping the Eighteenth Amendment: Temperance Reform, Legal Culture, and the Polity, 1880–1920*. Chapel Hill: University of North Carolina Press, 1995.

Hammond, Michael E. "Internet Gambling Regulation." University of Kentucky College of Law, April 17, 2000. Available at www.geocities.com/mehammo/netgambling.htm.

Hanes, W. Travis, and Frank Sanello. *The Opium Wars: The Addiction of One Empire and the Corruption of Another*. New York: Barnes and Noble, 2005.

Harcourt, Bernard E. "Criminal Law: The Collapse of the Harm Principle." *Journal of Criminal Law and Criminology* 90: 109–194, Fall, 1999.

Harris, David A. "Driving While Black: Racial Profiling on our Nation's Highways." American Civil Liberties Union Special Report, June 1999. Available at www.aclu.org/racialjustice/racialprofiling/15912pub19990607.html.

———. "Car Wars: The Fourth Amendment's Death on the Highway." *George Washington Law Review* 66: 556–591, March 1998.

Hart, H. L. A. *Law, Liberty, and Morality*. Stanford, CA: Stanford University Press, 1963.

Hausbeck, Kathryn, and Barbara G. Brents. "Inside Nevada's Brothel Industry." Chapter 13, pp. 217–44, in Ronald Weitzer, ed., *Sex For Sale: Prostitution, Pornography, and the Sex Industry*. New York: Routledge, 2000.

Hawkins, Gordon, and Franklin E. Zimring. *Pornography in a Free Society*. Cambridge: Cambridge University Press, 1988.

Heien, Dale M. "Are Higher Alcohol Taxes Justified?" *Cato Journal* 15 (2–3): 243–257, Fall/Winter 1995/96.

Heins, Marjorie. *Not in Front of the Children: "Indecency," Censorship, and the Innocence of Youth*. New York: Hill and Wang, 2001.

Herring, Bill. "The Next 20 Years: The Developmental Challenges Facing the Field of Compulsive Sexual Behavior." *Sexual Addiction & Compulsivity* 11: 35–42, 2004.

Herrnstein, R. J., George Loewenstein, Drazen Prelec, and William Vaughan, Jr. "Utility Maximization and Melioration: Internalities in Individual Choice." *Journal of Behavioral Decision Making* 6: 179–185, 1993.

"Hidden Slaves: Forced Labor in the United States," by Free the Slaves (Washington, DC) and the Human Rights Center of the University of California, Berkeley. *Berkeley Journal of International Law* 23: 47–111, 2005.

Hirschman, Albert O. *The Rhetoric of Reaction. Perversity, Futility, Jeopardy*. Cambridge, MA: Harvard University Press, 1991.

Hobbes, T. *Leviathan*. F. B. Randall, ed., New York: Washington Square Press, 1970 [1651].

Huemer, Michael. "America's Unjust Drug War." Chapter 14, pp. 133–44, in Sheriff Bill Masters, ed., *The New Prohibition. Voices of Dissent Challenge the Drug War*. St. Louis: Accurate Press, 2004.

Hughes, Donna M. "The Internet and the Prostitution Industry: Partners in Global Sexual Exploitation." *Technology and Society Magazine*, Spring 2000. Available at http://www.uri.edu/artsci/wms/hughes/siii.htm.

Husak, Douglas. *Legalize This! The Case for Decriminalizing Drugs*. London: Verso, 2002.

Institute of Medicine. *Marijuana and Medicine: Assessing the Science Base*. Washington, DC: National Academy of Sciences, 1999.

Irons, Richard, and Jennifer P. Schneider. "Differential Diagnosis of Addictive Sexual Disorders Using the DSM-IV." *Sexual Addiction and Compulsivity* 3: 7–21, 1996.

Johnson, Barclay Thomas. "Restoring Civility – The Civil Asset Forfeiture Reform Act of 2000: Baby Steps Towards a More Civilized Civil Forfeiture System." *Indiana Law Review* 35: 1045–1084, 2001/2002.

Johnson, David R., and David Post. "Law and Borders – The Rise of Law in Cyberspace." *Stanford Law Review* 48: 1367–1402, 1996.

Jürgens, Ralf. "Mandatory or Compulsory HIV Testing," in *HIV Testing and Confidentiality: Final Report*, Canadian HIV/AIDS Legal Network & Canadian AIDS Society, Second edition, March 2001. Available at http://www.aidslaw.ca/Maincontent/issues/testing/ootoce.html (accessed March 7, 2006).

Kaplan, John. "Taking Drugs Seriously." *The Public Interest*, No. 92, pp. 32–50, Summer 1988. Reprinted in Schaler (1998, pp. 92–108).

———. *The Hardest Drug: Heroin and Public Policy*. Chicago: University of Chicago Press, 1983.

Kearney, Melissa S. "The Economic Winners and Losers of Legalized Gambling." National Bureau of Economic Research Working Paper No. 11234, March 2005. Available at http://www.nber.org/papers/w11234.

Keller, Bruce P. "The Game's the Same: Why Gambling in Cyberspace Violates Federal Law." *Yale Law Journal* 108: 1569–1609, May 1999.

Kelling, George L., and Catherine M. Coles. *Fixing Broken Windows: Restoring Order and Reducing Crime in Our Communities*. New York: Simon and Schuster, 1996.

Kenkel, Donald S. "New Estimates of the Optimal Tax on Alcohol." *Economic Inquiry* 34: 296–319, April 1996.

Kenkel, Donald, and Willard Manning. "Perspectives on Alcohol Taxation." *Alcohol Health and Research World* 20 (4): 230–238, 1996.

Kerr, K. Austin. *Organized for Prohibition: A New History of the Anti-Saloon League*. New Haven, CI: Yale University Press, 1985.

Kleiman, Mark. "Dopey, Boozy, Smoky – and Stupid." *The American Interest Online* 2 (3), January–February 2007; available at www.the-american-interest.com/ai2/article.cfm?Id=224MId=7 (accessed February 24, 2007).

Kleiman, Mark. *Against Excess: Drug Policy for Results*. New York: Basic Books, 1992.

Klitgaard, Robert. "Gifts and Bribes." In R. J. Zeckhauser, ed., *Strategy and Choice*. Cambridge, MA: MIT Press, 1991.

Knapp, Caroline. *Drinking: A Love Story*. New York: Delta, 1996.

Knapp Commission Report on Police Corruption. New York: George Braziller, 1973.

Kondracke, Morton M. "Don't Legalize Drugs," *New Republic* 198, No. 26, June 27, 1988. Reprinted in Schaler (1998, pp. 109–14).

Krongard, Mara Lynn. "Comment: A Population at Risk: Civil Commitment of Substance Abusers After Kansas v. Hendricks." *California Law Review* 90: 111–163, January 2002.

Lang, Craig. "Note & Comment: Internet Gambling: Nevada Logs In." *Loyola of Los Angeles Entertainment Law Review* 22: 525–558, 2002.

Langum, David J. *Crossing over the Line: Legislating Morality and the Mann Act*. Chicago: University of Chicago Press, 1994.

Leitzel, Jim. "Secret Deviants: Comment on 'On Sadomasochism: Taxonomies and Language.'" *Carceral Notebooks* 2, 2006.

Leitzel, Jim. *The Political Economy of Rule Evasion and Policy Reform*. London: Routledge, 2003.

Leitzel, Jim, and E. Weisman. "Investing in Policy Reform." *Journal of Institutional and Theoretical Economics* 155 (4): 696–709, December 1999.

Lessig, Lawrence. *Code and Other Laws of Cyberspace*. New York: Basic Books, 1999.

Lester, Joseph L. "B-I-N-G-O! The Legal Abuse of an Innocent Game." *St. Thomas Law Review* 18: 21–52, Fall, 2005.

Leung, S.-F., and C. E. Phelps. "My Kingdom for a Drink . . . ? A Review of Estimates of the Price Sensitivity of Demand for Alcoholic Beverages." In M. E. Hilton, and G. Bloss, eds., *Economics and the Prevention of Alcohol-Related Problems: Proceedings of a Workshop on Economic and Socioeconomic Issues in the Prevention of Alcohol-Related Problems*. October 10–11, 1991, Bethesda, MD. NIAAA Research Monograph No. 25. Rockville, MD: National Institute on Alcohol Abuse and Alcoholism, 1993.

Levine, Phillip B. "The Sexual Activity and Birth Control Use of American Teenagers." National Bureau of Economic Research Working Paper No. 7601, March 2000.

Levine, Harry G., and Craig Reinarman. "From Prohibition to Regulation: Lessons From Alcohol Policy for Drug Policy." In Ronald Bayer, and Gerald M. Oppenheimer, eds., *Confronting Drug Policy: Illicit Drugs in a Free Society*. Cambridge: Cambridge University Press, 1993.

Loewenstein, George. "Out of Control: Visceral Influences on Behavior." *Organizational Behavior and Human Decision Processes* 65 (3): 272–292, 1996.

Loewenstein, George, Ted O'Donoghue, and Matthew Rabin. "Projection Bias in Predicting Future Utility." *Quarterly Journal of Economics* 118 (4): 1209–1248, November 2003.

Loewenstein, George, and Richard H. Thaler. "Intertemporal Choice." *Journal of Economic Perspectives* 3 (4): 181–193, Autumn 1989.

Lott, J. R., Jr., and R. D. Roberts. "Why Comply?: One-Sided Enforcement of Price Controls and Victimless Crime Laws." *Journal of Legal Studies* 18: 403–14, June 1989.

Lungren, Daniel. "Legalization Would Be a Mistake." In Timothy Lynch, ed., *After Prohibition: An Adult Approach to Drug Policies in the 21st Century*. Washington, DC: Cato Institute, 2000.

Lyon, Andrew B., and Robert M. Schwab. "Consumption Taxes in a Life-Cycle Framework: Are Sin Taxes Regressive?" *Review of Economics and Statistics* 77 (3): 389–406, August, 1995.

MacAndrew, Craig, and Robert B. Edgerton. *Drunken Comportment: A Social Explanation*. London: Thomas Nelson and Sons, 1969.

MacCoun, Robert. "Is the Addiction Concept Useful for Drug Policy?" Chapter 13, pp. 383–408, in R. Vuchinich, and N. Heather, eds., *Choice, Behavioral Economics and Addiction*. Oxford: Elsevier Science, 2003.

MacCoun, R. J., and P. Reuter. *Drug War Heresies: Learning from Other Vices, Times, and Places*. Cambridge: Cambridge University Press, 2001.

MacCoun, R. J., P. Reuter, and T. Schelling. "Assessing Alternative Drug Control Regimes." *Journal of Policy Analysis and Management* 15 (3): 330–352, 1996.

Malyshev, Nikolai. "Laundering of Money in the USSR through the Purchase of Winning Bonds and Lottery Tickets." In Studies on the Soviet Second Economy, Berkeley–Duke Occasional Papers on the Second Economy in the USSR, No. 11, December 1987.

Mann, Ronald J., and Seth R. Belzley. "The Promise of Internet Intermediary Liability." *William and Mary Law Review* 47: 239–307, October 2005.

Manning, W. G., L. Blumberg, and L. H. Moulton. "The Demand for Alcohol: The Differential Response to Price." *Journal of Health Economics* 14 (2): 123–148, 1995.

Manning, W. G., E. B. Keeler, J. P. Newhouse, E. M. Sloss, and J. Wasserman. "The Taxes of Sin: Do Smokers and Drinkers Pay Their Way?" *Journal of the American Medical Association* 261 (11): 1604–1609, March 17, 1989.

Manski, Charles F., John V. Pepper, and Carol V. Petrie, ed., *Informing America's Policy on Illegal Drugs: What We Don't Know Keeps Hurting Us.* Washington, DC: National Academy Press, 2001.

Markowitz, S., and M. Grossman. "The Effects of Beer Taxes on Alcohol Abuse." *Journal of Health Economics* 19 (2): 271–282, 2000.

Masoud, Shekel. "Note and Comment: The Offshore Quandary: The Impact of Domestic Regulation on Licensed Offshore Gambling Companies." *Whittier Law Review* 25: 989–1009, Summer, 2004.

Massing, Michael. *The Fix.* New York: Simon and Schuster, 1998.

Masson, David, ed. *The Collected Writings of Thomas De Quincey.* Vol. 3. London: A. & C. Black, 1897.

McNamara, Joseph. "The War the Police Didn't Declare and Can't Win." In Timothy Lynch, ed., *After Prohibition: An Adult Approach to Drug Policies in the 21st Century.* Washington, DC: Cato Institute, 2000.

Merz, Charles. *The Dry Decade.* Garden City, NY: Doubleday, Doran, 1931.

Mill, John Stuart. *On Liberty.* Elizabeth Rapaport, ed. Indianapolis/Cambridge: Hackett, 1978 [1859].

Milton, John. *Areopagitica.* In Great Books of the Western World. Chicago: Encyclopedia Britannica 1952 [1644].

Miron, Jeffrey A. "A Critique of Economic Estimates of the Costs of Drug Abuse." Drug Policy Alliance, August, 2003. Available at http://www.drugpolicy.org/docUploads/Miron_Report.pdf (visited November 25, 2006).

————. "Violence and the U.S. Prohibitions of Drugs and Alcohol." *American Law and Economics Review* 1: 78–114, Fall 1999a.

————. "The Effect of Alcohol Prohibition on Alcohol Consumption." National Bureau of Economic Research Working Paper No. 7130, May 1999b.

Miron, Jeffrey A., and Jeffrey Zweibel. "Alcohol Consumption during Prohibition." *American Economic Review Papers and Proceedings* 81 (2): 242–247, 1991.

Mollen Commission Report. "The City of New York Commission to Investigate Allegations of Police Corruption and the Anti-corruption Procedures of the Police Department," July 7, 1994.

Monet, Veronica. "Mandatory Testing: The Fear That Feeds the Falsehood," 2004. Available at http://veronicamonet.com/colleges.php (accessed on March 7, 2006).

Monto, Martin A. "Why Men Seek Out Prostitutes." Chapter 5, p. 67–83, in Ronald Weitzer, ed., *Sex For Sale: Prostitution, Pornography, and the Sex Industry.* New York: Routledge, 2000.

Morgan, John P. "The Jamaica Ginger Paralysis." *Journal of the American Medical Association* 248 (15): 1864–1867, October 15, 1982.

Morse, Edward A. "Extraterritorial Internet Gambling: Legal Challenges and Policy Options," March 9, 2006. Available at http://ssrn.com/abstract = 891851.

Mosher, William D., Anjana Chandra, and Jo Jones. "Sexual Behavior and Selected Health Measures: Men and Women 15–44 Years of Age, United States, 2002." *Advance Data from Vital and Health Statistics*, No. 362, September 15, 2005.

Musto, David F. *The American Disease: Origins of Narcotic Control*, third edition. New York: Oxford University Press, 1999.

Nadler, Janice. "No Need to Shout: Bus Sweeps and the Psychology of Coercion." Law and Economics Research Paper No. 03-1, Northwestern University School of Law, 2003.

National Commission on Marihuana and Drug Abuse. "History of Alcohol Prohibition." Available at http://mojo.calyx.net/~schaffer/LIBRARY/studies/nc/nc2a.html (accessed April 30, 2003).

National Gambling Impact Study Commission. "Lotteries." At http://govinfo.library.unt.edu/ngisc/research/lotteries.html (accessed April 5, 2002).

National Gambling Impact Study Commission. Final Report, 1999. At http://govinfo.library.unt.edu/ngisc/reports/finrpt.html.

National Institute on Alcohol Abuse and Alcoholism. *Economic Perspectives in Alcoholism Research* (Alcohol Alert No. 51), January 2001.

National Institute on Drug Abuse. *Heroin Abuse and Addiction*, NIH Publication 00-4165, reprinted September 2000.

Nelson, Jon P. "Cigarette Demand, Structural Change, and Advertising Bans: International Evidence, 1970–1995." *Contributions to Economic Analysis and Policy* 2 (1), 2003. Available at http://www.bepress.com/bejeap/contributions/vol2/iss1/art10.

Nyborg, Karine, and Mari Rege. "On Social Norms: The Evolution of Considerate Smoking Behavior." *Journal of Economic Behavior and Organization* 52: 323–340, 2003.

Odegard, Peter H. *Pressure Politics: The Story of the Anti-Saloon League*. New York: Oxford University Press, 1928.

O'Donoghue, Ted, and Matthew Rabin. "Studying Optimal Paternalism, Illustrated by a Model of Sin Taxes." *American Economic Review* 93 (2): 186–191, May 2003.

_____. "Risky Behavior among Youths: Some Issues from Behavioral Economics." In Jonathan Gruber, ed., *Risky Behavior Among Youth: An Economic Analysis*. Chicago: University of Chicago Press, 2001.

_____. "Addiction and Self-Control." In Jon Elster, ed., *Addiction: Entries and Exits*. New York: Russell Sage Foundation, 1999.

Ohsfeldt, R. L., and Morrisey, M. A. "Beer Taxes, Workers' Compensation and Industrial Injury." *Review of Economics and Statistics* 79 (1): 155–160, 1997.

Olson, Scott. "Betting No End to Internet Gambling." *Journal of Technology Law & Policy* 4 (1), Spring 1999. Available at http://journal.law.ufl.edu/%7Etechlaw/4/Olson.html.

Orphanides, Athanasios, and David Zervos. "Rational Addiction with Learning and Regret." *Journal of Political Economy* 103 (4): 739–758, August 1995.

Oxford Universal Dictionary. third edition. London: Oxford University Press, 1955.

Packe, Michael St. John. *The Life of John Stuart Mill*. New York: Macmillan, 1954.

Packer, Herbert L. *The Limits of the Criminal Sanction*. Stanford, CA: Stanford University Press, 1968.

Parke, Adrian, Mark Griffiths, and Jonathan Parke. "Can Poker Playing Be Good For You? Poker as a Transferable Skill." *Journal of Gambling Issues* 14, September 2005.

Peele, Stanton. "Is Gambling an Addiction Like Drug and Alcohol Addiction? Developing Realistic and Useful Conceptions of Compulsive Gambling." *Electronic Journal of Gambling Issues: eGambling* 3, February 2001.

Peele, Stanton. *Diseasing of America: Addiction Treatment Out of Control*. Lexington, MA: Lexington Books, 1989.

Peele, Stanton, and Richard J. DeGrandpre. "Cocaine and the Concept of Addiction: Environmental Factors in Drug Compulsions." *Addiction Research* 6: 235–263, 1998.

Plasencia, Madeleine Mercedes. "Internet Sexual Predators: Protecting Children in the Global Community." *Journal of Gender, Race and Justice* 4: 15–35, 2000.

Plato. *Protagoras*. In *The Dialogues of Plato*. Great Books of the Western World, Chicago: Encyclopedia Britannica, 1952.

Plato. *The Republic*. In *The Dialogues of Plato*. Great Books of the Western World, Chicago: Encyclopedia Britannica, 1952.

Polsby, Daniel. "Legalization Is the Prudent Thing to Do." In *After Prohibition: An Adult Approach to Drug Policies in the 21st Century*, Timothy Lynch, ed. Washington, DC: Cato Institute, 2000.

Pope, Thaddeus Mason. "Balancing Public Health against Individual Liberty: The Ethics of Smoking Regulations." *University of Pittsburgh Law Review* 61: 419–498, Winter 2000.

Posner, Richard A., ed. *The Essential Holmes*. Chicago: University of Chicago Press, 1992a.

Posner, Richard A. *Sex and Reason*. Cambridge, MA: Harvard University Press, 1992b.

Prime Minister's Strategy Unit Drug Report. *Phase 1: Understanding the Issues*. London, May 12, 2003. Available at http://www.strategy.gov.uk/downloads/work_areas/drugs/drugs_report.pdf (accessed August 15, 2006).

Reuter, Peter. "What Drug Policies Cost: Estimating Government Drug Policy Expenditures." *Addiction* 101: 315–332, 2006.

———. "The Limits of Supply-Side Drug Control." *Milken Institute Review*, pp. 14–23, First Quarter, 2001.

Reuter, Peter, and Harold Pollack. "How Much Can Treatment Reduce National Drug Problems." *Addiction* 101: 341–347, 2006.

Robinson, Jr., David. "*Powell v. Texas:* The Case of the Intoxicated Shoeshine Man. Some Reflections a Generation Later By a Participant." *American Journal of Criminal Law* 26: 401–454, Summer, 1999.

Robinson, Glen O. "Regulating the Internet." www.LegalEssays.com, 1999. Available at http://papers.ssrn.com/paper.taf?ABSTRACT_ID=205038.

Robinson, Terry E., and Kent C. Berridge. "Incentive-Sensitization and Addiction." *Addiction* 96: 103–114, 2001.

Robinson, Terry E., and Kent C. Berridge. "The Neural Basis of Drug Craving: An Incentive-Sensitization Theory of Addiction." *Brain Research Reviews* 18: 247–291, 1993.

Robson, Philip. *Forbidden Drugs*, second edition. Oxford: Oxford University Press, 1999.

Room, Robin. "Addiction Concepts and International Control." *The Social History of Alcohol and Drugs* 20: 276–289, Spring 2006a.

———. "The Dangerousness of Drugs." *Addiction* 101: 166–168, 2006b.

Rossow, Ingeborg, and Ragnar Hauge. "Who Pays for the Drinking? Characteristics of the Extent and Distribution of Social Harms From Others' Drinking." *Addiction* 99: 1094–1102, 2004.

Ruhm, C. J. "Alcohol Policies and Highway Vehicle Fatalities." *Journal of Health Economics* 15 (4): 435–454, 1996.

Ryan, Alan. *Mill*. New York: W. W. Norton, 1997.

Rydall, C. Peter, and Susan S. Everingham. *Controlling Cocaine: Supply Versus Demand Programs*. Rand Corporation, 1994.

Saffer, Henry, and Frank Chaloupka. "The Effect of Tobacco Advertising Bans on Tobacco Consumption." *Journal of Health Economics* 19: 1117–1137, November 2000.

Saffer, Henry, and Dhaval Dave. "Alcohol Advertising and Alcohol Consumption By Adolescents." National Bureau of Economic Research Working Paper No. 9676, May 2003.

Sanders, Teela. *Sex Work. A Risky Business*. Cullompton, Devon: Willan Publishing, 2005.

Santa Lucia, Naria K. "Ongoing Consent: A Proposed Model for Consent to Assault in the S/M Context." *Carceral Notebooks* 1: 133–150, 2005. Available at http://www.thecarceral.org/consent.pdf.

Satel, Sally. "Is Caffeine Addictive? – A Review of the Literature." *American Journal of Drug and Alcohol Abuse* 32: 493–502, 2006.

Savage, Dan. *Skipping Towards Gomorrah: The Seven Deadly Sins and the Pursuit of Happiness in America*. Plume, 2003.

Schaffner, Laurie. "Capacity, Consent, and the Construction of Adulthood." Chapter 11, pp. 189–205, in *Regulating Sex: The Politics of Intimacy and Identity*. Elizabeth Bernstein and Laurie Schaffner, eds. New York and London: Routledge, 2005.

Schaler, Jeffrey A., ed. *Drugs: Should We Legalize, Decriminalize or Deregulate?* Amherst, NY: Prometheus Books, 1998.

Schelling, Thomas C. "Coping Rationally with Lapses from Rationality." *Eastern Economic Journal* 22 (3): 251–269, Summer 1996.

———. "Economic Reasoning and the Ethics of Policy." In *Choice and Consequence*. Cambridge, MA: Harvard University Press, 1984.

———. "The Intimate Contest for Self-Command." In *Choice and Consequence*. Cambridge, MA: Harvard University Press, 1984.

Schneider, Jennifer P. "Sexual Addiction & Compulsivity: Twenty Years of the Field, Ten Years of the Journal." *Sexual Addiction & Compulsivity* 11: 3–5, 2004.

Schuckit, Marc A. "New Findings in the Genetics of Alcoholism." *Journal of the American Medical Association* 281: 1875–1876, May 26, 1999.

Schwarz, Joel Michael. "The Internet Gambling Fallacy Craps Out." *Berkeley Technology Law Journal* 14:3, Fall 1999. Available at www.law.berkeley.edu/journals/btlj/articles/14_3/Schwarz/html/reader.html.

Sgontz, Larry G. "Optimal Taxation: The Mix of Alcohol and Other Taxes." *Public Finance Quarterly* 21 (3): 260–275, July 1993.

Shapiro, Dan *Mom's Marijuana: Life, Love, and Beating the Odds*. New York: Vintage, 2001.

Simon, David, and Edward Burns. *The Corner: A Year in the Life of an Inner-City Neighborhood*. New York: Broadway Books, 1997.

Single, Eric. "Cost Estimates." International Center for Alcohol Policy, n.d. Available at www.icap.org/international/cost_estimates.html (accessed April 24, 2002).

Skog, Ole-Jørgen. "Hyperbolic Discounting, Willpower, and Addiction." In Jon Elster, ed., *Addiction: Entries and Exits*. New York: Russell Sage Foundation, 1999.

Skolnick, Jerome H. "The Social Transformation of Vice." *Law and Contemporary Problems* 51 (1): 9–29, 1988.

Slade, John. "Marketing Policies." Chapter 4, pp. 72–110, in Robert L. Rabin, and Stephen D. Sugarman, eds., *Regulating Tobacco*. Oxford: Oxford University Press, 2001.

Sloan, F. A., B. A. Reilly, and C. Schenzler. "Effects of Tort Liability and Insurance on Heavy Drinking and Drinking and Driving." *Journal of Law and Economics* 38 (1): 49–77, 1995.

Sloan, F. A., B. A. Reilly, and C. Schenzler. "Effects of Prices, Civil and Criminal Sanctions, and Law Enforcement on Alcohol-Related Mortality." *Journal of Studies on Alcohol* 55 (4): 454–465, 1994.

Small, Dan, Ernest Drucker, and Editorial for Harm Reduction Journal. "Policy Makers Ignoring Science and Scientists Ignoring Policy: The Medical Ethical Challenges of Heroin Treatment." *Harm Reduction Journal* 3: 16–29, 2006.

Smith, Adam. *An Inquiry into the Nature and Causes of the Wealth of Nations*. Edward Cannan, ed. Chicago: University of Chicago Press, 1976 [1776; Cannan edition, 1904].

Snadowsky, Daria. "The Best Little Whorehouse Is Not in Texas: How Nevada's Prostitution Laws Serve Public Policy, and How Those Laws May Be Improved." *Nevada Law Journal* 6: 217–247, Fall 2005.

Stevenson, Robert Louis Stevenson. *Dr. Jekyll and Mr. Hyde*. New York: Bantam Books, 1981 [1886].

Stevenson, Seth. "Know When to Hold 'Em, Know When to Log Off." *Slate*, November 15, 1999. Available at http://slate.msn.com/Features/netgambling/netgambling.asp.

Stigler, George J., and Gary S. Becker. "De Gustibus Non Est Disputandum." *American Economic Review* 67 (2): 76–90, March, 1977.

Strotz, R. "Myopia and Inconsistency in Dynamic Utility Maximization." *Review of Economic Studies* 23: 165–80, 1955.

Substance Abuse and Mental Health Services Administration. *Results from the 2005 National Survey on Drug Use and Health: National Findings.* Rockville, MD: Office of Applied Studies, NHSDA Series H-30, DHHS Publication No. SMA 06-4194, September 2006.

Substance Abuse and Mental Health Services Administration. *Results from the 2004 National Survey on Drug Use and Health: National Findings.* Rockville, MD: Office of Applied Studies, NSDUH Series H-28, DHHS Publication No. SMA 05-4062, 2005.

Sullum, Jacob. *Saying Yes. In Defense of Drug Use.* New York: Jeremy P. Tarcher, 2003.

Sunley, Emil M., Ayda Yurekli, and Frank J. Chaloupka. "The Design, Administration, and Potential Revenue of Tobacco Excises." Chapter 17, pp. 409–426, in Prabhat Jha, and Frank J. Chaloupka, eds, *Tobacco Control in Developing Countries.* Oxford: Oxford University Press, 2000.

Sunstein, Cass R., and Richard H. Thaler. "Libertarian Paternalism is Not an Oxymoron." *Univeristy of Chicago Law Review* 70, Summer 2003.

Talley, Louis Alan, and Brian W. Cashell. "Excise Taxes on Alcohol, Tobacco, and Gasoline: History and Inflation-Adjusted Rates." Congressional Research Report for Congress, April 22, 1999.

Temin, Peter. "The Origin of Compulsory Drug Prescription." *Journal of Law and Economics* 22 (1): 91–105, April 1979.

Thaler, Richard H., and Cass R. Sunstein. "Libertarian Paternalism." *American Economic Review* 93 (2): 175–179, May 2003.

Thomas, Joe A. "Gay Male Video Pornography: Past, Present, and Future." Chapter 4, pp. 49–66, in Ronald Weitzer, ed., *Sex for Sale: Prostitution, Pornography, and the Sex Industry.* New York: Routledge, 2000.

Thompson, Michael J. "Give Me \$25 on Red and Derek Jeter for \$26: Do Fantasy Sports Leagues Constitute Gambling?" *Sports Lawyers Journal* 8: 21–42, 2001.

Thornton, Mark. "Alcohol Prohibition Was a Failure." Policy Analysis No. 157, Cato Institute, July 17, 1991. Available at www.cato.org/pubs/pas/pa-157.html (accessed April 30, 2003).

UNAIDS. *2004 Report on the Global AIDS Epidemic.* Joint United Nations Programme on HIV/AIDS (UNAIDS), 2004. Available at http://www.unaids.orgbangkok2004//report_pdf.html (accessed February 9, 2006).

U.S. Department of Health and Human Services (USDHHS). *Reducing Tobacco Use: A Report of the Surgeon General.* Atlanta: USDHHS, Centers for Disease Control and Prevention, National Center for Chronic Disease Prevention and Health Promotion, Office on Smoking and Health, 2000.

Viscusi, W. Kip. "Principles for Cigarette Taxation in Africa." Harvard Law School, Public Law Research Paper No. 77, August 2003.

Volokh, Eugene. "The Mechanisms of the Slippery Slope." *Harvard Law Review* 116: 1026–1137, February 2003.

Waal, Helge, and Jørg Mørland. "Addiction as Impeded Rationality." In Jon Elster, ed., *Addiction: Entries and Exits.* New York: Russell Sage Foundation, 1999.

Walker, Ian. "The Economic Analysis of Lotteries." *Economic Policy* 27: 358–401, 1998.

Walters, Glenn D. *The Addiction Concept: Working Hypothesis or Self-Fulfilling Prophesy?* Boston: Allyn & Bacon, 1999.

Warburton, Clark. *The Economic Results of Prohibition*. New York: Columbia University Press, 1932.

Wechsler H., T. E. Nelson, J. E. Lee, et al. "Perception and Reality: A National Evaluation of Social Norms Marketing Interventions to Reduce College Students' Heavy Alcohol Use." *Journal of Studies on Alcohol* 64 (4): 484–94, July 2003.

Weitzer, Ronald. "Prostitution Panic: The Growing Hysteria over Sex Trafficking." *American Sexuality Magazine*, February 9, 2006. Available at http://www.nsrc.sfsu. edu/MagArticle.cfm?Article=5668PageID=0.

——. "The Politics of Prostitution in America. Chapter 10, pp. 159–180, in Ronald Weitzer, ed., *Sex For Sale: Prostitution, Pornography, and the Sex Industry*. New York: Routledge, 2000.

Weitzer, Ronald. "Prostitution Control in America: Rethinking Public Policy." *Crime, Law & Social Change* 32: 83–102, 1999.

Welldon, Estela V. *Sadomasochism*. Cambridge: Icon Books, 2002.

White, S. *Russia Goes Dry*. Cambridge: Cambridge University Press, 1996.

The Wickersham Report. Official Records of The National Commission on Law Observance and Enforcement, five volumes, Senate Document No. 307. Washington, DC: U.S. Government Printing Office, 1931.

Williams, J., L. M. Powell, and H. Wechsler. "Does Alcohol Consumption Reduce Human Capital Accumulation? Evidence From the College Alcohol Study." ImpacTeen Research Paper No. 18, University of Illinois at Chicago, 2002.

Wilson, James Q. "Against the Legalization of Drugs." *Commentary* 89: 21–28, February 1990. Reprinted in Schaler (1998, pp. 49–62).

Wilson, James Q. "Legalizing Drugs Makes Matters Worse." Slate.com, September 1, 2000; available at http://www.slate.com/id/88934 (accessed on September 8, 2006).

Wongsurawat, Winai. "Pornography and Social Ills: Evidence From the Early 1990s." *Journal of Applied Economics* 9 (1): 185–214, May 2006.

Wotton, Rachel. "The Relationship between Street-Based Sex Workers and the Police in the Effectiveness of HIV Prevention Strategies." *Research for Sex Work* 8: 11–13, June 2005.

Wu, Timothy. "Application-Centered Internet Analysis." *Virginia Law Review* 85: 1163–1204, September 1999.

Yandle, Bruce. "Bootleggers and Baptists: The Education of a Regulatory Economist." *Regulation*, pp. 12–16, May/June 1983. Available at http://www.mercatus.org/pdf/materials/560.pdf (accessed November 16, 2005).

Young, D. J., and A. Bielinska-Kwapisz. "Alcohol Taxes and Beverage Prices." *National Tax Journal* 55 (1): 57–73, 2002.

Zelenak, Lawrence. "The Puzzling Case of the Revenue-Maximizing Lottery." *North Carolina Law Review* 79: 1–43, December, 2000.

Zimring, Frankin E., and Gordon Hawkins. *The Search for Rational Drug Control*. Cambridge: Cambridge University Press, 1992.

Zinberg, Norman E. *Drug, Set, and Setting: The Basis for Controlled Intoxicant Use*. New Haven, CI: Yale University Press, 1984. Available at www.druglibrary.org and www.drugtext.org.

Zwyicki, Todd J. "Wine Wars: The 21st Amendment and Discriminatory Bans to Direct Shipment of Wine." Law and Economics Working Paper Series 0446, School of Law, George Mason University, 2004. Available at http://ssrn.com/abstract_id=604803.

Index

Made in the USA
Coppell, TX
06 January 2020

14168804R00175